PSYCHOLOGY OF
EFFECTIVE
LIVING

BROOKS/COLE PUBLISHING COMPANY
Monterey, California
A Division of Wadsworth, Inc.

NORMAN E. HANKINS
East Tennessee State University

ROGER C. BAILEY
East Tennessee State University

PSYCHOLOGY OF EFFECTIVE LIVING

Printed in the United States of America

10 9 8 7 6 5 4 3 2 1

Library of Congress Cataloging in Publication Data

Hankins, Norman E
   Psychology of effective living.

   Bibliography: p. 405
   Includes index.
   1. Success.   2. Psychology.   I. Bailey, Roger C.,
joint author.   II. Title.
BF637.S8H224   158   79-19044
ISBN 0-8185-0360-2

Project Development Editor: *Ray Kingman*
Manuscript Editor: *Rephah Berg*
Production Editor: *Sally Schuman*
Interior design: *Linda Marcetti*
Cover photo © *Jim Pinckney*
Cover design: *Jamie Sue Brooks*
Illustrations: *Alan May*
Technical art: *John Foster Tech Art Service*
Photoresearch: *Audrey Ross*
Typesetting: *Graphic Typesetting Service, Los Angeles, California*

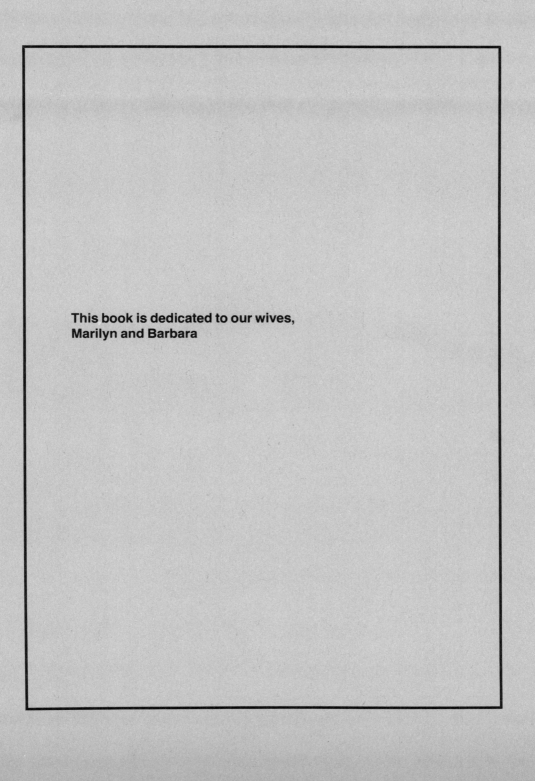

**This book is dedicated to our wives,
Marilyn and Barbara**

PREFACE

Some of the most popular books on the market are "do-it-yourself" books. These books provide instructions on how to change behavior, from breaking bad habits to becoming more assertive in interpersonal relationships and finding true romantic love. Their popularity reflects people's desire to know more about themselves and to find practical solutions to pressing everyday problems.

Our purpose in writing *Psychology of Effective Living* was to help meet the growing demand for more practical psychology among college and university students. We believe that the discipline of psychology has reached a stage of maturity at which both basic psychological principles and empirical research can be applied successfully to some common, everyday concerns.

Our approach in this book was to progress in content from the general to the specific. Section One, "The Study of Human Behavior," provides the reader with some understanding of basic concepts in psychology, such as personality, learning, perception, and motivation, and some understanding of the scientific approach to generating knowledge. Section Two, "Effective and Ineffective Living Patterns," and Section Three, "Interpersonal Behavior," should further equip the reader with basic conceptual tools for understanding the more application-oriented Section Four, "Behaving More Effectively." In this final section, the reader will find practical information on behavioral self-control, career choice, work motivation and job satisfaction, memory improvement, time management, and consumer behavior. To help the reader approach each chapter, we have provided a list of learning objectives for the chapter, a summary, and a list of key concepts with their definitions.

We are deeply appreciative of the many sources of support and guidance that spurred this effort on. Gratitude is expressed to Dr. Otto Zinser, who provided some helpful comments during the difficult early stages of this book. Special acknowledgment is also given to those who critically reviewed our book manuscript in its entirety: James C. Brown of Manatee Junior College, John C. Budz of Framingham State College, John M. Cozean of Central Piedmont Community College, W. G. Dey of Vancouver Community College, Pauline Gillette of Northern Virginia Community College, Wayne Hren of Los Angeles Pierce College, Duane Miller of Mississippi State University, Dan G. Perkins of Richland College, and Joan A. Royce of Riverside City College. Janelle Light and Joyce Larimer provided the typing expertise that brought this project to final manuscript form.

Norman E. Harkins

Roger C. Bailey

CONTENTS

ix

X

xii

PSYCHOLOGY OF EFFECTIVE LIVING

1

INTRODUCTION AND OVERVIEW OF THE BOOK

People are more knowledgeable about psychology than ever before. The popular magazines *Psychology Today* and *Behavior Today* are read by thousands of lay readers. This increased awareness among a more enlightened public, combined with a more service-minded breed of psychologist and more advanced and sophisticated research techniques, has resulted in the emergence of new horizons in applying psychology to practical problems. Because people are turning to psychology for solutions—or at least some help with problems in daily living—psychologists have begun to extend their investigations in areas with practical application.

Questions like the following reflect some of the contemporary concerns of the lay public as it turns to psychology for help: What can I do to make myself more attractive and interesting to other people? What can I do to keep from feeling so uptight all the time? How can I learn to manage my time more effectively? To what extent am I influenced by television? How can I become a more intelligent consumer? What can I do to bring my temper under control? Is there any way to stop smoking (or lose weight) that is both practical and effective?

Although these are difficult questions, they are neither too "practical" nor too perplexing to be beyond the realm of scientific investigation. In fact, some answers to most of these questions will be provided later in this book. In the last decade, for example, controlled scientific research has revealed that so-called involuntary functions of the autonomic nervous system can actually be brought under conscious control. This kind of breakthrough in our understanding of behavior has enabled psychologists to develop step-by-step self-control programs that people can apply to a wide array of undesired behaviors. Self-help programs are now available for various problem areas, such as the management of anxiety, anger, excessive smoking, or overeating.

In the broadest sense this book is concerned with finding ways of making human existence more meaningful and more enjoyable, social relationships more satisfying, human efforts more productive, and mastery of the self and the environment more complete. Although these objectives may seem broad and idealistic, psychology has now reached a stage of maturity at which general theories of human behavior have been tested and the application of such knowledge to real-life problems seems justified. In this book we hope to show how people can reduce vague or ubiquitous problems to clearly identifiable behaviors. And, when possible, we hope to provide techniques by which people can modify their behavior in more-desired directions.

SECTION ONE: THE STUDY OF HUMAN BEHAVIOR

The purpose of the first section of the book will be to present psychological concepts that will help the reader understand the material presented in the following sections. Chapter 2, "Understanding Human Behavior: Basic Concepts," will provide an overview of such concepts as personality, learning, motivation, and perception as they relate to human behavior. The concept of personality will be discussed in terms of three theoretical dimensions: consistency/variability, mind/body, and internality/externality. Learning will be examined both from a behavioral and from a cognitive perspective. The concept of perception will be discussed in order to better understand the ways people structure their experience and try to give meaning to it. The discussion of motivation will provide a means of understanding the underlying causes of human behavior. We will attempt to provide explanatory concepts for why people do what they do. A clear understanding of the concepts of personality, learning, perception, and motivation will provide a conceptual foundation for dealing with the topics covered in this book.

Chapter 3, "Understanding Human Behavior: The Nature of Research," will discuss the purpose and nature of research in psychology. The main purpose of research in psychology is to generate scientific knowledge and understanding about animal and human behavior. Although we recognize that there are many types of knowledge to which an individual may turn to explain human experience (for example, common-sense knowledge, logical knowledge, and religious knowledge), it will be the objective of this book to offer explanations that are grounded in scientific knowledge. But we should bear in mind that the understanding of human behavior is always confined to available evidence and that verification of scientific knowledge is a continuous process.

The understanding of human behavior is an enormously complex affair. Psychologists over the past century have striven to ask the right questions, develop the most trustworthy measures and procedures, and determine the usefulness of their findings for promoting human welfare. Such concerns have led psychologists to argue the pros and cons of "basic" versus "applied" research, "experimental" versus "nonexperimental" research, and the like. These are issues worthy of serious-minded debate. However, this book will draw generously from any and all available research that will improve our understanding of human behavior in the real world. Special consideration will be given to recent and innovative research that has practical appeal to a broad audience. However, you should be aware that there is a legitimate distinction between experimental research and nonexperimental research, based both on method and on the nature of the data. Chapter 3 will introduce you to the various experimental and nonexperimental methods of psychological research along with the strengths and weaknesses of each. This book will attempt to sample not only a wide range of practical human behaviors but the range of research methods used to study such behaviors. Therefore, we may expect that in our study of the new horizons of psychology we will on some occasions find ourselves inside the traditional laboratory setting and on other occasions in the home, classroom, office, or mental-health clinic.

In Chapter 3, we will try to define the term *science* and to understand how human behavior is studied scientifically. We shall look at various types of experimental and nonexperimental research as well as offer some criteria for assessing the trustworthiness of psychological research.

SECTION TWO: EFFECTIVE AND INEFFECTIVE LIVING PATTERNS

The major purpose of applied psychology is to use scientifically based knowledge in the promotion of human welfare. Without question, the single most concentrated effort by psychologists has been to aid individuals in improving their personal adjustment. In Chapter 4, "Human Development and the Effective Person," we will try to answer the question "What is an effective person?" We shall see that this question is best answered when we view effective personality functioning from a human-development perspective. The effective person is one who can adequately deal with the demands of living at his or her particular stage of biosocial development. Consequently, we shall examine some of the life demands and the techniques for coping with life demands at various stages of the human life cycle. Although all individuals pass through the same basic stages of development, each person will respond somewhat differently to the demands of living. Each person is uniquely different from all others. While searching for the general characteristics of the effective person, this fact must be kept in mind.

In any one year, over ¾ million persons are being treated for mental illness on an inpatient (residential) basis in the United States. Over half the hospital beds in the United States are occupied by people considered to be seriously mentally ill. Moreover, patients treated on an outpatient (nonresidential) basis would greatly increase these figures. At least one person in ten will sometime during his or her life seek the counsel of a mental-health specialist. Cates (1970) reported that 39% of psychologists were engaged in the clinical and counseling areas. If, however, we were to include the mental-health duties of other psychologists, such as school psychologists, psychometrists, and personnel psychologists, the percentage of psychologists involved in mental-health services would probably approach 50% or more.

In Chapter 5, "Ineffective Personality Patterns," we will examine some of the ways that characteristics of people may be judged to be expressions of unhealthy personality adjustment. We will review some of the major varieties of mental illness and discuss some of the personality and situational influences on such disorders. We will find, for instance, that even the normal or well-adjusted individual may behave inappropriately or maladaptively under certain circumstances. We will close Chapter 5 by looking at some of the attitudes that patients and mental-health specialists hold toward mental illness and the impact of such attitudes on individuals and on society.

SECTION THREE: INTERPERSONAL BEHAVIOR

The third section of the book will examine some of the ways psychological research has been applied to the area of interpersonal behavior. Our earliest experiences lead us to the awareness that other people are a source of security and comfort. We learn to value interaction with others. Throughout our lives we find most of our most rewarding experiences to involve relationships with others. We all have powerful needs for affiliation and attachment. Moreover, our own self-concepts are greatly influenced by a need to define reality in social terms and select the individuals who will maximize fulfillment of our personal needs. But why does an individual select this group rather than another? Why is one attracted to a particular person as a friend, date, or spouse? What factors lead to the establishment of a relationship and to the maintenance of a relationship over time?

In Chapter 6, "Social Perception and Interpersonal Behavior," we will present some conceptual tools for understanding social interaction. We will also examine some of the theoretical notions and empirical findings on why people like other people. Although most of us have a strong need for affiliating with others, we do not try to establish permanent relationships with everyone. Throughout our lives, we are selective about whom we prefer to interact with on an enduring basis. The chapter will look at some of the factors recognized as influencing the selection and maintenance of more-lasting relationships, like friendship, dating, and marriage. It will give particular attention to the development of the romantic relationship.

Chapter 7, "Living in Groups," will explore more fully the dynamics involved in larger-group interaction. We will define a group in terms of its goals, norms, and status relationships. Attention will be given to group structure and its effects on members' yielding to group pressure, leader-follower relations, and group satisfaction and group performance. This chapter will emphasize the conditions that lead to yielding to group influence (conformity and compliance) and those that lead to resisting group influence (independence and anticonformity).

In Chapter 8, we will examine the relation between social attitudes and social behavior. We will first define the concept "attitude" and present the case for the use of this concept in better understanding social behavior. We will discuss how the importance to a person of an attitude that he or she holds (that is, the ego involvement of the attitude) is related to attitude change and resistance to attitude change. This chapter will also deal with some of the more important social attitudes that may lead to prejudice and social stereotyping. We will also find it necessary to make a distinction between prejudice (which is an attitude) and discrimination (which is behavior). Common sense would lead us to believe that only prejudiced people will discriminate against the object of their prejudice, but we will find that this is not always so. In the final section of the chapter, we will look at how social behavior may have desirable social consequences (as in cooperating or helping behavior) or undesirable social consequences (as in violent or aggressive behavior).

SECTION FOUR: BEHAVING MORE EFFECTIVELY

Sections One, Two, and Three of this book will serve to build a conceptual and empirical foundation for the more practical psychology presented in Section 4.

Chapter 9, "Achieving Greater Self-Control," covers some of the basic principles for regulating one's own behavior. Self-control is a serious problem for many people. They realize that they are practicing bad habits but seem to lack the desire or the knowledge to break these habit patterns. Most people, for instance, would like to be physically strong and healthy and live to a ripe old age; yet millions smoke, drink alcoholic beverages to excess, use dangerous drugs, and drive recklessly on the highways. These are personal-choice behaviors that are not congruent with a long and healthy life. In fact, they are forms of self-destructive behavior. Some causes of heart disease, such as obesity, smoking, a diet high in fats and cholesterol, and lack of exercise, are fairly well documented, but you may have to look no farther than the person next to you, and possibly even yourself, to find an overweight, underexercised smoker who knowingly eats foods that are detrimental to health.

This chapter presents a model for achieving self-control. Some of the basic self-control strategies are also discussed. In this chapter we show how this model, together with the strategies we present, can be applied to problems of overeating and smoking.

In Chapter 10, "Managing Our Emotions," we focus on strategies for managing one's feelings more effectively. This chapter is based on the assumption that thoughts often precede actions and that when people learn to control their thoughts, they can also quite often change their feelings as well as their behavior.

Our discussion will be concerned mainly with the management of anxiety and anger. Fortunately, psychologists and other social scientists are studying these problem areas, and more and more psychological research is being made available to people who may profit from applying such findings to their own experiences. We will first present more-theoretical approaches to these problem areas and review some of the recent research that demonstrates the effectiveness of these approaches. Exercises for assessing the degree of one's anxiety or anger problem will be presented. This material will be followed by practical suggestions for dealing with excessive test anxiety, dating anxiety, and outbursts of anger.

Chapter 11, "Using Memory and Time More Effectively," deals with problems of memory and time management. These seem to be problem areas for many people. The part of the chapter devoted to memory improvement will emphasize the importance of attention to appropriate stimuli and organization of the information to be recalled. We will show how interference occurs in learning and forgetting and how it can be minimized. The use of mental imagery and other techniques will be discussed. Several mnemonic devices, including the "house method," or "method of loci," will be described. Exercises involving the use of these methods will be presented.

The rest of Chapter 11 will be devoted to time management, a problem frequently encountered by almost everyone. Time, like life, is irreversible and irreplaceable. To waste your time is to waste your life. If one can learn to master one's time, one is better able to master one's life and make the most of it. Effective time management begins with setting goals and priorities, both long-term and short-term. The importance of scheduling activities on a regular basis will be emphasized. Examples of schedules will be provided.

In Chapter 12, "Choosing a Vocation," we will try to show the importance of effective planning and decision making in this very important area. Unfortunately, the

8

Millions of people smoke in our society, although surveys indicate that many would like to stop smoking if they could. (Photo © Cornell Capa/Magnum.)

choice of one's vocation is an extremely important decision that is often taken too lightly. Many people tend to drift idly along until they find a job that will satisfy their current monetary needs, without regard to their life goals and values, the opportunity for growth and development in the job, or its ability to provide a sense of purpose and satisfaction. A decision that affects the way one spends one's working hours for 30 to 40 years of one's life deserves greater attention than it usually receives.

We will encourage systematic self-analysis, including an assessment of goals, values, interests, aptitudes, and personality traits as a starting point. A model for predicting job success from motivation, aptitude, and interests will be presented. We will also describe sources of vocational information and provide information on how to get and keep a job and how to advance in one's career.

In Chapter 13, "Motivation and Work Behavior," we will discuss some of the motivations of what Yankelovich (1978) calls the "new breed" of worker and the implication of these motivations for revised work incentives. For many people, according to Yankelovich, present work-incentive programs are so unappealing that, although workers still seek to hold a job, they are not motivated to put forth their best effort. While they complain about the job's lack of appeal and give less to it, they seem to demand more from it in wages and fringe benefits. A system has evolved in which employees are demanding more for doing less.

We will emphasize techniques designed to increase workers' motivation and perceived control over one's environment. Motivation will be discussed using Rotter's (1966) concept of the perceived locus of control of behavior. Discussing internal and external locus of control, De Charms (1972) uses the terms *origin* and *pawn* to distinguish between those who initiate activity and those who respond to external forces. We will present ideas designed to make workers feel more like "origins" than "pawns." We will discuss several theories of work motivation and show how they have been applied to work settings and with what results. The effects of job enrichment, flexible working hours, and differential reinforcement techniques will be included. We will close with a discussion of how such ideas relate to worker/management relations.

In the United States, leisure-time activities have become the number one industry. The average American today has more leisure time available and many rich opportunities for using it. For many, however, leisure time may be a mixed blessing, particularly if people do not know how to use such time in a meaningful and self-fulfilling manner. In Chapter 14, we shall deal with some of the problems and make some suggestions on how to live with leisure time.

One problem in the study of leisure time is that the concept has different meanings to different people. For one person, leisure time may mean the opportunity to do absolutely nothing; for another it may be an opportunity just to be with one's thoughts and relax. For still others, every moment of life must be devoted to productive activity, whether the activities be work-time activities or leisure-time activities. We shall also identify various psychological notions regarding the concept of leisure. Another objective of the chapter will be to examine how people tend to use leisure time at various stages of life in our society. In other words, the concept of leisure must be viewed from a developmental perspective. Each stage of biosocial development, from childhood to old age, brings with it unique leisure-time-use concerns.

Finally, Chapter 14 will present a conceptual model for helping you identify your own leisure behavior. It is assumed that the quality of leisure-time behavior is an influence on the effectiveness of personality functioning.

Because of an emerging need among consumers to analyze and evaluate advertising claims, we have included Chapter 15, "Becoming a More Knowledgeable Consumer." The purpose of this chapter is to help consumers become more efficient and perceptive participants in the marketplace. Many advertising claims are designed to persuade the consumer to make a decision on minimal information. This practice is particularly prevalent with products for which intense competition among producers causes the products to become strikingly similar. Since no product is clearly superior to others in a particular category, advertising is designed to create the illusion of superiority. The illusion of superiority is facilitated by our inability to distinguish between assertions and implications contained in advertising messages. Chapter 15 will provide exercises to help you distinguish between assertion claims and implica-

10

tion claims and will discuss some of the techniques used to create the illusion of superiority by implication. The chapter will also show how advertisements try to persuade through the use of fear, nostalgia, sex appeal, testimonials, endorsements, slogans and melodies, competitor putdown, and symbolism. We will identify and describe some procedures that involve deception as determined by the Federal Trade Commission and others that are illegal, including bait-and-switch advertising, quackery, and flimflam operations. Others that are misleading but not clearly illegal include pyramid sales techniques, land-development schemes, and appeals to vanity.

SECTION ONE

THE STUDY OF
HUMAN BEHAVIOR

2

CHAPTER OBJECTIVES

1. To understand the concepts of personality, learning, perception, and motivation as used by psychologists.
2. To differentiate the three major views of human nature (psychoanalytic, behavioristic, and humanistic) by identifying their basic assumptions about human nature.
3. To understand the concept of personality in terms of three dichotomies: consistency/variability, mind/body, and internality/externality.
4. To understand the difference between behavior that is learned and behavior that is not learned.
5. To understand the differences and similarities among classical conditioning, operant conditioning, and cognitive learning.
6. To understand what is meant by stimulus influences and personality influences on perception and motivation.
7. To be able to classify human needs into the following categories: biological needs, sociocultural needs, and psychological needs.

UNDERSTANDING HUMAN BEHAVIOR: BASIC CONCEPTS

In an attempt to understand why people behave the way they do, psychologists have developed a number of explanatory conceptual tools. The desire of psychologists to know not only *what* people do but *why* they do it has given rise to a broad spectrum of explanatory concepts. Many of the concepts attempt to encompass the broad and complex nature of personality, such as "personality"; many others pertain to more specific facets of personality, such as "learning," "perception," and "motivation." Whatever the level of abstraction, psychological concepts have emerged to explain observed human behavior. This chapter will discuss some of the more important concepts used by psychologists to better understand human behavior. In an attempt to unravel the complexity of human behavior, the chapter will first examine human personality in its broader sense and then examine more specific features of personality that have had lasting appeal to psychologists, such as learning, perception, and motivation.

THE CONCEPT OF PERSONALITY

The term **personality** has traditionally been used by psychologists to try to capture the totality of human behavior. Theorists have tended to use the term to explain human nature—that is, what people are naturally all about. Particularly during the last part of the 19th century and the first half of the 20th, a number of theoretical models of human nature were developed. Each theoretical model expressed explicitly or implicitly a set of basic assumptions about human nature, and these sets of assumptions eventually gave rise to a number of conflicting views of personality. Some theorists, such as Freud and other psychoanalysts, viewed the human personality as basically irrational, driven by powerful biological forces over which the individual had little control. Behavioristic theorists assumed little about the moral basis of human conduct, but they believed that human behavior is determined by environment and learning. Later the humanistic theorists, attempting to release the person from the bonds of any form of determinism, whether biological or environmental, emphasized the role of personal freedom and choice in human experience. The issues of whether people are good or evil, rational or irrational, and free or determined have remained basic themes in most theories of personality (Coleman & Hammen, 1974).

The observations made by psychologists, as well as by people in general, have led to a number of additional conclusions about human nature. One set of observations points to a remarkable degree of **personality consistency**, or consistency in behavior over time and in different settings, while other observations point to the opposite, **personality variability**. This behavioral *consistency/variability dichotomy* adds to the complexity in understanding human personality. We often see a great deal of consistency in individuals when they are observed over short periods. In fact, they seem to have personality predispositions that they carry across various situations. Therefore, we come to label a person as "impulsive" or "aggressive" or "prejudiced" because we assume that these traits do not fluctuate significantly within the person over time or over settings. If a person is prejudiced toward some object, person, or

16

*Personality includes things we can observe and things we cannot observe about people. (Photo ©
Bruce Roberts/Photo Researchers, Inc.)*

CHAPTER 2   UNDERSTANDING HUMAN BEHAVIOR: BASIC CONCEPTS

group today, we expect that person to harbor this prejudice tomorrow. It is such stability and consistency of one's traits and behavior that allow for predictions about the person. The behavioral scientist must assume that there is a regularity to behavior in order to discover the "laws" that govern behavior. Yet social psychologists have recently found out just how influential the present environmental setting may be in determining an individual's behavior. In various situations, a prejudiced person may not act in a prejudicial or discriminatory way, a highly ethical person may act unethically, an impulsive person may act conscientiously and cautiously, and a mentally healthy person may show signs of mental illness. Consequently, the social scientist must look not only for the stable features of human personality but also for the determinants that produce intra- and interpersonal variability in behavior.

Another conclusion about human personality that has been drawn from common-sense knowledge and empirical observation is that people "think" as well as "act." We sense, and intuitively confirm, the idea that when a person is sitting quietly reading a book, he or she is indeed experiencing something. Although we may not be able to directly observe at the moment any evidence of mental activity, it could be revealed by asking the person a question or giving him or her an examination. Accordingly, we may come to think of a person as something more than his or her observable behavior. This particular conclusion about human personality has been exemplified in a *mind/body dichotomy*. In fact, traditionally the term *personality* has been used to account for all the things we can observe (such as behavior) as well as not observe (such as thoughts, feelings, and motives) about a person.

We may also conceptualize personality in terms of the locus of influence on human behavior. On some occasions, behavior appears to be the result of **external influences**, or factors outside the person, whereas on other occasions behavior appears to be determined by **internal influences**. This *internal/external dichotomy* expresses a distinction between environmentally based influences and personally based influences on behavior. A person responding to a traffic signal, to the temperature of a room, or to other people would be demonstrating the effects of environmental, or external, determinants of behavior. A person's need for food or desire to go to college would appear to be a determinant located within the person. This tendency to attribute human behavior to either internal or external influences not only is the basis of many theoretical notions about personality but, as we shall see later, is a basic assumption of our common-sense notions of personality.

The consistency/variability, mind/body, and internal/external dichotomies have led to a plethora of theoretical speculation and empirical work designed to explain the "basics" of human personality. The fundamental assumptions about personality that are expressed in these three dichotomies will reappear in various discussions throughout this chapter and the remainder of the book.

At this point, attention will be diverted to some other important concepts psychologists use to understand human behavior. Learning, perception, and motivation are viewed as dimensions of human personality that have particularly broad explanatory value and practical usefulness to both the psychologist and the layperson. We will therefore examine these concepts in more detail at this point.

THE CONCEPT OF LEARNING

At the turn of the 20th century, the functionalist school of thought in the United States was emphasizing the importance of an individual's successful adaptation to the demands of the environment. Whether his or her environment was a college or a factory, the "successful" person was one who could adjust to environmental demands. Success in meeting these demands rested on the person's learning and experience. Early into the 20th century, the work of Thorndike, Pavlov, and Watson had seemed to increase the U.S. psychologists' interest in the learning process. Before long, psychologists were explaining all facets of human behavior via the learning process.

Definition of Learning

Hilgard, Atkinson, and Atkinson (1975, p. 194) define **learning** as "a relatively permanent change in behavior that occurs as the result of prior experience." It should first be noted that "learning" is a hypothetical concept used to explain observable changes in behavior. We can never see learning, but must infer learning from changes that occur in people.

The above definition of *learning* has three important features: that learning is a change in behavior; that it is relatively permanent; and that it is the result of prior experience. Let us examine each of these features.

Imagine that we observe someone at Time A and find that some particular behavior is absent. Then we observe this same person at Time B and find that the behavior is present. In between, something has occurred to allow the new behavior to be developed. What can explain this difference between no behavior being present and behavior being present? Two possibilities exist: The behavior has been learned, or the behavior has occurred as a result of something other than learning. For example, we often mistakenly speak of a child's "learning" how to walk or talk. By this we should not imply that the *capacity* for a child to walk or talk is learned. The capacity for walking and talking is the result of maturational readiness and is not brought on by training—although, in the case of talking, the language that one speaks is determined by training. This is a frustrating lesson most parents must learn. Their efforts to train the child to walk or talk earlier than is genetically determined are for naught. No doubt most parents, if they could actually teach their child to walk or talk, would do so at an age when the child would not be adequately prepared to exhibit such skills. Furthermore, the next-door neighbors, in order to display the precociousness of their child, would feel it necessary to train him or her at an even earlier age. The term *learning*, therefore, is not used to identify behavior changes that are direct products of biological maturation.

The critical phrase in this definition, then, is *prior experience. Prior experience* refers to things like "training," "practice," and "study." If a college professor were to administer a midterm examination on the first day of class, most students would no doubt do poorly. However, at the regularly scheduled time for the examination, most

19

Children do not "learn" how to walk, but holding on to a steady hand won't hurt. (Photo © T. C. Abell/Stock, Boston.)

20

students would do quite well. Why this difference in behavior from Time A (first day of class) to Time B (halfway through the term)? Obviously, the reason is not biological maturation. No, in this case we are looking at changes in behavior that are due to experience. It is only on those occasions when prior experience produces the behavior change that we use the term *learning*.

How does one define *learning* in terms of a "relatively permanent" behavior change? Suppose that a young man enters a phone booth and looks up a number in the phone book. He dials it, talks to his party, and then hangs up the phone. As he is leaving the phone booth, he is stopped and asked to report the telephone number he has just dialed. After a few unsuccessful attempts, it becomes apparent that he cannot accurately report the number he just called. Has this telephone number been learned? What if the person were hypnotized—could he then retrieve the number?

To answer these questions, we might examine the distinction between what psychologists call **short-term memory** and **long-term memory**. All the sensory information that finds its way to our consciousness passes through short-term memory. (See Figure 2-1.) Some information may be merely fleeting images that pass through our consciousness and then "right out our ears." Such information is not permanently processed and is therefore not retrievable. This does not mean the information cannot have temporary usefulness. When we have just read a telephone number out of the phone book, we may proceed to dial that number correctly. However, the number is retained consciously for only a brief period and then is lost. Even under hypnosis it may be expected that such information will not be recalled, since it may not have been permanently stored in the mind.

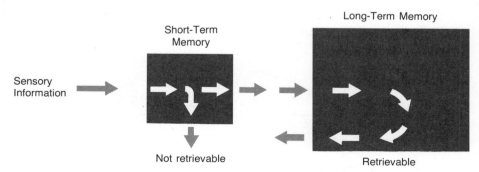

Figure 2-1. *Short-term and long-term memory.*

What, however, if the phone number is one that the person would like to recall at a future time (for example, the number of a prospective sweetheart)? In such a situation, the person might proceed to rehearse this number while the phone is ringing. For 5 or 6 seconds the number is held in consciousness. The effect of such a brief rehearsal may be to have this phone number transferred from short-term memory into long-term memory storage. As in an enormous efficient computer, this

21

number will be filed under "sweetheart phone numbers" and therefore becomes potentially recallable at a later time. The ease with which information is retrieved from long-term memory depends on many factors, such as the amount of prior practice and the preciseness of classification in long-term memory. In Chapter 11, we will present some suggestions for improving one's memory. However, the point to be made here is that the term *learning* is reserved for relatively permanently stored information in long-term memory.

Types of Learning

Classical Conditioning. The kind of learning which is primarily reactive and which accounts for most of our unconscious learning, such as acquisition of attitudes and some emotional responses is conditioning, classical and operant. For **classical conditioning** to occur, there must be some stimulus that regularly elicits some consistent response. For example, when meat is placed in a dog's mouth, the dog salivates. The meat serves as an unconditioned stimulus (UCS) eliciting the unconditioned response (UCR) of salivating. Pavlov (1927), the Russian physiologist famous for his investigation of the conditioned reflex, sounded a tuning fork shortly before presenting meat powder to a dog. Pavlov discovered that, after many repetitions of this sequence, the dog would salivate when the tuning fork sounded, even when no food was received. The tuning fork serves as a conditioned stimulus (CS), and the salivation elicited by the tuning fork is a conditioned response (CR). The conditioned stimulus may be presented simultaneously with or immediately before the unconditioned stimulus. After repeated pairing of the unconditioned stimulus with the conditioned stimulus, the CS develops the capacity to evoke the same response as the UCS. This procedure is illustrated in Figure 2-2.

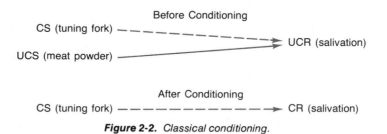

Figure 2-2. *Classical conditioning.*

In an early and classic study Watson and Rayner (1920) demonstrated learning by classical conditioning when they linked the sight of a white rat, which a child had previously not been afraid of, with a loud noise produced by striking a steel bar a sharp blow with a hammer. A few pairings of these two stimuli—the rat and the loud noise—were sufficient to produce a full-blown emotional response when the rat was presented. The child became frightened, whimpered, and withdrew from the animal.

A number of other furry stimuli, including a wad of cotton, a Santa Claus mask, a rabbit, and a woman with a fur collar on her coat, also elicited the fear response. All of us can think of similar cases. A sickly child, for example, soon makes an association between a painful shot in the arm or leg and the nurse who administers it, so that the sight of women in white dresses may come to elicit behavior similar to that elicited by the shot. Jones (1924), also using classical conditioning procedures, showed that a child's fear of furry objects could be eliminated by pairing them with a pleasant activity. The child was shown a white rabbit, a fear-eliciting stimulus, briefly and at a distance, while he was eating his favorite foods and playing with desired toys. Over a few weeks the rabbit was brought closer and closer to the place where the child was engaging in pleasurable activities. He soon learned to tolerate the rabbit's presence and eventually overcame his fear of it.

These studies show that, learning something about the regularity with which certain events go together, the organism is able to add structure to its environment and predict environmental events better. The first of a pair of stimuli can serve as a signal for the second, thereby eliciting an anticipatory response before the second stimulus event is experienced. This learning is especially valuable when the second stimulus is unpleasant or harmful. Imagine going to the dorm and taking a nice warm shower after a bad day at school. The warm water pouring down against your back helps you to relax and become oblivious to everything around you except the comfort of the water. Suddenly your state of relaxation is shattered by the awareness that the water has become scalding hot. Someone has flushed the toilet and used the cold water that tempers the shower. The water temperature abruptly returns to normal, but your back still burns and stings. You continue your shower but in a considerably less relaxed state, and as the water pressure drops again, on comes the red-hot flow to your already scalded back. This one association may be sufficient for you to learn that decreased water pressure is a signal for scalding water to follow.

You must now learn how to use this information in an adaptive way—that is, learn what will prevent this painful experience. It is not sufficient to learn to escape after the hot water starts. You must learn an avoidance response of getting out of the shower before the scalding water comes. By so doing you have demonstrated a learned response of moving out of the shower to the signal of a drop in water pressure. Your learned response has produced effective consequences and given you some control over your environment.

This example shows that learning what events in the environment are predictably related to each other is insufficient for adaptation and survival. We must also learn that consistent relations can be expected between our own action and subsequent events in the environment—that is, between our behavior and its consequences.

Operant Conditioning. A large portion of human behavior does not fit the classical conditioning paradigm, mainly because there is no identifiable eliciting stimulus. We are speaking of the broad class of behavior that appears to be voluntary: operant behavior. In **operant conditioning**, the consequences of a behavior determine whether that behavior will be repeated. The writing of this book, for example, is

23

operant behavior, because it is not an automatic response to something that happened before the behavior. It is a voluntary behavior, and whether it will be repeated depends on the consequences of our writing efforts. A feeling of accomplishment by the authors, recognition and approval from colleagues, a promotion, a pay increase, a reduced teaching load, a good review of the manuscript, or widespread use of this text would probably strengthen our writing behavior. If none of these results occurs, the outcome is less predictable, but it would seem to be a safe bet that we would approach the next manuscript with considerably less vigor, if at all.

Behavioral consequences may be pleasant or unpleasant, and they may consist of something added to or removed from the learning situation. When a response results in the addition of something pleasant to a situation, that response has been positively reinforced, and we say that **positive reinforcement** has occurred. **Negative reinforcement** occurs when behavior results in the removal of an unpleasant stimulus or condition. Jumping from the shower when the water pressure drops as a result of a flushing toilet is negatively reinforced because this behavior removes the person from the scalding water. All reinforcers, whether positive or negative, have a strengthening effect on behavior.

Punishment occurs when behavior produces an aversive or noxious condition (punishment type I) or results in the removal of something pleasant or desirable, such as paying a fine (punishment type II). Punishment generally weakens behavior. Behavior has no perpetual motion. For example, a factory worker will not continue working if he is taken off the payroll, and a fellow will not continue forever to drive long distances to see a girlfriend unless a smile, a kiss, or at least some comparable consequence is forthcoming. Behavior without purpose or results is at least senseless and possibly even maladaptive. Since behavior has no perpetual motion, it is likely to cease when it has no effect on one's situation.

A simple example can be used to illustrate each of the four preceding possibilities. Suppose you walk into a dark room and need to see your way around. You flip the light switch, and the lights enable you to see. The addition of this desirable consequence to the situation strengthens the response of flipping the switch (positive reinforcement). Let us now assume that the brilliance of the lights and the glare from them cause you to have a headache. You now flip the switch to turn them off or lower their intensity, and your headache disappears. In this case you have removed something unpleasant, and the response of flipping the switch is again strengthened (negative reinforcement). Now let us assume that you flip the switch and nothing happens one way or the other. Very quickly you will cease this behavior and try something else—try another switch, check the bulbs, and so on. In this case the response of flipping the switch is weakened (extinction). Finally let us suppose that there is a faulty connection, and when the switch is flipped you receive a shock. In this case the response has produced an undesirable consequence, and the behavior is weakened (punishment).

A basic concept in operant conditioning is reinforcement. A reinforcer is anything that strengthens behavior. Although psychologists are still a long way from identifying all the things that are or can become reinforcing to people, their concept of

The next time, this umpire may be less likely to call a player out. (Photo © Bob Clay/Jeroboam.)

what can reinforce behavior has been greatly expanded in recent years. It is common knowledge that food, water, sex, and other satisfiers of our physiological needs can serve as powerful primary reinforcers. Primary reinforcers are those that satisfy basic physiological needs. In an advanced technological society, however, little of our behavior in the course of a typical day is reinforced by primary reinforcers that have biological consequences. Far more important in controlling most of our behavior are stimulus events that have acquired the power to reinforce by being associated with primary reinforcers. Such stimuli, called "conditioned reinforcers," include smiles, pats on the back, good marks in school, and money. A gold star awarded to a student for good work is a conditioned reinforcer. It has little intrinsic value; rather, it is what this star represents or symbolizes that makes it an effective reinforcer. By the same token, money has significance only in relation to what it can be exchanged for or what it represents. People may continue to work for money long after their physiological needs are met, because money represents success and achievement, because it can be exchanged for something that does reflect status and success, or because it can be exchanged for some desirable outcome such as education, recreation, and labor-saving devices.

25

An opportunity to engage in a preferred activity can also serve as a behavioral reinforcer. Premack (1959) observed what animals did in a "free response" situation and found that rats deprived of water drank rather than exercising, while those deprived of exercise ran rather than drinking. Premack concluded that a high-probability (strongly desired) behavior can be used to increase the strength of a low-probability (less strongly desired) behavior if the former is made contingent on the latter. His water-deprived rats, for example, ran in order to get a drink of water, and the exercise-deprived rats would drink in order to get to run.

In a study of nursery school children (Homme, de Baca, Devine, Steinhurst, & Rickert, 1963), it was observed that, in the absence of aversive control, verbal instructions had little effect on behavior. When told to sit in chairs, the children often continued the activities in which they were engaged—screaming, pushing chairs, running around the room, and so on. In keeping with the Premack principle, these behaviors were labeled high-probability behaviors and were made contingent on low-probability, socially acceptable behaviors. For sitting quietly in chairs and looking at the blackboard, the children were given an opportunity to run and scream. At a later stage of training, the subjects earned tokens for low-probability behaviors which could be exchanged for the opportunity to engage in high-probability behavior.

Within a few days, control of the subjects was almost perfect. When they were told to sit and look at the blackboard (an activity that had previously been intermittently interrupted by the signal from the teacher for some higher-probability behavior), they were under such good control that, according to the experimenters, an observer new on the scene almost certainly would have assumed extensive aversive control was being used.

It may well be that, at least for humans, the basic reinforcer that sustains broad classes of behavior over long periods is the confirmation of one's competence (White, 1959). This source of reinforcement comes from attaining mastery over one's external or internal environment rather than satisfying appetites or minimizing aversions. Ruch and Zimbardo (1971) put it this way:

> From the infant's elation in learning to walk to the mountain climber's pride in conquering difficult and hazardous terrain, the perception of ourselves as active, capable agents is one of our greatest joys, whereas the perception of ourselves as helpless pawns controlled by others is one of the most galling of experiences. Students given all the privileges of affluence are not content with these gifts but go to painful lengths to get some control over their own education. No dictatorial regime has been able to indoctrinate its people beyond the point of at least underground resistance; sooner or later people who feel oppressed always rebel and demand to control their own destiny [p. 208].

Cognitive Learning. Much of our learning, however, cannot be explained by the conditioning models. Insight behavior, for example, involves more than mere conditioned responses. Proponents of **cognitive learning** theories tend to view behavior as purposive and goal-directed. A human being is seen as a very complex biological

26

What is reinforcing to children is best determined by watching children. (Photo © Lynn McLaren/ Photo Researchers, Inc.)

CHAPTER 2   UNDERSTANDING HUMAN BEHAVIOR: BASIC CONCEPTS

organism in a social environment. Learning is a result of trying various hypotheses and seeing what happens. Through this purposive living in a human environment, an individual develops as a person. The intelligently behaving person is one who acts as if he or she were pursuing a purpose and had some foresights as to how it was to be achieved. By observing the consequences of his or her behavior, the person develops expectancies of probable outcomes. Reinforcement is seen not as something that automatically strengthens behavior but as an outcome that affects one's expectations or foresights regarding the consequences of future actions. Basic to the cognitive learning position is the notion that an organism, rather than being an automaton, is capable of cognitively connecting the components of one situation or experience with those of another and deciding what relations are involved.

In cognitive learning great emphasis is placed on the internal processes of thinking and reasoning. A basic assumption about behavior is that since actions are preceded by thoughts, behavior can best be modified by first producing changes in the thought process. Shmurak (1974) was successful in helping male college students acquire more effective dating skills by teaching them to cognitively restructure a social situation involving a woman. Suppose, for example, that a couple on a blind date have gone to a movie and then for some coffee afterward. The young woman begins to talk about a political candidate, someone her date has never heard of, and then asks "What do you think of him?" The fellow might experience such thoughts as "She's got me now. I'd better try to bluff her, or she'll think I'm a dud. I hate politics anyway, so she's obviously not my type." This kind of thinking, or "self-talk," is very likely to generate behavior that is antagonistic to a desirable or enjoyable relationship between the couple.

Cognitive restructuring would involve a change in the way the young man perceives this situation—a change in the kind of "self-talk" that is occurring. Suppose he follows the self-statement above with this one: "Boy, that's really jumping to conclusions. This is only one area, and it really doesn't show what type of person she is. Anyway, what's the point of making up stuff about some politician I never heard of? She'll see right through me if I lie. It's not such a big deal to admit I don't know something. I'll just be honest and ask her to tell me more about where he stands on certain issues." When the situation is cognitively restructured in the manner reflected by these statements, the result is likely to be a more enjoyable form of verbal interaction between the fellow and his date.

Intelligence is a fundamental concept in cognitive psychology. It is seen as the ability to behave in present situations on the basis of anticipation of possible consequences and with a view to controlling the consequences that ensue. Within this frame of reference, behavior that produces a desired result is not considered intelligent behavior if it happened by chance or trial and error. Behavior is intelligent only when a person might have done otherwise and his or her actions reflected an understanding of what he or she was doing and why. Learning—the enhancement of intelligence—involves changes in the experiential situation of a person that give the person a basis for greater predictability and control in relation to his or her behavior.

Behavior is often the result of complex mental activity. (Photo © Karen Preuss/Jeroboam.)

THE CONCEPT OF PERCEPTION

Another concept that has occupied a prominent position in the understanding of human behavior is perception. Perception was one of the earliest concerns of prescientific thinkers and was to be the first major concern of scientific psychologists.

During the 17th and 18th centuries, a group of British philosophers reasoned that all mental events and mental activity were established on the basis of sensory experience. They pictured the mind at birth as merely a *tabula rasa*, or blank tablet, with the starting point of all knowledge being input from the world. There were no innate predispositions or unlearned emotional states. The content of the mind consisted of the raw material of our sensory images, called sensations, along with the unique ordering of such images. Therefore, all individual differences among people were explained by the variations in sensations received from their environments and the way these sensations combined in consciousness. These philosophers further assumed that the sensory images in the mind were exact mental duplicates of objects in the external world. Thus, these British empiricists, as they were called, believed that all human knowledge came by way of the senses and that such knowledge reflected identically the nature of the real world.

During the latter part of the 19th century, assumptions made by the British empiricists were subjected to more systematic analysis. The newly emerging field of experimental psychology was concerned mainly with why we see the world the way we do. The father of modern experimental psychology, Wilhelm Wundt, established the first laboratory in psychology for the purpose of investigating consciousness. By the time of Wundt psychologists were beginning to make a distinction between **sensation** and **perception**. Sensation was still viewed as the raw material of consciousness, but some were beginning to view the mind as something more than just the passive processing of sensory input. The mind was beginning to be viewed as a process that actively organized sensory information. Although the school of structuralism, which emerged from the Wundtian laboratory, showed some tendency toward viewing the mind as an active process, for the most part it remained in the tradition of British empiricism.

Others, however, were beginning to sense that the complexity of human mental activity could not be explained by sensations and their associations. They felt the mind was something more than just sensory input. Consciousness seemed to be a means whereby sensory information was actively processed. The mind seemed to selectively deal with the world and to consciously construct a meaningful picture of the world. There were many scientific and philosophical forerunners of this way of thinking, but it was the school of Gestalt psychology that was to epitomize the new approach to perception.

Gestalt psychology began mainly as a revolt against the structuralist school and the reduction of mental activity to association of sensations. The founders of the Gestalt school were Max Wertheimer (1880–1943), Wolfgang Köhler (1887–1967), and Kurt Koffka (1886–1941). These theorists reasoned that perception is basically an organizational process, that the mind actively organizes sensory input in such a way as to produce the most meaningful conscious organization possible. What is perceived is meaningful "wholes," not bits and pieces of sensory information.

What does one perceive if shown the following six dots?

.
. .
. . .

The Gestalt psychologists would argue that we do not merely perceive six discrete dots; rather, our mind makes an active (though not conscious) effort to organize such stimulation into a meaningful pattern. We see, therefore, not merely six dots, but a triangle.

This demonstrates two fundamental points about perception. One is that in perception, the whole may be greater than the sum of the parts. That is, perception is

30

a selecting and refining process, whereby stimulation from the external world may be organized into something more than its sensory characteristics. A second fundamental point about perception—related to the first point—is that there is not a one-to-one correspondence between external reality and the world of perception. Our minds do not simply duplicate what is out there. All information from the external world is processed and organized in the most meaningful way in perception. Sometimes reality and perception no doubt correspond very closely; at other times, as in the case of illusions, perception is very much at odds with incoming sensory information.

These assumptions of Gestalt psychology have found their way into much of our present-day thinking about human personality. We realize that humans are not passive receivers of information from their world, but that they filter information through their own personalities. Figure 2-3 presents a way of conceptualizing the factors that influence human perception.

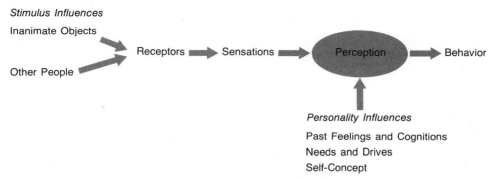

Figure 2-3. Influences on human perception.

Stimulus Influences

Figure 2-3 shows that there are two major categories of influences on human perception. First, there are influences outside the person, called "stimulus influences." Human beings are continually exposed to two types of stimuli in the world: inanimate objects and other people. Individuals do perceive inanimate objects and other people in a similar fashion. All external objects can be described along a number of physical dimensions, such as size, shape, and color. If we examine an apple, for example, we can know that object in terms of its physical dimensions.

Other people can also be perceived in terms of such physical dimensions as size, shape, and color. However, there is a very important distinction between our perception of an inanimate object and our perception of another person. With the apple, our perception must be limited to the object's physical dimensions. With human beings, however, we realize that they are something more than their physically observable characteristics. We assume that lying behind one's physical appearance or expressive motor or verbal behavior is a thinking and feeling person. When we pick up an apple, we do not ask "Does this apple find me attractive?" or "Does this apple think I am intelligent?" Moreover, if we take a big bite out of the apple, we are not concerned with whether we have injured the apple or hurt its feelings. This is because we assume that nothing lies behind the physical dimensions that we observed about an apple. With other people we assume that behind their behavior is a thinking and feeling organism. Consequently, our perceptions of people always combine stimulus information with inferences about the stimulus person's personality.

Once stimulus information is recorded by our sense organs, the information is transmitted across sensory fibers and enters the brain, where it is experienced as conscious sensations. As previously pointed out, the mind does not passively record sensory information but will actively organize the final conscious perceptions in ways that are most meaningful and consistent with the person's view of the world.

Personality Influences

The second major category of influences on human perception is personality influences, influences inside the person. There are many concepts used to identify the various personality influences. We often speak of "feelings," "attitudes," "thoughts," "needs," and "drives," to mention some of the more traditionally used terms. No one can directly observe these influences, but we all can intuitively attest to the reality of such influences in our perception. Experimentally, psychologists have found that such internal states do influence how people perceive and then respond to the world. In a later chapter we will examine some of the ways social and person perception influences people's interpersonal interactions.

THE CONCEPT OF MOTIVATION

The term *behavior* refers to what people do, while the term *motivation* is used to explain why people do what they do. *Motivation,* then, is concerned mainly with *causes* of human behavior.

The concept of motivation, like learning and perception, is an abstraction used to explain certain changes observed in human behavior. In the discussion of perception, it was pointed out that conscious perception is influenced by both stimulus and personality factors. In a sense, we might think of these stimulus and personality factors as the causes of conscious perception and, subsequently, the causes of human behavior. Let us examine more closely how these two sets of factors influence human functioning.

Stimulus Influences

The word *stimulus* has traditionally been used in psychology to refer to some feature of the external environment. The stimulus, then, is a feature of the physical world, and it impinges on the organism in the form of some physical energy. Environmental stimulation is brought about by one of our sensory receptors being influenced by some energy in the physical world. The only way that we can know the external world is by having a sensory organ that can detect energy changes in the world. For most individuals without sensory impairment, 95% of the input from the environment is recorded by the visual and auditory senses. We are constantly being bombarded by massive stimulation of light energy (producing sights) and changes in air pressure (producing sounds). Other sense organs, for taste, smell, and cutaneous (skin) sensations, are also intermittently recording various types of energy from the external environment.

We can know the physical world only to the extent that we have the appropriate sensory equipment to record physical energies. Indeed, much of our physical environment is not accessible to our sense organs. Our eye, for example, is sensitive to only a narrow range of energies along the electromagnetic spectrum. All the colors we observe in our world are restricted to this narrow visual spectrum. There are energies, such as ultraviolet and infrared rays, that lie outside our visual sensory capacity and are just as real—but we are unable to perceive them. Human hearing is restricted to changes in air pressures between about 20 and about 20,000 cycles/second. There are, of course, changes in air pressures that are above the threshold of human hearing, but they are not a part of experience because they are not perceived. We perceive and adapt to only those facets of the environment of which we are aware.

Suppose that students are sitting in a classroom. The temperature of the room is a comfortable 70° F, but the room temperature rises to 110° F in a matter of a few minutes. What will be the effect of this change in the environment on the students' behavior? We might observe that as the room temperature begins to climb, the students become more restless and begin to squirm in their chairs. As the room becomes warmer and warmer, other behaviors are observed. One student might proceed to shed some unnecessary clothing. Another student might use his or her notebook as a fan. Another might get up and check the air-conditioning unit. Another might leave the room. Another might request that the teacher take action to change the situation. Another in the meantime might collapse to the floor, and so on. What if the instructor were to give an examination during this class period? Would we expect the examination scores to be very trustworthy in such an environment? We can see that changes in the stimulus situation can produce changes in human behavior. In the situation just described, students are consciously aware of the excessive room temperature and are, therefore, motivated to adapt in various ways to this aversive situation.

The external environment can also influence us in ways we are not consciously aware of. What if all the doors and windows were closed in a classroom and all the oxygen were immediately extracted from the air? What changes would we observe in the students' behavior? Interestingly enough, not much of any change would probably take place, particularly as long as the air volume were maintained. The reason is that people are unaware of when they are not breathing oxygen. We do not have a sense organ that tells us when we are not breathing oxygen. Consequently, the students would probably lapse into unconsciousness one by one without realizing the reason. Students would not rush to the door and escape the room, as we might

33

imagine. Moreover, there are many types of environmental stimuli, such as radioactivity and lethal gases, that may cause serious injury or death because a person, being unaware of the danger, is not motivated to escape it. Some researchers even speak of "subliminal" perception, in which environmental stimulation may influence us without our conscious awareness, although this idea is seriously questioned. In any case, stimuli from the external world are major motivational influences on behavior.

Personality Influences

Much of human behavior can be explained as attempts to make adjustments to environmental stimulation. However, much of human behavior is motivated within the person. We call the internal determinants of behavior "personality influences." Such personality influences make for differences among people and include things like one's past feelings and cognitions and one's needs and motives. Personality influences, then, may be thought of as the sum total of life experiences as they come to bear on behavior patterns.

Past Feelings and Cognitions: Attitudes. Social psychologists have tried to identify the influence of past experience by way of the concept of **attitude**. Initially, an attitude was thought to be the simplest conceptual unit of one's consciousness, although eventually different components of an attitude needed to be specified. Included were both an affective (or feeling) component and a cognitive (or mental-content) component. Each component of the attitude has been subjected to measurement. Attitudes are always directed toward some object. Attitudinal objects may include a person, a group, or an inanimate object, such as a car or a B-1 bomber; attitudes may be held toward very concrete objects or more abstract objects, such as justice or a Martian. Whatever the mental content of the attitude, it is always tinged with some degree of emotion. Any object that passes across our mind elicits some degree of affect along a pleasantness/unpleasantness dimension.

Attitudes serve a number of important functions for the individual (Katz, 1960). They help us interpret the world and make it meaningful, they help us relate appropriately to other people, they help us express our value orientations, and they may serve to protect us from ego threats. It is on the basis of the attitudes we hold about things, other people, and ourselves that we are motivated to act in certain ways. Our attitudes may determine whom we ask for a date, whom we vote for, or what kind of car we choose to buy. They may motivate us to read a book, throw a rock, or seek a psychotherapist. Attitudes serve as one of our most important sources of internal motivation.

Needs and Motives. Another category of personality influences on behavior is a person's need states. There are many needs in human personality; they might be classified into the categories of biological needs, sociocultural needs, and psychological needs. Biological needs are ones that function to maintain a stable and balanced state in the internal biochemical environment of the body. In order for our

34

bodies to function adequately, we must maintain a fairly consistent biochemical condition in terms of water and food levels, chemical makeup, such as oxygen content, and temperature level, and the body must give off waste. Whenever there is a condition of deficit in the body's cells, a state of biological need will exist. Biological needs then give rise to a drive state, which leads to seeking out or avoidance behavior designed to eliminate the biological need. The body will then return to a balanced condition until the need arises again. During the course of a day, our internal biological needs are directing us toward places to eat or drink, toward more comfortable environments, and toward restrooms.

Because we have grown up in a particular culture, socialization into that culture has established in us a number of sociocultural needs. These needs are not directly tied to internal biological states, but are established and maintained through cultural expectations. From an early age, we learn what behaviors are appropriate and expected of us. Often such training is expedited by our awareness of cultural stereotypes. Age-role and sex-role stereotypes, for example, define for us what is appropriate behavior at a particular age and what is appropriate behavior if we are a certain sex. Socialization also involves coming to realize that there are other behavioral expectations of culture expressed through customs, taboos, and laws. We also learn that culture or society imposes penalties, or sanctions, on us if we fail to act according to cultural definitions. Such sanctions may result in our being ostracized from a group or imprisoned for a crime.

To list the sociocultural needs that may develop in individuals would be a virtually impossible task, and such needs would, of course, differ across cultures. However, in our own culture—and most Western cultures, for that matter—some sociocultural needs are almost universally enculturated. Two such highly conditioned needs are a *conformity need* and an *achievement need*.

Culture expects members to adapt and respond according to the prevailing norms. From early in life, we look to significant others to define for us both physical and social reality. We become dependent on others not only to reliably communicate the expectations of society but to structure our own self-concepts. It becomes stressful, therefore, for us to deviate from the behavior of others. Hence, to conform to the behavior of others is highly reinforced in culture and becomes a powerful means of maintaining cultural stability.

Another sociocultural need is the need for achievement. McClelland, Atkinson, Clark, and Lowell (1953) define achievement motivation in terms of one's desire to overcome obstacles and frustrations and to master the environment. Such motivation may lead to efforts to reach the goals the culture defines as desirable. For most, successful achievement motivation would be expressed by way of publicly recognized standards of achievement, such as earning college degrees, writing books, plays, or poetry, and succeeding at business enterprises. So, while conformity tends to encourage individuals to think and behave alike, achievement motivation encourages them to develop and cultivate their unique potentials.

In addition to the needs and motives that develop from our external world, internal biochemical environment, and culture, there are needs within the individual that serve to maintain one's psychological well-being. The fulfillment of such needs is crucial for maintaining an optimal level of mental health. Examples of such psychological needs are the need for a favorable self-concept, the need for sensory stimulation, and the need for knowing and understanding the world. We shall have more to say about important human psychological needs in Chapter 4.

SUMMARY

This chapter presented some of the basic psychological concepts used to understand human behavior. The concept of *personality* was viewed from three principal dichotomies: consistency/variability, mind/body, and internality/externality. The concept of *learning* has become one of the most fundamental to the understanding of human behavior. Learning was defined as a relatively permanent change in behavior that occurs as the result of experience. Learned behavior was discussed from the perspectives of classical conditioning, operant conditioning, and cognitive learning. The concept of *perception* was presented as a way of understanding how the mind processes incoming information. Factors outside the person (stimulus factors) and factors within the person (personality factors) that influence perceptual functioning were examined.

While the term *behavior* refers to *what* people do, the term *motivation* has been used to explain *why* people do things. In the final section of this chapter, we presented the stimulus and personality influences on *motivation*. In examining the impact of stimulation on motivation, we discussed environmental energy, receptor stimulation, and perception. We examined two kinds of personality influences on motivation: (1) attitudes and (2) needs and motives.

KEY CONCEPTS

Attitude a concept used by some psychologists to refer to a conceptual unit of consciousness, generally specified in terms of a cognitive component (mental content) and an affective component (feelings).

Classical conditioning the repeated pairing of a neutral stimulus (CS) with an unlearned stimulus-response reflex (UCS→UCR) such that the neutral stimulus (CS) comes to elicit the original response (CR).

Cognitive learning learning that occurs as the result of conscious mental processes such as thinking and reasoning.

External influences influences on human behavior that originate in one's external environment.

Internal influences influences on human behavior that originate in one's feelings, thinking, or physiological functioning.

Learning a relatively permanent change in behavior that is produced by training and not by biological maturation.

Long-term memory memory containing information that is permanently stored and is therefore potentially retrievable.

Motivation a term used by psychologists to explain why behavior occurs.

Negative reinforcement any aversive stimulus consequence that will strengthen a response.

Operant conditioning the strengthening of a response by following that response with a reinforcing consequence.

Perception the selective and organizational process whereby sensory input is made into meaningful conscious content aided by prior experience.

Personality a term traditionally used by psychologists to capture the totality of human behavior.

Personality consistency the consistency in human behavior across time and settings.

Personality variability the variability in human behavior across time and settings.

Positive reinforcement any stimulus with a positive consequence that will strengthen a response.

Punishment any aversive stimulus consequence that leads to a weakening of a response.

Sensation the raw material of consciousness resulting from sensory input.

Short-term memory memory containing information that is not permanently stored and is therefore not retrievable.

3

CHAPTER OBJECTIVES

1. To understand how psychologists study human behavior.
2. To list and define the steps in the scientific method.
3. To develop familiarity with the language of research.
4. To distinguish among laboratory, natural, field, baseline, and simulation experiments.
5. To identify some strengths and limitations of each of the experimental techniques in the previous objective.
6. To understand the concepts of validity and reliability.

UNDERSTANDING HUMAN BEHAVIOR: THE NATURE OF RESEARCH

Psychology has traditionally been defined as the scientific study of animal and human behavior. This definition, although few really stop to ponder its meaning, answers three important questions: "*What* is the object of study in psychology?" "*Who* is the object of study in psychology?" "*How* does psychology study its subject matter?" The subject matter, or "data," of psychology is behavior, and the objects of such study may be humans or lower animal forms. The method for studying behavior in humans and animals has been the method of science.

SCIENTIFIC METHOD

What does the term *science* mean, and what determines whether something is a scientific study? To many the term *science* has come to be synonymous with *advanced technology,* so that we vaguely sense that putting a man on the moon has something to do with science. Science, however, is basically a *method* of generating knowledge. The fundamental requirement to use this method of science is that you must have observable, and therefore measurable, events. Consequently, psychology is considered a science simply because we can apply this so-called scientific method to the observable and measurable events we call behavior.

The scientific method can be thought of as simply a set of steps or stages that leads one from mere observation about the world to verification of one's observation about the world and thus to what may be regarded as scientific knowledge. The scientific method has four basic steps:

> *Observation*—knowledge derived from the senses (common sense)
> *Hypothesis*—a clearly stated question that can be answered either yes or no
> *Experimentation*—trustworthy measures and procedures that provide an answer to the hypothesis
> *Verification*—confirmation of experimental finding by repeated experimentation (replication) or the laws of probability (statistical verification)

The first step is observation. The only way that anyone can know anything about the world is through information recorded by our sense organs. We may visually observe a beautiful sunset, auditorially observe a beautiful piece of music, olfactorily observe a rosebud, and so on. We spend our entire life recording such observations about the world. For most of us these observations will also lead to explanation of the events observed. For instance, the observation that a puddle of water gradually diminishes following a rain shower may mean to one person that the sun has evaporated the water, to another that the water is merely passing through porous ground. Each person has his or her own explanation for the event observed. If we were to stop at this first step of the scientific method, in which observations are explained by intuitive explanation, we would have what is called **common-sense knowledge**. Common-sense knowledge, quite simply, is knowledge generated from sensory observation. Imagine that one observes a woman trying to park in a small parking slot. In

40

B. F. Skinner has spent over 40 years experimenting on animal and human behavior. (Photo © Ken Heyman.)

the process she strikes a fender of another car. It is very easy for one to move from one's observation to the sweeping conclusion that "women are poorer drivers than men."

The scientist, like the person on the street, must not rely on such common-sense knowledge. Science requires that we proceed to a second step, called a "hypothesis." The scientist relies on observation merely as a way of generating questions to be answered about the world. For example, the scientist is required to ask "Has the puddle of water diminished because of the sun's heat?" or "Are men poorer drivers than women?" The hypothesis is simply a precisely stated question that has only two possible answers, yes and no. Science cannot deal with questions that cannot be answered by observation (such as "How many angels can dance on the head of a pin?"), nor can science deal with questions that cannot provide unequivocal answers (such as "Have you scolded your child lately?").

Once the scientist has asked a succinct question, the next step of the scientific method is to generate an answer. This is accomplished by the third step, experimentation. This step is the defining feature of the scientific method, and the terms *scientific method* and *experiment* are virtually interchangeable. It is the purpose of the experiment to provide a yes or no answer to the hypothesis posed by the researcher. Simple as this may sound, the capacity of a researcher to design and conduct an experiment that generates a trustworthy answer to the question under consideration is an enormously complex ability. Often even formulating the simplest hypothesis or conducting a seemingly simple experiment may require an enormous amount of training and preparation of the researcher. We will return to a more detailed discussion of the experimentation phase of the scientific method shortly. But let us first examine the fourth step of the scientific method.

Suppose that a researcher does conduct an experiment and does generate an answer to the hypothesis: "Are women poorer drivers than men?" This researcher has indeed found that, yes, women are poorer drivers than men. Where do we now stand relative to our objective of scientific knowledge? Can we now state confidently that it has been "proved" that women are poorer drivers than men? Have we now established a scientific "fact" or a scientific "law" regarding this aspect of human behavior? No. How, then, is something proved in science? The answer is that "proof" or scientific knowledge is generated by step four of the scientific method, called "verification."

One should be extremely careful not to associate "facts" with only one or even a few experiments. A recent advertisement of a widely used pain pill stated that it had been proved that Excedrin is a more effective pain reliever than the other medications studied. On what basis has this pain reliever been shown to be more effective? Because two studies, one in a famous hospital setting and one in a clinic, had shown it to be. Apart from the many questions that a scientist might raise about such findings, certainly no scientist should regard such "findings" as proof. If indeed something has been proved, there is hardly any need to continue investigating an area. The authors suspect, however, that few people are truly convinced that all future research on the relative effectiveness of the multitude of pain relievers should be discontinued. No, we would say, it is far from proved that Excedrin is the most effective pain reliever.

When we talk about "facts" or "laws" in science, we are talking about highly verified relations between variables. Suppose, for example, that while one researcher has conducted an experiment and generated a yes answer to a hypothesis, 99 other researchers testing the same hypothesis and using identical procedures have generated no answers. It seems likely that we would now question whether the first investigator's experiment has proved anything or offered the scientific community another "fact" to add to its collection. It should be apparent that this idea of verification is a more demanding notion. In psychology, as in science in general, two major types of verification have been used. The first type is called the "replication" and the second is called "statistical verification."

A **replication** is simply an attempt to repeat an experiment testing the same hypothesis as the original experiment did and using the same measures and procedures. This may be done by the same or different investigators. Although a replication is an attempt to retest a hypothesis under as similar conditions as possible, replications will almost always involve different samples of subjects. Therefore, in order to avoid

42

generating findings that differ from the original findings simply because of sampling differences, researchers should try to replicate experiments with as similar a sample of subjects as possible. If, however, researchers continue to verify a hypothesis across a wider range of subjects, the scientific knowledge generated will have a broader application.

If we were to survey the journals in psychology, it would become apparent that actual replications of experiments are seldom done. Occasionally an investigator will publish a replication, but usually only when the two experiments have produced dissimilar results. If verification is such an important step of scientific inquiry, why are there so few actual replications? The answer seems to be that psychologists have come to rely on the second means of verification—*statistical verification.*

Suppose that an investigator finds that children in School A have higher IQs than children in School B. The children in School A have a mean (average) IQ of 104, and the children in School B have a mean IQ of 102. Although there is a difference between the mean IQs of the groups, it is obvious that the difference is not very great. In fact, even if you had a large number of students from each school—say, 100 students from School A and 100 from School B—you would find that the difference between these two mean scores was not statistically significant. What if the students at School A, however, had an average IQ of 102 and students at School B had an average IQ of 80? This difference would probably be statistically, as well as practically, significant. The larger the difference between the mean IQ scores of the two groups, the more confidence we may have that this difference is a true difference. This investigator may be in a position to say she is 95% confident that the difference in IQs that she has observed between students in School A and students in School B is a true difference. How can this investigator express this degree of confidence in her findings? Why not 99% confident or 80% confident? The answer lies in probability theory. Statistical tables have been devised that allow investigators to determine the probability that their findings are genuine or indicative of only a chance difference. The greater the actual mean IQ difference between School A and School B, assuming that the variability within each group's scores is not great, the greater the probability that the investigator has identified a true difference between the ability levels of the two groups of students. Therefore, this investigator is in a position to say: If 100 other investigators were to replicate this study, I am confident that 95 of them would obtain the same results as I did.

THE EXPERIMENT

The **experiment** has as its purpose to relate some *cause* to some *effect.* If a psychologist wishes to know whether students' anxiety levels influence their examination grades or whether a particular drug influences a person's concentration or whether packaging a given product in a wrapper of a particular color increases sales,

43

he may arrange to study these concerns by way of an experiment. The investigator manipulates a cause (called an **independent variable**) to see whether it has an effect on a person's behavior (called a **dependent variable**). The independent variable may be a feature of the external environment (stimulus variable), such as temperature of a room or number of people in a room, or it may be a feature of the subject himself (organismic variable), such as age, sex, or level of anxiety. The researcher selects and/or manipulates the independent variable under investigation to see whether it influences some behavior.

The experiment is the cornerstone of the scientific method. In order to have an experiment, two requirements must be met: (1) you must have two groups of subjects, an experimental group and a control group, and (2) you must exercise what is called "scientific control" in the experiment.

The distinction between the experimental group and the control group is that the former is influenced by an independent variable, while the latter is not. Independent variables may be features of the physical environment (such as light, sound, or other people) or features that characterize the individual (such as level of anxiety, intelligence, or age and sex). The same experiment may study one or more independent variables. Moreover, each independent variable—a variable is something that varies along some dimension—may vary along quantitative levels (such as the amount of a drug or number of hours of sleep) or vary within a qualitative dimension (such as types of classroom instruction or types of TV advertisements). We cannot say for sure that an independent variable has caused an outcome unless we know whether that outcome would have occurred without the introduction of the independent variable. The control group allows us to do that.

For example, advertisers may claim that a group using Brand A toothpaste had 23% fewer cavities than the group using Brand B toothpaste. This may very well be true, particularly if Brand A toothpaste contains fluoride and Brand B does not. It therefore appears that the brand of toothpaste (independent variable) has influenced the number of cavities (dependent variable) that users have. But how would a control group perhaps qualify this finding? Well, the scientist must ask: Could it be that the number of cavities that people have is more related to the brushing than the toothpaste? How many cavities would people have if they merely brushed their teeth but used no toothpaste? What if we were to find that in the above study, a control group who brushed their teeth but used no toothpaste, did not have any cavities? Well, now we would be justified in saying that Brand A causes cavities, although admittedly fewer cavities than Brand B. Thus one can see the importance of a control group to our scientific understanding of cause-and-effect relations.

The second essential requirement of an experiment is **scientific control**, which may be defined as an attempt to eliminate all possible influences on the dependent variable except the independent variable. Scientific control is elimination of extraneous influences and therefore undesired variance in an experiment. If we wish to show that Cause A has produced Effect X, we must show that Effect X was not caused by some other variable, such as Cause B or Cause C.

Imagine that an investigator wants to conduct an experiment to show that

44

students' levels of anxiety during test taking affect their examination scores. The investigator might measure the students' arousal levels during the examination period by way of some physiological index such as heart rate. On the basis of the heart-rate measure, the researcher classifies students into a "high anxiety" group and a "low anxiety" group. He then determines that the high-anxiety group correctly answers significantly fewer test items than the low-anxiety group. It therefore appears that there is a causal relation between anxiety and examination performance.

And indeed there may very well be such a relation. But the question that should immediately come to mind concerning the above study is "Is anxiety the only reason that these two groups differed on examination performance?" Perhaps, after the fact, we ask these students how long they spent studying for the examination, and we find that the high-anxiety group studied an average of 2 hours, the low-anxiety group an average of 8 hours. Now it is apparent that the difference in examination scores for these two groups might be due to differences in anxiety level or differences in study time or perhaps both in combination. Obviously, the researcher does not wish to conduct an experiment that leads to such ambiguous interpretation. Therefore, in designing any study, the researcher must try to eliminate all the possible influences on the dependent variable except the one being manipulated.

Television commercials are a rich source of data for critical evaluation, particularly when so many commercials try to establish the worth of their product on "scientific" evidence. One should attempt, however, to apply the two basic requirements for an experiment the next time one hears that Brand A has been proved more effective than Brand B. When we ask "Where is the control group?" and "Is that the only reason for the effect?" we will often find that such commercials attempt to utilize and mimic the language of science but fail to adhere to the basic requirements of an experiment.

TYPES OF EXPERIMENTS

Every experiment involves selecting and manipulating an independent variable to determine whether it affects a dependent variable. An experiment may, however, involve more than one independent variable or dependent variable. In addition, experiments may be conducted in a variety of settings and for a variety of purposes. Generally, studies designed to identify cause-and-effect relations are classified as laboratory experiments, field experiments, natural experiments, baseline experiments, or simulation experiments.

Laboratory Experiments

Traditional experimental psychology has tended to emulate experimentation in the natural and physical sciences. There has been an emphasis on studying behavior in highly controlled situations where the experimenter can exercise maximum control over extraneous variables. Such artificial, "germfree" environments allow the experimenter to evaluate more precisely the extent to which the independent variable is operating on the dependent variable. Let us look at a hypothetical example of a **laboratory experiment**.

Suppose a psychopharmacologist—a psychologist who studies the effects of drugs on behavior—has synthesized a new drug that he believes may improve memory. Consequently, he wishes to design an experiment that will examine the influence of the new drug on memory. As pointed out previously, the experiment requires that we have two types of groups. One group receives the drug (experimental group), and another group does not receive it (control group). However, as is the case in most experiments, the experimenter may wish to gather as much information on the effects of this drug as possible in the experiment. One way of evaluating the efficacy of this drug would be to determine whether varying dosages of the drug have different effects on memory. Therefore, the investigator may wish to administer, say, three different drug dosages. In this case, only one independent variable will be studied, but it will be studied at three different levels. This experiment will, therefore, involve three experimental groups (three drug dosage levels) and one control group (no drug dosage). The investigator may then ask subjects to study some material (perhaps nonsense syllables, which have little retention value) while the drug is active in their bodies. One week later the subjects will be asked to recall the original material when the drug is not active in their systems. Table 3-1 is a summary of the experimental results.

This investigator would probably hypothesize that, as the drug dosage increases, retention for the nonsense syllables will increase. Therefore, the experimental findings directly support his prediction, and a publication is imminent. However, suppose the experimenter had not included a control group. Then he would not have been in a position to know whether the drug was having a positive influence. Even though retention for nonsense syllables seems to be increasing with drug dosages, it may very well be that a control group would have been able to recall 90% of the material. The conclusion would then have been that the drug inhibits, rather than enhances, recall.

What if the experimenter had obtained the results shown in Table 3-2? Then it would appear that the drug does improve memory in the first two groups but not in the high-dosage group. This finding might suggest that this dosage level is too potent and not only may impair memory but may possibly cause serious injury to the brain.

Table 3-1. Results of Hypothetical Drug Experiment

Group	Percentage of nonsense syllables recalled
Group 1 (low dosage)	60
Group 2 (medium dosage)	70
Group 3 (high dosage)	80
Control (no dosage)	50

46

Table 3-2. Alternative Results of Hypothetical Drug Experiment

Group	Percentage of nonsense syllables recalled
Group 1 (low dosage)	60
Group 2 (medium dosage)	70
Group 3 (high dosage)	20
Control (no dosage)	50

We see that a researcher must be very cautious about the manipulation given to subjects.

Let us suppose that this investigator has limited time, facilities, and access to subjects and decides to use only two experimental groups. He then obtains the results shown in Table 3-3.

On the basis of these experimental findings, the researcher concludes that there is no functional relation between his newly developed drug and memory. This researcher, then, discontinues this line of research and initiates a new research program. But what if the medium-dosage group had been included, and its percentage of retention had been 90? Well, now it is apparent that this researcher has missed a very important empirical finding simply because he failed to select the proper levels of the independent variable. In drug studies we often find that one group gets the drug (experimental group) and another group does not (control group). However, when experiments involve only one experimental group, there is always the risk of selecting the wrong level to study or failing to identify the relative influence of varying levels of the independent variable.

Often in studies designed to investigate the influence of drugs on human behavior it is desirable to include a second type of control group. What would happen, for example, if a group of subjects were led to believe they were taking a newly developed drug that was thought to improve memory, but the drug was in actuality an inert substance with no pharmacological properties? A *placebo* (literally meaning "I will please") group may provide a whole new perspective on the impact of an independent variable. Suppose we add a placebo group to our drug/memory study and obtain the results in Table 3-4. We can now see that the subjects' expectations about the drug's beneficial effects have outweighed the drug's actual effects.

Table 3-3. Results of Hypothetical Drug Experiment with Two Experimental Groups

Group	Percentage of nonsense syllables recalled
Group 1 (low dosage)	50
Group 2 (high dosage)	50
Control (no dosage)	50

Table 3-4. Results of Hypothetical Drug Experiment with a Placebo Group

Group	Percentage of nonsense syllables recalled
Group 1 (low dosage)	60
Group 2 (medium dosage)	70
Group 3 (high dosage)	80
Control (no dosage)	50
Placebo (believe they have received a drug)	90

It should be apparent that a laboratory investigation requires a great deal of thoughtful preparation to generate trustworthy data. In fact, there are many more questions that should concern us about the hypothetical experiment just discussed. For example, are the drug dosage levels the only influence on the retention scores? Did the experimenter try to control the amount of time the subjects spent studying the nonsense syllables? Did the subjects have an opportunity to rehearse the material between the original learning session and the retention test? Were there enough subjects in each group to make the findings trustworthy? Did the experimenter try to control such variables as the age, sex, and intellectual level of the subjects? Has the experimenter made provisions for assessing the possible negative or long-range side effects of the drug?

Psychologists have tended to rely on the laboratory experiment for discovering the "causes" of human behavior. One investigator has found that about 90% of all research in psychology has been of the laboratory-experiment type. Yet many investigators are beginning to wonder whether it might not be better to give up a degree of scientific control in order to study behavior in more natural conditions. In an effort to study human behavior in more "real-life" settings, psychologists have used the natural experiment and the field experiment.

Natural Experiments

Occasionally, special circumstances occur in the natural world that engender changes in behavior. These events are not manipulated by an investigator, but they may be regarded as a type of independent variable. For example, much of our understanding of how people behave in crisis situations has not resulted from planned experiments. Social scientists have simply conducted **natural experiments** by observing the ways people react to or cope with an emergency following some catastrophe.

These independent variables may be due to the forces of nature, such as hurricanes, tornadoes, or earthquakes, or due to such naturally occurring human events as elections, séances, or policy decisions. When possible, the researcher may obtain attitudinal information before and after the crucial event. However, if a tornado passes through a community decimating lives and property, we can be fairly confident that the observed behaviors are caused by this event. Ideally, it would be desirable to have a control group, such as another community of comparable size and likelihood of being struck by a tornado, but many situations make it extremely difficult to have one.

Few natural experiments have been reported by social scientists, simply because such studies are hard to plan and conduct. The investigator must typically seize an opportunity when it comes, and there must be a great deal of advance planning. Certainly, it is much more convenient for a researcher to design a laboratory study, which offers greater control over subjects and variables and promises immediately obtainable data. Still, some researchers have perceived that laboratory studies cannot provide the rich and illuminating information generated by natural studies.

How, for example, would an investigator design a laboratory study to examine individuals' reactions to the assassination of an American president? Following the assassination of President Kennedy, some researchers (Greenberg & Parker, 1965) gathered reactions from the American people on this unexpected tragedy and provided information that could not have been obtained otherwise. In another natural experiment, Lieberman (1956) studied factory workers' attitudes toward management and unions before and after naturally occurring changes in work roles. Some workers were promoted to foremen, while others were elected union stewards or remained in their same work roles. Lieberman found that the newly appointed foremen's attitudes became more favorable toward management, while the newly elected union stewards' attitudes became more favorable toward unions. These two illustrations of natural experiments show that such studies may or may not be planned before the event and may deal with a variety of concerns. They do offer the patient and innovative behavioral scientist another means of generating cause-and-effect information.

Field Experiments

Some have wondered whether it might not be possible for an experimenter to manipulate an independent variable in order to study its effects on behavior in settings closer to real life. In other words, one may strive to adhere to the rigorous demands for precise control of extraneous variables which characterize the laboratory experiment while trying to capture the naturalness of behavior in real-life situations. Such an objective has given rise to the so-called **field experiment**. Kurt Lewin (1951) was an early advocate of such an approach to scientific inquiry into human behavior. He identified a need for "action research," which would take the scientists of human behavior into the natural environment.

The defining characteristic of field experimentation is that an experimenter selects an independent variable and introduces it into an ongoing real-life situation. The subjects are unaware that they are under scientific scrutiny, and the independent variable is typically some event that does not arouse suspicion. It has been very forcefully argued (Bickman & Henchy, 1972) that such experimentation in the natural

49

context provides a freer and less constrained subject and, therefore, more trustworthy information about how people behave. Although laboratory experimentation is of immense value, reliance on it should not be total. Ideally, researchers should try to use the experimental methods of the laboratory and the field in a coordinated effort to expand our understanding of human behavior.

There has been an emerging interest during the past decade in field-research techniques. Many textbooks in social psychology have begun to devote considerably more space to a discussion of field experimentation than in the past. Many researchers have come to accept the value and validity of such an approach but have found it hard to discontinue their reliance on the traditional laboratory experiment. For example, during a three-year period (1968–1970), only 3% of the articles published in one of the most prestigious social-psychology journals were devoted to field experimentation. However, we can expect an ever-growing interest among applied psychologists, as well as basic researchers, in such research.

There are a number of important reasons why psychologists might prefer field experiments over laboratory experiments. First off, since subjects are not aware that they are subjects, we would not expect their behavior on the dependent variable to be influenced by that knowledge. Recently, investigators have come to realize just how important the problem of subject awareness is to the outcome of a study. Orne (1962) has argued that in laboratory experiments, where subjects are aware that they are being observed, they will seek to uncover the purposes of the experiment and behave in what they feel is an appropriate manner. They may observe cues by the investigator or solicit such cues or interpret the laboratory setting in such a way as to define their appropriate role behavior as a "good subject." Such speculation by the subjects may introduce extraneous sources of influence on the behavior under investigation and confound the experiment.

Unfortunately, the only successful means of eliminating subject influences, called *demand characteristics* by Orne, is to deceive the subject about the true nature of the experiment. Generally, the experimenter tries to remove a subject's suspicion or need for understanding about the experiment by generating an elaborate, though totally false, cover story about the purpose of the study. Thus, the subject is led to believe that some facet of his or her behavior is under observation, while in actuality another is. However, it is becoming harder and harder to deceive subjects— particularly college students (Kelman, 1967). In the field experiment, of course, there is no need for deception, since people are unaware that they are participating in an experiment.

There are other important reasons why psychologists may look to the methods of field experimentation as opposed to laboratory experimentation in studying human behavior. Schultz (1969) reviewed the research in a number of psychological journals and found that 80% of the subjects studied were college students. College students, however, make up only 3% of the general population, and they are not even a representative group of the general population on such dimensions as age, intelligence, and socioeconomic class. We must conclude that our scientific knowledge of

50

human behavior is really a psychology of college students. Obviously, there is a need in the science of psychology to understand human behavior across a wider range of subjects and life settings. Most field experiments are conducted in nonacademic settings and with a broader cross-section of the general population. Finally, many have questioned whether the psychological principles identified in the artificial settings of the laboratory can tell us anything about how people behave in the real world.

Baseline Experiments

The type of experimental study most frequently encountered in self-control research is the **baseline experiment**, an intensive design in which behavior is monitored repeatedly both before and after treatment procedures are initiated. This design is especially applicable to research in which the behavior of a single subject or group of subjects is intensively studied during exposure to one or more experimental variables. In intensive designs one is not limited to static measures as represented by averages for groups of subjects. Instead, the slope or drift of the data over time may be of primary concern.

A major feature of these intensive designs, which study changes over time, is that the subject serves as his or her own control for events before the experimental intervention. By repeatedly assessing, before the experimental intervention, the problem behavior to be modified, a baseline, or measure of the problem, is provided. In this way the stability of the target behavior during the baseline period can be determined. Without a stable baseline, inferences about the effects of the intervention procedure (treatment) are difficult. Two types of designs, the empirical case study and the empirical group study (Thoresen & Mahoney, 1974), are described here.

Empirical Case Study. The empirical case-study approach permits the target behavior of an individual subject to be studied both in the presence and in the absence of a particular self-control strategy (treatment). The measurements of the target behavior during the treatment and in its absence are compared. The effectiveness of a given strategy on smoking rate, for example, can be accurately assessed only if one has an index of smoking behavior both before and after the implementation of the treatment.

The most frequently used design in empirical case studies has been labeled "operant reversal" or "the ABAB design." The *A* represents observations of a behavior in the absence of treatment, and *B* represents observations during the treatment. This design generally includes these phases:

1. The specific behavior to be acquired or eliminated is clearly defined.
2. The subject is observed for a period of time, and the frequency of the target behavior is recorded. This record serves as Baseline I, against which the effectiveness of the experimental strategy is evaluated.

3. The experimental strategy is introduced (Treatment I). It may consist in some procedure for rewarding desirable behavior, ignoring or punishing undesirable behavior, a combination of these, or perhaps something else. The treatment is continued for a period of time.
4. During another period of observation, the frequency of the target behavior is recorded and compared with that of Baseline I. The increase or decrease in the frequency of the behavior under test can then be determined.
5. To ascertain that a change in the frequency of the target behavior, if found to exist, is due to the experimental intervention, the treatment is withdrawn for a time, after which another frequency count is made in Baseline II.
6. The last phase consists in a reintroduction of the experimental intervention (Treatment II).

The results of the ABAB design are usually expressed in graphic form. Figure 3-1 illustrates the effectiveness of some self-control strategy based on hypothetical data. In this figure the measure of the target behavior is its frequency. (The measure could be something other than frequency.) The figure shows that the target behavior was much less frequent during the treatment phases than during the baseline phases. The definite increase in frequency during Baseline II and the decrease during Treatment II indicate that the treatment rather than extraneous factors is responsible for the change in behavior. This reversal and reintervention provide a replication of any relation between observed behavior change and the introduction of the treatment variable that may have been found during Treatment I.

Perhaps the greatest problem encountered with this design is behavioral reversibility (Sidman, 1960). Behaviors, such as reading, that involve cognitive skills are unlikely to return to baseline frequencies when the treatment is removed. More pertinent to self-control is the fact that persons who have executed a successful self-control program may object to a return to pretreatment conditions. Someone who was able to quit smoking, for example, would hardly want to start again just to prove that he or she could quit again simply to satisfy the requirements of sound research.

One of the main advantages of the empirical case-study (single-subject) design is that it provides data on response trends during the treatment and baseline

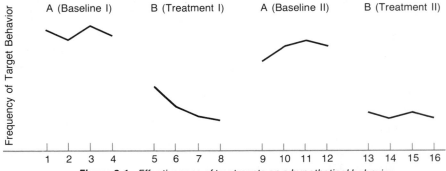

Figure 3-1. Effectiveness of treatments on a hypothetical behavior.

phases. This permits alterations in the experimental intervention procedure during the intervention, if practical or necessary. Group studies typically use only pre- and postmeasurements, thereby ignoring many intervening processes. A major disadvantage of single-subject designs is that they require many systematic replications for a comparison of the effects of two or more treatment procedures. A comparison requires that the procedures in question be applied separately to the same behavior. For example, one may wish to compare the effects of self-reward and self-punishment procedures on smoking behavior. After establishing a baseline, the self-reward procedure could be implemented for a few weeks. Following a return to the baseline condition, the self-punishment procedure could be implemented. One's conclusions from this design would be limited by the fact that the same subject had received a sequence of treatments. The effectiveness of a given treatment may be substantially altered by another treatment's having preceded it. It is hard to determine whether an observed behavior change results from a particular treatment or from a given sequence of interventions. Had the sequence been reversed, a different result might have occurred. Despite these limitations, this is the most frequently used single-subject design.

Empirical Group Study. It is often desirable to compare behavioral differences in groups of subjects in the presence and absence of certain variables. In the empirical group-study design, different groups of subjects are exposed to varying degrees of the treatment or intervention procedure. If we are interested in determining the effects of self-punishment on smoking, for example, we might have one group self-punish while another group (control) receives no treatment. Frequently an investigator will have several experimental groups, each receiving a different treatment and each being compared with a control group.

Perhaps the most crucial factor in evaluating group-based research is whether adequate controls have been used. If one conducted a study in which a self-reward resulted in a substantial reduction in smoking behavior, these questions should be asked: (1) how did this group compare with those who simply charted their progress, and (2) how did they compare with subjects who engaged in neither self-reward or self-charting? Of course the results of such a study are more meaningful when all possible independent variables have been isolated.

The empirical group study has the advantage of permitting comparisons among several treatment strategies. One disadvantage is that it does not usually permit an intensive study of behavioral variations within individual subjects.

Simulation Experiments

There has been intense debate among social scientists on the relative strengths and weaknesses of laboratory-based research and field-oriented research. Many investigators seriously question the ethics of deception and cover stories so often used in laboratory experiments as well as how revealing such research is about the real world. The laboratory-oriented psychologists, recognizing these drawbacks,

Smoking behavior has been a popular target of behavior modification studies. (Photo © Jeff Albertson/Stock, Boston.)

continue to argue for the intrinsic value of such research. Some, however, have studied human behavior in the laboratory while trying to reproduce the essentials of a natural situation. Experiments have been designed in which subjects in the artificial atmosphere of the laboratory are asked to imagine how they might behave in real-life situations. Subjects are asked to simulate in a hypothetical or abstract situation how they might behave. These studies are called **simulation experiments** (McDavid & Harari, 1974). Two general types of simulation experiments are commonly used: the scenario experiment and the role-playing experiment.

The Scenario Experiment. In the scenario experiment, subjects are presented with a description of a hypothetical situation and asked to predict how they might behave in such a situation. Such studies simply call for the subjects to read a short story (or "scenario") and then express how they would feel or behave in the

54

situation in the story. The independent variable in such studies is the stimulus material presented in the instructions, and the dependent variable is generally some measure of the hypothetical feelings or hypothetical behavior that the subjects report. A number of independent variables or a number of levels of a particular independent variable may be studied by presenting the subjects with scenarios that differ along a number of dimensions.

Bailey and Bartchy (1976) conducted a scenario experiment to study the attitudes of young male and female adolescents toward the acceptability of a man or woman as president of a large company. Subjects were given scenarios describing a vice-president of a large company who had recently been promoted to the company presidency by the company's board of directors. Each subject read one of four scenarios. These scenarios portrayed the new president as varying along two descriptive dimensions: the president was either male (Mr. Walker) or female (Ms. Walker) and was described as of either high or average competence. In the high-competence condition, the individual was described as often being praised for his or her original and clever ideas, and the company was said to owe much of its success to the thinking and planning of this vice-president. In the average-competence condition, the vice-president was described as doing well in the position, but his or her overall job record had not been outstanding, and he or she did not appear to be a substantially better prospect than the other company vice-presidents. However, the board of directors, having to make a decision, decided to promote Mr. Walker (or Ms. Walker). Once a subject had read a particular scenario describing a hypothetical person, he or she was asked to predict how well this person would perform in the role of company president (dependent variable) and to suggest an appropriate salary for the new president. The results showed that young male and female adolescents did not discriminate by sex on the salary measure but that certain sex-role stereotypes characterized these subjects' attitudes toward male and female presidents' predicted job performance.

The advantage of scenario experiments is that they can be conducted in a short time and can establish cause-and-effect relations among variables. Moreover, they generally do provide the subjects with a situation which they can readily identify and in which they probably do have a particular set of attitudes. Often in traditional laboratory studies, the subject is presented with a task that has little meaning or importance to him or her, such as memorizing nonsense syllables. Of course, in the scenario study, we still have the problem of demand characteristics, and we are not sure the attitudes expressed reflect how the subjects would in fact behave in a completely natural situation.

The Role-Playing Experiment. Another way of simulating real-life behavior in a laboratory setting is to ask a subject to "act out" how he or she might behave in some situation. A hypothetical situation is described to the subjects, and they are asked to behave in the way they would if the situation were real. In the scenario experiment we obtain attitudinal information from the subject's report, whereas in the role-playing experiment measurement is taken of the subject's behavior.

Kelman (1967), an early proponent of role playing in social-psychological

55

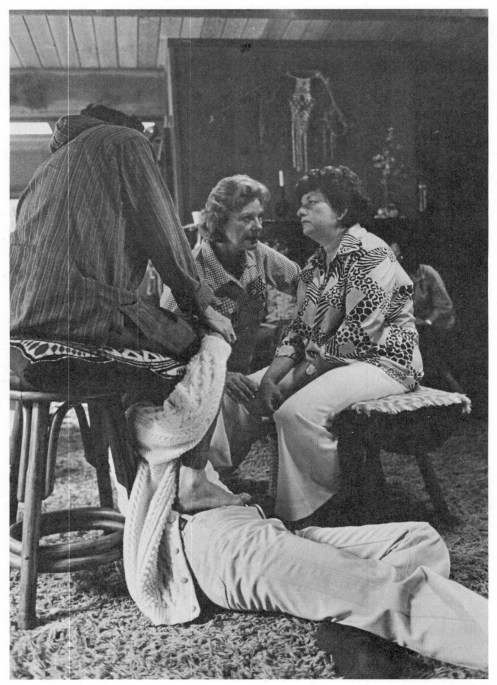

Is it possible to create emotions in a role-playing situation? (Photo © Karen R. Preuss/Jeroboam.)

SECTION ONE   THE STUDY OF HUMAN BEHAVIOR

research, believed that, although subjects knew the situation was not real, they would be more highly motivated to express their genuine behavior than in a mere laboratory exercise. Furthermore, the role-playing experiment would offer another alternative to laboratory deception.

One of the earliest types of role-playing research involved identifying subjects' opinions on some issue and then having the subjects argue, through role playing, a position that differed from their actual opinion. Such studies (for example, Janis & King, 1954; King & Janis, 1956; Scott, 1957) found that when subjects publicly expressed an opinion different from their own (as in a debate), subsequent measurement showed that the subjects' opinions shifted in the direction of their verbal arguments. Later development included studies on role playing in emergency, violence, conforming, and helping situations. Another version of role playing has been used in *games* research. A number of games have been developed to study conflict, competition, cooperation, bargaining, and decision making. Such games permit controlled interaction among subjects while providing the subjects with an opportunity to role-play very lifelike behavior. Moreover, role playing may be used as a treatment approach for the mentally ill.

Role-playing experiments have been subjected to the same basic criticisms as scenario experiments. Freedman (1969) has argued that there is no substitute for actual behavior in real-life situations. Thus, again a concern is being expressed as to whether laboratory-based behaviors are truly representative of how people will behave when the situation involves real losses of money or real threats of violence or real emergencies.

NONEXPERIMENTAL METHODS

The objective of experimental methods of research in psychology is to identify lawful relations between behavior and its antecedents. Such cause-and-effect relations, when highly verified, provide a basis for predictions about behavior. The researcher, however, may systematically record naturally occurring behavior without trying to change that behavior. In other words, we may study behavior in ways that do not allow us to specify why the behavior occurred. No experimental manipulation or independent variable is presented; the researcher merely hopes to observe some facet of behavior. Such nonexperimental methods do not provide scientific data, but they can provide data that have practical value and that can serve as a basis for formulating research hypotheses. The field study and the survey are two such methods.

The Field Study

The **field study** is an attempt to directly observe behavior without influencing the behavior under observation. The investigator merely records observations of behavior in some systematic fashion. Great care is taken not to disrupt or change the behavior being recorded. Usually the investigator is a *nonparticipant observer,* and he or she relies on unobtrusive observational techniques.

Field studies may be elaborate and comprehensive and generate an abundance of descriptive behavioral data. Barker and Wright (1954), for example, conducted a field study in a small town in Kansas. They had a number of nonparticipant observers record the daily community activities in this small town. Further observers followed single individuals throughout the day, recording in great detail the individuals' daily activities. This field study produced a massive amount of descriptive data. The researchers had planned in advance means of reducing their observations to a manageable number of behavioral categories.

One of the most important concerns in a field study is how to summarize massive amounts of descriptive behavioral data so that they can be communicated in a meaningful way. One must decide ahead of time what will define a unit of observation. Whether the investigators directly record behavior themselves or use some mechanical device, such as sound recorders or videotape cameras, they will subsequently have to reduce the observations to a manageable level without losing the natural flow of the observed activity. Some investigators have developed procedures not only for recording behavior but for categorizing or coding it. Bales (1950) has developed the most widely used system for coding directly observed behaviors. His approach is used mainly for classifying interpersonal behaviors in a social context. Others have developed coding methods for summarizing verbal behavior (Chapple, 1940) and complex social interactions (Freedman, Leary, Ossorio, & Coffey, 1951).

The field study may be a rich source of information for formulating hypotheses. However, the field study does not on its own provide experimental data. Most data analysis is correlational—that is, its purpose is to detect a relation between two variables. Since a field study does not collect data on an independent variable, it gives us no basis for determining why the behavior observed has occurred. Moreover, on many occasions the researcher cannot completely control the sample of subjects to be studied. Still, the breadth and depth of study on naturally occurring behavior provided by the field study make it an extremely valuable method of research.

The Survey

Another means of generating a large amount of nonexperimental data, but often in a vastly shorter time, is the **survey**. The survey involves asking people about themselves rather than directly observing their behavior. The survey attempts to measure attitudes or opinions by means of written or orally presented questions. It may vary widely in subject matter, and the questions to be asked, presented in a structured or open-ended questionnaire, may concern attitudes about behavior. Such a questionnaire may be administered over the telephone or in person or mailed to the respondent. Generally, mailed surveys are least preferred, since return rates are often less than 50%. The face-to-face interview is the most preferred method of administer-

58

ing a survey. The interview will not only result in a greater degree of participation but also allow the interviewer to observe the behavior of the respondent—that is, not only what he says but how he says it.

The purpose of the survey is to identify the attitudes, opinions, or predicted behavior of a particular group of individuals. Such a group—or *population,* as it is called—must have some essential characteristics in common, such as age, sex, race, socioeconomic class, or membership in a political party or organization. Sometimes the population is small enough that the researcher may wish to survey each individual. More typically, however, the researcher wishes the survey to provide information on a larger population. The population may be so large as to make testing each individual impossible. The researcher may then select a smaller group of individuals to examine, called a *sample.* If the sample selected is truly representative of the larger group, the data collected will give a very close approximation to the attitudes and opinions held by the population. Therefore, one may appropriately draw conclusions about the population on the basis of the sample data. There are several sampling procedures (for example, random sampling, probability sampling, quota sampling, and stratified sampling), and the skilled survey researcher will use the procedure that is suited to the nature of the study and that will assure the most representative sample.

The major advantage of the survey method is that one may collect a large amount of information in a short time and usually at little expense. However, the value of the survey approach rests on the representativeness of the sample studied and the trustworthiness of the respondents' self-reports.

THE TRUSTWORTHINESS OF PSYCHOLOGICAL RESEARCH

The purpose of all psychological studies, whether experimental or nonexperimental, is to measure some facet of the person. We may measure a person's behavior, or we may try to measure some dimension within the person, such as feelings, thoughts, attitudes, opinions, or motives. Whatever the target of the psychologist's inquiry, it must eventually be measured and communicated to others. Hence, the nature of research is intricately interwoven with the issue of the trustworthiness of measurement. All researchers try to reduce behavior or personality measurements to numbers. Such numbers are assumed to represent the true nature of the event being recorded. But how do we know that these numbers truly represent the event to be measured? Without the confidence that a number reflects a true and trustworthy dimension of human personality, the psychologist cannot apply such information in a practical or useful way.

A researcher must meet two minimal criteria in order for his or her measurement to be judged of value: **reliability** and **validity**. Reliability is essentially a matter of dependability of the observations; validity deals with the applicability of observations to some theoretical or practical concern.

May we have 20 minutes of your time? (Photo © George Kruse/Icon.)

Generally, when we speak of reliability, we are referring to the trustworthiness or accuracy of some measure of a personality dimension. When we convert a behavioral observation to a number, we hope that the number will represent the consistency assumed to characterize personality. Suppose that a researcher has constructed a new intelligence test. And now someone, perhaps a school psychologist, has decided to use this test in evaluating people's intellectual levels. Let us say a high school senior approaches the psychologist with the question "Can I graduate from a college or university?" The psychologist then administers this new intelligence test, and the student's performance is expressed in terms of an IQ score of 105. What would the psychologist recommend to the student on the basis of this IQ information? Well, on the basis of previous intelligence assessment of many people, we know that the average IQ of the general population is 100, the average IQ of high school students is about 110, and the average IQ of college graduates is about 120. Therefore, although this student's intellectual level is slightly above the average for the general population, it is below the typical high school student's and considerably below the typical college graduate's. On the basis of an IQ of 105, the psychologist would probably recommend that this student, if desirous of a college education, should carefully select the college to attend and the academic program to pursue. To determine whether this new intelligence test is reliable, however, the psychologist asks the student to retake the test in 2 weeks. On the second test, the student gets an IQ score of 140. On the basis of an IQ of 140, we would expect that this student not only would have sufficient intelligence to graduate from college but could probably achieve just about any academic goal he or she wished to pursue.

In the above example, the test scores on the two occasions are so discrepant that it would be hard to determine the student's "true" intellectual level from this instrument. This test is unreliable simply because the numbers it generates over time are too disparate to be useful; although we know that IQ scores may fluctuate slightly over time for a variety of reasons, we do not believe that actual intelligence increases or decreases by 35 points in a 2-week period. Consequently, this newly developed intelligence test is of questionable value to the psychologist.

We do not expect a person's test scores to be identical over time, but we do expect them to be sufficiently similar not to change a basic recommendation about the person. Why might a person's score on some measuring instrument vary from one occasion to another? There are three general types of influences on the reliability of measurements: environmental influences, personality influences, and features of the test itself.

It is generally recognized that the setting in which measurements are taken may influence the way a person behaves, whether we are taking measurements in a laboratory or natural environment, whether for the purpose of research or testing. We discussed earlier how the laboratory setting may call forth certain unwanted influences within a subject, called "demand characteristics." Moreover, in the testing situation, situational influences, such as lighting, size or temperature of the room, sex or race of the examiner, may affect a person's numbers on a measuring instrument. Rosenthal (1966) has also shown that an experimenter or test examiner may unwittingly influence performance in a measurement situation. Even in a psychotherapy or teaching situation, the behavior of the therapist or teacher influences the behavior of another in a desired direction. Accordingly, an awareness of the physical and social environments should be an important concern to the psychologist in any measurement situation.

A second category of influences comes from within the person being examined. Again, we discussed earlier how a subject's hypothesis about an experiment could introduce unwanted variance into experimental findings. Such hypothesizing by an examinee can occur in a testing situation as well. Moreover, many temporary states of a person, such as moods, physical problems, emotional problems, or situational problems, can alter behaviors over time. The perceptive researcher or test examiner will be on the lookout for such influences on behavioral measurement.

A final reason that numbers generated by a measuring instrument may be unreliable is that the instrument itself may be faulty. This is traditionally the major concern of psychologists, since without a trustworthy instrument, environmental or personality influences would make little difference in the overall accuracy of the measurement. The construction of good behavioral or personality measures in psychology is a highly sophisticated and technical area. In general, however, we expect any measure to have a sufficient range of scores and to have sufficiently unambiguous questions or instructions to provide accurate measurement of the dimension under study.

A second criterion of good measurement is validity. Any measurement should be logically, theoretically, and lawfully related to other relevant knowledge. If a measurement does indeed fit well with other knowledge, it should also be theoretically trustworthy and predict future observations. Terms like *anxiety, ego strength,* and *intelligence* are useful only if they support some theoretical notions, are consistent with known information, and allow for some prediction of relevant behaviors. Sometimes we say that a test is valid to the extent that it measures what it claims it measures. If a psychologist has constructed a new intelligence test, he must show that he is justified in naming the test an intelligence test. The test must be in agreement with what we know theoretically and empirically about intelligence, and it should be able to predict things that intelligence tests should predict. For example, knowing that someone has an IQ of 70 should allow us to make some prediction about how far this person might go in the formal educational system. Or if a test constructor develops a test designed to measure capacity to sell something, then we would be justified in expecting the scores on this test to predict actual selling performance.

Campbell and Stanley (1966) have introduced the concepts of *internal validity* and *external validity* to capture the essential requirements of experimental research. Internal validity is the overall precision of the experiment in generating accurate and reliable data. For an experiment to have internal validity, then, the experimenter must exercise great care in selecting and manipulating the independent variable, setting up experimental and control groups, eliminating extraneous influences in the study, and selecting a trustworthy measure of the dependent variable. Internal validity is a minimal requirement in order for data generated to be useful.

62

Yet a researcher may conduct a flawless experiment and still have a problem. A second requirement of experimental studies is that the research have what Campbell and Stanley call "external validity." External validity is concerned with the generalizability of the data. What if an investigator finds that highly anxious subjects (as measured by a test) have more difficulty recalling a list of nonsense syllables than low-anxiety subjects? Let us say this investigator has painstakingly set up this experiment and as a consequence has an internally valid experiment. We may still wonder whether these data can be applied to any particular setting in the real world. For example, does this finding generalize to different learning situations, such as an academic or vocational setting, or to different individuals, such as college students or factory workers? What would happen if one measured anxiety or retention differently? External validity, then, is concerned with the extent to which experimental results will generalize across differing populations, settings, and measurement variables. Obviously, establishing both types of validity should be a main objective of any experimental study.

SUMMARY

Psychology is defined as the scientific study of animal and human behavior. The scientific method is the method generally used to study behavior. It includes four steps: observation, hypothesis, experimentation, and verification.

An experiment is an attempt to relate some cause to some effect by manipulating independent variables and looking for changes in dependent variables. There are several types of experiments, including laboratory, natural, field, baseline, and simulation. Nonexperimental methods include field studies and surveys.

Traditionally most research in psychology has been of the laboratory type because of the degree of control that the procedure provides. Yet many investigators are willing to sacrifice a degree of scientific control in order to study behavior in more natural settings. They use the natural and the field experiments. Baseline experiments are especially applicable to research in which the behavior of a single subject or group of subjects is intensively studied during exposure to one or more experimental variables. A major feature of this design is that the subject serves as his or her own control for events before experimental intervention. Baseline experiments include the empirical case study and the empirical group study. Simulation experiments study behavior in the laboratory while trying to reproduce the essentials of a natural situation. Subjects are asked to simulate in a hypothetical situation how they might respond in a real-life situation.

Regardless of the kind of research being conducted, any findings must be trustworthy. This means that any method of measuring behavior must meet certain reliability and validity standards.

KEY CONCEPTS

Baseline experiment an experiment in which the same subjects are observed before and after the onset of the experimental treatment. The pretest data serve as the standard of comparison for assessing behavioral change.

Common-sense knowledge knowledge generated from sensory observation.

Dependent variable some outcome that is observed to see whether it is affected by the independent variable.

Experiment manipulation of some stimulus to see whether it has an effect on some outcome, which in psychology is often a person's behavior.

Field experiment an experiment in which an independent variable is injected into an ongoing real-life situation and its effects on subjects' behavior are studied without their awareness.

Field study an attempt to directly observe behavior without influencing it.

Independent variable some experimental condition that is controlled by the researcher.

Laboratory experiment an experiment conducted in a laboratory setting with some control over extraneous variables.

Natural experiment an experiment in which natural events, such as tornadoes, are treated as experimental variables and their effects on behavior are studied.

Reliability the extent to which a measuring instrument yields consistent results.

Replication an attempt to repeat an experiment testing the same hypotheses and using the same measures and procedures.

Scientific control an attempt to eliminate all the influences on the dependent variable except the independent variable.

Simulation experiment an experiment in which subjects are asked to indicate in a hypothetical situation how they would behave in the corresponding real-life situation.

Statistical verification the degree of confidence an experimenter puts in his or her research findings based on the predicted results of 100 identical experiments.

Survey a way of gathering data by asking people about themselves rather than directly observing their behavior.

Validity the extent to which a measuring instrument actually measures what it is designed to measure.

64

SECTION TWO

EFFECTIVE AND INEFFECTIVE LIVING PATTERNS

4

CHAPTER OBJECTIVES

1. To be able to identify and discuss critical life experiences and coping devices that characterize human developmental stages.
2. To be able to identify and discuss the factors that contribute to the uniqueness of human existence.
3. To be able to identify the characteristics of an effective person.

HUMAN DEVELOPMENT AND THE EFFECTIVE PERSON

What is an effective person? An effective person is one who can successfully cope with the demands of living. This definition rests on the following foundation of assumptions: (1) There are certain *stages* of personality development. (2) There are certain **demands** and critical life experiences at every stage of personality development. (3) People use various **coping devices** in meeting the demands of development. (4) One's **living effectiveness** is determined by how successful one is in coping with the demands of a developmental stage.

The above assumptions suggest that the mentally healthy, or effective, person is one who can adequately deal with the demands of living without resorting to habitual forms of self-defeating behavior. (We shall look at some varieties of ineffective personality patterns in the next chapter.) This viewpoint further assumes that to meet the demands of a stage of development, a person must have successfully coped with the demands of preceding stages. Failure to cope with the demands of an earlier stage will lessen one's capacity to take on the demands of a higher developmental stage. In other words, faulty development at one stage will disrupt the future course of development. Consequently, we would expect that the earlier biological or environmental demands are too great for one's available coping devices, the more devastating the effect on future personality development. If one has successfully reached adulthood with little disruption to the biosocial maturation process, then one will probably be capable of handling most later demands. Although one's development does not stop at early adulthood, most psychologists would perhaps agree that anyone who reaches adulthood with adequate coping skills will be equipped to deal with most of life's frustrations, disappointments, or traumas. The benefit of normal development is that the person is adequately prepared to meet the demands of early-adult, middle, and later stages of life.

We will now examine the course of human development within the following broad stages: infancy, babyhood, childhood, adolescence, and various stages of adulthood. You may wish to think of each of these stages of development with the concepts of demands, coping devices, and living effectiveness in mind.

STAGES OF HUMAN DEVELOPMENT

Infancy

The human organism never again experiences such a drastic change in environments as takes place at birth. The fetus resting comfortably in a quiet and warm world where all physiological needs are automatically regulated is suddenly expelled under great pressure into a world of massive stimulation. A number of years ago, the psychoanalytic writer Otto Rank spoke of the importance of this "birth trauma" in personality development. Recent research, however, suggests that the trauma of birth can be greatly reduced by simulating the prenatal environment as closely as possible

Life demands are different at different life stages. (Photo © Peter Simon/Stock, Boston.)

CHAPTER 4   HUMAN DEVELOPMENT AND THE EFFECTIVE PERSON

through placing the infant in warm water immediately, avoiding bright lights, and increasing the physical contact between mother and infant.

A prevailing common-sense notion is that the newborn is driven by the powerful biological urge for nourishment but is more or less insensitive to stimulation from the external world. Even developmental specialists have assumed that the infant's central nervous system was not sufficiently developed to process information from the world. Recent research, however, has revealed that the newborn is more responsive to the world than originally thought. For example, 2 weeks after birth the pupillary reflex is well established, and the infant responds with discomfort to an intense light after only 1 week. Infants are deaf immediately after birth, but this deafness is due to amniotic fluid in the ears, not to the ears' natural insensitivity to sounds. Five days after birth the infant will turn the head in the direction of a source of sound. Moreover, a few days after birth the infant will refuse a nipple coated with a bad-smelling substance. Taste, skin sensitivity, and sensitivity to pain are also fairly well developed a few short days after birth. Such research points to the importance of understanding the role that various environmental demands play at this time of development.

Babyhood

Hurlock (1968, p. 133) defines the babyhood stage as extending from the second week of life through the remainder of the first year. During the babyhood stage, the central nervous system develops to one-fourth the size of the adult brain. In the baby the head is one-fourth of the body length, as compared to the adult, whose head is one-seventh of the total body length. As the infant continues its biological development during the first year of life, new demands will mean that new adjustments will have to be made. The baby must learn to delay gratification and tolerate a certain amount of biological discomfort. Yet during this first year of life, the capacity to cope with the stresses of this age period results more or less from a joint effort of parents and child.

One of the most important psychological needs during the period of babyhood is the need for a **sense of security**. After the traumatic experiences associated with birth and early development, the child must come to accept the world as a safe and rewarding place to dwell in. Psychologists believe that a basic attachment must develop during the second half of the first year of life. Moreover, for healthy socialization to occur, this attachment must be established within a particular time period (that is, a **critical period**).

It has been suggested that some types of human psychopathology, such as schizophrenia or infantile autism, may in part result from an inadequately developed sense of security. If parents are perceived as a source of comfort and protection, however, the child becomes attached to them, and this attachment is the basis for later socialization. The child comes to value parents and hence will eventually come to

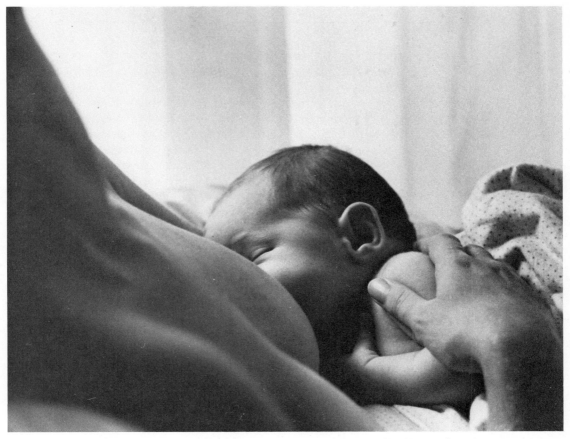

The infant needs contact with the mother in order to develop normally. (Photo © Ken Heyman.)

value people in general. Only when this attachment is fulfilled will a sense of security and basic trust develop in a child.

By the time the child is 6 months old, he or she has made many adjustments. Still, about the only way that a child can communicate displeasure during babyhood is by crying. Nature has provided the child with a very effective means of getting action. Since the baby cannot change his or her own diaper, prepare meals, regulate room temperature, or remove a diaper pin impaling the leg, crying is the basic coping device for meeting the demands of the world. For most babies the crying response results in more or less immediate action and thus becomes reinforced.

What if the child's crying does not result in the removal of discomfort? If crying does not produce adequate results, what is the child's next available coping device? The fact is that if the active response of crying fails to result in favorable consequences, the child has only passive coping devices available. Harry Stack Sulli-

71

The psychoanalytic theory of personality development stresses that male and female differences during the first 2 years of life are negligible. The needs and activities of the young boy and girl are more or less identical, and so there is little need to socialize masculinity or femininity at this age. Only during the emergence of the Oedipus complex do parents begin to respond differently to the biologically emerging male or female nature. The theory assumes that up to age 3 or so, the mother is the main influence in the young child's life, and the father is more or less a "peripheral parent." Eventually, the theory goes, a series of important interpersonal and biological maturation events will direct the boy toward identifying with the father (who will now become a central parent) and the girl toward a maternal identification, which presumably had been temporarily halted by the Oedipal situation.

Recently research has been directed toward understanding more fully the role that the father plays in early childhood socialization. Most developmental theories stress the role that the mother plays in development, and almost all the theories assign little impact to the father on development before age 3. Moreover, the discriminative attachment, characterized by an attachment to parents and a fear of

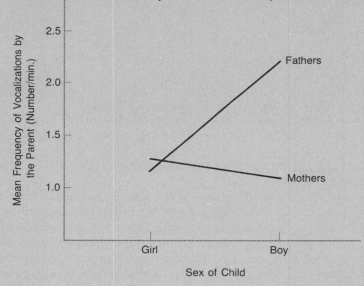

Figure 4-1. *Frequency of vocalizations by parents to infants during the second year of life. (From "The Development of Parental Preferences in the First Two Years of Life," by* M. E. Lamb, Sex Roles, *1977, 3, 495–497. Copyright © 1977 by Plenum Publishing Corporation. Reprinted by permission.)*

SECTION TWO   EFFECTIVE AND INEFFECTIVE LIVING PATTERNS

strangers, which occurs during the second half of the first year of life, is thought to result mainly in maternal attachment. Yet some investigators (Hetherington, 1966; Hetherington & Deur, 1971; Santrock, 1974) have shown that if the father is absent during the first 2 years of life, a child's psychological health may be impaired.

Lamb (1977) has provided one of the more valuable pieces of research on the development of childhood parental preferences in the first 2 years of life. A naturalistic home-observation study on ten male and ten female infants over a period of about 1½ years (7 months to 24 months of age) revealed the importance of the father in both male and female personality development. It was found that during the second half of the first year (that is, during the discriminative attachment period), more boys preferred fathers than preferred mothers, while girls preferred mothers or fathers about the same. Childhood preferences were measured by means of a number of attachment and affiliative behaviors, such as smiling, vocalizing, looking, laughing, offering a toy, touching the person, reaching for the person, and asking to be picked up.

Lamb felt that one reason for the male child's strong preference to interact with the father was the father's behavior. Figure 4-1 shows the frequency of vocalizations by fathers and mothers to little boys and little girls during the second year of life. As can be seen, mothers were equally active in communicating with their sons and daughters, but fathers were twice as active in communicating with their sons as their daughters. Thus, it seems that fathers strongly encourage and influence their sons' early socialization through active interaction. Other studies (Bronfenbrenner, 1961; Kohn & Carroll, 1960) have shown that fathers feel that sex-role training of their daughters is the responsibility of the mother. Moreover, girls do tend to shift almost universally to maternal parental preference around age 4 (Lynn & Cross, 1974).

van (1953) pointed out that a child who is continually exposed to intolerable anxiety must ward off stress with one of two passive defensive maneuvers: apathy and somnolent detachment. The infant may withdraw from the world by refusing to respond emotionally to his or her experiences (**apathy**) or by escaping stress through excessive sleep (**somnolent detachment**). Such defensive maneuvers by the child signal that a faulty foundation for personality development is being formed. It is most important that as the child completes the first year of life, a foundation has been formed whereby the child has come to trust people and to accept the world as a nonthreatening and safe place.

Childhood

Childhood has been defined as the time "when the helplessness of babyhood is over, at approximately the age of two years, and [extending] to the time when the child becomes sexually mature, at approximately thirteen years for the average girl and at fourteen years for the average boy" (Hurlock, 1968, p. 187). Childhood, then, is

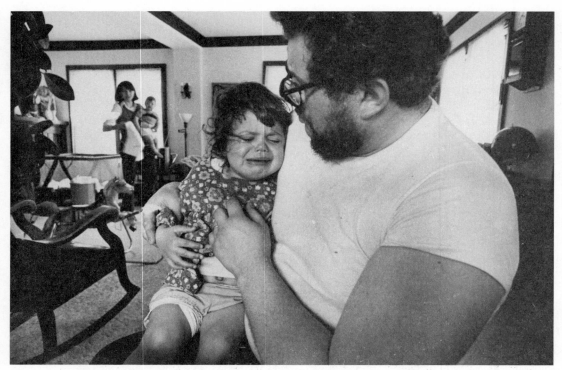

Parents can help soothe even the little pains in life. (Photo © Bohdan Hrynewych/Stock, Boston.)

a rather long stage of development, covering about 11 to 12 years. Some developmental psychologists have found it convenient to differentiate this lengthy period into phases of early childhood (ages 2–6) and late childhood (age 7 to puberty); although this division is somewhat arbitrary, it does reflect a distinction between a time when a child is mainly tied to parents and a time when the child broadens his or her contacts with the world outside the home environment.

Early Childhood. Early childhood consists of about 4 years of rather rapid physical and mental growth. It is a time when children must move from babyish concerns to more realistic life concerns. There will still be many residues of problems related to toilet training, discipline, and the control of impulses. The child's behavior may be marked by periods of warmth and affection, great understanding, and cooperation only to be followed by periods of extreme negativism, quarrelsomeness, and selfishness. It is a time of emotional upheaval and unrest that places great strain on the child's coping skills. Sleep disturbances, frightening dreams, and imaginary playmates reveal the wide range of tensions the child experiences at this time.

Psychoanalytic theory emphasizes that around age 3 the child experiences a particular form of stress brought on by an increase in sexual motivation and curiosity.

74

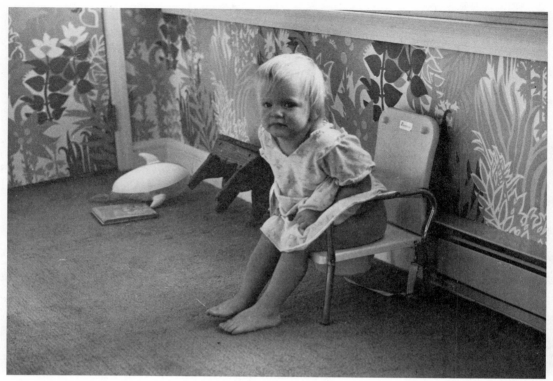

"Dad, would you bring me my coloring book?" (Photo © Ken Heyman.)

At this time the child also becomes aware of the anatomical differences between males and females. These developments give rise to a number of questions about the nature of birth and the mysteries associated with the mother/father relationship. It is not uncommon for children at this time to indulge in sexual exploration and observation and even express erotically tinged behavior toward parents. Freud spoke of an Oedipus complex that emerges at this time. This Oedipus complex involves an interpersonal situation in which the child becomes romantically attached to the parent of the opposite sex while harboring hostility and resentment toward the parent of the same sex. Obviously the associated behavior by the child tries the coping devices of both child and parents. While Freud may or may not have overstated the case for an Oedipus complex, it behooves parents of children at this age to be sensitive to the reality of certain needs in their children and be prepared to deal with them in a mature and reasonable manner.

     Many psychologists believe that the basic structure of one's personality has been formed by the end of early childhood. Many stable features of the person, such as the capacity to control and restrain sexual and aggressive impulses, the development of prejudices, the development of a positive or negative self-view, or the founda-

75

Parental identification is an important part of the socialization process. (Photo © Leonard Freed/ Magnum.)

tions for intellectual development, have been established by the end of this period. The makings of a basically healthy or basically unhealthy personality structure may exist by age 6, and attempts to correct faulty perceptual, motor, emotional, or intellectual development after this age have proved most difficult. This stage includes some of the most critical experiences during one's development.

BOX 4-2. THE IMPORTANCE OF TV IN EARLY CHILDHOOD

Surveys conducted during the 1960s showed that preschool children watch television an average of 1–2 hours a day and elementary school children 2–3 hours a day. Obviously the fact that children devote a sizable portion of their day to TV watching means that TV programs have the potential for influencing a child's early personality development. In particular, investigators have directed their attention to

76

how various behaviors depicted on TV might influence a child's cognitive functioning (reasoning and thinking) and helping and aggressive behavior.

Most intense among the issues of effects of TV has been the question "Does observing TV violence cause a child to act more aggressively?" In 1972 the Surgeon General's Scientific Advisory Committee on Television and Social Behavior studied this question. The resulting five-volume report implied that TV violence may lead to an increase in aggression in a small proportion of young viewers (Surgeon General's Scientific Advisory Committee, 1972, p. 7). In a review of the literature on TV violence and aggressive behavior, Kaplan and Singer (1976, p. 62) state that "the literature strongly suggests that the activating effects of television fantasy violence are marginal at most. The scientific data do not consistently link violent television fantasy programming to violent behavior." They feel that the television networks cannot be used as a scapegoat for violence in the world. After all, violence did not start with the advent of television. These writers are cautious to warn, however, that although a link between TV violence and aggressive behavior has not been convincingly demonstrated, further efforts should continue in this most important research area.

TV programming depicting violent and aggressive behavior is well documented. Coates and Pusser (1975) have also examined the impact on children's behavior of two of the most popular TV programs: *Mister Rogers' Neighborhood* and *Sesame Street.* They studied how these programs influence the cognitive, aggressive, and prosocial behaviors of children. They found that these two programs encourage mainly social behavior rather than cognitive behavior. That is, the programs place more emphasis on facilitating positive and warm interpersonal relations in children than reasoning and thinking skills. Further, it has been found that these programs influence the ways preschool children behave toward other children and adults (Coates, Pusser, & Goodman, 1976).

Late Childhood. If the child is able to cope successfully with the varied and troublesome demands of early childhood, he or she then enters the relatively quiet period of late childhood. This is not to say that late childhood is free of stresses and strains, but it does appear that the child who has successfully weathered the storm of early childhood enters into late childhood with a new lease on life. The child between the ages of 6 and 12 or 13 generally has the personality strengths to accommodate most stresses. If the child has not successfully coped with the stresses of early childhood, however, unresolved problems are likely to have a disruptive influence on this stage of development. Unresolved problems associated with feelings of insecurity or inferiority, the control of impulses, appropriate responses to authority figures, or the establishment of a stable moral code will indeed complicate the child's venture into a broadened social world.

In early childhood many stresses originate in the child's fanciful way of perceiving and understanding the world. In late childhood, however, the child's adjustments are more related to coping with environmental problems. The problems associated with a psyche in disequilibrium now give way to active attempts to respond to the world in an orderly and meaningful way. As the child matures, more and more of his or her thoughts become concerned with meeting the demands of the social and physical environment. The child's home life continues to be important, but the demands of school and the establishment of new relationships require that the child devote more and more of his or her thinking to understanding and predicting the world. The child is building a large vocabulary and learning to speak correctly. New interests and a lively imagination direct the child into seeking solutions to practical problems as well as seeking answers to profound questions about life, death, time, money, beauty, morals, and a host of other issues. New adjustment demands, however, lie on the horizon.

BOX 4-3. WHAT DO CHILDREN PERCEIVE AS GOOD BEHAVIOR AND BAD BEHAVIOR?

Developmental psychologists generally recognize that children progress through developmental stages of moral meaning. Hill and Hill (1977) found that 8-year-olds considered good behavior to be any behavior that was not bad. Being good is not hitting your little brother; being bad is hitting your little brother. By age 12, children have begun to judge behavior as good or bad in accordance with its consequences for people. Something you do that hurts someone is *bad;* something you do that helps someone is *good.* Actions are good or bad, and so are their consequences.

Puberty

The rather stable and consistent behavior patterns that tend to develop in late childhood are abruptly disrupted by the onset of puberty. Puberty is the relatively short period of life characterized by a series of physiological changes that prepare the person for adult sexual functioning. The pituitary gland, located in the brain, releases hormones that cause a general growth spurt, changes in the sexual organs, and a series of secondary sex characteristics.

One of the most difficult adjustments during this brief period is in regard to attitudes about one's body. Typically both males and females develop very negative attitudes toward their bodies while physiological changes are occurring. They become dissatisfied with their body size and body proportions. Moreover, such rapid physical changes result in incoordination and awkwardness, which further adversely affect one's self-concept.

78

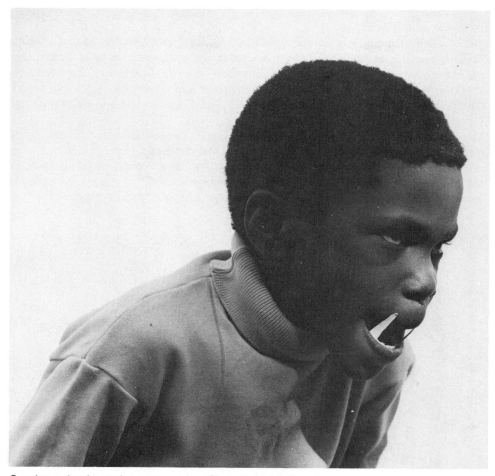

Growing up involves trying out new roles. (Photo © Audrey Ross.)

A number of other personality changes tend to accompany the physiological changes. The person may become withdrawn and seek out opportunities for solitude and isolation. Daydreaming and a preoccupation with sex may absorb one's energy, and one may develop a general disinterest in a world that just a few years before elicited keen interest and unrestrained curiosity. Now one becomes more easily bored and restless and develops an intense dislike for any type of obligation or work.

Puberty is an unhappy phase of life. There are few joys or pleasures, and one's conscious thoughts are taken up by worries, anxieties, and apprehension. Fortunately, puberty is brief and fades into the period of adolescence.

Early Adolescence

With the major impact of rapid physiological growth and emotional upheaval behind, one begins the stages of adolescence. Early adolescence begins right after puberty and continues for 2 years or so (to about age 15). There are many behavioral residues from puberty, such as unstable emotions and a tendency to devote time to daydreaming, but in general one's energy level and one's interest in the world have increased.

With the onset of early adolescence, one must now directly face the consequences of biological changes. Suddenly there is a heightened interest in members of the opposite sex. At this age, individuals often make rather awkward and at times amusing attempts to initiate contact with the opposite sex. A young adolescent male, for example, may crash into a group of girls standing idly about, scattering the girls in all

In addition to being with friends and that special someone, the adolescent needs time alone with his or her thoughts. (Photo © Ken Heyman.)

SECTION TWO   EFFECTIVE AND INEFFECTIVE LIVING PATTERNS

directions. One suspects that the girls may have had their part to play in eliciting this bizarre bit of behavior.

At age 13–15, adolescents often find themselves vacillating between childish ways of thinking and responding to the world and more adult ways of thinking and behaving. Most are not sure what being a man or being a woman really involves. Erikson (1963) says this age is characterized by **identity confusion**. Not only is it hard to give up the behavior patterns of childhood for more acceptable adult patterns, but the adolescent must also determine how males should act and how females should act and then adopt the sex-appropriate role. It is common to observe evidence of sex-role confusion in the adolescent's mannerisms, speech, appearance, and dress. While the adolescent may develop an obsessive concern for his or her physical appearance and dress, cultural guidelines for what is appropriate behavior and appearance are often unclear. The emergence of sexual interest and motivation and accompanying strivings for appropriate sex-role behavior may reawaken many unconscious childhood motives and feelings that have been dormant during the more or less quiet period of late childhood. Adolescence can be a particularly trying time if these revitalized memories, unresolved conflicts, and/or unrealistic needs and fantasies come to dominate one's behavior.

During this phase, the adolescent will be continuing his or her academic work. However, the new concerns of this stage and the energy expended in fantasy and worry may make academic work real drudgery. The young adolescent often has little patience for the theoretical or abstract and is instead more concerned with physical appearance, being accepted by peers, initiating the dating process, and even more distant worries about plans for the future. Thoughts about marriage, a possible future occupation, and religious and moral concerns all have their time in one's consciousness. Yet the full impact of going from childhood to adulthood must await the late adolescent stage.

Late Adolescence

The late adolescent period, lasting about 3 years (age 15–18 or so), is the period of "high school days" or "happy days" for most young people. Of course, the degree to which one has successfully come to grips with the adjustment tasks of prior developmental stages determines the ease with which one can manage the demands of late adolescence. At this time, the stresses brought on by biological growth and biochemical imbalance have diminished. The skeletal system has reached a plateau, and further biological and mental maturation has decelerated to an imperceptible rate. The person now has the biological and mental capacity for full adult functioning.

There are still new frustrations and worries, some short-range and some long-range. Concerns related to sex, physical appearance, and finances are still important, but they tend to be viewed more pragmatically and realistically. One can benefit from a number of years of experience and many opportunities to gather feedback from

81

	Very restrictive						Very flexible
How restrictive were your parents during your adolescence?	1	2	3	4	5	6	7
How restrictive do you think your parents should have been toward you?	1	2	3	4	5	6	7
How restrictive do you think you would be toward a 16-year-old daughter?	1	2	3	4	5	6	7
How restrictive do you think you would be toward a 16-year-old son?	1	2	3	4	5	6	7

friends, dates, teachers, and family members about one's physical and mental assets and liabilities.

People are still very important to the late adolescent. There still will be strong peer-group affiliations established during early adolescence, although the number of friends may not be as important as the kind of friends one has. Social snobbery tends to peak at this age as one becomes more identified with select groups. As part of this tendency to identify with groups comes the pressure to conform to group standards. Individual attitudes or opinions may become virtually synonymous with group standards. Typically, late adolescent groups tend toward liberal attitudes and develop a more critical attitude toward the broader culture. Late adolescent groups often tend to encourage more tolerant attitudes toward sexual behavior, cheating in the classroom, and use of drugs. Consequently, the adolescent may find that his or her new ways of viewing himself or herself or the world in general are at odds with the more conservative notions of parents.

BOX 4-4. ADOLESCENT/PARENT CONFLICTS

It is generally assumed that adolescence is marked by a great deal of interpersonal conflict between the young adult and his or her parents. Youths' demands for freedom and independence conflict with the parents' desire to give them the benefit of their years of experience. Bath and Lewis (1962) found that late adolescent girls

82

Learning how to relate to the opposite sex is an important part of the adolescent experience. (Photo © Christa Armstrong/Photo Researchers, Inc.)

Strong peer-group affiliations are established during early adolescence, and pressure to conform to group standards is strong. (Photo © Ken Heyman.)

(around age 20) reported few serious conflicts between themselves and their parents. When conflicts did occur, they were in situations in which parents were overly restrictive in attitudes toward their daughters. In fact, most of the subjects reported that they would treat their own daughters the same way their parents had treated them, although many felt they would be even more strict in limiting their teenage daughters' freedom. This study found that most adolescent/parent conflicts were a result of inconsistency in parental practices rather than restrictiveness of parental practices.

Although the adolescent is very much influenced by peer groups and the desire to be accepted by important others, most adolescents come out of this period with a new sense of autonomy and individuality. They have found it necessary to confront head on important life concerns like dating and face hard decisions about vocation or college. Assuming that one has managed to pass through this rather

84

lengthy and trying adolescent period with a favorable self-image and a sense of personal worth and confidence, one is adequately prepared to confront the new challenges of being an adult.

BOX 4-5. CHANGES IN ADOLESCENTS' SELF-IMAGE

Surprisingly few studies have traced the course of self-concept development through the adolescent period. Carlson (1965), however, conducted a longitudinal study (a study that follows the same subjects over time) of students from the sixth grade to the senior year of high school. He had previously identified two important and independent dimensions of self-image. The dimensions were the degree of social versus personal orientation and the degree of one's self-esteem, as measured by the congruence of self and ideal self. This study showed that although there were no sex differences at the preadolescent level, girls developed more of a social (or other) orientation than boys by high school, while boys had a more personal (or self) orientation. However, self-esteem was more or less independent of sex and tended to be relatively stable over this period.

BOX 4-6. EGO IDENTITY IN COLLEGE STUDENTS AND WORKING YOUTHS

Do college students differ from working youths in the development of self-identity?

Munro and Adams (1977) have shown that late adolescents who go to college and those who enter the work force differ in the formation of self-identity. Working youths were found to have attained a sense of self-identity, while college students had not. It seems that college students are not committed to a particular self-identity because they expect that college experience and future occupational endeavors will serve to define them more appropriately. These two groups did not differ in their commitment toward an occupational identity, but the working youths were more committed to a religious, political, and ideological identity than the college students.

BOX 4-7. THE NEED FOR INTIMACY IN LATE ADOLESCENCE

Erikson (1963) believes that the principal task of the late adolescent and young adult is to establish close, intimate relationships with others. This is fulfilled in the gaining of a few close friends and ultimately a spouse. There is a need for a "fusion of identity" with others. Intimacy is the capacity to develop a partnership with another based on trust and openness. Erikson suggests that the failure to develop and fulfill the affiliative need can only lead to the opposite and mentally unhealthy experience of *isolation,* in which one becomes absorbed in the self and is unable to experience the fusion of identity with another. According to Orlofsky, Marcia, and Lesser (1973), the degree of one's intimacy development can be measured by the following: (1) the presence or absence of close relationships with members of both sexes; (2) the presence or absence of a committed relationship with a dating partner or spouse; and (3) the depth (that is, the closeness, trust, and openness) or superficiality of peer relationships.

According to Erikson, the major problem of the adolescent is to establish a stable self-identity. This is a time when young men and women must seek appropriate courses of action from among many avenues (crisis) and eventually decide on a proper course of action (commitment). Marcia (1966) suggests that youths in later adolescence generally are in one of four ego statuses according to the degree of crisis resolution. The *identity achievers* have more or less resolved the crisis situation and have merged with others in stable, committed relationships. The *moratoriums* are still in the midst of the ego-identity crisis. The *foreclosures* have rushed to highly committed relationships, but without progressing through the refining influence of the crisis period. *Identity diffusion* is characteristic of those who have failed to make affiliative commitments and are making no progress in that direction.

Adulthood

In our society, one is considered an adult on reaching one's eighteenth birthday. Adulthood then characterizes the person for the remainder of life. Psychologists sometimes classify the adult years into three categories: young adulthood, middle age, and old age. Such labels are more a matter of convenience than clearly delineated developmental stages. Middle age, for instance, is often associated with physiological changes beginning about age 40, but young adulthood and old age are not initiated by specific biological changes. Often attempts to classify adults simply reflect significant changes in life's circumstances, such as retirement. For the purpose of discussion, however, we shall use these three categories of adulthood.

Early Adulthood. Simply because of the sheer number and variety of adjustments, the young adult years should be the most stressful of one's life. In the course of a few short years, a person may be required to make decisions about such varied concerns as whether to seek a college education or how long to go to college, whether to marry or when to marry or whom to marry, and whether to work, what kind of work to do, and what employer to work for. This may be followed by questions of desired size of family, whether to rent or buy a home, and where to live.

86

The making of difficult and important life decisions is one of the most defining features of young adulthood.

Setting realistic future goals and striving toward such goals become an important source of enjoyment and personal fulfillment. Yet unrealized goals can make this one of the most disappointing and frustrating times of life. For most young adults, the decisions made about college, occupation, or spouse will have enduring consequences, whether the outcomes are positive or negative. In a later chapter, we will discuss some of the information people may use in setting realistic goals at this time of life.

In addition to the adjustment problems associated with decision making and goal setting, the young adult has to accept a new set of adult roles. By age 30, most young adults have completed their education, begun an occupation, married, and become parents. One's education—whether high school or college—is designed to prepare one to successfully assume some productive place in society. Today education is almost entirely devoted to preparing people for occupational roles. Interestingly enough, little cultural training outside the family is devoted to preparing young adults for their dater/spouse/parent roles. Consequently, most young adults may find that once they become acclimated to the dater role, they are abruptly cast into a spouse role. Then, perhaps before they have had the opportunity to adjust to the spouse role, they have become parents.

BOX 4-8. DESIRED FAMILY SIZE IN YOUNG ADULTS

Haskell (1977) examined a number of correlates of desired family size in young college-age men and women. He found that men desired somewhat larger families (average, 2.04 children) than women (average, 1.91 children). Contemporary women seem to be more accepting of childless marriages, while men prefer larger families. Both men and women who preferred larger families had more traditional views. The percentages of men and women desiring no children or one child have increased over time.

With such an array of time commitments and interpersonal obligations, the young adult can no longer afford the luxuries of low energy, moodiness, procrastination, and daydreaming that were so common during adolescence. Life is suddenly thrust upon the young adult in full measure. Worries and anxieties are directed toward practical concerns like finances, quality of academic or occupational performance, the marital relationship, and child training. As one moves further and further into the young adult phase, idealism and liberal attitudes may be replaced by realism and conservatism. In other words, young adults tend to become more and more like the parents who just a short time ago appeared so irrational and out of touch with the real world.

87

Married couples will eventually need to confront decisions about family size. (Photo © Owen Franken/Stock, Boston.)

For many, the struggles, the disappointments, and the joys of young adulthood pass too quickly. This period is perhaps the fullest and richest of one's life. The agonies of study, not getting that promotion, medical bills, sleepless nights give way to a potentially quieter and less traumatic time of life, called middle age.

BOX 4-9. THE SEVEN-YEAR ITCH

The seven-year itch is a colloquial expression referring to a period of marital restlessness and disharmony that characterizes couples after 7 years of marriage. Although the "seven-year itch phenomenon" originated in common-sense knowledge, there is some evidence to support the notion that at about 7 years of marriage, couples do undergo a sort of life-review process. There are increases in extramarital sex, in thoughts of separation and divorce (Berman, Miller, Vines, & Lief, 1977), and in the rate of requests for outpatient marital counseling (Marmor, 1975). Berman et al. suggest that counseling of married couples during this crisis period should (1) emphasize the commonness of the seven-year itch in married couples, (2) help couples separate the real problems from the general restlessness and life-review process during this time, and (3) encourage and aid couples in determining each other's need patterns and improving marital communication.

Middle Age. The middle-age years are roughly between 40 and 60. The actual onset of this period is determined by the physical changes associated with the climacteric, or (in women) the so-called change of life.

Surprisingly little research has been conducted to understand the adjustment problems, let alone suggest solutions to the problems, of the middle aged. Traditionally, social scientists have concentrated their research efforts on understanding the span from birth to young adulthood. However, in recent years there has been a groundswell of interest in the old. This leaves the middle-aged group perhaps the least understood. Yet a number of adjustment areas of the middle aged have been identified. We hope that more research on and understanding of middle age will be provided in the future.

The middle-aged person by necessity must make some adjustments to physical changes taking place. There is a decline—although sometimes exaggerated—in sensory and motor functioning. Sensory functioning, such as seeing and hearing, may become more difficult as the gradual deteriorating process of aging continues. The body's glands and blood vessels may also become less efficient. The person may fatigue more easily. Such physiological changes will be accompanied by changes in physical appearance, physical attractiveness, and sexual capability.

Many dread middle age. Not only must one cope with the natural physiological changes associated with increased age, but changes in one's social and emotional life make for a broad spectrum of adjustment problems. Children have often reached adulthood and are leaving the home; new behaviors toward one's children, their dating partners or spouses, or grandchildren must be acquired. Moreover, this is often a period when adjustment stresses and general dissatisfaction with life may give rise to or be associated with marital disharmony and unhappiness. Many married couples separate at this time. Men, and more and more women, look back over their vocational histories with feelings of insufficient accomplishment. Work may seem unchallenging or routine. One may now have to confront the realization that certain occupational or other life goals will never be fully realized. There is something about being neither really old nor really young that has a depressing influence on people at this age.

In one sense, we might expect people to look forward eagerly to this period. Most will be at or near their peak earning capacity and generally will have fewer

89

family and financial obligations. They may have more leisure time on their hands and greater opportunities to use their time enjoyably. Obviously many use such opportunities to enrich their lives. However, for the person who looks to middle age as a time to be dreaded, these opportunities for personal growth may be overlooked.

Old Age. *Old age* is a label given to that part of the life cycle that runs from the end of middle age to death. For some it will be the shortest period of one's life, for others the longest (perhaps 30 years). Age 60 has often been arbitrarily used to identify the onset of this period, although 65 or even 70 has often been used in making retirement decisions in our society. Certainly the great strides in improving living conditions and promoting better mental and physical health for the elderly have produced some ambiguity in deciding when a person is old.

Social scientists have recently increased their efforts to understand the needs and problems of the elderly. More and more, one sees discussions devoted to the elderly on television, in magazines, and in books as well as in professional conferences and scientific journals. Research has increased rather dramatically in the areas of *gerontology* (the science that studies aging) and *geriatrics* (the area of medical practice devoted to improving the life of the aged).

As with the other age periods, our society has generated social stereotypes that tell us what old people are like; however, like all social stereotypes, they include some accurate information and perpetuate some misinformation. Such stereotypes often treat the elderly as if they were all alike, and the wide range of individual differences that characterizes any age group is often ignored.

The high value that the American culture places on strength, speed, and physical attractiveness is continually reinforced in the mass media. The mass media often portray the elderly in ways that emphasize our less favorable impressions. Often the helplessness of the elderly or the inappropriateness of their actions is emphasized.

More and more, empirical research with the elderly suggests that these persons are more capable and mentally competent than our cultural stereotypes would suggest. Unfortunately, aged persons may find themselves adopting the behaviors that society deems appropriate, and a kind of self-fulfilling prophecy may occur. The acceptance of such "appropriate" behavior may give rise to a less favorable self-concept than one would otherwise have, and such an unfavorable self-concept may further restrict one's capability to deal with the world successfully. This circular effect of the self-concept may be particularly troublesome for people at this age.

One problem that the elderly must face is continuing physiological changes that had an insidious beginning in the middle years. The aging process never stops and may actually accelerate at this time. As one moves into one's sixties and seventies, there are often tasks that cannot be done with the same speed or accuracy or occasionally tasks that one cannot perform at all. Blood circulation has declined even more from middle age, and one is even more susceptible to diseases and poor health. For many we can add some degree of malnutrition brought on by a natural reduction in

90

One attitude about the elderly is that one is just as old as one feels. To feel youthful, one must lead an active life. Another attitude assumes that elderly people should grow old gracefully, with more passive interests. (Photo © Arthur Grace/Stock, Boston.)

CHAPTER 4 HUMAN DEVELOPMENT AND THE EFFECTIVE PERSON

the appetite. Moreover, such physiological changes are occurring in people who may be facing the death of a spouse or the permanent separation from an occupation.

The elderly may also have to make adjustments to new living arrangements and new standards of living. The children of the elderly are more mobile than a decade or two ago and more prone to feel that the proper place for their mothers and fathers is in nursing homes. Even the elderly may see this separation from children as inevitable, although they can remember a time when such a practice was uncommon.

Two attitudes toward the elderly prevail in society. The first attitude assumes that one is just as old as one feels. Therefore, if one remains active, has hobbies and social interests, and maintains a daily exercise program, one should not feel old. The other attitude is that the elderly should act their age and avoid trying to compete with the more youthful members of society. Aged persons are thought to be happiest if left to their own thoughts and cared for by skilled personnel. The attitudes that society advocates may reflect the most convenient solutions for facing the problems of and obligations to the aged. Perhaps it is too easy for the more youthful segments of society to assume they know what is best for persons at this time of life. We should seek not only the most realistic, but equally the most compassionate, solutions to the needs and problems of the elderly. This can happen only if we are aware of their adjustment problems.

THE UNIQUENESS OF HUMAN EXISTENCE

Now that we have made a quick survey of human personality development, some additional comments should be made. You should realize that although we viewed human development within various stages, no one individual will progress through these stages in exactly the same way or make exactly the same adjustments to them. In fact, if there is one main characteristic of the human species, it is this: each one of us is unique.

In addition to each person's being uniquely different from all others, we are unique as a species. The human species has developed the capacity to adjust to a wide variety of physical and social environments. We have attributes and capacities for adjustment that far exceed those of any other species. Such an adaptation capacity has contributed to the uniqueness and diversity of human behavior. However, many of the attributes that set the human so far apart from lower animals may act to hinder as well as aid one's adjustment. Zimbardo and Ruch (1975, p. 610) have presented some of the unique human attributes that not only can help people meet the demands of a hostile environment but also can become a source of breakdown and maladaptation. Here we will examine three human attributes that may have either positive or negative influences on our adjustment. These three attributes are memory, time sense, and use of language. Next we will look at three important psychological needs in human personality.

Important Human Attributes

Memory. Human brain tissue is a great storeroom of experience. In fact, it has been estimated that we probably use as little as 5% of our total capacity to file away information in the brain. Hence, the brain may be regarded as, for practical purposes, an unlimited reservoir of knowledge. The importance of this capacity is understandable when we note the length of time it takes to progress from infancy to adulthood. About one third of one's life (20 years) is required to develop one's physical and mental capabilities to their fullest. No other animal takes so long to develop from infancy to adulthood. But, then, other animals can typically rely on instinct to help them meet the demands of the world. For humans, successful adaptation depends on the amassing of knowledge.

The purpose of memory is to provide an organism with a backlog of experience that can be retrieved with, in many cases, split-second proficiency. Memory, although not always as efficient as we would like, does provide us with the capacity to deal with most immediate concerns. But memory can also be the source of complications in our lives. By way of memory, we are capable of carrying grudges, retaining prejudices, and suffering from past emotional traumas. We may compulsively rely on maladaptive learning rather than creatively and spontaneously responding to the world with new and perhaps more adaptive behaviors. Thus we can suffer as well as profit from a highly developed memory capacity. It would be interesting to speculate how much mental illness would exist if the brain could routinely erase all negative memories at week's end.

Time Sense. The human is unique in the perception of time. In a split second one may mentally survey the past, imagine one's self into the future, or experience the immediate present. The human brain allows one to deal with time as an abstraction, whereas lower animals apparently are restricted to experiencing the here and now. In fact, humans have become so accustomed to dealing with past or future time that they have difficulty grasping that fleeting moment of present time. Many Eastern philosophies and religions recognize that people must experience the here and now to appreciate and comprehend existence.

Our highly developed time sense allows us to unify our experiences. We can review our past and structure it into a meaningful chronological unity. We can identify ourselves with a past history that gives our existence continuity. One facet of self-definition is that one can perceive the present in relation to that which has gone before. We may reflect on our first day in school, our first part in a high school play, or our first date, and all these experiences, although widely separated in time, still remain "my" experience. It was still me at ages 6, 18, 20, and 25. Our time sense gives continuity to our concept of "self" and makes our lives more meaningful.

Many of our fantasies dwell on past experiences, but probably most of our thoughts and fantasies are oriented toward the future. We are concerned with long-range concerns—future occupation, future spouse, education, retirement, and so on.

At other times our concerns are with the more immediate future: "Will I get a date for Friday night?"; "Am I going to be able to study adequately for that test next week?"; "I must get my dress to the cleaners"; "I must remember to pay that bill." The advantages of the capacity to deal with the future before it arrives are that we can plan our lives, set goals for ourselves, and predict our lives well in advance.

There can be, however, undesirable consequences to living in the past, as well as to being preoccupied with the future. As we mentioned in regard to memory, a person may dwell on past experiences to the degree of disrupting his or her life. If one's life is continually tinged with fear or guilt originating in past threats or disappointments, the person cannot function properly. However, our highly developed sense of time also allows us to be preoccupied with what might happen to us in the future. Apprehension about the future is what psychologists call *anxiety*. It is a dread of the unknown and is usually triggered by thoughts of all the bad things that might happen in the future. Consequently, if a person's capacity to imagine the future results in mere anxiety and not in the constructive setting of goals or planning of future courses of action, it too may be a two-edged sword.

Use of Language. Perhaps the most sophisticated of all human attributes is the ability to communicate verbally with others. To be able to communicate our thoughts and feelings with language is one of the most important features of human learning. Language allows us to express our own wishes and needs and to evaluate the feelings and needs others have toward us. We can benefit not only from our own past experiences but from the past experiences of others. We may use others to help us evaluate and assess present circumstances, such as whether to go to the doctor or whether to ask a person for a date, or to plan and predict the future. Sometimes using language is a rewarding activity in itself, as when we meet and converse with an old friend. Language is essential to the socialization process and education in general. It is only through the highly specialized and publicly agreed-on use of symbols that huge storehouses of knowledge, such as libraries and bookstores, can be made available to us all. It is hard to imagine any other event that would return the human species so close to its lower-primate relatives as the removal of human language.

Yet, like so many of the human's unique attributes, language can be a mixed blessing. If, for example, proper language development does not occur, whether because of congenital or environmental problems, the human will fail to become socialized and will not be capable of functioning successfully in his or her social world. In the schizophrenic, for example, language does not serve a social function but has become a form of idiosyncratic communication. The neurotic may use language to solicit excessive attention. The psychopath may use language to exploit others. Even in the normal person, language may be used in unhealthy ways. We can use language to spread rumors, to embarrass someone or inflict psychological harm, or to distort our true feelings and motives. Sometimes words take on a magical quality and often result in confusion of the object itself and its mental representative the word. Psychologists have found that most words carry both denotative and connotative meaning. For example, the word *pig* may denote a four-legged animal with a curly tail or may be used to refer to a dirty, coarse, or gross person. In the latter instance, the word *pig* is being used beyond its literal meaning. Different individuals or groups may attach their own unique connotative meanings to words. Many of our stereotypes about people are based on these subtle connotative meanings.

Other Attributes. Zimbardo and Ruch (1975) have identified a number of other human attributes that may have either a positive or a negative influence on adjustment. For example, our creativity capacity gives us the potential for planning, solving problems, and creating something new, but this capacity can give rise to fantasy-dominated thinking, misperceptions about ourselves and others, and even delusional thinking. The human capacity for free choice and judgment allows us to act independently in the world and experience the pride of success and accomplishment. Nevertheless, such freedom of choice places heavy responsibility on us to make correct choices. Choices give rise to conflicts and decisions, which in turn may give rise to feelings of failure, guilt, and inadequacy. In addition, the quality of a person's decisions may have positive or negative consequences on other people's lives.

Needs for affiliation, dependency, and love may also be a two-edged sword. People may be a source of comfort, security, and knowledge about the world. However, a proper balance between dependency and independence must be maintained. One must not be hopelessly dependent on others for one's self-identity and self-esteem, but at the same time one should not exaggerate independence at the expense of cultivating warm, affectional relationships with others.

Important Human Needs

Need for a Favorable Self-Concept. At about 6 months of age one becomes aware of the distinction between oneself as an object and other objects in the world. We come to realize that there are certain things that are "me" and certain things that are "not me." Probably the first awareness of the self as a distinct object in the world comes in the form of a **body image**. Through an extensive exploration process, the child identifies the physical dimensions of his being. He reaches down and squeezes his toe and he feels it. He squeezes his teddy bear's toe and he doesn't feel it. The child's capacity to discriminate among things eventually results in a clear awareness of his body as a separate object different from other objects in the world.

The notion of one's self as a distinct object in the world probably includes more than just the awareness of one's body. The child also views himself as a thinking and feeling being. Later the words *I* and *me* come to refer to one's physical and psychological being. Internal perceptions of body and being will eventually blend into a comprehensive view of the self, called the **self-concept**. As we develop from childhood to adulthood, the self-concept progresses toward greater and greater stability and crystallization. When we reach adulthood, the self-concept has become a relatively enduring and stable facet of human personality that provides consistency to experience and a unity to our self-identity.

95

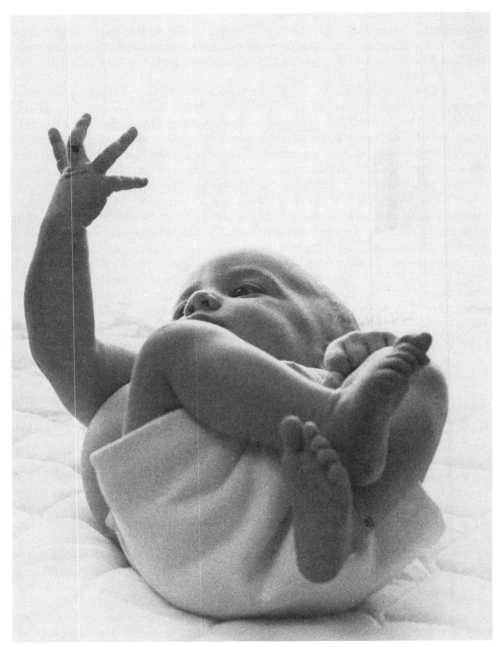

Through the process of self-exploration, an infant comes to define the boundaries of the body. (Photo © Ed Lettau / Photo Researchers, Inc.)

SECTION TWO   EFFECTIVE AND INEFFECTIVE LIVING PATTERNS

In general, self-concept development seems to progress along two development tracks. Along one track an individual develops a favorable self-concept; the other track results in an unfavorable self-concept. It is thought that parents are the initial and most critical influence on a child's developing self-image. If a child receives such parental feedback as "Susie, you sure are a cute and intelligent little girl," it will not be long before Susie is saying to herself "Gee, I sure am cute and intelligent." Conversely, as we may imagine, negative feedback, whether given explicitly or implicitly, may result in an unfavorable self-image. Although such self-perceptions will undergo some degree of change throughout life, many psychologists believe that the basic structure of the self has been formed by around age 6 and is hard to change after this age. Later we will examine the role of the self-concept in mental health and interpersonal relationships.

Need for Sensory Stimulation. People are constantly being bombarded with stimulation from the physical world. Only recently have psychologists come to realize how important such stimulation is for normal psychological functioning. Apparently sensory stimulation has a critical role in maintaining one's mental health.

We all know how uncomfortable it is to be bored. Boredom usually occurs in situations that provide little novelty or interest to us. But usually in the most boring and routine situations, we are receiving a large amount of stimulation from the environment, although the mind seems relatively unstimulated. Some researchers have investigated the effect of more limited sensory environments on behavior in a series of sensory-deprivation studies (sometimes called perceptual-isolation studies). People who have been shut off from normal environmental stimulation for a prolonged period showed dramatic changes in behavior.

In one of the pioneer studies on sensory deprivation, Heron, Doane, and Scott (1956) paid volunteers $20 a day simply to do nothing. Subjects were left alone in a small room, wearing translucent goggles, so that all they could see was diffuse white light, and gloves and cardboard cuffs to reduce tactile stimulation. They were exposed to a monotonous roar that sounded something like a waterfall. Many of the participants expected that the experiment would provide an opportunity to do some deep, serious thinking. In actuality, however, few subjects could tolerate this state more than a couple of days. Subjects who did endure this state for more than a couple of days began to show marked personality changes. They developed a distorted sense of time, had difficulty concentrating, and experienced a number of hallucinatory distortions. Subjects reported flight of bright colors, depersonalization and a loss of body image, and various agitated emotions. In short, the subjects were displaying signs of severe mental illness. The dramatic changes in personality brought about by sensory deprivation have been replicated (Heron, 1961; Zubek, 1969). Lilly (1956) found similar behavioral effects when subjects were submerged in a tank of warm water for several hours. It seems apparent that we should not take lightly the importance of our external environment. The brain is programmed to receive and process massive input from our world. Even when we are asleep and least sensitive to external

97

stimulation, the brain appears to need periodic stimulation in the form of dreams. The brain cannot tolerate prolonged inactivity. People have a psychological need to actively seek out and interact with their world.

Need to Know and Understand the World. In addition to a need for a favorable self-concept and a need for sensory stimulation, people also have a need to make some sense out of the world. As pointed out earlier, the infant in the first few days of life shows evidence of a desire to perceive the world. As the child gets older, very strong drives toward exploration and curiosity unfold. Children enjoy picking up and examining objects. Piaget (1952) noted that even at age 1, infants have become skilled investigators of their world.

As children develop effective means of locomotion, they are into everything. They are intensely curious not only about things but about other people and themselves. They explore their bodies with the same interest they show in exploring their world. By age 2 or 3, children are asking rather searching questions about themselves and the world. Some researchers have shown that whether children receive satisfactory answers to their inquiries has a lot to do with the future development of the curiosity motive.

Typically, by the time a child reaches late childhood, his or her curiosity wanes somewhat. One reason, no doubt, is that the once new and novel world has taken on the character of the familiar. Further, the child has now learned to read and can obtain many answers through his or her own efforts. As the young move into adolescence, they become more concerned with understanding appropriate sex-role behavior, and they develop a renewed interest in their body image. By late adolescence, they have broadened their concerns to areas of independence and life careers. Moreover, the need to know and understand the world may include more abstract and philosophical concerns. The person may now wish to understand what human nature is all about or to understand his or her place in the scheme of things. The curiosity motive may now take the form of redefining one's self-identity and searching for a meaning to experience. Social psychologists point out that the adult personality includes a motive to maintain consistency in our attitudes. It is stressful for our thoughts or our thoughts and behavior to be discrepant. We need to feel that the world is orderly and predictable and that we have control over our world in order to function in a psychologically healthy manner.

CHARACTERISTICS OF AN EFFECTIVE PERSON

Now that we have examined human personality development and discussed some examples of human attributes and human needs, we will briefly summarize some of the major characteristics of the effective person.

Schultz (1977) has suggested a set of characteristics after looking at theories of healthy personalities by well-established personality theorists. He reviewed popular models of the healthy personality developed by Allport, Rogers, Fromm, Maslow, Jung, Frankl, and Perls. Schultz found that differences among these viewpoints abounded; similarities were harder to find. He did, however, manage to identify a number of areas of agreement among these diverse viewpoints. Below are some general areas of agreement among personality psychologists on what is the healthy personality (Schultz, pp. 143–146):

1. The psychologically healthy person is capable of being *in the world of physical reality and social reality.* The person is capable of making objective judgments about himself or herself, others, and inanimate objects.
2. The psychologically healthy person is *consciously in control* of his or her life. Although one is never completely aware of all motives for one's behavior, nor is one entirely rational all the time, one must be largely in control of one's destiny.
3. The psychologically healthy person should *know who he or she is.* We all may be required to assume social roles, but we should have some inner sense of identity that goes beyond mere social roles. We should be acceptant and tolerant of our weaknesses and confident in our strengths.
4. The psychologically healthy person must be firmly *anchored in the present.* Although no one is immune to influences from the past or demands of the future, for life to be rich and meaningful it must be experienced in one's immediate existence.
5. The psychologically healthy person must seek *contact with the environment.* One must desire diversity in both sensory and imaginal stimulation. Most real problems are in the real world, and finding realistic solutions to such problems must be an ongoing process.

Schultz goes on to point out that there is probably no such thing as *the* healthy personality. In other words, there is no universal ideal we can use as a model for everyone. If there is one thing that studies in personality have revealed, it is that each of us is unique. Such uniqueness may be occasionally viewed as maladaptive, although we should be careful to see the richness provided by human diversity. Another important consideration in understanding healthy personalities is that psychological health cannot be viewed independently of the developmental process. As we grow older, our needs and aspirations vary. We change. What course of action we should take is probably different for each of us. The next chapter, however, will look at some of the ways that the differences among people may be judged to be expressions of unhealthy personality adjustment.

SUMMARY

This chapter presented a discussion of living effectiveness by outlining the demands and coping devices at various stages of personality development. Different adjustments characterize infancy, babyhood, childhood, puberty, adolescence, and various adult stages.

Several factors make for the uniqueness of human experience. Many uniquely human attributes that are adaptive may also be maladaptive. The positive and negative consequences of human memory, time sense, and language were considered in particular.

Fulfillment of various human needs is important to living effectiveness, such as the need for a favorable self-concept, the need for sensory stimulation, and the need to know and understand the world.

Finally, we listed the characteristics of an effective person. Most psychologists would probably agree that an effective person is one who is in contact with physical and social reality, knows who he or she is, and interacts actively with the environment.

KEY CONCEPTS

Apathy a way of withdrawing from the world by refusing to respond emotionally.

Body image the concept of one's self as a physical object.

Coping devices ways in which an individual attempts to meet the demands of living.

Critical period a particular time in development when appropriate environmental stimulation must occur if some aspect of the person, such as the forming of an interpersonal attachment, is to develop.

Demands factors outside or within the person that create stress.

Identity confusion confusion in adolescence surrounding the questions of what one is and what one should be.

Living effectiveness how successful one is in meeting the demands of living.

Self-concept how one views oneself.

Sense of security the feeling that one exists in a safe and rewarding world.

Somnolent detachment a way of withdrawing from the world through excessive sleep.

100

5

CHAPTER OBJECTIVES

1. To understand the nature of anxiety and its role in ineffective personality functioning.
2. To understand the major types of defense mechanisms used to ward off anxiety.
3. To understand the major types of mental illness.
4. To understand the role of situational factors as well as personality factors in ineffective personality functioning.
5. To understand how people view the causes of psychological problems.

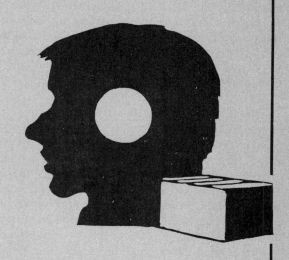

INEFFECTIVE
PERSONALITY
PATTERNS

In the last chapter we pointed out that successful adaptation requires that a person be able to cope with the demands of living. We examined some of the adjustment demands that tend to characterize various stages of personality development. Adjustment demands may originate in one's environment or one's personality. A person confronted with severely taxing demands will respond with feelings of **anxiety**. Anxiety is the reaction to any situation or circumstance that threatens the person's well-being. In this chapter we will look at the variety of consequences of unsuccessful coping with the demands of living.

THE CONCEPT OF ANXIETY

Freud believed that anxiety was a conscious feeling experienced in response to various threats to one's ego. He identified three general areas of threat to one's ego. First, the ego may be pressured by immediate demands from the environment. Such threats as seeing a bear jumping out at you in the woods, taking a college examination, or being interviewed for a job produce **objective anxiety**. We would expect the stress on the ego to be in direct proportion to the extent of external threat. Once the person has confronted the external threat and dealt with it successfully, we would expect the anxiety to vanish. Objective anxiety is a reaction to realistic problems and a person must deal with it on a more or less continuing basis. This form of anxiety is not a pathological or maladaptive response, but is, rather, a normal reaction to the demands of normal living.

Freud described two other types of anxiety that may have a more lasting and potentially more disruptive influence on behavior. **Moral anxiety**, or guilt, is the feeling that results when the ego comes under pressure from a second structure in personality, called the "superego" (roughly, the conscience). According to Freud, the superego develops mostly from parents' moral, instructional, and disciplinary teaching. The parents make few attempts to socialize a child during the first year of life. However, as the child moves into the second year of life, the parents begin to instruct the child that some things are good, some things are bad, some things are clean, some things are dirty, some things are right, and some things are wrong. Such standards are internalized, and these internalized standards serve to evaluate the more pragmatic activity of the ego. If the ego violates these internalized standards of conduct, the superego immediately passes judgment on the ego, and that quiet though forceful voice of conscience brings the ego under scrutiny. For the ego to act unacceptably, or merely think unacceptable things, produces guilt feelings.

People need a stable and rational set of internal standards. It is hard to imagine what social order would prevail if the development of individual conscience did not occur. Yet, for most of us, the raw material of the superego is the uncritically accepted standards derived from childhood experience and fantasy. As an adult, one must come to balance the need for internal control with a rational view of the world. Either an overly punitive superego or an insufficiently punitive superego can lead to inadequate ego functioning in the adult.

104

A mentally healthy person is not someone who is free of life stresses and strains. We all must occasionally experience objective anxiety. (Photo © Arthur Grace / Stock, Boston.)

From a mental-health point of view, the most disabling form of anxiety is **neurotic anxiety**. Freud believed that around the 5th to 6th year of life, one undergoes an extensive repression (motivated forgetting) of childhood experiences, particularly traumatic ones. This massive repression "locks in" early childhood experiences into the subconscious. It is assumed that such experiences retain their original emotional character and are striving for conscious expression. Hence, the ego must erect barriers to prevent such experiences from overwhelming it. The pressure that such unconscious conflicts exert on the ego gives rise to neurotic anxiety. Since the causes of this anxiety are outside one's awareness, one is unable to confront and deal with such problems rationally and effectively. Consequently, many maladaptive behaviors, or **symptoms**, as they are called, are indications of the ego's desperate attempts to deal with overwhelming unconscious internal demands.

TECHNIQUES THAT PROTECT THE EGO AGAINST ANXIETY

The ego uses two general types of coping devices to ward off anxiety: *adaptive devices* and *maladaptive devices*. An adaptive coping device is one in which the person tries to deal with the source of stress head on. It involves using one's intellectual and rational skills to remove the source of anxiety, whether the source be external (such as studying harder for an upcoming examination) or internal (such as removing obstacles to one's own self-confidence). Adaptive coping devices, however, can be used only when one is aware of the cause of anxiety and is willing to seek a realistic solution. Sometimes—in neurotic anxiety, for example—one is not aware of the source of the anxiety and is therefore not capable of dealing with the anxiety directly. It is then likely that one will use an unhealthy coping device, or defense mechanism.

Freud referred to the more maladaptive devices for coping with anxiety as **defense mechanisms**. Defense mechanisms are devices used by the ego to ward off anxiety. They have two major purposes. First, a defense mechanism is used because it reduces the level of anxiety experienced by the ego. Second, the use of a defense mechanism allows one to retain some level of self-esteem in spite of threats to one's self-esteem. Very simply, defense mechanisms allow one to reduce anxiety while maintaining a degree of self-esteem. The problem is that such a response is always at the expense of reality. Defense mechanisms are generally regarded as unhealthy, or pathological, because in using such devices the person must resort to self-deception. Such self-deception may range from denying a problem to misidentifying the source of a problem.

Sigmund Freud, and later his daughter Anna Freud, identified a number of ways the ego may try to protect itself from anxiety. People may use different defense mechanisms depending on whether the threat is external or internal, whether the threat is mild or severe, whether one has high or low ego strength, whether the stress originated earlier or later in development, and so on. We would expect, however, that the more intense the anxiety, the more unconscious its source, the weaker the ego, and the earlier the origin of the demand, the more habitual will become the use of a defense mechanism.

We now describe four examples of defense mechanisms.

Rationalization

In the defense mechanism of **rationalization**, a person offers a seemingly rational, or reasonable, explanation for some anxiety-arousing event. More often rationalization is used when the source of anxiety is external and the anxiety is not too disabling. Consequently, rationalization is a commonly used defense and is generally not a sign of severe pathology. If, for example, a student flunks an examination, it is easy for the student to explain away his or her performance by saying "The professor simply gives examinations that are too hard" or "If I had had more time to study, I would have got a high grade." The girl who anxiously awaits being asked to a dance but is not asked by anyone may find it comforting to say "Well, I didn't really want to go anyway, because there are only crummy people going and there is a crummy band playing." The girl has managed the anxiety of not being asked while retaining a measure of self-esteem. But the price has been to distort the true state of affairs.

Reaction Formation

Another type of defense mechanism is the **reaction formation**. The person comes to consciously think or feel something that is just the opposite of his or her true feelings. In other words, a conscious thought or feeling may serve to disguise an unconscious thought or feeling. Sometimes a conscious feeling of love, hate, or sympathy may hide an unconscious feeling of hate, love, or hostility. Suppose a woman gives birth to an unwanted child. Consciously facing her negative feelings toward the child would give rise to intolerable moral anxiety. Accordingly, to ward off such anxiety, the mother may repress her negative feelings toward the child, and excessively favorable reactions may come to the conscious surface. To convince herself and others that she really loves the child, the mother may become overly solicitous toward the child and overdriven to prove to others she genuinely loves the child.

How does one know whether a conscious feeling is genuine or merely a substitute for a hidden opposite feeling? Obviously, this is not always easy to determine. Typically, however, if a reaction formation is operating, the person is compelled to prove to himself or herself and others that the conscious feeling is the genuine feeling. There is a quality of desperation about the person's behavior.

Displacement

Sometimes a person will try to cope with internal stress by displacing the feeling onto the environment. Imagine that you have been severely criticized by a supervisor. You probably would like to challenge the supervisor and vigorously de-

107

fend yourself. However, because of the risk of losing your job or other reprisals, you do not use a direct coping device. Instead you pent up this hostility and later release it on a less threatening object. For example, you may go home and kick your dog or provoke a quarrel with your spouse. In such an instance, you have exhibited the displacement mechanism. People often displace their hostility onto objects other than the original one that produced the frustration. Such "displaced aggression" often characterizes discriminatory or violent behavior toward minority social groups. Displacement may also underlie many of our irrational fears, or phobias. The feared object may simply be a symbolic substitute for some unconscious threat.

Projection

A person may displace an unconscious feeling onto another person or group and then extend the process to the point at which the person feels that the other person holds such feelings toward himself or herself. This sequence of distortion in **projection** produces a shift from the notion that "I hate others" to the conscious view that "Others hate me." Typically one must then take "rational" steps to protect oneself from such insensitive and dangerous people. The defense mechanism of projection often underlies the paranoid personality. Paranoids feel that they are living in a dangerous and threatening world where people are constantly plotting against them. Even normals may occasionally extend displacement to a projection and feel that others are to blame for one's misfortunes. However, the habitual use of the projection mechanism almost always indicates serious maladjustment.

EXERCISE 5-1. WHAT ARE YOUR MOST MALADAPTIVE BEHAVIORS?

List what you consider your most maladaptive behaviors during your lifetime. Do such behaviors seem to be permanent features of your personality, or are (or were) they products of environmental circumstances? Is there any relation between the maladaptive behaviors you listed and a particular age or stage of development?

What are the most severe maladaptive behaviors that you have personally witnessed in others? List them.

EXERCISE 5-2. IDENTIFYING THE SEVERITY OF MALADAPTIVE BEHAVIORS

Hinkle, Redmont, Plummer, and Wolff (1960) have made a distinction between the "severity" and the "seriousness" of an illness. *Severity* refers to the incapacitating or distressing aspect of the illness, whereas *seriousness* refers to the likelihood that the disorder will result in death. Some disorders are severe but not serious, such as a migraine headache. Others may produce little discomfort or pain but are potentially life-threatening, such as the early stages of hypertension. Psychological problems are not generally threatening to one's life, but they are characterized by varying degrees of severity.

Below are some examples of maladaptive behaviors we will be discussing in this chapter. Rate each behavior in accordance with how you perceive its severity (that is, degree of incapacity or personal stress). After reading the section "Varieties of Mental Illness," you may wish to reevaluate your judgments.

Record your judgments on a separate piece of paper. Use a 1 to indicate the least severe maladaptive behaviors and a 5 to indicate the most severe maladaptive behaviors.

1. A person reports that he or she is "going crazy."	1	2	3	4	5
2. A person is afraid of the number 13.	1	2	3	4	5
3. A person appears to have a private and incoherent language.	1	2	3	4	5
4. A person lives like a hermit in a cave.	1	2	3	4	5
5. A person commits crimes for the thrill of it.	1	2	3	4	5
6. A person feels compelled to wash his or her hands every few minutes.	1	2	3	4	5
7. A person believes others have implanted a radio transmitter in the brain to monitor his or her thoughts.	1	2	3	4	5
8. A person is blind and deaf, but there is no physical impairment.	1	2	3	4	5
9. A person is depressed and is contemplating suicide.	1	2	3	4	5
10. A person appears to have more than one personality.	1	2	3	4	5

VARIETIES OF MENTAL ILLNESS

It may be assumed that mentally ill persons are attempting to defend the ego against anxiety. It should be pointed out, though, that concepts like "neurotic anxiety" or "defense mechanisms" are hypothetical constructs. They are merely intellectual constructions that have been developed to explain what is thought to be going on inside the person. The diagnosis of mental illness, however, is not determined by inference. Mental illness is determined by the presence of maladaptive behavior, called "symptoms." Symptoms are behaviors and are, therefore, observable. A person is judged neurotic or psychotic because he or she displays particular categories of behavior. When a set of related symptoms hang together to form a syndrome, we may

109

One must be careful not to regard all eccentric behavior as maladaptive. (Photo © George Malave / Stock, Boston.)

110

use a general identifying label such as *hysteria* or *paranoid schizophrenia*. Let us examine some of the common syndromes of mental illness.[1]

Neuroses

During the 18th and 19th centuries, the term **neurosis** was used to characterize a wide variety of diseases thought to be associated with the central nervous system. By the 20th century, the term was restricted to disorders associated with high levels of manifest anxiety—anxiety of which the person is aware (Knoff, 1970, p. 80). This is pretty close to the modern use of the term.

Generally, mental-health specialists regard the neuroses as the milder forms of mental illness. Most laypersons, when introduced to such disorders, do not feel the disorders are mild. It is hard to imagine how people who complain that they feel they are about to "fall apart" or "go crazy" or "have a nervous breakdown" are experiencing a mild disorder. Yet such statements are characteristic of people experiencing anxiety symptoms. In a clinical sense, the neuroses are milder forms of mental illness because neurotics are rarely institutionalized. Moreover, although they may be incapacitated over prolonged periods, they are capable, for the most part, of functioning within the bounds of reality. Yet the range of symptoms exhibited by neurotics is quite varied. The major syndromes of neuroses are anxiety neurosis, phobic neurosis, obsessive-compulsive neurosis, and hysteria.

Anxiety Neurosis. The main symptom of **anxiety neurosis** is nonspecific anxiety, or what is called "free-floating anxiety." The person experiences states varying between mild apprehension and sheer panic. Unfortunately, the person is unable to attach the anxiety to any environmental event. Being unable to rationally explain one's panic leads to further apprehension. The unpredictable and disguised nature of the anxiety gives rise to the belief that the person must be going crazy. The psychoanalytic view of neurosis would assume that the source of the subjective discomfort is neurotic anxiety. The actual source of danger is some childhood conflict buried beneath repression. The only conscious expression is the raw, unbound anxiety.

Rimm and Somervill (1977) have challenged the notion that the anxiety neurotic suffers from "free-floating anxiety." They contend that this view rests on merely the psychoanalytic theoretical notion. They argue that in actuality, such anxiety is tied to environmental cues that have gone unidentified. They suggest that often

---

[1] At the time of this writing, the American Psychiatric Association has proposed a new classification of psychiatric disorders, the *DSM-III*, to replace the current classification, the *DSM-II* (American Psychiatric Association, 1968), and trial "field sites" have been established to assess the value of this new system. Two psychologists, Thomas Schacht and Peter E. Nathan (1977) have outlined their views of some of the strengths and weaknesses of the new *DSM-III*, and they suggest some potential problems of the new classification for nonmedical mental-health specialists.

111

the clinician assumes the source of anxiety is unconscious and internal without fully exploring the situational determinants of anxiety. In any case, the anxiety is quite real and disabling to the neurotic, whatever the origin.

Phobic Neurosis. The main symptom of **phobic neurosis** is the presence of disabling and irrational fears. Sometimes a person's fear of an object is completely out of proportion to the actual threat. To another person the fear merely seems an exaggerated reaction to a genuine danger. In one sense, the phobic has a distinct advantage over the anxiety neurotic, whose anxiety is more free-floating and unpredictable. The anxiety neurotic is generally at the mercy of the anxiety states, with no clear understanding of what precipitates the fear. A phobia, however, is directed toward a specific object. Consequently, a phobic can successfully avoid intense anxiety states by avoiding the object. Unfortunately, sometimes a fear is of an unavoidable object. Phobics may, for example, fear heights or people or confining spaces; it is hard to imagine how a person could completely avoid such objects as steps, people, or confining spaces, such as restrooms, during the course of a normal day.

If the feared object is merely a conscious substitute for some hidden, unconscious threat, we would assume that even if one could successfully avoid the feared object, the inner stress would have to be released in some manner. This often seems true of the phobic. For instance, a person who fears heights may work out the inner tension by constantly worrying about entering situations that would involve high places. You might simply plan your typical day and identify the number of times you would be confronted with situations that involve threatening heights. Such planning and worry may serve to release some of the pent-up anxiety.

Another way in which the anxiety may find expression is that the primary phobia can generalize to a class of objects. For example, a person may initially be afraid of the number 13. As long as one avoids the number 13 in print or in speech, we might assume the anxiety would be avoided. But the person may come to fear people with 13 letters in their names, or fear walking up steps if there are 13 steps, and so on. Eventually the person may come to create a world full of the number 13. In such a case, again, the person may have to create additional opportunities to work out the anxiety in manageable amounts so as not to be overwhelmed with excessive anxiety.

Psychologists disagree on what are the necessary conditions for the development of phobias. The psychoanalytically oriented clinician has tended to assume that phobias are merely symptoms or surface manifestations of childhood unconscious fears. The consciously feared object is simply a substitute object, and the substitution was brought about by a displacement defense mechanism. The most intense challenge to this psychodynamic viewpoint has been from the behavioristically oriented psychologists who rely heavily on learning principles as explanatory concepts. Such researchers argue that phobias are maladaptive behaviors learned by the same basic principles as any other form of learning. One may learn to fear a snake just as one may initially learn to tie a shoestring. Phobias are sustained or extinguished in the same way that any other behavior would be strengthened or weakened. Such a viewpoint

112

would assume that if the phobic symptom were extinguished in some fashion, the disorder would disappear, since there is no underlying or hidden "cause" within the person. The psychoanalytic clinician, however, would argue that this is merely a form of symptom removal and that if the underlying unconscious cause is not removed, another symptom will merely come along to replace the first symptom. In the final analysis, the development of human phobias may stem from multiple causes, such as repressed childhood traumas or the accidental pairing of some aversive experience and a neutral object.

Obsessive-Compulsive Neurosis.
The characteristics of **obsessive-compulsive neurosis** are repetitive and irrational thoughts and behaviors. Most of us on occasion find ourselves thinking strange thoughts or doing irrational things. Sometimes, to our surprise, we find ourselves doing or thinking the same thing repeatedly. Have you ever broken up with a sweetheart and said to yourself "That's it. I'm not going to think about him (or her) again!"—only to find in a matter of minutes the image of that person forcing its way into your mind? Or have you ever studied for hours before a big exam and then gone to bed only to find that psychology, or biology, or chemistry, or whatever keeps forcing its way into your mind? These are examples of *obsessional thought*. We all experience such thinking from time to time. In the obsessional neurotic, however, such persistent and recurring thoughts are quite often irrational and negative, and the person feels unable to control them. Many times the content of such neurotic obsessions centers on negative and disturbing themes, such as death, sexual immorality, aggression, suicide, or homicide. Obsessives become so preoccupied with the thoughts that they will kill themselves or contract a terminal illness or kill a loved one that their lives completely deteriorate. The person realizes the irrationality of such thoughts and would like to push them out of his or her mind but finds it impossible to do.

Whereas an obsession is an irrational and recurring thought, a *compulsion* is an irrational and recurring act. A person feels an uncontrollable urge to behave in a certain way. Again, even normal people occasionally find that their actions defy rational explanation. Imagine that you have lost an item, perhaps a shoe, in your bedroom. During your search you look under the bed and it is not there. You proceed to search other areas of your bedroom, but before you know it, you are looking under the bed again. You may find you repeat this two, three, four, or maybe five times. If you were a totally rational being, you would simply stop and ask yourself this question: "Is it under the bed?" You should be able to give yourself a very straightforward answer, "No, it's not under the bed!" Yet you, like most people, feel compelled to look just one more time. Many other everyday occurrences have a compulsive character, such as stepping over cracks in the sidewalk, doodling on a workbook, or straightening one's tie or dress.

Sometimes compulsions reach the point of rituals. Such rituals may be very elaborate and have a magical or superstitious quality. If a person follows a series of predetermined steps, then the future might be favorably influenced. For example, a baseball pitcher may follow a particular ritual of handling the ball, rearranging the hat, taking a spit, picking up dirt, and so on before delivering the ball. This may serve to satisfy the gods before the pitch.

In the neurotic, compulsions may develop into comprehensive rituals that control one's life. One may use a series of irrational actions in hopes of warding off dangerous and threatening impulses. The behavior becomes fixed and stereotyped. A behavior that often reaches a neurotic degree is the handwashing compulsion. The person feels compelled every few minutes to wash his or her hands. Generally it is found that obsessions and compulsions appear together and are cognitively interrelated. Obsessions usually involve very negative thoughts, while compulsions generally involve some positive corrective action. The person may harbor murderous or immoral thoughts, but then such thoughts are followed with compulsive handwashing or compulsive prayer. This thought-and-action sequence may be repeated many times during the day.

Sometimes obsessional thought is actually beneficial, as in memorizing the lyrics to a song or overlearning for an examination.

Obsessional thoughts and compulsive behavior serve the same basic purpose as other neurotic symptoms—namely, to reduce the level of disturbing anxiety. Typically, the person does not actually carry out the negative obsessions into behavior. The obsessional person does not tend to act on his or her murderous or sexually assaultive fantasies. They merely serve as a release from anxiety. However, obsessional thinking may occasionally combine with various antisocial characters, and the obsessional thoughts may be carried out in direct action. Such is the case with the pyromaniac (a person with an intense urge to set fires), the kleptomaniac (a person with an intense urge to steal), and the nymphomaniac (a person who compulsively indulges in indiscriminate sexual behavior).

Hysterical Neurosis. Psychiatry has traditionally classified hysteria into two types: conversion hysteria and dissociative hysteria. Hysteria was first described by the early Greeks. (The term *hysteria* comes from the Greek word for uterus.) They observed symptoms of deafness and paralysis in young women and attributed these symptoms to an overexcited uterus that wandered throughout the body, clogging up various body functions. Even during the latter part of the 19th century, physicians considered such psychosomatic symptoms to be characteristic of females only. Freud was one of the earliest physicians to suggest that hysterical symptoms may appear in either sex, as contemporary investigators have found (Chodoff & Lyons, 1958).

We shall consider **conversion hysteria** first. Freud was the first person to use the term *conversion hysteria*. He thought that in hysterical patients the method of coping with unconscious problems was to "convert" the anxiety into some loss of bodily function. The loss might be in the sensory sphere (as in hysterical blindness, deafness, or loss of skin sensitivity) or the motor sphere (as in hysterical paralysis or mutism). Such apparent physical disorders, however, were not due to physiological or neurological dysfunctioning, but merely served the psychological function of any symptom (that is, to reduce manifest anxiety).

114

But how does one know for sure that such symptoms as blindness, deafness, or paralysis are psychologically based disorders, not organically based ones? Could not a diagnosis of hysteria be given to a patient when further physical examination might identify a true organic basis for the disorder? Although a premature diagnosis of hysteria is always a possibility, there are many strong indicators that a disorder is truly hysterical. Below are some diagnostic cues that may suggest that a sensory or motor loss is hysterical:

1. First and foremost, a complete physical examination must be given. Quite often a physical examination will point to the psychological basis of the symptoms. For example, if a person is organically blind, the organic impairment must be along the sensory neurological pathways from the eye to the brain. There will be some structural damage to the eye itself, the optic nerve, the optic chiasma, or the occipital cerebral lobe which processes visual information. Such dysfunctions can be identified by physical examination. Further, EEG recordings of the occipital-lobe area show that hysterically blind patients are actually receiving visual input from the eye. The brain is receiving the messages, but the person is apparently not consciously experiencing them.

2. Another indication that a disorder is hysterical is that the disturbances disappear during sleep or under hypnosis or merely after strong suggestion from a clinician. We know that truly organic blindness, deafness, or paralysis cannot be removed by hypnosis or powerful suggestion.

3. Sometimes a sensory or motor disturbance is inconsistent with available knowledge about neurological functioning. In "glove anesthesia," for instance, the patient has a hand paralysis or hand desensitivity from the wrist outward, while the rest of the arm retains its normal function. The way nerves that feed the hand are distributed through the arm makes it impossible to have an organically paralyzed hand without some part of the arm being affected as well. Such "anatomical nonsense" often characterizes hysterical disturbances; the disorders seem to reflect the person's own naive view of how the body works.

4. Another indicator that a disorder is hysterical is the patient's indifference toward the disturbance. We would assume that a person who was blind, deaf, or paralyzed would be highly motivated to seek every possible medical avenue to correct the condition. However, the hysteric's attitude toward such disabling symptoms is total indifference. The person seems perfectly willing to include the disability as part of his or her life. In fact, he or she may actively resist any physical or psychological attempts to correct the disorder. In the final analysis, the hysteric may prefer blindness, deafness, or paralysis to the more painful alternative of facing the unconscious origins of the anxiety.

The term *hysteria* has also been applied to a group of disturbances that involve some type of loss of self-identity, called **dissociative hysteria**. One's consciousness becomes dissociated, and some memories remain conscious while others are repressed. The official diagnostic manual of mental disorders used in this country (American Psychiatric Association, 1968) classifies hysterical amnesia, fugue states, and multiple personality under this category.

In *hysterical amnesia* the person forgets those memories that serve to identify the self. One may forget one's name, one's address, one's family and friends, and where one works. Such massive forgetting is limited to things that are associated with one's self-identity and do not involve a loss of one's vocabulary or the ability to drive a car. It is assumed that such forgetting is a defensive maneuver designed to help the person cope with intolerable anxiety. Such memories are potentially recoverable by means of psychotherapy, hypnosis, or so-called truth serums. Hysterical amnesia should not be confused with organic amnesia, in which the memory loss is due to injury or destruction of brain tissue and the memories are therefore not recoverable.

The *fugue* is a special case of hysterical amnesia. The person represses his or her old self-identity, but a new self-identity comes to replace it. The fugue (literally "flight") is characterized by the person's adopting a new identity and fleeing from the present environment to a totally new environment. The mystery of such a disturbance—which would distinguish its victim from the more common child deserter or spouse deserter—is that the person may be unaware of this transition from an old to a new self-identity and environment.

We all occasionally feel as if we were different people at different times or feel that there is another side to us. Yet most of us realize this is simply a matter of perspective and a product of our fantasy. We "feel" like two persons but "know" we are not. In *multiple personality* the person actually comes to develop two or more distinct selves. In perhaps the best-known case (which became popularly known and publicized as "The Three Faces of Eve") a young woman developed three more or less distinct selves. Sometimes one self was aware of another; another self was totally unaware of the other two. Intermittently the patient would seem to be under the controlling influence of a particular self. As Eve White, the woman was very rigid and proper in her posture and mannerisms, and her speech was restrained and gentle. As Eve Black, she became more flighty, provocative, and childlike and spoke more coarsely. Not only did these two personalities differ in appearance and behavior, it was found that one had an allergy to nylon and the other did not. Later a more mature and maternal personality called Jane emerged during the course of treatment. Although everyone has various conflicting parts of personality—as shown when one part says "Do that" and another says "Don't do that"—most of us live with such conflicting natures consciously. In the multiple personality, it seems that the person comes to develop separate selves to accommodate the various conflicting dispositions. Another nonfictional case of multiple personality has been described in the best-selling book *Sybil*.

Psychophysiological Disorders

In conversion hysteria, an apparent physical symptom is not linked to tissue damage or organ dysfunction. The cause of the disorder appears to be psychological. In the psychophysiological disorders, the person does suffer from an actual bodily disorder. Some clinicians think that emotional problems may actually cause physical

116

problems; others have emphasized psychological or emotional factors as merely precipitating influences. The term **psychosomatic disorder** is used to characterize physical disorders in which there is a reciprocal interplay between mind and body.

The basic psychosomatic hypothesis was an outgrowth of Freud's psychoanalytic theory of psychopathology. It was assumed that the autonomic nervous system (which controls various involuntary functions, such as heart rate, respiration, and gastrointestinal activity) responds to internal unconscious threats (such as unconscious guilt, anger, and fear) in the same ways as it responds to external threats (such as a bear jumping out at you in the woods). However, the person cannot run away from or directly deal with internal threats, unlike external ones. Consequently, the person may remain in a state of autonomic stress, and eventually such stress may cause a physical breakdown in the body.

Two theoretical views of psychophysical disorders have developed. One is the *somatic compliance* notion, which assumes that the bodily disorder will develop in the weakest area of the body. Under autonomic stress, disturbance will occur in the "weakest link" of the body. The other view is that the type of physical problem that develops is traceable to the type of unconscious internal stress. This *emotional constellation* view assumes that only certain types of personalities develop certain kinds of physical problems. Although the evidence for the emotional-constellation view is at best tentative and inconclusive, some investigators have found evidence that ulcerative-colitis patients are hostile and immature, with intense dependency needs (McKegney, Gordon, & Levine, 1970), that duodenal-ulcer patients have conflicts between conscious needs for independence and achievement and unconscious dependency needs (Alexander & French, 1948), and that essential-hypertension patients have a strong need to avoid threatening interpersonal situations that provoke latent hostility (Sapira, Scheib, Moriarty, & Shapiro, 1971).

One must be careful not to overpsychologize physical dysfunctioning. It is indeed risky for a person not to seek medical attention at the earliest signs of a physical problem. Yet more and more medical specialists are becoming aware of the impact of the patient's emotional life on physical well-being.

Psychoses

A **psychosis** is the most severe form of psychopathology. The psychotic's behavior has become so disorganized and impaired that he or she is unable to function in the real world. The term *psychosis* is a psychiatric designation. Sometimes a person is judged insane by the courts. The term *insanity* is a legal term, although such a legal judgment is generally made after careful diagnostic study by psychologists and/or psychiatrists. In order to classify a person as legally insane, it is necessary to show that the person is not capable of assessing what is real and what is unreal and is not capable of differentiating what is right from what is wrong.

The cause (or combination of causes) of psychosis is far from settled. Generally, however, psychoses are classified as either *functional* or *organic* in origin. Func-

117

tional psychoses are due to psychological factors, such as early child-training practices or early traumatic emotional experiences. Organic psychoses are disorders in which there are clearly definable structural or biochemical problems in the central nervous system. For example, if psychotic behavior is traceable to brain injury, brain tumors or infection, or toxic substances in the brain environment, then an organic-psychosis label is appropriate. In the absence of such clearly identifiable causality, a functional-psychosis diagnosis will be used. That is, the functional-psychosis label is used when obvious organic origins of the behavior have been eliminated.

Traditionally, psychiatrists have distinguished between two categories of psychosis: schizophrenia and manic-depressive psychosis.

Schizophrenia. **Schizophrenia** is a label applied to a wide range of deviant behavior. In fact, the symptoms used to define schizophrenia are so numerous and diverse that it probably would be more appropriate to speak of "schizophrenias" than to lump such a range of behaviors under a single syndrome.

Four general types of schizophrenia have been traditionally designated. *Simple schizophrenia* is characterized by extreme social withdrawal and emotional apathy; the bizarre behaviors associated with schizophrenia may be absent. Simple schizophrenics have simply withdrawn from the world. Such a person may remain in society as a hermit or vagrant. Society may perceive the person as "weird" or "eccentric" but not as dangerous or threatening to the community.

Paranoid schizophrenia is characterized by highly suspicious and persecutory thoughts. Such thoughts may attain the proportions of a delusion, as when a person believes that others have implanted radio transmitters in the brain to read his or her thoughts. Or paranoids may believe that people are poisoning their food or are out to murder them. Such persons are always poised for defense against a hostile and dangerous world. The paranoid's delusional thoughts are usually the result of the projection defense mechanism. The paranoid may assign his or her hostility feelings to others and then feel "I must get them before they get me." Consequently, the paranoid schizophrenic must be regarded as a potentially dangerous person.

Catatonic schizophrenia is characterized by immobile and rigid stupor states. A person may assume some fixed body posture and remain in that position over long periods of time. Then, unexpectedly, this stupor state may be broken by a state of wild excitement in which the person may become highly aggressive.

Hebephrenic schizophrenia is perhaps the most deteriorated of the four types of schizophrenia. The hebephrenic schizophrenic is characterized by very immature and primitive behavior combined with delusional and hallucinatory thoughts. In many ways, such persons do not seem to progress much beyond the mental development of a 1- or 2-year-old child. They often soil or wet themselves, play with imaginary companions, and exhibit stereotypic behavior such as rocking or swaying. The most distinct symptom, however, is the hebephrenic's incessant laughing and giggling. Usually, such patients are the more dependent and deteriorated in mental hospitals, and the prognosis for improvement is very poor.

118

Manic-Depressive Psychosis. The schizophrenic process results in general deterioration in all facets of personality, such as perception, emotion, motivation, intellectual skills, and interpersonal relationships. Although *schizophrenia* is a label attached to a broad range of maladaptive behaviors, the principal disturbance is in the area of thought and speech. The schizophrenic is most easily identified by idiosyncratic ways of thinking and communicating with others. The term **manic-depressive psychosis**, in contrast, has been reserved for those whose most obvious area of disturbance is in emotional, or mood, states. There may be occasional evidence of bizarre thought processes or extreme dysfunctioning, but the most disturbing influence on one's life functioning is uncontrolled and varied moods.

Most of us have our occasional "ups and downs." We go from periods of joy to periods when life appears unchallenging, boring, or mundane. For the manic-depressive psychotic, such mood swings become so extreme that the person's life becomes completely disorganized.

The *manic* states are characterized by a great energy level and hyperactivity. Thoughts (and speech) and motor activity become so greatly accelerated that speech runs together and behavior becomes disorganized and confused. The person often makes grandiose plans but fails to carry them out. The manic states have a euphoric character, the person feels that all is just great with the world. The behavior may include whistling, singing, and shouting joyously. However, such feelings of euphoria may suddenly give way to just the opposite feelings. In the *depressive* states, the person plummets into the depths of despair and despondency. Suddenly life becomes the worst of all possible worlds. The patient sees no purpose to life and feels life is not worth living. The confidence and joy that characterized the manic phase are now replaced with extreme feelings of worthlessness and discouragement. Such persons may become so depressed that they refuse to speak, eat, or move and may attempt suicide. Sometimes they have to be fed intravenously to sustain life.

Personality Disorders

In the categories of ineffective behavior we have discussed so far, the person is mainly characterized by self-suffering. Anxiety symptoms and escapes from reality result in extreme forms of subjective discomfort or highly inappropriate behavior. Such maladaptive behavior leads one to seek aid from a mental-health specialist (such as a psychiatrist, psychoanalyst, or clinical psychologist), or one may be required by society to submit to such aid.

In this final group of ineffective behaviors, we find a substantially different situation. Persons who suffer from character disorders, also called "personality disorders," do not exhibit the disabling symptoms of the disorders previously discussed. Their problem seems to be more a failure of the socialization process. Such persons do not have the troublesome anxiety symptoms (such as phobias or obsessions) of the neurotic, the problems with reality of the psychotic, or the disturbances in body

119

functioning of the psychophysiological patient. The basic problem of such persons seems to be that they have not come to adjust to the necessary requirements of social living. They have not incorporated into their personalities internalized ethical controls or the affective reactions that are necessary to moderate their amoral behavior.

The term *personality disorder* has become something of a wastebasket label for disorders that involve "acting out" internal conflicts on the environment. Traditionally, this classification has included such diverse disorders as sexual deviations (like exhibitionism, voyeurism, and pedophilia), personality-trait disorders (like compulsive gambling or bedwetting), and antisocial personality disorders (like the psychopathic personality). We will leave a more complete discussion of these various disorders to an abnormal-psychology text. Here we will briefly examine one example of a personality disorder, the psychopathic personality.

Have you ever met a person who initially seems like a good candidate for a friend? This person is very likable and intelligent, has a carefree attitude toward life, and has many entertaining "war stories" to tell. Nothing seems to bother this person. He or she never complains about headaches, anxieties, or tensions, like the rest of us seem to experience routinely. You feel that the person is genuinely enjoying your company and would like to be your friend. You plan a number of activities together. He or she says "Why don't we go to the movies tonight? Just meet me in front of the theater about 7:00. Don't worry about bringing any money, I'll pay your way." So you show up in front of the theater at 7:00, but your "friend" fails to show. After a series of such disappointments, it becomes apparent to you that this person is not at all as he or she initially appeared. In fact, the more you come to know this person, the more apparent it becomes that he or she doesn't "like" you. This person's social behavior is very shallow, with no meaningful commitment. This person actually seems incapable of developing a relationship built on trust, affection, or loyalty. All these traits are characteristic of **psychopathy**.

The psychopath also has a very defiant and hostile attitude toward all authority in society. Psychopaths feel immune to the rules and regulations of a society. They appear to lack inner emotional restraints, such as guilt and anxiety, that would inhibit impulsive action. Consequently, the psychopath often becomes involved in antisocial or outright criminal behavior. However, the psychopathic personality appears to be distinctively different from the typical criminal personality. The criminal type is usually a part of a well-organized criminal subculture that includes clearly defined role positions. High cohesion, loyalty, and responsibility prevail among the members. Criminal behavior is directed toward maximizing illicit profit while minimizing getting caught. The psychopath, in contrast, seems incapable of becoming part of an established group, where loyalty and responsibility toward the group are expected. Moreover, the psychopath commits crimes for the sheer thrill of doing it, not for financial profit.

One simply need look at the front page of the newspaper to see examples of psychopathic crimes. The typical psychopathic crime is an unprovoked and vicious attack on an innocent victim. There is little premeditation to the psychopath's antisocial behavior. He is easily apprehended and convicted of crimes. Once released from

120

prison, the psychopath will quickly repeat the same self-defeating behavior. Mental-health specialists see such a person to be not only a threat to society but a person seriously in need of help. Unfortunately, most psychopaths end up in penal institutions, not mental hospitals.

A NOTE ON THE SEVERITY OF MALADAPTIVE BEHAVIOR

In Exercise 5-2 you were asked to rate the severity of ten maladaptive behaviors. You may now wish to review your judgments. Statements 1, 2, 6, 8, and 10 are examples of neurotic symptoms, or the milder forms of mental illness. Did you rate these maladaptive behaviors as less severe than the others? People particularly think of statement 10 as indicative of severe pathology. Did you? Statements 3, 4, 7, and possibly 9 are suggestive of more severe mental disorders (that is, psychoses). Statement 5 is characteristic of the psychopath, who often appears less disturbed than he or she is.

SITUATIONAL INFLUENCES ON MALADAPTIVE BEHAVIOR

So far we have presented a brief summary of some of the more common forms of psychiatric disturbance. These neurotic, psychotic, psychophysiological, and personality disorders were viewed as types of abnormal personalities, resulting from various antecedent influences, such as childhood traumas or maladaptive learning. Such a view assumed that there are certain "abnormal" persons and there are certain "normal" persons. Even the normal or well-adjusted person, however, may occasionally exhibit maladaptive behavior.

Maladaptive Behavior in the Normal Person

A number of years ago, Kurt Lewin, a social and personality psychologist, stated that any behavior is the joint product of those stable predispositions (such as needs and attitudes) we call personality and the influences of the immediate situation in which a person finds himself or herself. In other words, Lewin was saying the following:

Behavior = function of (personality × situation)

Behavior is never just the result of personality predispositions or just the result of situations, but is, rather, the joint product of these two influences in combination. One of these two influences may outweigh the other on some occasions, but in all behavior both play some role.

121

The phenomenon of streaking popularized on college campuses in the mid-1970s demonstrates socially deviant behavior. (Photo © Mark Jones/Jeroboam.)

BOX 5-1. SITUATIONALLY DEVIANT BEHAVIOR

Chances are that, if most people were asked whether public nudity was a deviant behavior, the answer would be yes. However, during the spring of 1974, the phenomenon of "streaking" became popular on many college campuses. Students in groups, and occasionally alone, disrobed and ran gleefully within public view. After such an incident on a large university campus, researchers (Grimes, Pinhey, & Zurcher, 1977) found that the majority of nonstreaking students (81%) did not consider such behavior deviant. Most saw such behavior as a way of releasing springtime tension and participating in a fad.

The important implication of this notion for this discussion is that any behavior may appear under certain circumstances. Earlier parts of this chapter identified several behaviors that are generally judged by mental-health specialists to be maladaptive either for the person or for society. Traditionally we have looked inside the person to identify the causes of such behavior. Such behaviors as anxiety attacks, irrational fears, hallucinations, and antisocial behaviors like lying, cheating, or stealing were regarded as permanent features of the person. But can such maladaptive or socially inappropriate behaviors occur in the normal person under certain circumstances? If Lewin is correct, we would expect that under certain environmental conditions even the well-adjusted person will exhibit maladaptive behavior. Interestingly, psychologists have conducted studies that do show that many of the abnormal behaviors we have examined in this chapter can be exhibited by almost anyone under certain circumstances.

A number of studies by social psychologists have shown how situations influence behavior. Like Lewin, most social psychologists have attempted to link behavior to the immediate setting. As indicated earlier, psychotics do not have a firm grip on physical and social reality. Hence, we would not be surprised if a psychotic reported that this line ——— is the same length as this line ——————. We would not expect a normal person to give such a report. This was, however, exactly what was found by Asch (1956) in a classic study on conformity. About one third of the subjects in this experiment gave a verbal statement of line lengths that contradicted their notion of physical reality. Still other investigators have (1) produced psychoticlike behavior, such as hallucinations and distorted time judgments, in a normal person by simply depriving the person of his or her usual environmental stimulation; (2) elicited socially undesirable behavior, such as lying or cheating, in highly moral people; and (3) arranged the situation in such a way that reluctant subjects administered what they thought were painful, if not near-fatal, electric shocks to someone toward whom they harbored no ill feelings. Such evidence shows dramatically that the so-called normal person is capable of displaying a wide range of pathological behaviors in various situations.

In abnormal-psychology texts, a situationally related disturbance is called a **transient situational disorder**. Such disorders may be in response to natural disasters, such as earthquakes, tornadoes, hurricanes, and the like, or to personal traumas, such as the death of a loved one, divorce, or news of a serious illness. In such situations, the maladaptive behavior continues until the particular source of stress has been removed or coped with. One need only recall the devastating effects of prolonged confinement and physical and mental torture of American prisoners of war during the Vietnam war to confirm the importance of situations to behavior.

Life Stresses

Most of us do not have to cope with the kind of extreme situational stress suffered by the POWs. However, our lives are full of lesser crises that require our best psychological effort to cope. The news that we have lost a job or failed a particular examination—and a hundred and one other situations—seems to push us to our adaptive limits.

Holmes and Rahe (1967) developed the Social Readjustment Rating Scale (see Table 5-1) to measure some of the common stressful life events that most people experience. The scale lists 43 stressful life experiences and assigns each life event a relative stress weight. For example, death of spouse (100) and divorce (73) have the highest stress values; Christmas (12) and minor violations of the law (11) have the lowest. A total life-stress score can be obtained by simply summing the number of life-stress points over a 1-year period. A score between 150 and 199 indicates *mild* life stress; a score above 300 indicates *major* life stress. Substantial evidence has been presented that life-stress scores are related to physical and psychological health problems.

Table 5-1. Social Readjustment Rating Scale

Rank	Life event	Mean value
1	Death of spouse	100
2	Divorce	73
3	Marital separation	65
4	Jail term	63
5	Death of close family member	63
6	Personal injury or illness	53
7	Marriage	50
8	Fired at work	47
9	Marital reconciliation	45
10	Retirement	45
11	Change in health of family member	44
12	Pregnancy	40
13	Sex difficulties	39
14	Gain of new family member	39
15	Business readjustment	39
16	Change in financial state	38
17	Death of close friend	37
18	Change to different line of work	36
19	Change in number of arguments with spouse	35
20	Mortgage over $10,000	31
21	Foreclosure of mortgage or loan	30
22	Change in responsibilities at work	29
23	Son or daughter leaving home	29
24	Trouble with in-laws	29
25	Outstanding personal achievement	28
26	Wife begins or stops work	26
27	Begin or end school	26
28	Change in living conditions	25
29	Revision of personal habits	24
30	Trouble with boss	23
31	Change in work hours or conditions	20
32	Change in residence	20
33	Change in schools	20
34	Change in recreation	19
35	Change in church activities	19

124

Table 5-1. Social Readjustment Rating Scale *(cont.)*

Rank	Life event	Mean value
36	Change in social activities	18
37	Mortgage or loan less than $10,000	17
38	Change in sleeping habits	16
39	Change in number of family get-togethers	15
40	Change in eating habits	15
41	Vacation	13
42	Christmas	12
43	Minor violations of the law	11

From "The Social Readjustment Rating Scale," by T. H. Holmes and R. H. Rahe, *The Journal of Psychosomatic Research, 11,* 213–218. Copyright 1967 by Pergamon Press, Ltd. Reprinted by permission.

PRESTIGE OF MENTAL-HEALTH SPECIALISTS

How does our society perceive the prestige of various mental-health providers? Gravitz and Gerton (1977) asked 100 pedestrians on a major street in Washington, D.C., to rank the kinds of mental-health professionals they would prefer if they needed to consult a mental-health provider for an emotional problem. They were also asked whether they would prefer to consult a male or a female or had no sex preference. Table 5-2 shows the rank order of prestige ratings and the preferred sex of mental-health professionals given by the respondents. The three most prestigious professions were psychiatrist, psychoanalyst, and psychologist, in that order. Social

Table 5-2. Preferred Specialists and Preferred Sex of Mental-Health Workers

Professional	Percentage of respondents preferring males	Percentage of respondents preferring females
1. Psychiatrist	52	29
2. Psychoanalyst	68	20
3. Psychologist	48	28
4. Counselor	56	36
5. Pastoral counselor	85	8
6. Marriage counselor	44	23
7. Psychiatric nurse	6	63
8. Paraprofessional worker	31	12
9. Psychiatric social worker	22	58
10. Social worker	6	81

Adapted from M. A. Gravitz and M. I. Gerton, "Public Prestige and Preferred Gender of Mental Health Providers," by *Journal of Clinical Psychology,* 1977, *33*(3), 919–921. Reprinted by permission.

125

Although we all have unique stresses in life, Holmes and Rahe have identified some common stressful life events experienced by most people. (Photo © Elliott Erwitt/Magnum.)

126

workers and paraprofessional workers were the lowest in rated preference. Respondents preferred a male specialist to a female specialist in the high-prestige professions. Female specialists were more preferred as psychiatric nurses and social workers.

PERCEIVING THE CAUSES OF PSYCHOLOGICAL PROBLEMS

In any therapy or counseling situation, there are two sets of perceptions about the causes of the patient's behavior: the clinician's perception and the patient's perception. The specialist's view of the causes of certain types of behavior will stem from some theoretical position. The psychoanalytic therapist, for instance, will tend to look for internal, unconscious causes in the form of intrapsychic conflicts, unconscious fears, or repressed childhood experiences. The behavioristically oriented psychologist will tend to perceive the problem in environmental reward-and-punishment contingencies. The social-oriented therapist will find causes in the patient's milieu, society, or interpersonal relationships. The humanistically oriented therapist will view the problem in terms of an identity crisis or a need to confront life's stresses more realistically.

Knowing what the patient sees as the causes of his or her problems can have important consequences for the course of treatment. One can imagine the difficulties that might develop if therapist and patient place the cause of a problem in different realms. For example, a therapist may see the problem in the patient's personality (such as an unconscious conflict), while the patient may feel the problem is that people do not understand him or give him enough love (environmental causes). Usually, over the course of treatment, the patient will tend to relinquish his or her view of the problem in favor of the clinician's view.

BOX 5-2. PATIENTS' ATTITUDES TOWARD MENTAL ILLNESS

Two mental-health models have been disseminated in our society over the past few decades. One is the medical model, which views mental illness from a traditional disease perspective. The other is the psychosocial orientation, which views mental illness as a product of problems in living. These two prevailing psychiatric models have come to influence the way patients think about their disorders and their role in the treatment process. The patient who accepts the medical model will expect to be a passive recipient of the doctor's treatment techniques. The patient will expect to sit passively by while the doctor "fixes me up." The patient who has been influenced by the psychosocial orientation will see the mental-health specialist as merely supportive of self-corrective tendencies. Morrison, Bushell, Hanson, Fentiman, and Holdridge-Crane (1977) have found that psychiatric patients who accept a medical model of mental illness are more prone to be dependent on therapists; patients with a psychosocial orientation have more independent attitudes. The fact that mental-health specialists themselves tend to be more accepting of the medical model (Morrison & Nevid, 1976) might lead us to conclude that such helpers may actually foster patients' dependency on them.

BOX 5-3. HOW DO COLLEGE STUDENTS SEE THE CAUSES OF PSYCHOLOGICAL PROBLEMS?

Selby, Calhoun, and Johnson (1977) presented undergraduate students with a set of statements describing potential causes of psychological problems and asked the students to indicate whether they thought that such potential causes would or would not contribute significantly to psychological problems. A mathematical procedure was applied to the students' responses to determine whether these various causes could be grouped into general categories. It was found that the students tended to use the following four categories to describe causes of psychological problems: (1) internal personality dispositions, such as need for security or need for self-esteem; (2) organic causes, such as genetic abnormality or hormonal imbalance; (3) situational problems, such as financial or natural disasters or marital crises; and (4) childhood family conditions, such as a child's being raised without one parent.

BOX 5-4. EMOTIONAL DISORDERS AND ATTRIBUTION

Valins and Nisbett (1971) suggest that people tend to view others' emotional disorders as originating in personality rather than in the environment. As a result of the popularity of Freudian psychology, people in our society tend to look for the causes of life's problems in hidden predispositions in the personality. We have become a society of amateur psychodiagnosticians continually looking for that complex, conflict, or hidden motive that accounts for our own and others' behavior. Particularly when we judge a piece of behavior as "bad" or pathological, we tend to look for the hidden causation in the individual's personality rather than in his or her life's circumstances.

BOX 5-5. ETHICAL PROBLEMS OF PSYCHOLOGICAL JARGON

Edwin Newman (1975), a noted news reporter, wrote a best-selling book, *Strictly Speaking,* criticizing social scientists for their excessively obscure communi-

128

cations. Hallenstein (1978) has further discussed the ethical problems that can result from psychological jargon that hinders effective communication. Below are some dangers of overuse of psychological jargon:

1. *Psychological jargon may distort truth and understanding.* High-sounding words may be used by psychologists and laypersons alike to substitute for simpler expressions that more accurately communicate feelings and thoughts. In therapy situations, a client may believe he or she must learn the jargon before any benefit can come from the therapeutic experience. Then, simply because clients use the jargon, they may believe they understand and are in control of their problems. One may think that perceiving that one "has low ego strength" or "needs to do one's own thing" means one has a grip on both the cause of the problem and the solution to the problem. In actuality, all one has is a bag of empty phrases.

2. *Psychological jargon may produce an elitist class of specialists.* The major purpose of most mental-health efforts is to increase people's understanding of themselves and others. Yet quite often psychological jargon may serve only to convince a naive society that mental-health specialists have special knowledge and understanding that lie outside the typical person's comprehension. Psychologists and psychiatrists may thereby create the impression that only highly trained specialists like themselves can use such knowledge to bring about personality change.

As Hallenstein (1978, p. 116) points out: "The charge of the profession is to increase people's understanding of themselves and others." Consequently, he suggests that psychologists might try to reduce the problem of psychological jargon in the following ways: (1) use words that accurately describe events and one's own feelings; and (2) learn to recognize when others are using words that block the truth.

IS MENTAL ILLNESS REAL?

Is mental illness real? This may seem a very unlikely question after just examining some forms that mental illness takes. For over a century, psychiatrists and other physicians have treated some illnesses as physical and some illnesses as mental. In both cases a "disease" model has been used to explain illness. Evidence of disease is revealed through the presence of some physical dysfunctioning, such as a heart disorder, or some mental dysfunctioning, such as a hysterical blindness. In order to treat such disease, we must identify the cause of the disorder. This medical model assumes that mental illness is just as real as physical illness but that the underlying causes of mental illness are different.

Thomas Szasz (1960), a psychiatrist, has challenged these traditionally accepted notions about mental illness. He argues that mental illness just does not fit a disease model even though clinicians tend to treat it as such. For example, if mental illness were a type of disease, then one could "catch" a mental disease from others and

129

"transmit" that disease to others, or the disease could be traced to a specific cause. This, of course, does not happen. A person is actually judged mentally ill only when some clinician (for example, a psychiatrist or a psychologist) makes a subjective value judgment that a person is mentally ill based on the clinician's view of reality and what is "good" behavior and what is "bad" behavior. The clinician makes a socioethical judgment about a person and then assumes the role of what London (1964, p. 156) calls a "secular priest." The "salvation" of the mentally ill person means restoring that person's behavior in line with the clinician's view of the moral and social order.

To Szasz, what we call the mentally ill are actually people with problems in communicating with the world and defining their proper place in the world. We are talking about *problems of living,* not mental problems. People need to be encouraged to face problems head on and to learn to make difficult moral choices about their lives. For a person to accept the notion that he or she is mentally ill only serves to allow that person to avoid confronting problems directly. One must be willing to face personal, social, and ethical problems of life, rather than assuming that mental health can be achieved merely by removing tension headache, periods of depression, fatigue, or anxiety. Szasz feels that we might be better off in the long run if the term *mental illness* were not used at all and people were encouraged to confront the totality of existence.

Some believe that mental illness is merely problems in living. (Photo © Suzanne Arms / Jeroboam.)

130

SUMMARY

Freud identified three types of anxiety: objective, moral, and neurotic. The ego has various maladaptive ways of defending itself against anxiety (defense mechanisms), such as rationalization, reaction formation, displacement, and projection.

The major forms of mental illness are the neurotic disorders, such as anxiety neurosis, phobic neurosis, obsessive-compulsive neurosis, conversion hysteria, and dissociative hysteria; psychosomatic disorders; and the psychoses (schizophrenia and manic-depressive disorders). In addition, there are personality disorders, such as the psychopathic personality. The behavior typical of neurotic, psychotic, psychosomatic, or personality disorders is viewed as resulting from an abnormal personality. Yet in certain situations even the so-called normal person may exhibit abnormal behavior.

An individual's common-sense notion about the causes of mental illness can influence his or her perception of a mental-health specialist and of psychological treatment. Ethical concerns have recently emerged about mental-health professionals. One of these concerns is the use of psychological jargon on the part of mental-health professionals to distort or disguise truth and understanding. Another concern centers around the mental-health professional's role as a provider of moral values. Some writers have gone so far as to question whether mental illness is actually real.

KEY CONCEPTS

Anxiety the reaction to a situation or circumstance that threatens the person's well-being.

Anxiety neurosis a disorder characterized by vague, or "free-floating," anxiety.

Conversion hysteria a neurotic disorder in which the person "converts" anxiety into an apparent physical disorder.

Defense mechanisms maladaptive coping devices that serve to ward off anxiety and help one maintain self-esteem.

Displacement a defense mechanism in which a motive is displaced from its original object to some substitute object.

Dissociative hysteria a neurotic disorder in which a person suffers a partial or complete loss of self-identity.

Manic-depressive psychosis a psychotic disorder that involves extreme mood swings.

Moral anxiety in psychoanalytic theory, anxiety resulting from a conflict between the ego and the superego; roughly, guilt.

Neurosis the milder forms of mental illness, in which the person is rarely institutionalized but experiences rather severe anxiety.

131

Neurotic anxiety anxiety resulting from unconscious threats to the ego.

Obsessive-compulsive neurosis a disorder characterized by repetitive and irrational ideas or acts.

Objective anxiety anxiety resulting from threats in the environment. The term *objective anxiety* is similar to the commonly used term *fear.*

Phobic neurosis a neurotic disorder characterized by irrational and disabling fears.

Projection a defense mechanism in which one displaces one's unconscious feelings onto another and then assumes that the other person has those feelings toward oneself.

Psychopathy a personality disorder characterized by seemingly unmotivated criminal behavior and an inability to develop lasting interpersonal relationships.

Psychosis the most severe form of psychopathology, in which a person is unable to assess or function in reality.

Psychosomatic disorder a physical disorder that has an accompanying or precipitating psychological cause.

Rationalization a defense mechanism in which a person offers a seemingly reasonable explanation for some anxiety-arousing event.

Reaction formation a defense mechanism in which one consciously feels something that is just the opposite of one's unconscious feeling.

Schizophrenia a group of psychotic disorders generally involving a break with reality and disturbed speech.

Symptom any maladaptive behavior.

Transient situational disorder maladaptive behavior in response to some temporary environmentally based threat.

SECTION THREE

INTERPERSONAL BEHAVIOR

CHAPTER OBJECTIVES

1. To understand the distinction between viewing social interaction from a strictly stimulus-response perspective and from a behavior/personality perspective.
2. To understand how people assign causes to behavior both within themselves and in others.
3. To be able to identify some of the important influences on whether liking develops in interpersonal relationships.
4. To understand how romantic love may be defined and how it may relate to one's own level of self-esteem.
5. To understand the reasons why people marry and stay married.
6. To understand some factors related to the occurrence of divorce and adjustment to it.

SOCIAL PERCEPTION AND INTERPERSONAL BEHAVIOR

THE NATURE OF SOCIAL INTERACTION

We live in a social world, and our most important behaviors are toward people rather than objects. Imagine you see an apple resting enticingly on a bowl of fruit. You pick up this apple and begin to eat it. The decision to pick up and eat this apple was not determined by whether the apple found you attractive or by whether the apple would be offended by your consuming it. You did not have to concern yourself with whether the apple would hold a grudge. An apple is not an animate being that has feelings, thoughts, and actions. Consequently, this rather uneventful encounter with an apple reveals little about our social nature.

The major characteristic of our relations with people, however, is that they do involve social interaction. Every bit of behavior emitted (whether verbal or nonverbal) by the partners in a social interaction serves as a stimulus in the interaction. Each piece of stimulus information is processed before the next behavior is emitted. Figure 6-1 suggests how a reciprocal exchange of stimulation and behavior between two persons may be conceptualized.

A social interaction can be extended by a smile and a comment such as "It's so nice to see you." (Photo © Richard Kalvar/Magnum.)

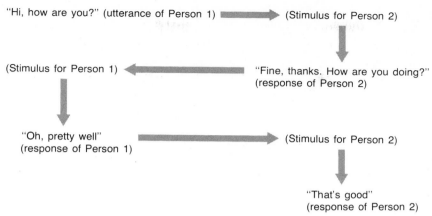

"Hi, how are you?" (utterance of Person 1) ⟶ (Stimulus for Person 2)

(Stimulus for Person 1) ⟵ "Fine, thanks. How are you doing?" (response of Person 2)

"Oh, pretty well" (response of Person 1) ⟶ (Stimulus for Person 2)

"That's good" (response of Person 2)

Figure 6-1. *Responses as stimuli in social interaction.*

A social interaction may be of short duration: Person 1 says "Hi, how are you?" and Person 2 responds with "Fine, thanks." One person has initiated a verbal exchange, and the other person has responded appropriately. Person 2 might extend this social exchange merely by saying "Fine, thanks. How are you doing?" to which Person 1 may respond with something like "Oh, pretty well." How long this verbal exchange continues will, of course, be determined by the participants' desire to continue it.

The amount and type of such verbal exchanges can be studied from strictly a stimulus-response (S-R) point of view. Many psychologists, however, feel that such an S-R analysis is insufficient for a full understanding of social interaction. From our point of view, social behavior cannot be fully understood from just an analysis of the observable features of the social interaction. Suppose your doorbell rings and you open the door to find an attractive young man standing there. He proceeds to introduce himself and comment on various and sundry topics—the weather, the attractiveness of your home, and the like. You perhaps have a strained smile on your face as you give the necessary "yes," "no," "thank you" responses to the stranger's questions and comments. But what else are you doing as you stand in the doorway (no doubt behind a locked screen door) listening to this person? Chances are you are saying to yourself "What's this fellow after?" or "When is he going to begin his sales pitch?" In other words, although you are conducting an appropriate behavioral exchange with this person, what is going on inside your mind is a series of questions about this stranger's real purpose for standing on your doorstep. You are quite frankly just as concerned about "why" the person is there as "what" he is saying.

We realize that we are something more than what we say or do, and we realize that other people are more than what they say or do. People are not only behaving organisms, they are thinking and feeling organisms. We are constantly processing behavioral information from others to help ourselves understand what they are really like. Accordingly, a more complete way of viewing human social interaction is to

137

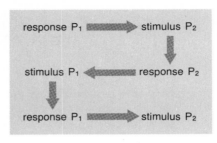

Unobservable Events
Person 1

1. Person 1's thoughts, feelings, and motives.

2. Person 1's inferences about Person 2's thoughts, feelings, and motives.

Observable Events

response P₁ ➡ stimulus P₂

stimulus P₁ ⬅ response P₂

response P₁ ➡ stimulus P₂

Unobservable Events
Person 2

1. Person 2's thoughts, feelings, and motives.

2. Person 2's inferences about Person 1's thoughts, feelings, and motives.

Figure 6-2. *Social interaction from a behavior/personality perspective.*

consider the role that inferences about personality play. Figure 6-2 presents a way of conceptualizing social interaction that goes beyond the behavioral level to the level of inferences about unseen personality influences. Each person in a social situation not only emits behavior but is continuously processing stimulation through (1) his or her own thoughts, feelings, and motives and (2) his or her inferences about the interaction partner's thoughts, feelings, or motives.

In this chapter we will be concerned with the ways people perceive themselves and others. We will examine some of the basic perceptual processes that operate in social interaction. This chapter will be concerned mainly with how such perceptual processes make for interpersonal attraction and more lasting relationships, like friendship, dating, and marriage. In later chapters we will examine additional facets of social life.

PERCEIVING THE CAUSES OF BEHAVIOR: ATTRIBUTION THEORY

The causes of behavior and other events are generally not directly observable, and therefore people must make inferences about why things occur. Heider (1958) reasoned that, like the scientist, the person on the street moves around in his or her world assigning causes to events that influence the self and others. One needs to identify the *cause* of an event to truly understand it.

Heider's **attribution theory** proposed that people tend to attribute events to two main categories of causes—what he called *personal,* or *internal,* causes and *environmental,* or *external,* causes. Heider pointed out that internal causal attributions are often to ability and/or effort, whereas external causal attributions are often to task ease or difficulty and/or good or bad luck. For example, if a student gets an A on an examination, she might see the cause of that grade within herself (ability or effort expended) or outside herself (easy exam or good luck). Conversely, if she gets an F on an examination, she might attribute that grade to poor effort or low ability (internal causes) or to exam difficulty or bad luck (external causes). It is an important feature of Heider's view that people feel responsible for an outcome only when they see the cause of an event within themselves (internal cause). Consequently, assigning an internal cause for an examination grade should lead to a feeling of personal responsibility for the grade.

Weiner, Frieze, Kukla, Reed, Rest, and Rosenbaum (1971) have developed an attribution model that closely parallels that of Heider but is more suited to understanding perceived causality of achievement-related outcomes. They propose that perceived causes of success or failure at some achievement task can be organized within a 2 × 2 matrix. This matrix includes the internal/external **causality dimension** outlined by Heider, but they would add a second dimension, stability/instability. The **stability dimension** of an attribution deals with the extent to which the attribution is to a stable cause and therefore leads the person to expect that outcomes of similar tasks in the future will be about the same as the outcome that the attribution explains. Stable attributions lead people to expect that outcomes will be unchanging over time, and unstable attributions lead them to expect that outcomes might vary over time. For example, suppose our student gets an A on her exam and attributes this outcome to high ability. This attribution is stable because one does not expect one's ability to change very much. The student will probably expect to get high grades on future exams in the same course. But what if she attributes her A to having studied hard for the exam? This attribution is unstable because amount of studying can vary greatly from one occasion to another. The student will not necessarily expect to do well on her next exam, because she might not study so hard next time.

Table 6-1. Achievement-Attribution Model

		Causality dimension	
		Internal	External
Stability dimension	Stable	Ability	Task ease or difficulty
	Unstable	Effort	Good or bad luck

Table 6-1 shows this 2 × 2 achievement-attribution model by Weiner et al. From Table 6-1 we can see that ability and task ease or difficulty are stable attributions, and effort and luck (good or bad) are unstable attributions. An internal cause may be stable (ability) or unstable (effort). Similarly, an external cause may be stable (task difficulty) or unstable (luck). This theoretical model, then, would view Heider's four perceived causes in the following way:

Ability = internal, stable factor
Effort = internal, unstable factor
Task difficulty or ease = external, stable factor
Luck = external, unstable factor

139

The model of Weiner et al. holds that the causality dimension determines the degree of shame or pride experienced after an achievement outcome. One will experience more intense feelings of pride (or shame) when the achievement outcome is perceived as due to internal causes (ability or effort) rather than external causes (task difficulty or luck). The reason is that internally caused outcomes are thought to be under one's control and externally caused outcomes are not. If a student attributes a grade of F on an examination to examination difficulty, the model would predict that the student would feel little shame about this grade, since examination difficulty is outside the student's control. If the student perceives a grade of F as due to poor effort, the model would predict that this student would feel greater shame.

Do people assign the same causes for other people's success or failure as for their own? In general, it appears that people are more prone to assign internal causes for their own success experiences and external causes for their own failure experiences. However, they assign external causes for others' successes and internal causes for others' failures. It seems that we are more prone to place the weight of personal responsibility on others when they fail. This may be one reason that a teacher/student conference about a student's academic performance may prove unproductive. The student may think his or her F is the result of the professor's difficult examinations, but the professor sees the performance as due to the student's low effort.

EXERCISE 6-1. PERCEIVING THE CAUSES OF SUCCESS AND FAILURE

---

1. The next time you receive a college grade, assign one of Heider's causes to the grade. Then estimate the degree of pride or shame you feel about the grade and estimate how you expect to perform on the next examination. Determine whether the reason you gave for the grade predicted your feeling and future expectations as the model of Weiner et al. suggests.
2. Ask someone to give the reason his or her friend or classmate received a particular grade. Do you find that people tend to give external reasons for others' success and internal reasons for others' failure?
3. Imagine that your college or university has just played a considerably larger school in a sporting event and your school's team won. Which of the following reasons would you check as the best explanation for the victory?
   We won because:
   _____ we were the better team (high ability)
   _____ we were more highly motivated (high effort)
   _____ they were a weak team (task ease)
   _____ we were lucky
   Now imagine that your team lost this sporting event. Which of the following reasons would be the best explanation for the failure?
   We lost because:
   _____ we were a weaker team (low ability)
   _____ we were less motivated (low effort)
   _____ they were too strong a team (task difficulty)
   _____ we were unlucky

140

Are the reasons you gave for success or failure in the above situations consistent with the achievement-attribution model? Are your feelings of happiness or disappointment following victory or loss a function of the perceived causes you gave? Are your feelings about beating or losing to this same team in the future a function of the perceived causes?

4. Why is it that when a team wins a contest, the individual members wish to give the credit to other team members and not themselves? Why do team members and coaches tend to take a disproportionate amount of the responsibility for team failure? In some circumstances, do people tend to assign internal causes for their own failure and external causes for their success?

WHY DO WE LIKE SOME PEOPLE AND NOT OTHERS?

In discussing early childhood development, we pointed out how important it is for the early parent/child relationship to be satisfying and rewarding. If the child comes to perceive the parents as predictable and reinforcing, interpersonal attachment and a sense of security will develop. From the early acceptance of parents comes a more generalized acceptance of people. One becomes aware that others, as well as parents, can be a source of satisfaction for a wide range of physical and psychological needs.

Although most of us develop a strong need for affiliating with others, we do not try to establish permanent relationships with everyone. Throughout our lives, we are selective in forming relationships; we like some people, but others we dislike.

BOX 6-1. THE NEED FOR OTHERS IN TIMES OF STRESS

We seek out the company of others for many reasons. Schachter (1959) has identified one important reason that individuals may be drawn together. He found that when college women were made anxious (by being given the impression that they would shortly receive painful electric shocks), they preferred to wait in a room occupied by other people rather than wait alone. He concluded that individuals have a high need to affiliate when in a state of high anxiety, or, as the old saying goes, "Misery loves company." In a related experiment, Schachter gave the high-anxiety subjects the opportunity to wait with students who were waiting to see their adviser and were unrelated to the experiment or to wait with other subjects who would be undergoing the painful shocks too. In this study, he found that subjects preferred to wait with other subjects in the experiment. Therefore, it appears that not only does "misery love company," but "misery loves miserable company."

Liking may be encouraged by similarity of interests, physical closeness, and self-disclosure. (Photo © Stephen J. Potter/Stock, Boston.)

In this section we will examine some of the important factors that determine whether liking for another person develops. If two persons come to like each other, it is more probable that a social relationship will be established. If a social interaction develops into a permanent relationship, the factors that maintain the relationship will become more varied and more complex. Some factors that have been recognized as influencing the selection and maintenance of liking relationships are (1) **propinquity**, or physical closeness of persons, (2) **self-disclosure**, or people's sharing information about themselves with others, (3) the *similarity* or *dissimilarity* of personal characteristics and interpersonal perceptions that persons hold about themselves and others, and (4) *physical attractiveness* and *intelligence*.

Propinquity and Liking

Although there are many important influences on attraction, attraction typically will not take place unless people come into contact with each other. Independent of other influences, it appears that the more opportunities for interaction, the more likely is interpersonal attraction to take place.

Propinquity (physical closeness) has been found to be a particularly important influence in dating and marriage attraction. (Photo © John R. Maher/EKM-Nepenthe.)

Many studies point to the importance of propinquity (physical closeness) in attraction. It has been found that friendships are more likely to develop between persons who live closer to each other in apartment complexes (Caplow & Forman, 1950) or students who are on the same dormitory floor (Simon & Lawton, 1967) or classmates who sit next to each other in a college classroom (Byrne, 1961).

Why does increasing contacts with other people increase liking? One reason seems to be that such contact elicits social responses, like conversation, salutations, smiling, and head nods. There are many situations in which we feel obligated to be cordial and polite even to a stranger. A social exchange may be lengthened merely by responding to a "Hello" with "Hi, do you live in apartment B1?" or, in a classroom, with "Hi, have you read Chapter 2 yet?" The acknowledgment of another's presence often brings more interaction.

Zajonc (1968) proposed that merely increasing contact with something will increase positive reactions to it. It has been found that this attraction effect occurs for objects and words (Zajonc, 1968) as well as people (Wilson & Nakajo, 1965). Moreover, Darley and Berscheid (1967) have found that when someone expects to meet a stranger, he or she begins to emphasize positive traits of this person before the actual meeting.

143

Propinquity is also an important factor in dating and mate selection. Clarke (1952) interviewed a few hundred applicants for marriage licenses and found that the majority of the couples lived within 16 blocks of each other. Although most feel that there is that one special someone just made for us, it is amazing how often this person is in our own neighborhood or university.

We should point out that although frequent exposure to another may result in liking, it may have just the opposite effect. Probably many of our most disliked acquaintances are family members, neighbors, fellow students, and the like. Increased opportunities for social interaction may intensify both positive and negative feelings toward others.

EXERCISE 6-2. PROPINQUITY AND LIKING

What evidence can you find in your own life that liking for others is influenced by propinquity?

Try this little test. List your three best friends. In comparison to other people you know, do they tend to live closer to you? How about your dating partner or spouse, if you have one? Is this person from your own neighborhood or home town? Was your opportunity to meet this person determined by the closeness of your physical locations?

Are the people you dislike most also influenced by physical closeness or the number of opportunities for contact?

Self-Disclosure and Liking

The psychoanalyst Carl Jung said that people tend to put on a social mask, or *persona,* to hide from public view their innermost thoughts and feelings. Jourard (1971) has suggested that people are more likely to reveal their true thoughts and feelings to others if they trust others. **Self-disclosure** is one indication that a person is attracted to another. People tend to respond positively to those who are willing to make disclosures about themselves. For someone to confide in you means he or she must perceive you as a trustworthy and likable person. Accordingly, self-disclosure is often a necessary ingredient for the establishment of more enduring relationships, like friendship, dating, and marriage, in which affection and trust are predominant.

Jourard (1971, p. 5) describes the following consequences of self-disclosure: (1) people can determine the degree of similarity or dissimilarity in interests, thoughts, and feelings, (2) they can determine each other's or express their own needs to help ensure need fulfillment, and (3) they can determine each other's moral or ethical standards. In other words, the chief way we can know how another thinks or feels, or what types of needs he or she has, or what his or her moral character is, is by the information he or she gives us.

144

Another interesting hypothesis by Jourard is that "no man can come to know himself except as an outcome of disclosing himself to another person" (p. 6). When a person comes to share his or her innermost self with others, that person gains self-understanding and can relate to the world in a more realistic and confident way.

Research has shown, however, that self-disclosure does not necessarily lead automatically to interpersonal attraction. First off, *how much* you disclose to another may not be as important as *what* you disclose. Altman and Haythorne (1965) say that the depth, rather than the breadth, of self-disclosure influences one's response to the divulged information. Generally, the more intimate the information, the more positive the response to the self-disclosure. Some types of information are intimate because they deal with a person's inner self; others are intimate because there are social mores against such disclosures (Schneider, 1976).

In the real world, most of our self-disclosures are toward people we have close relationships with, such as family members and friends. There are perhaps, however, situations in which a person is more prone to self-disclosure to a stranger than to a close friend or relative. Occasionally we meet a stranger on an airplane and divulge information that we would not share if we thought we would meet that person again. In addition, people are generally willing to share their inner feelings and thoughts with doctors and mental-health specialists. Sometimes we would prefer to put our trust in others we do not have intimate relationships with. In general, though, research (Taylor, 1968) has shown that self-disclosure increases as the length of the

---

BOX 6-2. GOSSIPING: DISCLOSURE ABOUT OTHERS

In addition to disclosing information about oneself to another, one can disclose information about someone else. One form of such disclosure may be regarded as gossip. Fine and Rosnow (1978) report that this form of disclosure has generally escaped attention by psychologists, even though some form of gossiping probably characterizes most social interactions. The layman essentially regards gossiping as a type of idle talk based on hearsay information. Fine and Rosnow (1978, p. 161) define *gossip* as "*a topical assertion about personal qualities or behavior, usually but not necessarily formulated on the basis of hearsay, that is deemed trivial or nonessential within the immediate social context*" (italics in original). This definition implies that gossip is usually of a local interest, it may be about oneself as well as others, it may be factual or nonfactual, and it may be positive or negative. Moreover, what is gossip in one context may not be gossip in another context. Fine and Rosnow think that gossip may serve three main functions in social situations: it may provide an informational, or news-bearing, function; it may provide a means of influencing or gaining control over others; or it may merely serve an entertainment function (being a means of escape from boredom or routine activities).

relationship increases. In fact, a person who discloses something very personal early in an acquaintanceship may be viewed as immature and maladjusted or perhaps as a phony (Wortman, Adesman, Herman, & Greenberg, 1976).

Similarity or Dissimilarity and Liking

Another influence on liking is the similarity or dissimilarity between persons' attitudes and needs. Two theoretical notions have guided most research on interpersonal perception over the past four decades: the similarity hypothesis and the dissimilarity hypothesis.

The **similarity hypothesis**, simply stated, says we tend to like others who are similar to ourselves. There are, of course, many ways that a person may be similar to someone else. People may be similar along various demographic dimensions, like age, sex, race, socioeconomic status, and occupational or religious affiliation. Studies of interpersonal attraction in friendship, dating, and marriage have shown that similar demographic backgrounds increase the likelihood that people will affiliate.

Although demographic similarity may serve as an initial condition for attraction, other factors must be operating, since we do not automatically desire close relationships with everyone we meet who shares our demographic characteristics. Many psychologists believe that similarity of personality characteristics is the most important influence on liking. We are attracted to people who seem to think or feel the way we do or to have needs similar to our own. Psychologists use the terms *attitude similarity, trait similarity,* and *need similarity* to identify such apparent personality compatibility. Research points to the importance of both demographic similarity and personality similarity in contributing to liking.

Whereas the similarity hypothesis is expressed in the common-sense adage that "birds of a feather flock together," the **dissimilarity hypothesis** is expressed in the saying "opposites attract." The idea is that people are attracted to others with different attitudes, traits, or needs. Winch (1958) proposed a theory of interpersonal attraction based on differences between persons. To Winch, complementarity exists when one person's needs interlock with a partner's needs. For example, a person with a strong need to dominate others would be attracted to a person who has a need to submit to a dominant partner. The couple's personal needs for dominance and submission would complement each other.

Complementarity may also exist when role partners are at the opposite extremes on some dimension. Bailey, Finney, and Bailey (1974), for instance, found that men tend to select friends either more or less intelligent than themselves. Moreover, the friend in such a relationship generally agrees with—and therefore complements—the individual's perception. It seems that men select a friend of more or less intelligence so as to reinforce their view of their own intelligence.

Another example of complementarity can sometimes be seen in female friendships. Imagine two female friends, one very attractive and one not so attractive, vacationing at a beach. Would the difference in the friends' physical attractiveness be beneficial or harmful for attracting male dates? Probably, beneficial. The very attractive woman might enhance her perceived attractiveness by being compared with the unattractive friend. Her benefit, of course, would be to have first choice of a male companion—no doubt from an unhandsome/handsome male pair. But how does the less attractive woman benefit from such a friendship? Quite simply, she gets dates; although she may have to settle for the less handsome male, she probably does improve her opportunities for heterosexual contact over what they would be if she were roaming the beach with an unattractive female partner.

Physical Attractiveness

Some of the most readily available information about another person in an initial social encounter is that person's age, sex, and race. Another readily available characteristic is the person's physical attractiveness. Recent studies have paid increasing attention to physical attractiveness and have shown that there is general agreement among people on what is an attractive or unattractive female or male (Berscheid & Walster, 1974).

Investigators have found that physical attractiveness influences a wide variety of judgments made about a person. Lerner and Lerner (1977) found that a child's physical attractiveness influenced how teachers responded to and evaluated that child. The more attractive a child, the more positive was the teacher's appraisal of the child's academic ability and personal adjustment. Dion (1972) also found that adults assigned more antisocial and unfavorable dispositions to an unattractive, socially deviant child than to an attractive, socially deviant child.

In adults, Byrne, London, and Reeves (1968) found that liking for a stranger was greatest when the stranger was very attractive. In this study even greater liking occurred when the stranger was very attractive and also had attitudes similar to the subject. Pavlos (1978) found that watch repairmen in a large metropolitan area gave a lower cost estimate for a watch repair when the customer was a physically attractive female than when the customer was a physically unattractive female.

A number of studies have shown that information about a person's physical attractiveness may shape judgments about his or her personal adjustment. For example, college students' impressions of other students' personal adjustment (Cash, Kehr, Polyson, & Freeman, 1977) and college students' impressions of professional counselors (Cash, Begley, McCown, & Weise, 1975) were influenced by the attractiveness of these persons. Moreover, Barocas and Vance (1974) discovered that professional counselors' judgments of their clients' personal adjustment and prognosis for improvement were influenced by the clients' physical attractiveness.

Pavlos and Newcomb (1974) found that physical attractiveness influenced one's belief about whether a seriously ill patient's thoughts of suicide were justified. They found that subjects considered suicide less justified for an attractive than an unattractive female who had a dreaded but treatable disease (such as treatable cancer). However, if the disease was terminal, subjects felt that the physically attractive patient

147

Research has shown that physically attractive children sometimes receive more attention and more favorable evaluations from teachers. (Photo © Burt Glinn/Magnum.)

was more justified in considering suicide than the unattractive patient. The investigators believe that physically attractive people are more valued and that this attitude might influence society's healers (physicians, psychotherapists) in their treatment of patients.

In addition, a college student's physical attractiveness may have a bearing on academic and occupational success. Landy and Sigall (1974) reported that poorly written college essays were judged more favorably if the student was more attractive. Cash, Gillen, and Burns (1977) found that good-looking applicants for a job received more favorable personnel decisions.

The most extensive investigation of the role of physical attractiveness in attraction has been with dating couples. Walster, Aronson, Abrahams, and Rottmann (1966) hypothesized that participants in a computer-dating situation would prefer to date a partner of about their own level of physical attractiveness. However, when they were asked to express their preference in a dating partner, most desired to date the most attractive partner available. When prospective dating partners were given an opportunity to meet and interact before stating their preferences, though, it was found that they were more cautious in stating a preference, since the partner selected might not reciprocate the choice. Here people tended to express preferences for a partner

148

who more closely matched their own level of physical attractiveness. This research, therefore, suggests that at a fantasy level people entertain the hope of dating the most attractive partner possible; in practice, however, the fear of being rejected by a more attractive partner leads most to seek out a person about as attractive as themselves.

Attractiveness similarity also seems important to married couples. Similarity of physical attractiveness in married partners (Murstein & Christy, 1976) and daters (Murstein, 1972) exceeds what we would expect by mere random pairing of partners. Moreover, a group of raters can pair up photographs of unknown husbands and wives more accurately than if they guessed randomly (Terry & Macklin, 1977). Hence, it seems that in the heterosexual attraction situation, people tend to select and maintain relationships with similar rather than maximally attractive partners.

BOX 6-3. WHAT IS BEAUTIFUL IS NOT ALWAYS TO ONE'S BENEFIT

Dion, Berscheid, and Walster (1972) believe there is a **physical attractiveness stereotype** operating in our society. This stereotype assumes that what is beautiful is good. Being attractive means one must be happy, well adjusted, and successful.

But are there situations in which a physically attractive person is viewed less favorably than an unattractive person? The answer from a number of simulation studies appears to be yes. It has been found that highly attractive females described in scenarios are often judged to be more egotistical and to be riskier choices as wives because of a presumed greater likelihood of extramarital affairs and divorce (Dermer & Thiel, 1974). Moreover, a hypothetical physically attractive female swindler is given a more severe penalty for her crime than a less attractive swindler (Sigall & Ostrove, 1975). Seligman, Brickman, and Koulack (1977) have also found that a female described as physically attractive is rated a more likely rape victim than an unattractive female by subjects; however, the unattractive female was assigned greater responsibility for the rape, presumably because she must have been acting provocatively for the rape to occur.

Intelligence

The studies just discussed show how important physical attractiveness is in interpersonal behavior. One reason physical attractiveness plays such an important role in social behavior is that it is one of the most readily discernible aspects of people. However, Solomon and Saxe (1977) suggest that personal characteristics other than physical attractiveness may have an important influence on interpersonal perceptions if such characteristics are salient features of the interpersonal situation. They present evidence that intelligence is one such characteristic and that information about one's intelligence may be as important in impression formation as attractiveness.

149

Solomon and Saxe manipulated both the physical attractiveness and the level of intelligence of a female student presented on videotape. The student was supposedly having a conference with a college placement counselor. She was made to appear attractive or unattractive by means of cosmetics and clothes changes. Her intelligence level was manipulated by having the placement counselor comment on the student's low grade-point average (2.25) and Graduate Record Examination scores (below 400) or else comment that the student's grade-point average was high (3.75) and her GREs were high (above 600). Four videotapes were made, covering all possible combinations of high or low attractiveness and high or low intelligence.

After viewing one of these four videotapes, subjects were asked to rate the student in accordance with (1) the extent to which they would enjoy interacting with this student, (2) the extent to which they felt she would be successful in her chosen career, and (3) the extent to which she would probably find social happiness.

Table 6-2 presents the average ratings. Both physical attractiveness and intelligence influenced the subjects' judgments about the student, and the more attractive or more intelligent she was, the more favorable the impressions. Intelligence raised the ratings of social desirability, occupational success, and future social happiness. Attractiveness raised the ratings of social desirability and social happiness but not occupational success. The most favorable impressions on all three dimensions occurred for the highly intelligent and highly attractive female. Overall, intelligence affected impressions more than physical attractiveness did.

Table 6-2. Ratings[a] of a Person Perceived as High or Low in Physical Attractiveness and Intelligence

Perceived traits of person rated	Social desirability	Occupational success	Future social happiness
Unintelligent, unattractive	2.64	2.28	2.58
Unintelligent, attractive	2.74	2.25	2.69
Intelligent, unattractive	2.98	3.34	2.76
Intelligent, attractive	3.39	3.53	3.41

Adapted from "What Is Intelligent, as Well as Attractive, Is Good," by S. Solomon and L. Saxe, *Personality and Social Psychology Bulletin*, 1977, *3*, 670–673. Copyright © 1977 by the Society for Personality and Social Psychology. Reprinted by permission.
[a] Ratings were made on scales running from 1 (little promise of the characteristic) to 7 (much promise of the characteristic).

Interpersonal Perceptions of Self and Others

Social theorists have devoted many years to identifying the perceptions that operate in social-interaction situations. Helm (1974) has reviewed the literature on interpersonal perceptions and has suggested that social interaction may include at least

To have a partner who supports one's own self-image is important in relationships. (Photo © Owen Franken/Stock, Boston.)

three viewpoints: (1) one's perception of one's own abilities, feelings, and motives; (2) one's perception of the abilities, feelings, and motives of one's partner; and (3) one's perception of the abilities, feelings, and motives attributed to one by the partner. These perceptions may then be compared to determine the congruency between one's self-view and one's view of the partner (**perceived similarity** or **perceived dissimilarity**) and the degree of congruency between one's self-view and the view of oneself that one believes one's partner to have (**self-concept support** or nonsupport).

In addition to these self/other perceptions, one may also hold more idealized perceptions of oneself or the partner. The similarity between the self-view and the ideal-self view can be used as an index of satisfaction with oneself. Likewise, the similarity between one's perceptions of the partner and one's perceptions of the ideal partner can be used as an index of satisfaction with one's partner. For traits or needs that can be assessed by an objective measurement (such as intelligence), it is possible to examine the **accuracy of self-rating**.

A series of studies using such pairs of persons as friends, daters, and married couples have found that the most important perceptions in liking were those that lead to self-concept support. We apparently become attracted to others who verify our view of ourselves. To have support for one's self-view was even more important than

151

having a partner who matched one's self-view. One study (Bailey, DiGiacomo, & Zinser, 1976) found that people select friends who support—that is, agree with—rather than match their self-view of intelligence. In marriage, typically a husband will desire that his wife support his concept of his intelligence to a high degree, while a wife is less concerned about self-concept support for her intelligence but is more concerned that her husband's intelligence level match her conception of an ideal husband's (Bailey & Mettetal, 1977). However, a wife is concerned that her husband provide support for her self-view of physical attractiveness (Bailey & Price, 1978).

ROMANTIC LOVE

Although the romantic love relationship is perhaps the most intense and in many ways the most significant of our many relationships, relatively little research attention has been given to it. Traditionally, researchers felt that romantic love transcends objective measurement, and accordingly the description of the love relationship was left to poets and novelists.

Rubin (1970), however, breaking with this tradition, assumed that romantic love was merely a special form of attitude and could be measured like other attitudes. He constructed two questionnaires from a large pool of statements: one to measure *liking* and the other to measure *loving* of another person. These two questionnaires were sufficiently different to be regarded as measuring distinctly different attitudes.

Rubin was interested in determining whether love scores would predict interpersonal behavior. He hypothesized that college dating couples who had high love scores would spend more time gazing into each other's eyes than couples with low love scores. He found that couples who were more "in love" did spend more time looking at each other. Another study (Goldstein, Kilroy, & Van de Voort, 1976) reported similar results.

Loving and Liking: Friends and Lovers

Rubin had these same dating couples provide loving and liking scores for their dating partners and for a close same-sex friend. Table 6-3 gives the subjects' scores on the loving and liking scales for both partner and friend. Men and women reported essentially the same love scores for their partners. Women reported liking their boyfriends somewhat more than men reported liking their girlfriends. It was found that both men and women *liked* their same-sex friends about equally, but women loved their friends (average score, 65.27) substantially more than men loved theirs (average score, 55.07). This last finding agrees with the social norm that allows more open expression of affectional feelings between women than between men.

One final observation from Table 6-3 is that although subjects of both sexes liked their same-sex friends about the same as they liked their dating partners, they tended to love their partners more than they loved their friends.

Table 6-3. Loving and Liking Scores for Date and Best Friend

Scale	Women	Men
Love for partner	89.46	89.37
Liking for partner	88.48	84.65
Love for friend	65.27	55.07
Liking for friend	80.47	79.10

Adapted from "Measurement of Romantic Love," by Z. Rubin, *Journal of Personality and Social Psychology,* 1970, *16*(2), 265–273. Copyright 1970 by the American Psychological Association. Reprinted by permission.

I Love You because You Make Me Sad, Mad, or Glad

One reason love is so hard to understand is that it is so hard to define. Most people, if asked to define love, will find themselves rambling on, modifying this, qualifying that, and so on. After a few exasperating minutes, one will have to admit that one does not really know what love is. Unfortunately, most of us begin the dating process with little understanding of what to look for to define a state of romantic love. Then, once we "fall in love," we still do not know what it is.

Since the conditions or defining features are unknown, we define love the best way we know how. Consequently, "falling in love" may be a label attached to a variety of circumstances. Consider the following situation.

Johnny B. is taking a girl out on his first date. They drop by a pizza parlor for an early dinner and then take in a movie. While sitting in the movie theater, Johnny decides it is time to make an initial move toward physical intimacy. He places his hand on top of his date's hand. Suddenly, Johnny experiences a series of unusual and intense feelings in the pit of his stomach. "Wow," says Johnny, following this first physical contact with the date. Johnny just knows this is the real thing. Love surely is a many-splendored thing.

What Johnny has failed to realize is that the dramatic physiological sensations he is experiencing are not the result of "love in bloom" but an overworked gastrointestinal system finding it difficult to digest a high-powered pizza. Without knowledge of what true love entails, many a romance may have begun on stomach rumblings at a critical moment of physical contact.

Walster and Berscheid (1971) postulated that any state of arousal may be labeled love if the situation is appropriate. Hence, a romantic attraction may develop

153

toward a member of the opposite sex who elicits strong emotions whether those emotions resulted from reward or from rejection. Walster (1970) indicated that such widely diverse experiences as sexual arousal, gratitude, anxiety, guilt, loneliness, hatred, jealousy, or confusion may produce a physiological arousal state that is experienced as love. Perhaps this is the reason that daters often say "I couldn't stand him (or her) when we first met. He (she) was so arrogant and self-important I just despised him (her)." Next thing you know, they are married!

BOX 6-4. ATTRIBUTION AND ROMANTIC LOVE

Some people (called "externals") tend to view the causes of events that affect them as lying in the environment—and therefore out of personal control—while others ("internals") view events as originating within the person. Dion and Dion (1973) have examined the relations between internal/external control and romantic love. They reasoned that "externals" would be more likely to perceive love as a mysterious phenomenon and due mainly to fate, whereas internals would view romantic love as due to personal causes. They found support for the following statements: (1) internals were less likely to have experienced romantic love than externals, (2) internals were less likely to experience romantic love as a mysterious or unexplainable phenomenon than externals, and (3) internals were more opposed to an idealistic view of romantic love than externals were.

Is Romantic Love More Likely if We Dislike Ourselves?

One set of theories has assumed that the more self-accepting, self-aware, and emotionally healthy the person, the more capable that person is of loving others. Various self-actualization theorists (for example, Fromm, 1939; Maslow, 1970; Rogers, 1959) have advocated this view. The opposite viewpoint is that the lower one's self-esteem and sense of self-worth, the more likely one is to seek fulfillment in romantic love. This view rests on the psychoanalytic notion of why people need and seek affection. The more inferior one feels, the more readily one will identify with a strong partner.

Some researchers have found that lowering a person's self-esteem will make that person more receptive to a member of the opposite sex. Walster (1965) experimentally lowered the self-esteem of females and found that these females were more receptive to a male's request for a date than females with higher self-esteem. Dion and Dion (1975) have also reported: "Persons possessing low self-esteem expressed inter-

154

personal attitudes of greater love, greater liking, and more trust for their partners; they also more favorably evaluated their romantic partner than did the high self-esteem individuals. Moreover, those low in self-esteem reported generally more intense experiences of romantic love and described them as being less 'rational' and, therefore, more genuine" (pp. 52–53).

MARRIAGE AND DIVORCE

When young unmarried adolescents are asked whether they intend to marry, over 94% indicate they do, and most expect to marry as young adults (Martin, 1974; Rubin, 1973). In actuality, over 95% of American men and women will marry at least once. Nearly half these first marriages, however, will end in divorce, although 80% of these divorced people will remarry at least once (U.S. Bureau of the Census, 1976).

It has also been found that 30% of married people express some degree of dissatisfaction with their marriage (Birchler, Weiss, & Wampler, 1972). Although these figures are somewhat dated, there are indications that they could probably be revised upward virtually every year. It seems that unmarried people look forward to marriage, but once they are married, divorce, separation, and marital dissatisfaction characterize a disproportionate percentage of their marriages.

In this final section of the chapter, we will briefly examine some of the reasons why people marry and try to understand some of the factors that relate to the occurrence of and adjustment to divorce.

Why Do People Marry?

If you are typical of most adults, either you are married or you expect to be married shortly. Marriage is and has always been a popular institution in our society, and despite occasional trends toward free love, "trial" marriages, or communal living, chances are that marriage will retain its popularity. We have been conditioned to look forward to marriage, and many of us feel that complete self-fulfillment and personal satisfaction can be achieved only when one is married. In fact, there is a negative stereotype of the male or female over 30 who is not married.

Most people seldom think of the reasons they wish to marry but just assume it is something they will do. However, when people are asked why they plan to marry, three reasons are commonly given (Coleman & Hammen, 1974): (1) because marriage is the end result of being romantically in love with another, (2) because marriage will provide an escape from aloneness, and (3) because marriage will provide an opportunity for personal fulfillment. These popularly held reasons for marrying suggest that people expect the marriage to fulfill a broad spectrum of human needs.

155

Husbands and wives must be sensitive to each other's needs and be willing to share in each other's joys and sorrows. (Photo © Burt Glinn/Magnum.)

Why Do People Stay Married?

Once married, a person may expect the spouse to serve a number of additional need-fulfilling roles. Nye (1974) has identified three important roles that one expects one's partner to serve in the marriage:

1. A *therapeutic role*—the spouse is expected to alleviate one's stress and provide advice and counsel.
2. A *recreational role*—the spouse is expected to share and help plan the couple's leisure time.
3. A *sexual role*—the spouse is expected to meet one's sexual needs.

The reasons that people get married may or may not be the same as the reasons people stay married. Moreover, as Box 6-5 shows, married and unmarried males and females differ in opinion on what is important to a successful marriage.

156

Most people do marry in early adulthood. As we mentioned in Chapter 4, early adulthood is a time when people are confronted with a variety of new adjustments, demands, and responsibilities. This is particularly true for the young married adult. Married couples might have expected continual marital bliss, but the daily demands and responsibilities of marriage can strain the coping capacity of even the heartiest couple.

It cannot be overemphasized how important flexibility of attitudes is to marital success. Few people fully appreciate the effort required for two individuals to live in an intimate relationship over time. Two distinctively different personalities, with different socialization histories and usually some degree of difference in age, socioeconomic status, religion, and philosophy of life, are suddenly united in an intimate and supposedly everlasting relationship. Many probably fail to give sufficient attention to the role of the past or the future in marital success. Although couples do assess each other during the dating relationship, they seldom give adequate attention to the range, or scope, of prospective married life. Questions about sex-role obligations, child-training theories, and the partners' perceptions of responsibilities and duties for self and spouse may be given only the sparsest consideration. Whatever the preparation for marriage, a flexible attitude toward problems is of paramount importance. Husbands and wives must be able and willing to cultivate communication skills and show respect for the partner's feeling and thinking about things.

In general, the more emotionally healthy and mature the partners, the better the chances for marital success. Further, the more time and effort given to serious talk about marriage during dating, the more positive will be the couple's approach once they are married. Assuming that being in love will solve all problems or that simply being married will bring personal happiness is a signal of an immature attitude toward marriage (Olson, 1972). One should never assume that a marriage will be successful without one's best efforts to make it so.

157

Divorce

When most people marry, they expect their commitment to be lifelong. Only a small percentage of people feel that "if it doesn't work out, we will get a divorce." With almost half of all marriages ending in divorce (over 1 million divorces occurred in 1975 in the United States), it can be safely concluded that a sizable number of couples who divorce do so reluctantly.

A number of reasons have been cited for the high divorce rate in the United States, including concern about overpopulation, improved contraceptives, the effects of the feminist movement, and a general movement toward greater freedom in virtually all spheres of society. Moreover, many states now have no-fault divorce laws, and readily available and inexpensive legal counsel can be obtained by all segments of society.

BOX 6-6. FACTORS RELATED TO DIVORCE

Divorce is more likely:

1. at lower education levels than higher education levels
2. among lower socioeconomic groups than professional groups
3. among couples raised in unhappy homes and/or having divorced parents
4. in non-White marriages than White marriages
5. among nonchurchgoers than churchgoers
6. for those who had brief courtships
7. for those marrying in their teens

Adapted from *Contemporary Psychology and Effective Behavior,* by James C. Coleman and Constance L. Hammen. Copyright © 1974 by Scott, Foresman, and Company. Reprinted by permission.

Whatever the causes or justifications presented for divorce, there is no question from a psychological perspective that it is a stressful experience for the partners and quite often for children and other relatives. Feelings of guilt and inadequacy, combined with a prevailing negative social stereotype of divorced persons, make divorce one of the most trying of adult life demands. Regaining a sense of self-acceptance and self-confidence may be a major task. In most cases, professional counseling is desirable, but although such counseling may help to heal the hurt and wounds, emotional scar tissue will almost always remain.

Research has shown that divorce is traumatic for both women and men. Generally, however, socialization has more adequately prepared males for unmarried adult life than females. Bohannan (1970, 1972) has identified six significant areas of crisis the contemporary woman may have to undergo during and after a divorce. Many of these crises may, of course, be equally traumatic for men. They are:

158

1. *Emotional crises* resulting from feelings of hurt, anger, rejection, or abandonment
2. *Legal crises* resulting from a bewildering legal process that often is accompanied by recrimination or intimidation by spouse or lawyers
3. *Economic crises* resulting from the division of money or property and often an increase in financial insecurity
4. *Parental crises* resulting from guilt and worry about children
5. *Social crises* resulting from a loss of social contacts and the need to establish new interpersonal relationships
6. *Psychic crises* resulting from feelings of loneliness and apprehension about facing the future alone

Aslin (1976) has suggested that the counseling of "single again" women must be addressed to these crises. She emphasizes the following in helping the single-again woman meet the divorce-related crises: (1) the counselor should help the client make immediate contact with others to share her feelings and regain a sense of personal identity; (2) the counselor should use assertiveness training in preparing the client to confront legal problems and aid her in getting legal information; (3) the counselor should help the client find job-training opportunities and help her develop a more competent view of her abilities; (4) the counselor should help the client work through emotional problems pertaining to children, other relatives, and loss of spouse; and (5) the counselor should help the client face the future and develop and plan new directions in life.

SUMMARY

We live in a social world where our most important behaviors are toward other people. In order to conceptualize social interaction, a behavior/personality model was developed. This model assumes that a view of social interactions must take into account both the behavior and the feelings, thoughts, and motives of the participants.

The causes of behavior and other events are not generally observable, and so people assign causes to events. Attribution theory classifies along two dimensions the causes that people use to explain events: internal/external and stable/unstable. Internal causes are within the person; external causes are within the environment. Stable causes are consistent over time; unstable causes are subject to change. Attribution theory holds that (1) we feel more pride or shame about the outcome of a task if we attribute that outcome to an internal than to an external cause and (2) we are more likely to expect the outcomes of similar future tasks to resemble the present outcome if we attribute the present outcome to a stable than to an unstable cause.

We all like some people but not others. Some factors that encourage liking are propinquity, self-disclosure, interpersonal perceptions, physical attractiveness, and intelligence. There are theories that people are attracted to others who are similar to themselves—and there are theories that people are attracted to others who differ from themselves. Self-concept support has been found to encourage liking: we like people who reinforce our view of ourselves.

Romantic love is hard to define. Some psychologists believe that any strong emotion may be interpreted as love.

Almost all adults marry, but almost half of all marriages end in divorce; many others become unhappy. The reasons people marry and the reasons they stay married are not necessarily the same. Building a satisfying marriage requires mental health, maturity, hard work, communication skills, mutual respect, and flexibility of attitudes. The more the partners prepare for marriage by serious talk about their future during the dating stage, the better.

Divorce is traumatic for both partners and for other family members. Professional counseling can be helpful.

KEY CONCEPTS

Accuracy of self-rating the correspondence between one's rating of oneself on some dimension and an objective measure on that dimension.

Attribution theory a theory developed by Heider stating that people tend to attribute events to causes either within the person (personal causes) or outside the person (environmental causes).

Causality dimension in the achievement-attribution model of Weiner et al., the internality or externality of causal attribution.

Dissimilarity hypothesis the hypothesis that differences between two persons on various dimensions will lead to mutual liking.

Perceived dissimilarity the degree of dissimilarity between one's self-view and one's view of one's partner.

Perceived similarity the degree of similarity between one's self-view and one's view of one's partner.

Physical attractiveness stereotype a view shared in society that the more attractive a person, the happier, the better-adjusted, and the more successful that person.

Propinquity the physical (that is, geographical) closeness of persons.

Self-concept support the degree of similarity between one's self-view and the view of oneself that one thinks one's partner has.

Self-disclosure the process of giving information about one's thoughts and feelings to another.

Similarity hypothesis the hypothesis that similarity between two persons on various dimensions will lead to mutual liking.

Stability dimension in the achievement-attribution model of Weiner et al., the stability of changeability of a causal attribution.

160

7

CHAPTER OBJECTIVES

1. To be able to define and identify various types of groups.
2. To understand how group goals, group norms, and group status relations contribute to "groupness."
3. To understand the types and functions of group leaders.
4. To understand the factors that lead individuals to yield to or resist group influence.
5. To understand the factors that affect who is liked and who is disliked in a group.

LIVING
IN GROUPS

The last chapter discussed some of the factors that determine with whom we choose to interact on a more or less permanent basis, as in particularly close relationships like friendship, dating, and marriage. Yet our social existence involves more than selecting and maintaining close relationships with relatives, friends, or love partners. During the course of a normal day, we pass through many situations in which we are in physical proximity to others. A 5-minute walk down the main street of a city will result in hundreds of such encounters. We meet people on the sidewalk, on the stairs, and on the bus. Everywhere we are, there are others also. Some may be friends, others acquaintances, some strangers. How the presence of other people in our world influences us is the concern of this chapter.

DEFINING THE TERM GROUP

Group is an abstract term representing an intellectual construct used to mean that individuals have become part of the same general setting and that some degree of

In a crowded stadium, our behavior may be influenced by people both near and far. If someone yells "Fire!" we may look to others for the appropriate course of action. (Photo © Elizabeth Hamlin/Stock, Boston.)

SECTION THREE   INTERPERSONAL BEHAVIOR

BOX 7-1. DO YOU KNOW A FAMILIAR STRANGER?

The social psychologist Stanley Milgram (1977) describes an interesting social phenomenon common in urban settings. For years he stood at the same commuter railroad station with essentially the same group of people, although they never spoke to one another. He observed that he had been interacting with these people as though they were total strangers, while in actuality they were not. In one sense, however, Milgram did know these strangers. He often had thoughts and fantasies about them; he speculated about their life-styles, whether they were married or not, what occupations they had, and the like. In fact, he had constructed an implicit view of each person's personality. Milgram coined the term **familiar stranger** to refer to a person to whom we repeatedly come into physical proximity but with whom we do not maintain a social relationship.

Even though we do not maintain an actual behavioral interaction with a familiar stranger, behavior toward a familiar stranger is different from behavior toward a total stranger. First, if two familiar strangers happen to meet in a physical setting other than the one where each is known, they will acknowledge each other and perhaps engage in conversation almost like old friends. Second, if circumstances suggest that a familiar stranger is in need of emergency aid, one will respond immediately to offer assistance to the familiar stranger. Third, if a person is in need of some less urgent help, such as a light for a cigarette, he or she will avoid making a request to the familiar stranger and will make the request to a total stranger instead.

The familiar-stranger phenomenon points out a number of fascinating features of social living. Moreover, it demonstrates the need for social science researchers to realize that a full understanding of social behavior must include more than just the observation of some behavior.

interrelationship exists among the individuals. The main feature of a group is that people are in physical proximity and/or have psychologically identified with other people for a period of time.

Sitting in a football stadium packed with thousands of people, we probably do not feel a part of a group. We are probably relating to only a small number of such a collection of people in any meaningful way. However, if we hear someone yell "Fire, run for your life," we may suddenly find ourselves scanning this mass of humanity for some cue as to what course of action to take. If others seem to be ignoring this cry, chances are we will do likewise. But if we see people rushing toward the exits, we will become alarmed and follow suit. Our behavior has suddenly been influenced by this crowd of people.

There are many ways of thinking about groups. Some social researchers use the term *aggregate* to refer to an assemblage of people who have no prior established relationships and reserve the term *group* for a collection of people with some degree of

165

established relationships. Others have distinguished between groups that have close and intimate relationships (**primary groups**) and groups that have transitory or less personal involvement (**secondary groups**). There are groups to which one belongs (*in-groups*) and groups to which one does not belong (*out-groups*).

One may hold membership in a group (**membership group**), or one may have some psychological identification with a group but not have actual membership (**reference group**). An example is a sophomore student who plans to be a doctor. This student's membership group is the sophomore class in college, but her reference group is doctors: she thinks and feels the way she thinks doctors do. Research has shown that one's reference group may affect behavior as much as one's membership group does. One's self-identity may be grounded in one's status as a college sophomore and in the thought of being a prospective physician.

DEFINING "GROUPNESS"

However we choose to conceptualize a group, all groups may be thought of as existing along a continuum of "groupness," or what is called **cohesiveness**. *Cohesiveness* refers to the sum of all the influences that keep individuals within a group (Festinger, 1950). Although this definition is a general one, it does seem that the degree of cohesiveness, or groupness, is influenced by three specific aspects of a group: the goals of the group, its norms, and its status relations.

Group Goals

Every group has some reason for existing. Groups emerge out of the needs of their members. And we would assume that people are attracted to a group because they hope for fulfillment of needs that could not be fulfilled without the group.

Sometimes individuals collect together in order to achieve some specific objective. The group comes into existence to fulfill some **instrumental goal**, and usually the group dissolves when the goal is attained. For example, students may group to study for an examination. Community workers may group to gather signatures on a petition or collect donations for a fund drive.

Other groups come into existence to satisfy various psychological needs. The **psychological goal** may be tied to affiliation, dependency, or security needs or ego needs, such as self-esteem. Individuals may group for no other reason than the goal of "having fun."

Group Norms

Another influence on the cohesiveness of a group is **group norms**. Every group has some widely agreed upon explicitly or implicitly communicated rules. Such rules, or social norms, reflect the acceptable and unacceptable ranges of thinking and behaving in group members. The social norms designate what group members ought to do and ought not to do. Group norms may be well formalized or may emerge out of the informal social organization. Generally, the group provides various means of reinforcing acceptable behavior (such as praise, promotion, or other forms of recognition) and various means of punishing, or *sanctioning*, unacceptable behavior. Such sanctions may take the form of mild rebukes, like kidding, or more decisive rebukes, like ostracization.

Group Status Relations

All groups are characterized by a status hierarchy, and the more cohesive the group, the better-defined are the group members' status positions. Each group member will come to occupy a **status position** in the hierarchy. Moreover, each status position will carry with it a set of expected behaviors (or what are called **role expectations**). **Role behaviors** are the actual behaviors exhibited by a person occupying a status position. If a person's role behaviors are consistent with role expectations for that position, the person will be well accepted by the group. If, however, a member's role behavior does not conform to the role expectations for the position, sanctions will be imposed to bring the member's conduct in line with role expectations.

One important consequence of a person's status position is that it determines the person's influence over other members of the group. Usually the person with the highest status in the hierarchy will become the leader. This person generally adheres closely to the values and norms of the group and can influence goal setting and initiate group action. Although the leader is expected to adopt and even enforce the norms of a group, he or she may have somewhat greater freedom and autonomy in some areas than other members of the group. Hollander (1967) points out that a leader or other high-status person who is perceived as highly competent and faithful to the group may accumulate "credits" that allow for some assertive or innovative behavior. Such a person has **idiosyncrasy credit** and is allowed greater latitude for nonconformity. A number of studies (Berkowitz & Macaulay, 1961; Harvey & Consalvi, 1960; Wiggins, Dill, & Schwartz, 1965) have shown that high-status group members are permitted more nonconforming behavior.

Typically, the lower one's status position in the hierarchy, the less influence one has on setting group goals or initiating group activity. For example, a person in a very low-status position may not be expected to make suggestions or recommendations to the group. Such a person is often the group clown, whose acceptance in the group is contingent on ability to entertain the group. This person always has a joke to share and at social gatherings may be expected to act the fool. However, if such a person assumes a more serious-minded manner or offers recommendations regarding appropriate behavior of the group members, he or she may be sanctioned by the group.

Most groups have two leaders. Because most groups serve the dual function of working toward instrumental goals and fulfilling psychological needs, two types of

167

Group activities may be encouraged by both a task leader and a socioemotional leader. (Photo © Jerry Berndt/Stock, Boston.)

leaders may emerge. Bales (1958) has indicated that most well-established groups have both a **task leader** and a **socioemotional leader**. The task leader is usually the highest in status, and his or her duties are to initiate new ideas and police other members in achieving instrumental goals. An established task leader is perceived as being high in intelligence and competence, although he or she may not be the most-liked member of the group. The socioemotional leader has the responsibility of arranging opportunities for group members to satisfy their psychological needs. The socioemotional leader encourages cordial and friendly exchanges among members, and he or she must be skilled at soothing hurt feelings.

BOX 7-2. DOES EVERYONE WISH TO BE A LEADER IN A GROUP?

It is probably not true that everyone in a group would like to be the leader. Leaders are typically people who are articulate and extroverted. They may also have powerful needs for status, affiliation, or dominance over others. Not everyone fits this

SECTION THREE   INTERPERSONAL BEHAVIOR

"leadership type," although research indicates that in some circumstances virtually everyone may exhibit leadership behaviors. Another reason that many people may find leadership positions unattractive is that leadership has costs as well as rewards. The privileges and high status of the leader usually go along with large time and service commitments. Many people may find the low-status, low-responsibility "follower" role more desirable than the high-status, high-responsibility "leader" role.

BOX 7-3. ACCEPTANCE OF LEADERS' INFLUENCE

People do not accept all leaders equally. Anderson, Karuza, and Blanchard (1977) have identified two variables that affect a leader's ability to influence group members. These investigators manipulated the method of choosing leaders (election versus appointment) and the desirability of the leadership position (desirable versus undesirable). Once elected or appointed, a leader was either given money and extra course credit for the leadership assignment (desirable position) or simply asked to perform the leadership duties for no payment or credit (undesirable position). This study found that acceptance of the leader was greatest when the leader was elected, and the leadership position was undesirable. It seems that group members are more willing to be influenced by a leader they have elected. And they are more willing to be influenced if the leader is not receiving special personal benefits.

To return to the concept of cohesiveness, we may now think of the degree of "groupness" in a group in terms of the three characteristics of a group just discussed. The degree of cohesiveness of a group will be directly related to (1) the extent to which the group has well-defined goals (whether instrumental or psychological), (2) the extent to which it has well-established norms, and (3) the extent to which it has well-defined status relations.

GROUP INFLUENCES

Imagine yourself in the following group situations. How do you think you would behave?

1. You walk into an elevator occupied by three persons. Unlike the typical group of elevator riders, these three are facing the right wall rather than the door of the elevator. Would you turn and face the elevator door as usual, or would you face the right wall with the other three riders?

169

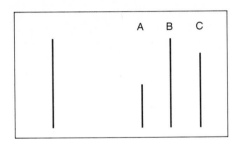

Figure 7-1

2. You are sitting in the third row of a classroom when a psychology instructor brings a small vial into class. He announces that this vial contains some liquid and that after the cork is removed from the vial, each student is to indicate when he or she detects the odor emanating from the vial. The vial is uncorked, and students in the front row begin to hold up their hands; now students in the second row begin to hold up their hands. What do you do sitting in the third row, straining your olfactory sense but not really smelling anything?

3. You have volunteered for an experiment and arrive at the designated room to find six other subjects. The experimenter introduces the experiment as a study designed to measure students' capacity to judge the length of lines accurately. The experimenter then holds up a card like the one illustrated in Figure 7-1. Subjects are then asked which of the three lines on the right is the same length as the line on the left. Six students report that B is the same length as the standard line, and you, occupying the seventh position in the group, also report B. A number of such cards are presented to you and the other subjects, and all subjects are pretty much in agreement about the correct pairing of lines. But now (using the above card) the first subject reports that she thinks line C is the same length as the standard line, and to your surprise five other students preceding you also say C. Now it is your turn. What will you say?

4. Imagine that you are participating in a different psychology experiment supposedly intended to study the effect of punishment on learning. Following a coin toss, you are assigned to be a "teacher" and another student is assigned to be a "student" in this learning situation. The student is placed in a chair, and his hand is strapped to a shock plate. You are then taken to the next room, where you are seated in front of a shock generator that will deliver shocks of between 15 volts and 450 volts to the student. The study begins. The student begins to make many errors in the verbal-learning task, and you therefore must increase the magnitude of punishment for the errors. At the 150-volt level you hear the student in the next room crying out that he would like to discontinue his participation in the study. He complains of symptoms of a heart condition. However, the experimenter urges you to go on. After you reach the 300-volt level, you hear no sound from the next room, but the experi-

170

menter strongly urges you to continue with the experiment. You now find yourself being asked to give severe and perhaps fatal shocks to a person whom you have just met and who may be unconscious from the preceding shocks. What will you do now? Will you insist that the experiment be terminated and the student examined, or will you continue to administer even stronger shocks to the student?

Interestingly enough, when people are asked to predict what they would do in the situations described above, most feel they would behave independently and autonomously. They do not feel that the situation or the presence of other people would cause them to behave unusually. And, indeed, many people would resist yielding to the pressures in these situations. Surprisingly, however, a substantial number would give way to group pressure and would say or do things that they would not say or do were the group not present.

In one of the earliest conformity studies, Clark (1916) showed how individuals may yield to group influence. He found that when students were tested individually, they rarely reported detecting an odor from the open bottle. But in a class of 168 students, 33 reported detecting an odor within a couple of minutes. Moreover, the students reporting an odor were more likely to be seated closer to the bottle and were more likely to be seated closer to other students who reported smelling an odor.

The classic conformity study by Asch (1956) served as an impetus for a number of empirical studies of conformity during the late 1950s and 1960s. Subjects were asked to select which one of three lines was equal in length to a comparison line. In a group of seven subjects, six were planted subjects, or confederates of the experimenter, and only one was a real subject. Confederates were told when and how to give wrong judgments throughout the experiment. Asch found that 32% of the real subjects erred in the direction of the incorrect majority, even though the majority opinion contradicted the subject's own view of physical reality. These subjects showed obvious signs of tension but went along with the group anyway. It is encouraging, however, that about two thirds of the subjects did not report such faulty judgments. In subsequent studies, Asch found that yielding to group influence could be greatly reduced if at least one person other than the subject resisted the majority. Yielding to group pressure was at its greatest when the person was a minority of one.

After World War II, the world became aware of the Nazi atrocities toward European Jews. At the Nuremberg trials, many officers of the Nazi high command who had been directly involved in the extermination of Jews gave as a defense "I was simply following orders." As a consequence of such trials, social scientists began to raise questions about the circumstances and personalities that allowed such horrors to happen.

Adorno, Frenkel-Brunswik, Levinson, and Sanford (1950) believed that perhaps there might be a particular type of individual who would accept such military orders unquestioningly. These investigators tried to identify such an "authoritarian personality" with a short questionnaire called the "Fascism scale" (or "F scale"). Years of research on the F scale have shown that there are individuals who more readily submit to authoritarian commands.

171

But are authoritarian personalities the only individuals who submit to authoritarian commands? In 1964 Stanley Milgram began a series of studies identifying situational factors that can influence one's tendency to submit to authority figures. In Milgram's studies, the authority figure was merely a researcher prodding a subject to administer higher levels of shock to a partner making errors on a simple learning task. The goal of this research was to determine whether the experimenter's prods would influence the subject to continue giving increasingly severe shocks to a partner even if the partner was in apparent pain or danger from the shocks. An interesting aspect of Milgram's study was that he initially asked mental-health specialists to predict what percentage of the subjects would comply with the experimenter's requests and actually continue to the highest shock level (450 volts) on the shock generator. These experts on human nature predicted that certainly not more than 1% of the subjects would administer such severe shocks to another human being toward whom they held no malice. In actuality, 65% of the subjects delivered the maximum shock on the generator.

Milgram's studies have raised many questions about the ethical requirements of social-psychological research. For instance, the studies have been criticized because subjects were led to believe they were giving real shocks when they were not and because subjects could have suffered a loss of self-esteem because of their compliance. Nevertheless, the trustworthiness of Milgram's findings has been firmly established across a wide range of settings and subjects. One important finding from these studies was that the willingness to submit to legitimate authority in our society is not limited to a particular personality type. In fact, the "obedience effects" identified by Milgram appeared to be characteristic of people in general, not of some particular type of emotionally disturbed person, like an authoritarian personality or a sadistic psychopath. Such research points out how the social situation may override generally stable personality characteristics, like our sense of what is right and what is wrong. As in the situation of the three elevator riders, people often find it easier to go along with a crowd than to behave independently.

Yielding to Group Influences

Psychologists have studied two ways in which individuals yield in group situations. One type of yielding to group influence is called **conformity**, and another type is called **compliance**. In conformity individuals bring their behavior in line with the group norms and tend to internalize those norms into their own personalities. The person comes to think and feel like other members of the group, and he or she comes to behave like the others both within and outside the group. In compliance, in contrast, the person alters his or her behavior to accommodate the pressures of the group, but permanent changes in thoughts and feelings do not occur. This person thinks or behaves differently when alone than when in the group.

When alone a person probably would not face the right wall of an elevator, judge two lines of different lengths to be equal, or give painful or near-fatal shocks to another human being. Yet under the influence of group pressure people may exhibit such behavior. Consequently, the studies by Asch and Milgram demonstrate the extent to which some people will *comply* with situational demands.

BOX 7-4. DO WOMEN CONFORM MORE READILY THAN MEN?

There is a widely accepted notion that women are more easily persuaded than men and more readily conform to group influence. Eagly (1978) examined reviews and studies on sex differences in persuadability and conformity and found that virtually all the reviews of this literature concluded that there is "strong," or "clear," or "well-established" evidence that women are more easily influenced than men. Her critical analysis of the evidence, however, suggested that there is actually little evidence that women are more prone to yield to group pressure than men. Most of the studies that have identified a sex difference involved conformity situations in which women have little background knowledge to base their judgments on. She concludes that the empirical evidence is not sufficiently strong to support the social stereotype that women are basically passive, dependent, and suggestible in most group situations. Moreover, researchers have probably tended to attribute female group behavior to personality factors when situational explanations might be more appropriate.

Resisting Group Pressures

Not everyone will be swayed by group pressure, although not everyone who resists group pressure will do so for the same reasons. Two forms of resistance to group pressure are anticonformity and independence.

Have you ever been in a group situation in which one person always seems to oppose other members, regardless of the issue or circumstance? Whenever agreement prevails among the members, this person always has just the opposite viewpoint. Such a person might be an **anticonformer**. Initially, the anticonformer may be seen as independent or perhaps just opinionated. However, as one comes to know such a person better, the more apparent it is that the anticonformer is against everything just for the sake of being different. Such a person uses the norms of the group as a standard by which to determine his or her actions. Since this person tends to disagree with the group about anything, his or her membership in the group may be short-lived. Unlike the leader, who may be allowed some degree of deviant behavior as a result of idiosyncrasy credit, the anticonformer does not have such status, and his or her actions are perceived as disruptive and without benefit to the group.

There is another kind of nonconformity, called "independence." Most people view themselves as independent, but the truly independent person is uncommon in

173

groups. The **independent** is a person whose thinking and behavior originate from internal standards (that is, values), not from group pressure. Often such a person seeks out membership in groups whose norms and goals are consistent with his or her own value system. The independent person is accepted by the group because he or she is "his own man" or "her own woman." As long as the independent's behavior is not continually at odds with group norms and goals on important issues, the independent will be viewed as an asset to the group.

WHO IS LIKED AND WHO IS DISLIKED IN A GROUP

Imagine that you are a member of a seven-person discussion group. Today this group will be discussing the hypothetical case of Johnny Rocco. "Johnny Rocco" is a 14-year-old boy who has been in and out of trouble in society for a number of years. Johnny has been recently apprehended for yet another crime, and your discussion group must make a recommendation to a juvenile-court judge on what course of action should be taken with this boy.

On a blackboard in the room are seven possible courses of action that your group may recommend:

Recommendation 1: Johnny should be given more unconditional love with no punishment for his behavior.
Recommendation 2: Johnny should be given a lot of love with some punishment for his behavior.
Recommendation 3: Johnny should be given more love than punishment.
Recommendation 4: Johnny should be given equal amounts of love and punishment.
Recommendation 5: Johnny should be given more punishment than love.
Recommendation 6: Johnny should be given a lot more punishment than love.
Recommendation 7: Johnny should be given severe punishment with no love.

After lengthy discussion you and most of the other members of the group decide that Recommendation 2 would be the most desirable course of action.

Then the group leader announces that the size of the discussion group is somewhat unwieldy and it will be necessary to reduce the group from seven to five. Every person is to write down the names of the four people he or she would prefer working with in future discussions. Which of the following group members do you think are most likely to be rejected by the other members?

Person A began the discussion supporting Recommendation 2 and at the end of the discussion still supported Recommendation 2.

Person B began the discussion supporting Recommendation 2, but by the end of the discussion Person B had changed his or her position to Recommendation 7.

Person C began by supporting Recommendation 7 but by the end of the discussion had switched to Recommendation 2.

174

Person D began by supporting Recommendation 7 and at the end of the discussion still supported Recommendation 7.

If you believe that Person B and Person D would probably be rejected by the other group members, you are probably correct. Evidence indicates that we tend to accept those whose attitudes are similar to ours and reject others who disagree with us. Group members would prefer interacting with others who support the group decision.

We have described four types of individuals who may be part of a group. Person A is an individual who adopts the group norm early and keeps his or her behavior in line with the group norm throughout the social interaction. Such an individual might be called a **conformer**. The conformer fits very smoothly into the group and is generally well liked.

A second type of group member is a **heretic**. The heretic agrees with the prevailing group position early in the discussion, but by the end of the discussion his or her attitude has changed to the extreme opposite of the group's. The heretic is most threatening to a group and will become the most disliked person in a group. (You might recall how you rated Person B.) The heretic may break away from a group and try to establish a competing social group with new goals and norms. Group members perceive a heretic as supporting a false doctrine. Iwao (1963) found that this was the reaction of divinity school students toward a fellow student who challenged their basic religious beliefs.

Person C represents the **slider**. The slider initially disagrees with the prevailing group norm but eventually comes to accept the group norm. Such a person is often the most-liked member of a group. The slider is perceived as flexible, intelligent, and responsive to the group's collective wisdom. Group members take great satisfaction in having been capable of influencing the opinion of such a critical-minded person. The social fate of the slider is that he or she will rise in status and influence in the group, often to a leadership role.

The last person in our exercise is the **deviant**. The deviant adheres to a nonconforming position throughout the group discussion. Group members may initially attempt to dissuade the deviant from his or her position. However, as it becomes more and more apparent that the deviant is stubbornly retaining his or her opinion, the group will more or less write this person off. If it is not possible to exclude the deviant from a group, he or she will be assigned the more irrelevant and boring tasks of the group. Such a person is disliked but not to the extent of the heretic.

Table 7-1 summarizes a group's response to these four types of members.

Table 7-1. Acceptance and Rejection of Group Members

	Most liked	Most disliked	Accepted	Rejected
Conformer			X	
Slider	X		X	
Deviant				X
Heretic		X		X

175

Groups may have negative influences on human behavior. Yet many of our important human needs find expression in group activity. (Photo © Charles Harbutt/Magnum.)

WOULD HUMANS DO BETTER WITHOUT GROUPS?

According to Buys (1978), social-psychological studies of group influence suggest that individuals would be better off if they did not participate in groups. Buys' review of the literature finds the following negative influences of groups on individuals: a loss of self-identity (often called *deindividuation*), a loss of a sense of personal responsibility for actions, a tendency to model others or follow the lead of others unquestioningly, a tendency for individuals to make more risky decisions and act more impulsively, a tendency to act more panicky in emergency situations, a tendency for people to be swept away by mass (social) movements, and a tendency for people to say things and do things they might not do otherwise (as in conformity studies). Consequently, group membership has a wide and often negative influence on one's assessment of social and physical reality. In fairness to groups, Buys does point out that conformity and group membership may have many beneficial effects, such as enhancement of survival or goal attainment, and groups may serve as sources of reliable and useful information. In any case, it is probably safe to conclude that groups are here to stay.

SUMMARY

A group exists wherever people are gathered together. Social scientists distinguish several kinds of groups: primary groups and secondary groups, in-groups and out-groups, membership groups and reference groups.

The "groupness," or cohesiveness, of a group depends on the group's goals, norms, and status relations. Groups have two types of goals, instrumental (to accomplish some task) and psychological (to fulfill psychological needs of members). Corresponding to these dual goals are two types of leaders—task leaders and socioemotional leaders.

Individuals yield to group pressure in two ways. In one type of yielding to group influence, conformity, individuals come to adopt the group's norms. In a second type, compliance, individuals bring their behavior in line with group norms but not their feelings and thoughts. In some classic studies on compliance, such as those by Asch and Milgram, alarmingly high percentages of subjects submitted against their better judgment to group opinion or orders from an authority figure.

People resist group pressure for different reasons. The anticonformer merely disagrees with group norms regardless of the circumstances; the independent may disagree with group norms because of personal values.

Who is liked and who is disliked in a group? The conformer, who agrees with a group throughout, and the slider, who disagrees at first but later comes to agree, are most accepted by the group. The deviant, who disagrees with a group throughout, and the heretic, who agrees at first but later comes to disagree, are most rejected.

Although groups have several negative effects on individuals, they serve useful functions, and they are no doubt a permanent feature of human life.

KEY CONCEPTS

Anticonformer a person who is always opposed to the norms of a group.

Cohesiveness the sum of all the influences that keep individuals within a group.

Compliance yielding to group pressure behaviorally without change in thoughts and feelings.

Conformer a person who brings his or her behavior in line with group norms throughout an interaction.

Conformity yielding to group pressure while internalizing the norms of a group.

Deviant a person who adheres to a nonconforming position throughout an interaction.

Familiar stranger a person to whom one repeatedly comes into physical proximity but with whom one does not maintain a social relationship.

Group an abstract term used to mean that individuals have become part of the same general setting and that some degree of interrelationship exists among them.

Group norms rules that reflect the acceptable and unacceptable ranges of thinking and behaving in a group.

Heretic a person who initially agrees with a group but later comes to disagree with the group.

Idiosyncrasy credit the greater latitude for nonconforming behavior allowed high-status group members, such as leaders.

Independent a person whose thinking and behavior originate from internal standards of conduct, not group norms.

Instrumental goal a group goal that is directed toward some specific task.

Membership group a group in which a person holds membership.

Primary group a group characterized by close and intimate relationships.

Psychological goal the satisfaction of basic psychological needs associated with group membership.

Reference group a group with which a person psychologically identifies but in which he or she does not actually hold membership.

Role behaviors the actual behaviors exhibited by a person occupying a status position.

Role expectations the expected behaviors associated with a particular status position.

Secondary group a group characterized by transitory or little interpersonal involvement.

Slider a person who initially disagrees with a group but eventually comes to agree with the group.

Socioemotional leader a group leader with the responsibility of arranging opportunities for group members to satisfy their psychological needs.

Status position an individual's rank in a group's status hierarchy.

Task leader a group leader whose duties are to initiate new ideas and encourage group members to achieve instrumental goals.

CHAPTER OBJECTIVES

1. To understand the concept of attitude and factors related to attitude change.
2. To understand the concepts of prejudice, social
   stereotypes, and discrimination.
3. To understand the reasons why people help or cooperate with others.
4. To understand the reasons why people harm others.

SOCIAL
ATTITUDES AND
SOCIAL
BEHAVIOR

181

The last two chapters discussed some factors that might lead to interpersonal relationships. Some of our relationships are close, intimate, and enduring, while others are casual, impersonal, and temporary. Sometimes we select the people with whom to interact, and at times our affiliation with others is unexpected or undesired. From door-to-door salespeople to television personalities, our world is full of people.

As pointed out previously, we do not enter social interactions with our minds set at zero information. Rather, we bring into every social situation a storehouse of attitudes about ourselves, what other people are like, and how we should respond to others. The present chapter will examine social attitudes in more depth and try to show how such attitudes are related to positive social behavior (such as cooperation and helping) and negative social behavior (such as discrimination and aggression).

THE CONCEPT OF ATTITUDE

An **attitude** is a predisposition to behave in a particular way toward an object. Attitudes are cognitive (mental) representatives of our thinking, feeling, and motivational tendencies toward something. We hold attitudes toward all objects of which we

Individuals may structure their time around their most ego-involving attitudes. (Photo © Jean-Claude Lejeune.)

182

are aware. Such objects may be ourselves, other people, inanimate objects (such as cars or snow), or abstract ideas (such as justice or democracy). *Attitude* is an extremely broad term designed to capture the content of human consciousness. In one sense, we might think of human personality as a collection of attitudes.

One way to think about attitudes is to view them along an *ego-involvement* dimension. The more ego-involving the attitude, the more important the attitude is. A person's attitudes vary in ego involvement, or importance. Highly ego-involving attitudes may serve to determine one's self-identity and values about the world. We define ourselves and our place in the world in terms of what is important to us. In general, the more ego-involving an attitude, the more resistant that attitude is to change.

In Table 8-1 some attitudes of a hypothetical person are ranked according to their importance to the person (that is, their ego involvement) and their resistance to change.

Table 8-1. Ranking of Attitude Importance and Resistance to Attitude Change in a Hypothetical Person

Attitudes	Ego involvement	Resistance to change
Believe in God	High	High
Believe I am a truthful person		
Believe my race is superior to other races		
Believe white sugar is bad for health		
Believe that I should make high grades in college	Moderate	Moderate
Believe that my brand of toothpaste is best		
Believe that I should pick up trash off the sidewalk		
Believe that Martians are purple	Low	Low

TRYING TO CHANGE OTHER PEOPLE'S ATTITUDES

Our world is full of attempts to change our thinking and feeling about things. Your parents or friends may try to change your attitudes about drugs or rock music. Teachers may try to influence your way of thinking about human nature, the nature of the physical universe, or international affairs. We are bombarded by magazine, TV, radio, and newspaper advertisements trying to get us to buy a particular car, toothpaste, deodorant, or pain reliever. However, we are not equally influenced by all persuasion attempts. A TV commercial may influence you to invest a dollar in a new brand of toothpaste that promises to increase your sex appeal, but it is hard to imagine a 60-second TV message that would change one's belief in God. One can afford to risk mistakes in choosing toothpaste, but changes in ego-involving attitudes require modifications in one's self-identity. The loss of a dollar or the risk of making a mistake about toothpaste is far less serious than changing our stable and ego-involving beliefs.

We will now look at some of the factors that influence attitude change. Hovland, Janis, and Kelley (1953) have suggested a model similar to the one shown in Table 8-2 for thinking about the attitude-change situation.

Table 8-2. Model of Attitude Change

Stimulus influences	Cognitive processing	Behavior
Characteristics of the communication Characteristics of the communicator	1. Attention 2. Comprehension 3. Acceptance	Response toward object

Characteristics of the Communication

The most important feature of a communication is the content of the message. Influence messages must be relevant to our attitudes before they will be seriously entertained. However, there are times when the way a message is presented is as important as what it says. The same message may, for example, be given in a rational or emotional manner. Sometimes an emotional presentation will bring about attitude change and a rational presentation will not. With a different audience, a rational presentation may be more effective. Generally, the more intelligent the audience is and the better informed it is about an issue, the more receptive it is to logical and well-thought-out messages.

Janis and Feshbach (1953) have shown that the extent to which a message is fear-arousing can influence its acceptance. They presented one group of subjects with a mildly threatening message, such as statistical data on the relation between poor oral hygiene and oral-health problems. Another group of subjects was presented with graphic, fear-arousing information, such as photographs of diseased gums. The mildly threatened subjects improved their oral-hygiene habits more than the severely threatened subjects. Janis and Feshbach concluded that an intense fear appeal may be a good attention getter, but people may avoid recalling such a message because of its punishing effects. In general, weak or moderate emotional messages are more effective in producing attitude or behavior change than more-threatening messages.

Some situations involve more than one message. In a debate situation or political campaign the audience is exposed to opposing arguments. Or occasionally the same person may wish to present his or her own point of view and an opposing point of view. Suppose you are trying to influence your classmates on an issue like whether to have beer on campus. Which of the following approaches do you feel would be most effective in producing attitude change in your audience? (1) Give the strong points of your position, and omit any reference to the opposing position. (2) Give the strong points of your position and the weaknesses of the opposing position. (3) Give the strong and weak points of both your position and the opposing position, but emphasize the strengths of your position.

The fact is that whether one should present a one-sided or a two-sided argument may vary with the circumstances and the audience. One can imagine, for instance, the commanding officer of a military company presenting a two-sided argument before sending troops into battle. The approach that "we have our point of view and the enemy has its point of view" may not have the most-desired effect on motivation and morale. In general, however, it appears that the more intelligent and the more knowledgeable the audience, the more effective is the two-sided presentation. Chances are that in the above situation with college students, the two-sided argument slanted toward your own position would be most effective.

If you are to present both your argument and a counterargument, which should come first? Should you take advantage of your listeners' early heightened attention, or should you present your point of view at the end so that your message is fresh in their minds? Studies on memory have found that people tend to recall the first items in a list (**primary effect**) and the last items (**recency effect**) more easily than the middle items. This suggests that the sequence of material in a presentation may have an important influence on retention. Evidence (Lund, 1925; Rosnow & Robinson, 1967) suggests that primacy is more powerful in attitude change than recency, particularly if the message is highly appealing and familiar. However, recency may be more effective than primacy when the communication deals with unfamiliar information and when important conclusions are given at the end of the presentation. As a practical suggestion, it might be best to present one's own viewpoint first, followed by the opposing view, and then restate one's viewpoint at the close of the presentation. Your message would benefit from both the primacy and recency effects, while the opposing viewpoint would be weakened by being presented in between.

Characteristics of the Communicator

We all have occasion to realize that *who* is presenting a message is often as important as what is communicated or how it is communicated. In the college classroom, for instance, a student's receptiveness to course material may be more influenced by the lecturer's reputation as a famous scholar. Similarly, a television commercial message may be more favorably viewed if it is presented by a celebrity.

A number of communicator variables have been studied in experiments. Studies show that we are more receptive to a communication if we perceive the communicator as highly attractive, highly credible, highly knowledgeable, and similar to ourselves in feeling and thinking. Of course, the influence of the communicator's attractiveness or expertise will vary with situation and type of audience.

185

The importance of a communication may be determined by what is being said, who is saying it, and how it is being said. (Photo © Peter Gerba/Jeroboam.)

There is also research evidence that the initial acceptance of a message or the communicator may not hold up over time, particularly if the attitude concerned is highly ego-involving. One may be swayed by the circumstances, but over time one's more basic ways of feeling or thinking tend to prevail. Moreover, Hovland and Weiss (1951) have found that attitude change resulting from the influence of a highly credible communicator tends to disappear, a tendency they called the "sleeper effect." They found that people tend to forget a communicator faster than what he or she communicated, particularly if the communicator was a highly credible source.

Cognitive Processing of Information

Hovland, Janis, and Kelley (1953) have suggested that both the message and the communicator must be cognitively processed before attitude change can occur. Such cognitive processing has three steps. First, the person must attend to the stimulus (both message and communicator). Features of the message, of the communicator, or of both must be sufficiently appealing to get one's attention. Second, the message must be understood. Have you ever laughed uproariously at a joke someone

186

told you but later asked yourself "What did that joke mean?" Most people are reluctant to modify their feelings or thinking on the basis of poorly understood or misunderstood information. Third, one must then evaluate the information and decide to reject it or accept it. Such decisions are complexly tied to our personality and history of past experiences.

Behavior Change

Most people who want to influence us are more concerned with what we do than what we feel or think. A politician has little to gain by convincing you that he or she is the best candidate if you do not go out and actually vote for that candidate. Likewise, the millions of dollars in TV, radio, and magazine advertising are for naught if a person accepts the message but does not have the need and inclination to buy the product. A person may accept the message that a $25,000 Mercedes-Benz is an excellent car but have little or no behavior potential toward buying one. Social psychologists have well documented the finding that there is not always a one-to-one correspondence between what one thinks and feels and what one does. Sometimes a person may even reject a message but find himself or herself responding favorably to the object because of situational influences, such as group pressure.

Resisting Attempts at Influence

Many attempts to influence us are beneficial. Parents try to get their children to be considerate, cooperative, and altruistic. Teachers try to get students to learn new ideas and think creatively and critically. However, many persuasion attempts are not directed toward improving a person's life, but are designed to manipulate or exploit the person. Someone may be interested in getting us to buy an undesirable product, vote for an undesirable candidate, or join an undesirable cause just to fulfill his or her own selfish desires. Accordingly, we must be capable of predicting the short-term and long-term consequences of our acceptance or rejection of communications. Chapter 15, on consumer psychology, will examine specific illustrations of attempts to influence us.

SOCIAL ATTITUDES

For most people, the most ego-involving attitudes are toward oneself. Attitudes toward our body, our intelligence, our physical attractiveness, and so on serve to define our self-identity, and they are most resistant to change. However, people also hold ego-involving attitudes toward groups to which they belong (in-groups) and groups to which they do not belong (out-groups). In this section we will examine some important social attitudes and try to relate them to social behavior.

Unjustified Social Attitudes: The Concept of Prejudice

Above we defined an attitude as a predisposition to behave in a particular way toward some object. The object may be oneself, other people, an inanimate object, or an abstraction. We also pointed out that a person's ways of feeling or thinking about various objects vary along a scale of ego involvement (or importance). In this section we will be looking at a special group of highly ego-involving attitudes that are highly resistant to change. They are called "prejudices."

A **prejudice** may be defined as an unjustified positive or negative attitude that is highly resistant to change. We all harbor unjustified attitudes about ourselves and our world. However, most of these attitudes will change if we are presented with conclusive evidence that they are incorrect. We may not like to confront the knowledge that we are a weak student in this or that course, that our dating partner is not trustworthy, or that a political figure is involved in illegal activities, but if the evidence is sufficiently convincing, we will change our attitudes. So not all our unjustified ways of thinking and feeling about the world are prejudices.

What sets prejudices apart from other incorrect ways of viewing the world is that prejudices resist change even when evidence contradicts them. One may refuse to accept the evidence that challenges one's beliefs, no matter how conclusive or overwhelming it is. Prejudices are habitual ways of feeling and thinking that are remarkably insensitive to rational arguments or objective evidence. For this reason, prejudice may be regarded as a pathological perceptual process like that observed in hallucinations and delusions. A person just knows that there are little pink elephants climbing the wall (hallucination) or that he is Napoleon (delusion). No matter what the source of contrary evidence, the psychotic may reject it in favor of his own conception of reality. For most people their prejudices are not as resistant to change as the psychotic's delusions or hallucinations, but for others they are.

We usually think of prejudice as involving an unjustified negative attitude toward some out-group. Thus, we associate prejudice with a member of one group holding a negative view of members of some other group. However, when prejudice is operating, there are always two unjustified attitudes—one toward the out-group (usually negative) and one toward one's in-group (usually positive). The two attitudes may be equally irrational and equally resistant to change. For a White person to say that all Blacks are lazy and stupid is to imply that all Whites are industrious and intelligent. The more extreme and unjustified one's attitude toward another group, the more distorted will be one's attitude toward one's own group.

One reason that prejudices are so resistant to change is that they are typically established in the socialization process. From early in life, one learns to think and feel about oneself and others in particular ways. As we grow older, we may find support for our conceptions in culturally established stereotypes. For some (the authoritarian personality, for example), prejudices are resistant to change because they serve as a basis for self-identity.

188

Racial prejudice may be difficult to change because such beliefs serve as the basis for one's self-identity. (Photo © Charles Harbutt/Magnum.)

Social Stereotypes

Stereotyped thinking develops out of the normal perceptual processing of the world. In our perceptual and cognitive processing of information, we need to categorize and classify information in ways that give our world consistency and order. **Social stereotyping** is a means by which we classify people into understandable categories. If you were asked to describe the typical male, the typical female, the typical college professor, the typical politician, and so on, you would rely on your social stereotypes. Of course, the danger in such stereotypic thinking is that every member of a group becomes synonymous with that hypothetical "typical" person. Even if our social stereotypes were accurate appraisals of the average person in a group (and research indicates that most stereotypes are not), they would not recognize the entire range of individual differences in a group. Social stereotypes fail to encompass the complexity and variability that characterize any group.

EXERCISE 8-1. IDENTIFYING YOUR SOCIAL STEREOTYPES

A. Imagine that you are the personnel officer of a large company and you are about to interview an applicant for a position with the company. Not having met the candidate and having no background information about him or her, could you give five characteristics of this person if you knew only that the person was (1) female or (2) Black or (3) physically handicapped or (4) Jewish or (5) 40 years old?

B. Can you give five characteristics of the following types of individuals? (1) A male college professor. (2) A female college professor. (3) A male hairdresser. (4) A female hairdresser. (5) A male politician. (6) A female politician.

Let us look at two forms of social stereotyping that are common parts of our everyday living.

Sex-Role Stereotypes. **Sex-role stereotyping** is the tendency to over-categorize all members of a sex into a "typical male" or "typical female." The fact that males and females behave differently across a wide range of situations is firmly established. One exhaustive review of the literature (Maccoby & Jacklin, 1974) documents many reliable differences between males and females by the time they have reached adulthood. On the average, males are found to be more aggressive, to see events in their lives as caused within themselves rather than outside themselves, and they have higher scores on mental-health and self-acceptance measures. In addition to personality differences, males and females exhibit some differences in intellectual abilities. There is little difference between males and females on overall IQ scores, but females seem to do better on verbal tasks, whereas males tend to do better on visual and spatial tasks. In the social area, males tend to prefer larger and more activity-oriented groups,

190

while females tend to prefer smaller social groups, such as friendships or dating relationships.

Few would question that substantial research evidence exists to document differences between the sexes. However, why such cognitive and behavioral differences exist is a moot question. Two distinct theoretical views of human nature have emerged to explain such differences. One emphasizes biological causation, and the other emphasizes the socialization process.

Probably the most influential of the biological approaches has been the psychoanalytic theoretical model. Freud thought that not only were anatomical differences between the sexes inborn, but so were differences between male and female temperaments. Males were born with an active and assertive nature, females with a more passive and submissive nature. Consequently, males were biologically programmed with drives for curiosity and mastery of the environment. The passive feminine nature was a biological preparation for childbearing, child rearing, and cultivation of the home environment. The normal, or emotionally healthy, man or woman would be one whose behavior aligned with his or her "basic nature."

The viewpoint that stands in least accord with an emphasis on male and female "basic natures" is the social-learning model. This viewpoint explains the differences observed in male and female thinking, feeling, and behaving as results of the socialization process. That is, an individual must learn what is appropriate behavior for males and females. This theoretical viewpoint assumes that parents in raising their children draw on the acquired and accumulated wisdom of culture. Culture has established sex-role ideals to which parents may turn for properly socializing a child. These sex-role stereotypes may be transmitted in the mass media or in direct interaction with others (as wisdom passed along from one's parents, relatives, friends, and so on). Embedded in such sex-role stereotypes is not only how the child should behave but also how the parent should behave toward the child. From the first moment that parents learn the sex of a newborn, they become the agents of culture for socializing the child in line with cultural expectations. From this perspective, the normal, or emotionally healthy, person is one whose behavior aligns with culturally defined sex-role stereotypes.

BOX 8-1. SEX-ROLE MESSAGES IN TV COMMERCIALS

Many of our sex-role stereotypes are supported by the mass media. Courtney and Shipple (1974) examined the sex-role messages presented in TV commercials in the early 1970s. They found that men's voices were most often used to narrate commercial messages, although women's voices were almost always used when the product was a domestic item. A later study (O'Donnel & O'Donnel, 1978) found that even after the impact of the feminist movement, traditional sex-role stereotypes were still dominant in the style and content of TV commercials.

191

BOX 8-2. SEX-RELATED STEREOTYPES IN TODDLERS' BEHAVIOR

Men and women without children were asked to rate behaviors of toddlers (children 18–30 months old) according to sex-appropriateness. The childless adults generally perceived most observed behaviors as appropriate for either sex, although adults of both sexes perceived aggressive behavior as appropriate for male toddlers and playing with dolls as appropriate for female toddlers. Moreover, it was found that men made more sex-typed discriminations than women (Fagot, 1973). Fagot (1974) has also shown that parents of toddlers respond to little boys and little girls differently. She found that boys were more prone to manipulate and play with blocks, while girls were prone to play with dolls. Girls sought help more often from parents, and parents responded more often with praise and punishment to girls. Boys were given more freedom and left alone to play more than girls.

BOX 8-3. PREVAILING MYTHS ABOUT WHY WOMEN WORK

Crowley, Levitin, and Quinn (1973) examined the trustworthiness of some commonly held notions about why women work. Some of the prevailing myths about why women work that were contradicted by research evidence were as follows:

1. Women work only for "pin money."
2. Women work merely to fulfill their socioemotional needs.
3. Women would not work if economic wants did not force them into the labor market.
4. Women are more content with an intellectually less demanding job.
5. Women are less concerned with being viewed as successful or competent at their jobs.

Their research found that about 40% of working women were economically independent and many were the sole breadwinners of their households. The women sampled in this study also expressed a desire to be fully competent and to "get ahead" at their jobs.

One area that has been given considerable attention over the past decade is the nature of sex-role stereotypes for male and female occupational achievement. Research has shown that there are sex differences in occupational achievement motivation, whether these differences are viewed from a biological or a socialization perspective. Typically, females do not strive toward occupational achievement with the same vigor as males (Epstein, 1970). In fact, Horner (1968) has suggested that many adult

Many beliefs about why women work have developed out of prevailing sex-role stereotypes. (Photo © Abigail Heyman/Magnum.)

women have a "fear of success," especially in traditionally masculine occupational areas.

BOX 8-4. MOTIVE TO AVOID SUCCESS

Horner (1968) studied attitudes of males and females toward female achievement. In one study, she had male and female college students write stories about a hypothetical male or female student who stood academically at the top of his or her medical school class. She found that 66% of the females wrote negative stories about the female student's success and only 9% of the males wrote negative stories about the male student's success. Horner believes that the females have learned to avoid too much success, particularly in situations that involve competition with males. Too much success is perceived as a threat to femininity. Horner maintains that many capable females experience negative feelings that are barriers to achievement success.

193

The barriers to female achievement may be external (such as sex discrimination) or internal (such as fear of success or low self-esteem). That many of the barriers (whether self-imposed or culturally imposed) limiting the achievement performance of women are learned seems without question. Moreover, many of the psychological barriers to female achievement motivation are probably established very early. For example, Pollis and Doyle (1972) found that first-grade girls tended to underestimate their ball-throwing performance even when it was comparable or superior to the boys' performance. Obviously, the belief among females that they should not outperform males is established very early in training.

Darley (1976) hypothesizes that much of the difference between males' and females' career achievement can be explained by situational influences. She argues that males and females do not inherently differ in competitiveness, assertiveness, or competence; rather, culture tends to limit the ways the sexes may express these traits. Culture has provided males with opportunities to channel their energy and competence through competitiveness and occupational achievement. Females, however, must limit their competitive and achievement strivings to culturally defined areas like

---

BOX 8-5. MOTIVE TO AVOID FAILURE

Feather (1975) has shown that the occupations perceived as more prestigious in our society are dominated by males. Such occupations as company director, doctor, or school principal are high in status and high in male dominance. Feather reasons that if such occupations are considered male territory, males should have greater fear of failure and a higher motive to avoid failure in such areas than females. Feather asked college students to evaluate the feelings of males and females following success or failure at prestigious achievement pursuits. For example, Feather used the following scenarios:

In a highly competitive final year of law school examinations, David and Mary both pass at the same level and thus qualify to become solicitors [lawyers]. Who would feel happier about the success?

In a highly competitive final year of medical school examinations, Anne and John both fail at the same level and thus do not qualify to become doctors. Who would feel unhappier about the failure?

Table 8-3 shows how students (male and female combined) rated male and female scenario characters' happiness about occupational success and their unhappiness about occupational failure. As Feather predicted, when the occupations were typical male-dominated ones, male characters were rated as happier about success and unhappier about failure than female characters. To fail at a masculine occupation was particularly distressing for males.

194

Table 8-3. Mean ratings of Male and Female Characters' Happiness and Unhappiness with Occupational Success and Failure

Occupation	Happiness with success[a]		Unhappiness with failure[b]	
	Male	Female	Male	Female
Company director	12.07	11.88	13.49	10.50
Lawyer	13.39	12.66	13.55	12.36
School principal	12.78	11.85	13.22	11.16

Adapted from "Positive and Negative Reactions to Male and Female Success and Failure in Relation to the Perceived Status and Sex-Typed Appropriateness of Occupations," by N. T. Feather, *Journal of Personality and Social Psychology*, 1975, *31*(3), 536–548. Copyright 1975 by the American Psychological Association. Reprinted by permission.
[a] Responses were scored from 1 to 15 in the direction of increasing happiness.
[b] Responses were scored from 1 to 15 in the direction of increasing unhappiness.

domestic or social performance. For both males and females, attempts to achieve outside one's sex-appropriate area may be followed by social sanctions of rejection and overt hostility.

The contemporary emphasis has been on the problems associated with females' sex-role development. However, some (Bardwick, 1971; Sexton, 1969) have highlighted the complication of male sex-role development. Sexton believes that male acquisition of sex-role identity may be more complicated and difficult than female acquisition of sex-role identity. She points out that males throughout early development are overexposed to feminine role models, such as mothers and female teachers, and they do not get sufficient opportunities to learn the behaviors necessary for successfully fulfilling the demands of their sex role. In any case, it behooves the researcher not to ignore the complications of masculine sex-role development.

Whatever the nature of sex-role stereotypes, we should not forget that there is wide variability among both sexes on virtually all personality dimensions. Although the average male is taller and heavier than the average female, considerable overlap exists between males and females on height and weight. The same holds true for personality dimensions, such as aggressiveness, achievement motivation, or self-acceptance. Moreover, we should keep in mind that one's personality characteristics are not necessarily comparable across all situations. A male may be aggressive and assertive in one situation but passive and dependent in another. The same is true for females.

EXERCISE 8-2. QUESTIONS ON SEX-ROLE STEREOTYPES

Discuss the following set of questions with other people. You might wish to ask these same questions of people you know who have highly ego-involving attitudes

195

about male and female differences (such as a member of the women's liberation movement or a member of a fundamentalist religious group).

1. Should parents try to make male and female sex roles more pronounced or less pronounced?
2. Should children be given an opportunity to explore both male and female sex-role behavior?
3. Should school curricula be changed to reduce or to enhance sex-appropriate behavior?
4. Are some occupations more suited to one sex than the other?

Ethnic Stereotypes. Researchers have found that "in-groups" and "out-groups" are often established on the basis of racial or ethnic identification. Like sex-role stereotyping, **ethnic stereotyping** is apparently learned very early. Early in development, it appears that the color white is judged favorably and is associated with positive characteristics, while the color black is associated with negative characteristics. In a series of classic studies, Clark and Clark (1947) found that young Black children preferred to play with a White doll rather than a Black doll. Surprisingly, many of these Black children chose a White doll when asked to select a doll that most looked like themselves. It was apparent from these studies that the Black children perceived "Whiteness" of a doll more favorably than "Blackness." Such evaluations of skin color no doubt originate in the socialization process, since children may learn not to associate the label "Black" with negative characteristics (Williams & Edwards, 1969).

Years ago it was observed that one's ethnic stereotypes were related to the degree of contact one desired with members of ethnic groups. Bogardus (1924–1925) devised a "social distance" scale that assessed the desired distance between one's self and a particular racial or ethnic group. Individuals were asked into which of the following categories they would willingly admit members of 39 ethnic groups:

1. To close kinship by marriage
2. To my club as personal chums
3. To my street as neighbors
4. To employment in my occupation
5. To citizenship in my country
6. As visitors only to my country
7. Would exclude from my country

Bogardus (1947) compared the social-distance rankings of White respondents in 1927 and in 1946. He found a remarkable agreement in social-distance preferences in these two years. Generally, the least social distance was expressed toward Anglo-Saxon groups (English, American, Canadian) and the greatest social distance toward Blacks and Orientals.

196

Research has shown that Black children often prefer to play with a White doll rather than with a Black doll. (Photo © Ken Heyman.)

In another early study of ethnic stereotypes, Katz and Braly (1933) had 100 university students select from a list of 84 adjectives those that best described various national, racial, and ethnic groups. These students described Negroes as "lazy" and "ignorant," Jews as "shrewd" and "ambitious," Italians as "impulsive," and Americans as "progressive." A similar study was conducted nearly two decades later (Gilbert, 1951) and it was found that students again expressed agreement about characteristics of particular groups, but the adjectives used reflected less bigotry. Some 20 years later, a third assessment of ethnic attitudes among university students (Karling, Coffman, & Walters, 1969) revealed even less negative attitudes. There was evidence, for example, of an emerging positive Black stereotype, perhaps reflecting the liberal climate of university campuses during the 1960s. Some (Sigall & Page, 1971), however, cite evidence that students may have become reluctant to express anti-Black attitudes because of normative or situational influences. The extent of actual attitude change toward Blacks might be considerably less once students leave the university setting.

How can racial prejudice be reduced? To the layperson, the way to go about changing racial attitudes is to present a person with a strong argument that results in a rational modification of existing negative attitudes. Surprisingly, however, research in social psychology has shown that strong persuasion has not proved effective in bringing about changes in racial attitudes. While prejudices are highly resistant to change, studies showing positive change in racial attitudes have generally created favorable circumstances for interracial interaction. If one behaves favorably toward a person or group, one's attitudes toward that person or group may shift in a more favorable direction.

Not all forms of interracial contact will result in acceptance, and some may only serve to validate one's prejudice. One situation that seems to promote mutual interracial acceptance is when two different ethnic or racial groups cooperate to achieve a joint goal (Cook, 1969). Sherif and Sherif (1969) have described how a **superordinate goal** may bring conflicting groups into mutual regard. They define superordinate goals as *"goals that are compelling for the groups involved, but cannot be achieved by a single group through its own efforts and resources"* (p. 255). In general, studies have shown that when racial groups are brought together in cooperative efforts, mutually favorable attitudes may evolve. Edinger, Bailey, and Lira (1977), for example, have found that in highly competitive task situations, Black and White teammates display interracial acceptance.

DISCRIMINATION

People often confuse the concept of prejudice with the concept of **discrimination**. *Prejudice* refers only to unjustified *attitudes*, not to unjustified behavior. Up to this point we have limited our discussion to the unjustified feelings and thinking that one may have toward oneself or the group to which one belongs (in-group) or toward

Interracial cooperation may result from working together toward mutually desired goals. (Photo © Rohn Engh/Van Cleve Photography.)

some out-group. In our society it is not illegal to feel and think in certain ways about ourselves or others. It is, however, illegal to behave in certain ways toward others, particularly if the behavior is aggressive or exploitive. It is important to keep in mind that prejudice involves attitudes about people and discrimination involves behavior toward people.

What Is Discriminatory Behavior?

You may wish to complete Exercise 8-3 before reading further.

EXERCISE 8-3. WHAT IS DISCRIMINATORY BEHAVIOR?

Read the following descriptions and then determine where discrimination is operating.

199

1. A college student wishes to enroll for seven college courses in one term, but the university has a policy that students cannot enroll in more than five courses per term.
   _____ I believe this is an act of discrimination.
   _____ I do not believe this is an act of discrimination.
   Suppose the university administration decides that, because this student is a sophomore and has a straight-A grade-point average, he or she should be allowed to take seven courses even though the university policy states that only five courses can be taken.
   _____ I believe this is an act of discrimination.
   _____ I do not believe this is an act of discrimination.
2. A motorist is spotted by a highway patrolman and given a traffic citation for driving at 70 mph on a highway marked at 55 mph.
   _____ I believe this is an act of discrimination.
   _____ I do not believe this is an act of discrimination.
   Suppose many motorists are exceeding the posted limit, but only one person is stopped and given a citation.
   _____ I believe this is an act of discrimination.
   _____ I do not believe this is an act of discrimination.
3. A student applies for admission to medical school but is rejected because the student is female.
   _____ I believe this is an act of discrimination.
   _____ I do not believe this is an act of discrimination.
4. A family of a minority race moves into a neighborhood, and some individual families move out of the neighborhood because of the minority family's arrival.
   _____ I believe this is an act of discrimination.
   _____ I do not believe this is an act of discrimination.
   A family of a minority race moves into a neighborhood, and the majority members of the neighborhood begin to harass the minority family by throwing rocks at its home.
   _____ I believe this is an act of discrimination.
   _____ I do not believe this is an act of discrimination.

Many people use the term *discrimination* whenever some decision about a person results in an undesirable outcome. For example, a person may feel discriminated against if he or she is turned down for medical school or gets an F in a course or receives a traffic citation. Obviously, it is important that some standard be applied to determine what is a discriminatory act and what is not. Unless we can clearly distinguish between discrimination and nondiscrimination, these terms will lose their usefulness for social, legal, and research purposes.

Perhaps the safest approach to discrimination is the legal one. Current rulings by U.S. courts state that no decision about a person may be made on the basis of the person's sex, race, ethnic origin, or religion. To do so constitutes an act of illegal discrimination. Who should be admitted to universities, graduate schools, or medical schools? Who should be hired for a particular job? However such decisions are made, they are not to be made on the basis of one's sex, racial or ethnic origin, or religion.

In our society the idea of discrimination has come to mean more than legal discrimination. Various "social" or "moral" definitions are also prevalent in our society. Many of our behaviors toward others may not involve aggressiveness or exploitive outcomes but may be judged as moral discrimination. If parents forbid their child to play with a child from a minority family, they are not necessarily committing an act of illegal discrimination. In our society we regard individuals as having the right to associate (or not associate) with whomever they choose. Yet, although the parents' behavior cannot be regarded as an act of illegal discrimination, one may view it as morally or socially inappropriate. In social science research, care should be taken to distinguish between legal and moral definitions of discrimination. If, for example, in the course of an experiment a subject expresses a desire not to be photographed with a member of another racial group, this might be viewed as an act of social, but not legal, discrimination.

Do Only Prejudiced People Discriminate?

Common sense would lead us to believe that prejudiced people will discriminate against the objects of their prejudice and nonprejudiced people will not discriminate. However, as we pointed out when discussing attitude change, behavior cannot always be predicted from attitudes, and this holds true for prejudice and discrimination. The inconsistency between social attitudes and social behavior was observed a number of years ago by LaPiere (1934). He mailed questionnaires to restaurants and sleeping establishments and asked whether they had any policy against accommodating a Chinese couple. Over 90% of the respondents indicated that they could not accommodate this couple. However, when the Chinese couple accompanied an American couple to these same establishments, invariably the Chinese couple was served. Other studies have found a similar discrepancy between attitudes and behavior. Kutner, Wilkins, and Yarrow (1952) used a procedure similar to LaPiere's to study attitudes and behavior toward a Black customer, with similar results. Williams (1964) has also found that although a number of bartenders indicated they would not serve Blacks, they did serve the Black customers when they appeared in person.

In another study, DeFleur and Westie (1958) asked White students to consent to be photographed with a Black person for a picture to be used in a nationwide publicity campaign. Students' willingness to be photographed with a Black were compared to scores on a prejudice questionnaire they had filled out earlier. It was found that many of the prejudiced persons did not discriminate and many of the nonprejudiced persons did. However, in a later study (Green, 1969), subjects who expressed favorable attitudes toward Blacks were more likely to sign a consent form to be photographed with a Black than subjects with unfavorable attitudes toward Blacks were.

201

Some researchers have ascertained that pervasive anti-Black attitudes still exist in American culture (Allen, 1975; Clarke, 1970). When White people are asked to express their attitudes toward Blacks on self-report questionnaires, the majority express nonprejudiced attitudes toward Blacks. In fact, many Whites express an overfavorable attitude toward Blacks and extreme friendliness. Gaertner (1974) believes that many White Americans have well-organized anti-Black attitudes as a result of socialization but have developed a belief that they are fair-minded. Consequently, they must "bend over backward" to show their acceptance of Blacks. Such extreme friendliness or favorability may actually serve to convince a person that he or she does not harbor prejudice. This veneer of equalitarianism may disappear and more deeply embedded feelings surface when the person is asked to help a Black (Gaertner, 1973) or to volunteer time to aid a Black cause (Dutton & Lake, 1973). Such discrepancies between attitudes and behavior are revealed toward other racial groups. For example, Bahr and Chadwick (1974) have found that Whites want American Indians to be a part of the mainstream of culture, but they prefer that their children not have close associations with Indians.

BOX 8-6. PERCEIVING THE CAUSES OF SOCIAL INJUSTICE

Why is it that people so often see social injustice in everyone but themselves? It is much easier to perceive religious, ethnic, and racial discrimination in others' behavior than in one's own. Attribution theory predicts that one tends to perceive another person's socially unjust behavior as caused by the person (for example, "That person is prejudiced"). But when one or some member of one's in-group exhibits the same socially unjust behavior, one tends to attribute the behavior to external causes ("It is just natural that some people are more intelligent, competent, and so on than others").

Rothbart (1973) points out the difficulty people have in perceiving social injustice when the social injustice is close to home. He cites, for example, how Northern Whites often feel indignant about Southern discrimination while failing to perceive similar discrimination in the North. Moreover, he says, it is easier for one to attribute the cause of pollution to big industry than to one's own contributions. As Rothbart (1973, p. 292) puts it, "There appears to be some psychological mechanism that prevents us from perceiving proximal events as immoral or unjust, yet allows us to perceive the same or similar circumstances as morally wrong when distant from self."

In two studies, Rothbart (1973) demonstrated the validity of such a hypothesis. He examined the relation between acceptance of a prison-reform program or a proposed public housing project for low-income families and distance of one's home from the proposed project locations. The closer one lived to the locus of reform, the more negative one's view of such social reforms. The farther from the locus of reform, the more liberal the attitudes toward social reform.

202

How are we to deal with these findings that people do not always behave toward an object consistently with the way they feel and think? If indeed attitudes are rather stable predispositions, we would expect greater agreement between attitudes and behavior. Wrightsman (1972) has suggested several possible reasons that attitudes and behavior may diverge. First, many studies measure attitudes toward very broad and general categories of people and things. When one is confronted with a specific person, one's stereotyped notions may be inappropriate. Moreover, behavior may be determined not solely by personality influences, like attitudes, but by the demands of the situation as well. Very strong normative pressures exist in our society not to exhibit blatant negative responses to others in various situations. For example, no matter what one's feelings and attitudes toward a minority-group member, one would probably not refuse to share a seat on a bus or take a college course with such a person. Consequently, if one does hold an unfavorable attitude toward a group, it is much easier to express that attitude on a questionnaire than in real social situations. The possible costs of embarrassing oneself or appearing to be a bigot may discourage overt negative behavior toward another.

SIGNIFICANT SOCIAL BEHAVIOR TOWARD OTHERS

In this final section of the chapter, we shall look at two additional forms of important social behavior. We shall look at social behavior that has a desirable and positive social consequence (cooperative or helping behavior) and social behavior that has an undesirable and negative social consequence (violent and aggressive behavior).

Cooperative and Helping Behavior

In the 17th century, a group of British social philosophers argued that humans are by nature pleasure-seeking organisms, driven by sheer self-interest. In the 19th and 20th centuries, writers began to emphasize that the human is by nature a social organism driven as much by social interest as self-interest. Today social researchers are less concerned about whether human nature is selfish or social but are more concerned with identifying the conditions that make for socially desirable or undesirable behavior.

Cooperative behavior is characterized by two or more individuals working together in the pursuit of some common goal. Chapter 7 pointed out that groups can help the individual satisfy psychological needs or help the individual achieve instrumental goals that would be impossible by his or her own effort. It perhaps is easy to understand how cooperative behavior might be explained in selfish terms: we tend to cooperate with others because we have benefits to gain from cooperation.

Altruistic behavior means offering aid or assistance to another where there is no expectation of personal benefit. It is harder to interpret altruistic behavior in terms of self-interest than cooperative behavior. One offers aid to another without any measurable benefit to oneself. For a helping act to be truly altruistic, it must meet three requirements (Leeds, 1963): (1) the behavior must be an end in itself, with no direct gain to the person; (2) the behavior must be performed voluntarily; and (3) the behavior must accomplish a good result. Therefore, if one helps another for some personal gain (as in making a charitable gift in order to get a tax deduction) or under coercion (as when an employee is required to give to the United Fund or risk losing his or her job), or if one's assistance results in unintended harm to another (such as giving a dollar to a wino and thereby further damaging his physical condition), then the behavior would not be considered altruistic.

Obviously, this definition of altruism includes not only one's behavior but also an inference about the intention behind one's behavior. Such inferences, even by social scientists, are hazardous. Moreover, it is hard to determine what may be the short-term effects, let alone the long-term effects, of one's helping another. In research it is often best to simply deal with "what" a person does rather than make inferences about "why" the person does it. For these reasons, many social scientists prefer to speak of "helping behavior" rather than altruism. The former concept simply refers to what a person does, without any inference about why it is done. Still others feel that a complete explanation of helping behavior must include an understanding of the reasons for the behavior.

BOX 8-7. SOCIAL TRAPS

Sometimes individuals' behavior in a group is to their own advantage but is damaging to the group. Such behavior produces immediate personal gain to the individual but in the long run is detrimental to both the individual and the group. Platt (1973) uses the term *social trap* to refer to situations in which an individual continues to place personal interest above the benefit of group members. Platt cites an example in which a piece of common pasture land in early New England was eventually overused by individual farmers to the point of destroying this common grazing ground so that it was no longer of benefit to anyone. A similar "social trap" may occur during an energy crisis when individuals hoard the available energy supply, thereby only compounding the problem.

Platt also describes one-person traps, in which an individual's behavior has positive short-term consequences but negative long-term consequences. Examples of one-person traps are excessive use of cigarettes, alcohol, or drugs: immediate gratification may lead to serious health problems. Another one-person trap is seen when a coal miner or a factory worker works for immediate gains but over the long run risks serious illness or death.

204

Why do people help others? There are both reasons within the person (internal reasons) and reasons outside the person (external reasons) for helping another. Some *internal reasons* are *empathy, self-esteem,* and *normative influences.* Empathy is one's capacity to imagine oneself in the same situation as someone else; we may tend to identify with another's pain, stress, or confusion. Another reason for helping someone else is that it brings us some internal satisfaction, such as a heightening of feelings of self-esteem. Further, we tend to incorporate cultural norms, or values, and behave consistently with them. Such norms include a *responsibility norm* (we are responsible for helping others who are in need of aid), a *reciprocity norm* (we help others because we may be in need of help ourselves sometime) and an *equity norm* (people should be given aid in line with their own efforts to find a solution to the problem).

Michelini, Wilson, and Messé (1975) have also shown that helping another is influenced by the helper's level of self-esteem. The higher one's self-esteem, the more prone one is to aid another, independent of the situation. They suggest that one reason situational factors in helping have been found to be so important is that most people's self-esteem is too low. It might be possible to train people to be more sensitive to helping situations and to derive self-esteem from a helping act in the same way people may be trained to increase their achievement motivation. Such training to encourage helping could produce important benefits in society.

BOX 8-8. PERCEIVING THE CAUSE OF NEED AND HELPING

Horowitz (1968) found that people show a greater tendency to help those whose need stems from external causes rather than internal causes. That is, if we think a person is personally responsible for his or her problem (someone absent-mindedly forgot and left her money at home; someone falls because he is drunk), we are less prone to offer assistance than if we perceive the problem as outside the person's control (someone stole the victim's money; someone falls because of an epileptic seizure).

We all carry into any helping situation the stable predispositions (such as attitudes, level of self-esteem, values, and needs) that are called personality. However, many times our behavior may be more influenced by the nature of the situation than our personality predispositions. That is, our behavior is under the influence of external factors. In recent years, field experiments have identified some of the situational influences on helping. Research has shown that the following factors influence one's tendency to help another:

1. Whether the person in need is dressed like a "hippie" or a "straight" person (Emswiller, Deaux, & Willits, 1971)

2. Whether a person who collapses on the floor of a subway train appears intoxicated (Piliavin, Rodin, & Piliavin, 1969)
3. Whether someone feels responsible for causing someone else's problem (Konecni, 1972)
4. Whether someone has offered help to the potential helper recently (Goranson & Berkowitz, 1966)
5. Whether the person in need of help appears severely injured (Piliavin & Piliavin, 1972)
6. Whether the potential helper has observed someone else helping another recently (Bryan & Test, 1967)
7. Whether a person is alone or in the presence of others (Darley & Latané, 1968)

One rather extensively studied area has been differences between urban and nonurban individuals' tendency to help others. Milgram (1970) has suggested that city-dwellers have more or less desensitized themselves to others because of the massive information overload of city life. They have adopted an attitude of indifference and noninvolvement as a means of adapting to too much stimulus input. Consequently, it is thought that city-dwellers will tend to exhibit less helping behavior than people in smaller towns, and there are studies supporting this notion (Altman, Levine, Nadien, & Villena, cited in Milgram, 1970; Korte & Kerr, 1975; McKenna & Morgenthau, cited in Milgram, 1970).

BOX 8-9. IS THERE SAFETY IN NUMBERS?

In 1964 a young woman named Kitty Genovese was attacked twice and killed by a lone assailant in front of her apartment building. Many of the apartment residents heard her cries for help, but no one offered any assistance. Almost daily we hear of similar accounts of individuals beaten or raped in the presence of others who stand idly by. Latané and Rodin (1969) have found that people in groups—even groups of two persons—were less likely to offer assistance to an injured person than if alone. So there may not be safety in numbers, particularly if the victim is unknown to the group. Latané and Darley (1968) suggest that the inhibitory effect of other people in helping situations may be partly due to diffusion of a sense of personal responsiblity.

However, Levine, Villena, Altman, and Nadien (1976) found there is more to this urban/small-town effect. They, like many others, found that small-town residents were more willing to let strangers gain entry into their homes than city residents. However, they suggest that this response by city residents does not indicate coldness or indifference but is merely the consequence of being in an environment where residents are more vulnerable to threat. Although many city residents did not show the same degree of trust as small-town residents (by inviting the stranger inside

206

their houses), they did appear equally willing to help the stranger (by calling a number to verify an address).

Aggressive Behavior

Aggression is usually defined as behavior that results in harm or injury to another. Behavior is judged aggressive if it has harmful or injurious consequences (whether physical or psychological). What if the action is accidental rather than intentional? If a person injures another in a car accident, can that behavior be regarded as an aggressive act? In order to determine whether a behavior should be regarded as aggressive, we must go beyond the behavior itself and make inferences about it. Aggressive behavior becomes more meaningful if we can understand the antecedent causes of the act as well as the act itself. Therefore, a more useful definition of aggressive behavior might include intent to harm another. Perhaps a more useful definition of aggression might be "an action whose intention and goal is to inflict injury and harm [on] another person or persons" (Severy, Brigham, & Schlenker, 1976, p. 263). Moreover, if a person throws a rock at someone but misses, this might also be regarded as an aggressive act even though no injury occurs.

Biological Explanations for Aggression. The basic postulate of biologically oriented explanations of aggression is that humans have an innate predisposition to engage in aggressive behavior. Such behavior is energized by instinctual energy that must find modes of release. Freud believed that if aggressive energy was not released in some culturally acceptable form, it would have to be expressed in socially unacceptable forms, like violence. During the course of socialization, individuals must learn ways of working off aggressive energy in small amounts (that is, through catharsis) or channeling this energy into socially prized forms of behavior (that is, sublimating). Cathartic outlets might take the form of participating in or viewing sports activities. Sublimation might involve channeling aggressive energy into an occupational pursuit, as in becoming a professional boxer or football player or perhaps a surgeon.

Instinctual approaches to human aggression were popular around 1900. Then the concept of instinct fell into disfavor among American psychologists following the rise and popularization of behaviorism. The notion of instinct was virtually banished from American psychology, and an emphasis on environment and learning took hold. However, many European investigators, called "ethologists" (students of animal behavior), continued naturalistic research on innate mechanisms of behavior. Within the past couple of decades, the research and theories of ethology have found their way into popular works, such as Ardrey's *African Genesis* and Morris' *Naked Ape*. These books introduced to a broad audience principles of contemporary instinctual psychology and biology.

Lorenz (1966) has dealt specifically with the instinctual basis of aggressive behavior from an ethological point of view. He points out that aggression may be expressed toward members of the same species (intraspecies aggression) or members of a different species (interspecies aggression). Although intraspecies and interspecies aggression have different biological purposes, both promote survival of a species. Interspecies aggression typically is for the purpose of gathering and protecting a food supply or protecting offspring or mates. Intraspecies aggression is often for the purpose of establishing dominance hierarchies. Lorenz thinks that lower animals have developed various instinctual inhibitors against intraspecies killing.

Lorenz contends that humans, like all animals, have instinctive urges toward aggression. However, while lower animals have natural inhibitors against killing members of their own species, humans are characterized by unrestrained intraspecies killing. Perhaps the human species has lost its natural inhibitors of intraspecies killing. One reason may be that humans have the intellectual capacity to create means of injuring another without coming into contact with the victim. Once humans introduced *weapons* as means of harming others, the natural inhibitors of aggression became ineffective. When a human first picked up a stone and struck another, we were on our way toward massive and extremely effective means of killing. Today, in the thermonuclear age, we can see how "successful" we have been in our creation of weapons. Now that we are capable of destroying all life on this planet many times over, the problem is that we may not have any natural inhibitors for successfully restraining use of weapons.

Another perplexing feature of human aggressiveness is that such behavior may not serve a survival purpose, as it does in lower animals. Although we may not like to watch animal aggression, we can appreciate the necessity for it. In humans, however, we often observe aggression or violence that apparently has no survival purpose. Unlike any other species, humans kill one another because of differences in thinking. If we survey the basis for most violent confrontations across the earth today (for example, those in Ireland, the Middle East, Africa, and Indochina), we can see that most human killing originates from ideological and religious differences among people, not from striving for personal survival.

From the ethological perspective, the combination of natural aggressiveness, inadequate natural inhibitors of intraspecies aggression, and the creation of highly efficient weapons for massive intraspecies killing makes the human the most dangerous of all living species.

208

Learning Explanations for Aggression. Not all psychologists accept the assumption that humans have an aggressive instinct. Many believe that aggressive behavior is learned and therefore can be explained by learning principles. Two approaches for explaining aggressive behavior from a learning perspective are the *social-learning approach* and the *frustration-aggression approach*.

Albert Bandura at Stanford University has developed the most popular social-learning view of human aggressive behavior. Bandura (1969, 1973) emphasizes the importance of learning by observation. He believes that people learn the instrumental value of aggressive behavior by imitating others. In other words, people are not innately aggressive; they learn to be from appropriate "models," like parents or siblings.

One interesting feature of Bandura's theory is that an individual's own behavior does not have to be punished or rewarded for learning to occur. Simply observing the rewarding or punishing consequences of another's behavior may be sufficient to establish learning. Consequently, if one sees violent or aggressive behavior lead to tangible rewards like status or financial profit (as is often the case in the mass media), one might be expected to adopt such behavior.

BOX 8-11. MODELING OF AGGRESSIVE BEHAVIOR

Bandura, Ross, and Ross (1961) studied the effect of observed aggressive behavior on children. They had children watch an adult vigorously punch a 5-foot inflated plastic doll. Later the child was left alone for 20 minutes in a room with the plastic doll along with other toys. In comparison to a group of children not exposed to the aggressive adult model, the "modeling" children struck the plastic doll more often and more vigorously.

Another point of view in psychology on how aggression may be learned is the frustration-aggression approach. This approach assumes that aggressive behavior is always the result of frustration. Frustration is the unpleasant subjective state that results when a barrier blocks some goal that a person has. The goal might be to run the 100-yard dash in 9 seconds, to get an A in psychology, to get a college degree, to be the most beautiful person who ever lived, or something else. A goal is anything that one desires to obtain. There are different types of barriers that prevent one from reaching a goal. There may be biological barriers to running 100 yards in 9 seconds or being the most beautiful person who ever lived. There are physical barriers, such as the bars of a prison, which limit a person's freedom. There are sociocultural barriers, such as feelings of guilt. The degree of one's feeling of frustration will be directly related to the attractiveness of the goal and the strength of the barrier blocking the goal.

One feature of the frustration-aggression explanation is that once frustration develops, it may take on the characteristics of a *drive state*. Frustration produces a more or less enduring arousal condition that energizes aggressive thoughts and actions. Until the feeling of frustration is removed (for example, by satisfactorily achieving the desired goal), the person will have a potential for aggressive behavior. This behavior may be directed toward the object of one's frustration (in what is called **direct aggression**) or toward some substitute object (in **displaced aggression**).

It is probably safe to state that the reasons aggressive behavior occurs are not fully understood. Some emphasize inborn explanations, others learning explanations, and still others some interaction of heredity and environment; the picture is far from being clear. Some have shown that the mere sight of a gun in a room can rouse one to greater aggression. Others have found that features of the environment, such as the presence of others or the temperature of a room, have an effect. We know that many drugs can either trigger or cause aggressiveness in people. Still others believe that one's chromosomal makeup can produce a predisposition toward overcontrol or undercontrol of aggressiveness. Whatever the present state of theory and empirical evidence, we are far from being able to successfully manage violence and aggressive behavior in our society. There is still much to be known about the conditions that make for antisocial behavior as well as socially desirable behavior. With the ever-increasing population of not only our society but the world, the answers to many of the questions about both cooperative and aggressive behavior take on added urgency.

SUMMARY

This chapter examined the relation between social attitudes and social behavior. An attitude is a predisposition to behave in a particular way toward an object. In one model of the attitude-change situation, the elements are stimulus influences (the communication and the communicator), cognitive processing (attention, comprehension, and acceptance), and behavior. Our most ego-involving attitudes—that is, the ones most important to us—are the most resistant to change.

Prejudices are among our most ego-involving attitudes. Prejudices are unjustified attitudes, highly resistant to change, toward objects. Most typically, these objects are oneself and other people. A person who is prejudiced against some out-group will necessarily be prejudiced in favor of his or her own in-group as well.

In social stereotyping we form an oversimplified view of a group of people. Two common forms of social stereotyping are sex-role stereotyping and ethnic stereotyping. Researchers have established many differences in personality and abilities between the average male and the average female; theorists disagree on whether these differences are innate or learned. Ethnic stereotyping can begin in early childhood. Racial prejudice is most likely to be reduced when people are given an opportunity to behave favorably toward the objects of their prejudice or when the antagonistic groups cooperate to achieve a shared goal.

210

People often confuse prejudice with discrimination. *Prejudice* refers to attitudes, whereas *discrimination* refers to behavior. Some behavior is morally (or socially) discriminatory although it falls outside a legal definition of *discrimination*. People may be prejudiced against a racial group but not discriminate against members of that group, and people who are not prejudiced may discriminate.

Two important forms of social behavior are cooperative and helping behavior and aggressive behavior. People have internal reasons for helping others, such as empathy with others or the prospect of raising their own self-esteem, but helping behavior is also influenced by external, situational factors. Aggression is not well understood. Some social scientists have attributed aggression to biological causes (instinct), others to learning.

KEY CONCEPTS

Aggression action whose intention and goal is to inflict injury or harm on another person or persons.

Altruistic behavior offering aid or assistance to another without expectation of personal benefit.

Attitude a predisposition to behave in a particular way toward an object.

Cooperative behavior behavior exhibited by two or more individuals working together toward a common goal.

Direct aggression aggression directed toward the object of one's frustration.

Discrimination a legal or moral concept of unacceptable behavioral decisions regarding another.

Displaced aggression aggression directed toward a substitute object rather than the actual object of one's frustration.

Ethnic stereotyping the tendency to overcategorize all members of an ethnic group into a "typical member" of that group.

Prejudice an unjustified positive or negative attitude that is highly resistant to change.

Primacy effect the tendency to recall information that appears at the beginning of a list.

Recency effect the tendency to recall information that appears at the end of a list.

Sex-role stereotyping the tendency to overcategorize all members of a sex into a "typical male" or "typical female."

Social stereotyping the normal perceptual process of overcategorizing some social group into an abstract "typical member" of that group.

Superordinate goal a goal which is desired by two or more groups but which cannot be achieved by a single group through its own efforts and resources.

SECTION FOUR

BEHAVING
MORE
EFFECTIVELY

CHAPTER OBJECTIVES

1. To understand the nature of programs designed to help us achieve greater self-control.
2. To list the steps included in self-control programs.
3. To clearly identify and define behavior to be brought under greater self-control.
4. To accurately collect and record information on the frequency of the target behavior and the context in which it occurs.
5. To identify and describe some strategies for developing self-control programs.
6. To develop some self-control programs for specific problem areas.

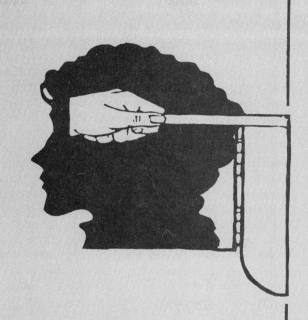

ACHIEVING
GREATER
SELF-CONTROL

Most of us wish to live a long and healthy life; yet much of our behavior is not compatible with that goal. We may eat to excess, smoke to excess, and not get enough exercise. You may have to look no farther than yourself to find an overweight, under-exercised excessive smoker. We are all aware of the hazards of various excesses, but we just cannot seem to bring such behavior under control. We are like many students who know that academic performance is related to later opportunities for advanced education or employment but still do not manage to perform academically at their potential. Even greater frustration occurs when we try to exercise some willpower or good judgment in regard to undesirable behaviors and find that the behaviors persist anyway.

Psychologists realize that willpower and good judgment are necessary for positive behavior change. Yet changing behavior significantly and maintaining the change may require something more. It may be necessary to know more about the nature of one's behavior and how to bring it under some means of self-control. In the present chapter, we will offer some suggestions on how to achieve greater control of one's behavior. We will develop a conceptual model for understanding self-control and then suggest some self-control strategies people might apply to behaviors they want to change—namely, excessive eating and excessive smoking. In the next chapter we will expand our discussion to the area of managing one's emotional life. You may wish to review some of the concepts in Chapter 3 in preparation for the discussion on achieving greater self-control.

SELF CONTROL: A PLAN OF ACTION

Achieving self-control depends on an orderly, systematic plan of action. Hankins (1979) has developed a four-step plan of action for achieving greater self-control:

1. Define the problem in terms of specific behavior.
2. Collect baseline data on how often the specific behavior occurs in specific situations.
3. Develop a program for modifying the behavior.
4. Develop a means of evaluating the behavior-control program.

1. Defining the Problem

The first step in a self-control program is to precisely identify the **problem behavior**. The problem behavior might be excessive eating, excessive smoking, or poor examination performance. Some problem areas, such as anger, shyness, or anxiety, may be harder to define. For example, with anger a person might say "I get angry

Some of the material in this chapter first appeared in *How to Become the Person You Want to Be*, by Norman E. Hankins. Copyright 1979 by Nelson-Hall Publishers, Chicago, Illinois 60606. Used by permission.

Virtually everyone has the need for greater self-control over some aspect of behavior. (Photo © Elliott Erwitt/Magnum.)

too easily" without having a clear understanding of the kinds of stimuli that arouse anger. Until one has been able to narrow the problem area to a specific situation, one cannot establish specific goals for achieving greater self-control. With many emotionally based problems, the best thing to do is to identify some specific situations in which that particular emotion has been a problem. Describe each example in writing, including the event that led up to the behavior in question and the consequences of that behavior. Then try to determine whether there is a common element in these situations. It might be that you find you are getting angry, for example, with members of your immediate family or some particular person, or it may be that you are getting angry when someone competes with you or makes you feel inadequate. Identifying the problem situation makes it possible to deal directly with the problem behavior.

2. Collecting Data and Establishing a Baseline

The second step is to determine how much of a problem you have in various circumstances when the behavior occurs. For a smoking problem, you would begin by counting the cigarettes smoked per day. You would do this for at least a week before

217

Hour	Date		Date		Date		Date		Date	
	A.M.	P.M.	A.M.	P.M.	A.M.	P.M.	A.M.	P.M.	A.M.	P.M.
12										
1										
2										
3										
4										
5										
6										
7										
8										
9										
10										
11										

Figure 9-1. Tally sheet for collecting behavioral data.

trying to alter your smoking habits. You would also keep a record of when and in what circumstances you smoked. You might find that you are smoking mostly after meals, when studying, while driving, or with a cup of coffee. The period during which you record the problem behavior without trying to change it is called the **baseline phase** of the self-control program. The purpose of establishing a baseline is to show the frequency of the problem behavior so as to assess any behavior change that occurs when the treatment is introduced. It is hard to determine whether you are smoking less or losing weight unless you know how much you previously smoked or weighed.

One popular self-observing device is the wrist counter originally developed for golfers. Lindsley (1968) has adapted the wrist counter for monitoring behavior in virtually any environment, such as the home, school, or workplace. With each occurrence of the problem behavior, a button on the counter is pressed, and a cumulative total of the responses is available to the person at any time. The counter can be reset at any time. In addition, various kinds of tally sheets and behavior charts can be used for recording behavior. Figure 9-1 is a sample tally sheet that might be used for collecting behavioral data. Figure 9-2 is a form that might be used for recording some antecedents and/or consequences of the problem behavior.

It is important that the frequency and time of occurrence of the behavior and the antecedents and consequences of that behavior be recorded. The information on behavioral antecedents and consequences will be especially helpful when you begin developing a self-control program to deal with your problem.

218

Date	Significant Antecedents and/or Consequences

Figure 9-2. *Chart for recording circumstances in which problem behavior occurs.*

Let us assume that a person has counted the cigarettes smoked each day for a period of 1 week and has recorded these data on a form similar to Figure 9-1. The baseline data can now be presented in graphic form, as shown in Figure 9-3. From the hypothetical data given in Figure 9-3, we can see that during a 1-week period this person's daily cigarette consumption ranged from 18 to 24, with an average of about 21. The figure also shows that more cigarettes were smoked on the weekend than during the rest of the week. When the program to reduce smoking is initiated, the daily smoking rate can be recorded in the same manner.

3. Developing and Implementing the Self-Control Program

Once the baseline data for the problem behavior have been carefully recorded and the circumstances in which the behavior occurred have been identified, an analysis of the data should be made. This analysis should include a search for patterns in the occurrence of the problem behavior. An inspection of Figure 9-3, for example, shows a higher rate of cigarette consumption on the weekend than during the week. Data recorded on charts similar to Figures 9-1 and 9-2 might contain useful informa-

219

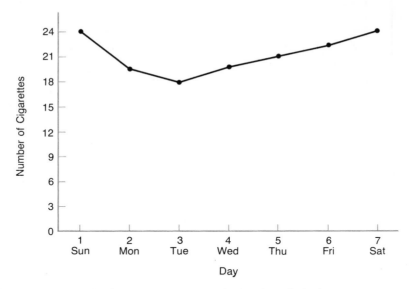

Figure 9-3. *Baseline data for daily cigarette consumption by a hypothetical person.*

tion about the situations in which the behavior occurred and its consequences. Careful recordkeeping might show that most smoking is occurring after meals, while driving, and in certain other situations. This information helps one pinpoint the problem and formulate some plan for coping with it.

When the self-control program has been developed and initiated, the recording procedures discussed in Step 2 should be continued. A note should be made on all graphs and charts indicating the date on which the program was begun. This point indicates a transition from the baseline phase to the **treatment phase** of the program.

4. Evaluating the Program

The evaluation of the self-control program consists mainly in comparing data gathered during the baseline and treatment phases. Figure 9-4 shows the frequency of smoking during each of the phases. These data show that the self-control program used here was successful, as the frequency of smoking was decreasing almost daily. Most treatment periods should be much longer than 1 week, the period shown in our example.

In many cases the frequency of problem behavior will differ little, if at all, between the baseline and treatment phases. This indicates that the program is not producing desired results and probably should be modified. When this happens, return to Step 2 and reexamine the data for clues that might suggest a more effective approach. Alter the program and continue collecting data. Repeat this process until an effective solution is found.

220

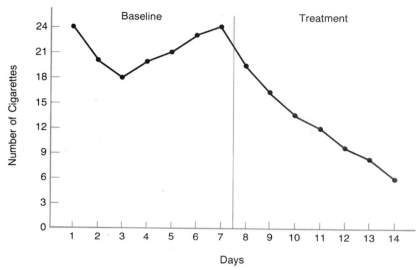

Figure 9-4. *Baseline and treatment data for daily cigarette consumption by a hypothetical person.*

With many problem behaviors, the self-control program should not be discontinued when the goal is reached. Weight reduction is an example. Once some people reach their desired weight, they may be tempted to discard their program and return to their previous eating habits. If they do, they soon discover that they again have a weight problem. When a goal is reached, a new one should be set and the self-control program modified accordingly. Once the desired body weight has been reached, for example, the goal is changed from weight reduction to weight maintenance.

STRATEGIES FOR SELF-CONTROL

Self-control programs are usually established on the basis of one or more basic strategies. These strategies involve helping a person control behavioral antecedents, acquire incompatible responses, and/or alter response consequences. Data recorded on forms similar to Figures 9-1 through 9-4 should suggest which particular strategy or combination of strategies should be most productive. Figure 9-5 describes three basic self-control strategies.

Controlling Behavioral Antecedents

One strategy, controlling behavioral antecedents, is based on the assumption that certain stimulus events, called **behavioral antecedents**, precede and serve to maintain a problem behavior. Many years ago, such learning theorists as Pavlov (1927)

Figure 9-5. Self-Control Strategies

Strategy	Goal
Controlling behavioral antecedents	Identifying and bringing under self-control the environmental cues that elicit some problem behavior
Acquiring incompatible responses	Acquiring new behaviors that compete with existing problem behavior
Altering response consequences	Learning to recognize and bring under self-control the reinforcing consequences of one's problem behavior

and Guthrie (1935) recognized that behavior is controlled by antecedent stimuli. For example, Guthrie expressed this notion when he said that "a combination of stimuli which accompanies a movement will on its recurrence tend to be followed by that movement" (p. 30).

The first practical application of **stimulus control**—the regulation of behavior through the control of behavioral antecedents—was by Ferster, Nurnberger, and

Eating behavior can be elicited by food-related environmental cues. (Photo © Gregg Mancuso/Jeroboam.)

Levitt (1962), who applied this strategy to the management of body weight. Ferster et al. emphasized that eating behavior is frequently elicited by environmental cues, such as watching television, studying, or the sight of a sandwich bar or vending machine. These researchers recommended that weight watchers restrict eating to only a few situations, such as mealtimes.

Like eating, smoking can be attached to numerous environmental cues, such as getting up in the morning, completing a meal, having a cup of coffee, driving an automobile, or studying. Nolan (1968) reports success with a strategy of having smokers restrict smoking to a "smoking chair," particularly when the smoking chair is located at an inaccessible and boring location, such as the garage. The smoker must go to the garage, sit in the smoking chair, smoke the cigarette alone, and then return to the house. This strategy serves to narrow smoking behavior to a single situation. Nolan found that when smoking was limited to this one situation, smoking behavior was more easily brought under control.

To the extent that you can identify the antecedent influences on problem behavior, you will be in a better position to avoid such stimuli. However, it is not always possible or practical to avoid certain situations. In such cases, control of antecedent influences must be combined with other strategies.

Acquiring Incompatible Responses

Another strategy is to acquire **incompatible responses**—behaviors that are incompatible with problem behavior. When obese persons find themselves desiring food between mealtimes, they might use such a desire as a signal to engage in some other activity. The competing activity may be behavioral, such as drinking a glass of water, or it may be mental, such as thinking how slender and attractive one will soon be. Sometimes a smoker may find a suitable competing response by chewing a piece of gum or placing a toothpick in the mouth or doing ten pushups. There are a number of situations in which this strategy seems particularly suited. For example, it is useful when the problem behavior is the last response in a response chain. This is often true of excessive use of alcohol.

What is a response chain? After a busy day, perhaps, a man finds himself at home with nothing much to do. He reads the newspaper and then finds television boring. He begins to think of something to do. He puts on his coat, walks out of the house, and begins a nightly routine. He enters the bar, orders a drink, and eventually completes the evening after six drinks. The consumption of the first drink is actually the termination of a chain of related behaviors. How can one disrupt this behavioral sequence? Evidence shows that the earlier a competing response is introduced, the greater the likelihood of avoiding the terminal response. This chain could have been interrupted by reading a good book or planning a home project. It is easier to introduce a competing response before leaving home than it would be after one enters the tavern. This point seems rather obvious, but many people fail to realize it. Some people behave as if the only control over behavior were one's capacity to withstand

223

intense temptation. In actuality, the mark of successful self-control is the ability to avoid extreme temptation by early interruption of the behavioral chain that leads to the tempting behavior.

The incompatible-response strategy is probably the hardest to use effectively. Quite often the substitute stimuli will not actually reduce the craving for food, alcohol, or cigarettes, particularly if some degree of physiological addiction is operating. In such cases something more than self-control procedures is called for.

Altering Response Consequences

Whether behavior is repeated depends largely on the consequences of that behavior. **Response consequences** (or behavioral consequences) have a greater effect on most human behavior than antecedent stimuli do. The learning theories of Thorndike (1911) and Skinner (1938) were based on the assumption that behavior is determined mainly by its consequences. Consequences that strengthen behavior are called **reinforcers**. What is unique about the response-consequence strategy is that people can generally determine the consequences of their own behavior. Psychologists have found that people can alter behavior consequences to change behavior through (1) self-reinforcement following desired behavior, (2) removal of reinforcers following undesired behavior, and (3) self-punishment following undesired behavior.

Mahoney, Moura, and Wade (1973) studied the effect of self-reward, self-punishment, and self-monitoring (merely observing behavior and collecting data) on weight reduction. All groups were given instructions in the use of stimulus-control procedures. When subjects in the self-reinforcement group lost weight, they gave themselves money, which could be used for purchasing desired items and entertainment. Subjects in the self-punishment group imposed monetary fines on themselves for weight gain. These investigators found that self-reward was more effective than self-punishment or self-monitoring in producing weight reduction.

In a more recent study Mahoney (1974) randomly assigned obese persons to one of three experimental groups. Subjects kept records of their eating habits and body weight throughout the treatment period. After a 2-week baseline period, experimental subjects practiced different forms of self-control for a period of 6 weeks. A *self-monitoring* group set weekly goals for weight loss and improvement of eating habits. In addition to the self-monitoring and goal setting, a *self-reward-weight* group awarded themselves money or gift certificates whenever they achieved a predetermined weight loss. A *self-reward-habit* group received money or gift certificates contingent on the improvement of eating habits rather than weight reduction. A followup assessment 4 months later found self-reward procedures to be more effective than the self-monitoring procedure. Moreover, the self-administered reinforcers were found to be more effective in producing weight reduction when made contingent on improving eating habits than when made contingent on weight reduction.

What are effective reinforcers? Although money was the reinforcer used in the two studies (Mahoney, 1974; Mahoney et al., 1973) cited above, there are many

224

Research has shown that obese individuals are particularly sensitive to food stimuli. (Photo © Rene Burri/Magnum.)

kinds of reinforcers. One of the problems with relying on natural behavioral consequences in self-control is that the pleasant consequences of engaging in some habits occur immediately, whereas the reinforcement for not engaging in that behavior is long delayed and therefore much less effective. When smokers light a cigarette, they experience immediate gratification. But if they decide to stop smoking, it may be weeks before they begin to feel better and possibly years before discovering that they are not suffering from lung cancer or heart disease. Likewise, those with weight problems find immediate reward in the taste of food. When they try to limit the unnecessary calories, reinforcement in the form of a more pleasing physique, verbal compliments, admiring glances from other people, and greater physical stamina may not be experienced for weeks or months. For this reason, more-immediate rewards are necessary in behavioral self-control.

Anyone developing a self-control program should begin by making a list of reinforcers. One's list might include such activities as going shopping, attending a party, playing tennis, going swimming, reading a book or magazine, going for a drive, taking a bath, or relaxing on the couch or in a favorite chair. Although such a list could be lengthy, one must determine which activities are really personally rewarding.

225

Remember that what others find reinforcing may not be for you; determining reinforcers is an individual matter. Watson and Tharp (1972) suggest three things to consider in choosing reinforcers: (1) The consequence has to be a reinforcer for you. You need to select consequences that are tailored to your particular situation and needs. (2) The consequences you select must be available and accessible to you. They must be under your control. (3) They should be relatively strong reinforcers. The more powerful the reinforcer, the more likely it is to be effective in helping you change your behavior. Watson and Tharp recommend that in evaluating the strength of a potential reinforcer we ask ourselves this question: "Do I really think that I will stop performing the undesirable behavior—or start performing the desirable behavior—just because I will gain X (the reinforcer)?"

CONTROLLING MENTAL ACTIVITY: COVERANT-CONTROL PROCEDURES

Much of the emphasis in self-control procedures is on coming to control one's ways of thinking and feeling. Our thoughts and mental images exert a significant amount of control over our behaviors. Homme (1965) believes that thoughts—or coverants, as he calls them—can be thought of as internal behavior subject to the same learning principles as overt behavior. Homme describes the use of **coverant control** with a smoker who makes a list of thoughts about the consequences of smoking that he personally finds aversive. These consequences include lung cancer, coronary disease, bad breath, discolored teeth, and shortness of breath. When the smoker feels the urge for a cigarette, he engages in an aversive thought, or coverant, such as "Smoking causes lung cancer," "Smoking produces bad breath," or "Smoking makes it hard to breathe." The primary advantage of the use of coverants is that these representatives of aversive consequences can be experienced immediately, whereas the actual consequences, as we previously emphasized, may be long delayed. When the coverant is sufficient to prevent undesirable behavior, it should be followed by a positive reinforcer, such as a cup of coffee, a piece of gum, or even a positive thought: "My food will taste so much better now," "How fresh and cool it feels when I take a deep breath," or "My girlfriend or boyfriend will now enjoy my kisses so much more!"

There are many ways that mental images can be used constructively. One lady with a weight problem had a "sweet tooth," especially for chocolate pie. She tried to construct an aversive image to associate with the sight of her favorite dessert. She recalled what had been for her a very repulsive scene while working as a surgical nurse. During an operation on an obese patient, the surgeon had had to cut through and roll back layer after layer of fat on the patient's stomach before getting down to the diseased organ. From that time on, when she was tempted with dessert, especially chocolate pie, she produced this mental image. After several pairings of this aversive image with chocolate pie, she was able to resist it without great difficulty. Every time she did forgo her favorite dessert, she further reinforced her behavior by imagining how slender and attractive she was becoming.

Coverants and mental images are particularly useful in self-control because they can be produced on demand and can serve as an immediate behavioral consequence. Two keys to the success of these techniques are the extent to which they are actually aversive to an individual (what is aversive to one person is not to another) and the clarity or intensity with which they can be called up.

INTERVENTION PROGRAMS FOR SPECIAL PROBLEM AREAS

Up to this point, we have examined three basic approaches to self-control: control of behavioral antecedents, development of incompatible responses, and alteration of response consequences. We will now suggest how these self-control procedures might be applied to two problem areas, overeating and smoking.

You will recall that according to our self-control model previously outlined, the first step is to clearly identify the specific problem behavior. Next, one gathers data on the magnitude of the problem behavior, the behavioral antecedents, and the behavioral consequences. When one has established baseline behavior, one will need to develop and implement an intervention program. This section of the chapter will offer some suggestions that should be useful in developing your own self-control program. It is recommended that you follow only those suggestions that are best suited to your individual situation and that you are capable of maintaining over time. These suggestions are grouped under the three strategies previously discussed.

OVEREATING

Controlling Behavioral Antecedents

Remove from sight ready-to-eat or readily prepared foods. Avoid open display of such foods as cookies, cakes, pies, potato chips, and candy in the house, thereby reducing cues for eating. Many other foods requiring little or no preparation, such as bread, cheese, and instant cereals, should be bought in small quantities. Leftover items should be frozen so that time and effort are required before they can be eaten. The more effort required to prepare food, the more discouragement for the impulsive eater. When preparing a food that needs to be cooked, prepare only one serving. Clear food and dishes after meals so that they will not trigger later eating behavior. Any reasonable measure to make food less accessible should be considered.

Establish a specific location for eating. A major goal is to separate the satisfaction derived directly from eating from the satisfaction derived from other activities

227

while one is eating. The enjoyment that one thinks one gets out of eating may actually be due to good company, a TV program, or even pleasant memories.

Serve your meals on a salad plate rather than a larger plate. A full small plate creates the feeling that one is eating more.

Eat slowly. Think about the fact that you are eating. Eat soup with a teaspoon rather than a soup spoon, and make sure it is served hot so it takes longer to consume. Use eating utensils for everything, even sandwiches. It is much harder and more time-consuming to cut a sandwich than to pick it up and devour it. Try the "one bite at a time" method: Pick up the knife and fork. Cut one piece of meat. Put it in your mouth. Put down the knife and fork. Begin chewing. Do not touch your utensils until you have finished that bite. Repeat this procedure.

You might also have several pauses of 3–5 minutes during a meal. This helps you learn to be in the presence of food without constantly eating. Make a conscious effort to increase the amount of time you use for eating. This allows you to begin digesting food while you are still eating, and you will feel "full" before having eaten so much. Satiation can also be increased by drinking water with your meals and by beginning your meals with bulky items like lettuce, celery, and other raw vegetables, which go a long way toward curbing your appetite without making you eat more than you need or want.

Always leave some food on your plate. Most of us have been taught to clean our plates, and in an attempt to do the "proper" thing, we eat to excess. You may wish to start by leaving only a small amount of food on your plate and gradually progress to larger amounts.

BOX 9-1. HOW MUCH SHOULD YOU WEIGH?

Many people try to determine how much they should weigh by reading height/weight tables, but since many such tables show average weights rather than optimum weights, the figures tend to be too high. There is, however, a formula for estimating your healthiest weight.

Women of average build can compute their ideal weight by multiplying their height in inches by 3.5 and then subtracting 110 from the product. Thus, a woman who is 5 feet tall should weigh about 100 pounds ($60 \times 3.5 - 110 = 100$). For men of average build the formula is height in inches times 4 minus 130. A 6-foot man should weigh about 158.

It is reasonable to make allowances for bone structure and muscularity: even if Woody Allen and Rosie Grier were the same height, they should not weigh the same amount. But be careful that in making these allowances you do not mistake fat for muscle. And remember that if you are 30 pounds overweight, it is unlikely that the difference is all in your bones.

The amount of food you need to maintain your ideal weight depends on how active you are. Begin by rating yourself on the scale below:

very inactive	13
slightly active	14
moderately active	15
relatively active	16
frequently, strenuously active	17

If you are a sedentary person (for example, an office worker), you should rate yourself as a 13. If your physical exercise consists of occasional games of golf or an afternoon walk, you are a 14. A score of 15 means that you frequently engage in moderate exertion—jogging, calisthenics, tennis. A 16 requires that you be almost always on the go, seldom sitting down or standing still for long. Do not give yourself a 17 unless you are a construction worker or engage in other strenuous activity frequently. Most adult Americans should rate themselves 13 or 14.

To calculate the number of calories you need to maintain your ideal weight, multiply your activity rating by your ideal weight. A 150-pound office worker, for example, needs 2300 calories a day; a 150-pound athlete needs 3100 calories.

To estimate how many calories you are getting now, multiply your current weight by your activity level. If your weight is constant at 140 pounds and you are inactive, you are consuming about 1820 calories a day (13 times 140). Subtract the number of calories you need for your ideal weight from the number of calories you are consuming, and you will know the size of your energy imbalance.

To reach your ideal weight, we recommend that you correct your calorie imbalance slowly. It is a bad idea to lose more than 1% of your current weight a week. Cut your daily calorie consumption by 2 times your current weight, and you should achieve that goal. Regardless of your weight, you should not get less than 1200 calories a day. Reducing by much more than 1% of your body weight a week could mean destruction of muscles and organs as well as fat. The same is true of diets that prohibit all fats and carbohydrates.

Adapted from "Fight Fat with Behavior Control," by M. J. Mahoney and K. Mahoney, *Psychology Today,* May 1976, 43. Reprinted by permission from Psychology Today Magazine. Copyright © 1976 Ziff-Davis Publishing Company.

When you have finished eating, leave the table, even if others are still eating. Many people, having finished their own meal, continue to nibble away at food while waiting for others to finish. If you cannot resist such temptations, excuse yourself and leave the table.

Do grocery shopping only from a list made out in advance, and eat only foods prepared from this list. Go shopping after a meal rather than when hungry. This precaution will help reduce excessive food purchases, and you will later find fewer food cues in your home.

229

Acquiring Incompatible Responses

It is common for such emotions as anger, frustration, and depression to trigger an eating response. Penick, Filion, Fox, and Stunkard (1971) report a case of a 30-year-old housewife who, for the first time in her life, recognized that anger stimulated her eating. Following that discovery, whenever she became angry she left the kitchen and wrote down how she felt. This exercise reduced her anger and subsequently her appetite.

If your eating has an emotional base, then any means of reducing the feelings could decrease your desire for food. Exercise routines are an excellent outlet for anger and frustration. Pushups, situps, walking or jogging around the block, riding a bicycle about the neighborhood, and so on may serve not only as a distractor but as a means of reducing the eating desire. Such activities also burn up calories. Exercise programs combined with stimulus-control procedures can produce added benefits.

BOX 9-2. THE ANGUISH OF THE OBESE—FAT FOLK BEFORE THE IRON JUDGE

As a maligned minority, obese people suffer from a mean form of bigotry. Popular theory treats them like flabby exhibitions of weak character, and they often accept this view in self-contempt. Each pound adds to their burden of guilt.

To understand their suffering, I did a sociological study of Calorie Counters, my fictitious name for a national organization of the obese. C. C. is to heavy people what A. A. is to heavy drinkers.

In the Midwestern C. C. chapters I have studied, the moment of agony comes in the weighing ceremony at the weekly meeting. The group leader brings out a set of medical scales, a cold and precise instrument that each member approaches like a criminal before the bar of justice.

The dieter, usually a woman, looks at her group leader, then the scale. She drops her purse, then bows humbly before the omniscient truthgiver and removes her shoes. Jackets, coats, sweaters, earrings fall to the floor. Some members, in a kind of nonverbal confession of guilt, remove girdles; one woman snatched off her wig and tossed it on the pile of rejected accessories.

The scale often stands in silent disapproval of a member's mass, and some deny its verdict. "My home scale says that I weigh three pounds less than this one; there must be something wrong with this scale." Others go back to the scale a half-dozen times in an hour; perhaps it has changed its mind. They treat it like a person, a judge. "He is terrible," one woman said of the scale. "That thing . . . over there in the corner . . . is looking at me. He knows if I have cheated or not. Oh, I can get him to fudge a little by shifting my weight or letting out my breath, but he usually wins."

One 16-year-old girl burst into tears when the scale announced that she had gained five pounds. "I wasn't that bad. I really didn't think I had done that bad. I don't know what to do. It was only a little chicken." Her group leader pressed hard for more information about the size of the little chicken. In despair, the agonized girl held her arms at right angles to her body and exclaimed "Here, dammit. This is a little chicken." Her arms defined a chicken that in her memory was now as big as an ostrich.

Other dieters submit to the iron judge as if caught in a dirty act. The fault, they confess, is in themselves. But they plead extenuating circumstances. "I had an automobile accident four days ago," argued one, "and you wouldn't believe how upset I've been. I've just been frantic and I certainly didn't stick with (my diet) program."

And some blame those around them. One group leader thought a dieter's chief problem was her husband. "What you ought to do," she counseled, "is get rid of that bastard; then you could lose some weight." The next week the dieter had lost five pounds. "I really lost 185 pounds," she chortled. "I took your advice and got rid of him. I figured that he was deliberately trying to keep me fat so that he could have a good time needling me about my lack of willpower. It took me 20 years to figure it out, but I'm well rid of him."

"Fat Folk before the Iron Judge" as it appeared in *Psychology Today* from *Put Down and Ripped Off: The American Woman and the Beauty Cult,* by Nora Scott Kinzer (TYC). Copyright © 1976, 1977 by Nora Scott Kinzer. Reprinted by permission of Harper & Row, Publishers, Inc.

Because eating is usually the endpoint of a series of preparatory responses, the chaining principle can be effectively used in modifying eating behavior. A number of sequential behaviors take place before you actually put the food in your mouth. You prepare the food, place it on the table, come to the table, sit down, pick up a utensil, cut the meat, and so on. Each activity forms a link in the chain of eating. If one can disrupt the behavioral chain, one may successfully avoid the terminal behavior. If you know that walking into a coffee shop with friends starts a chain that ends with eating doughnuts or a hamburger, you may have to avoid the coffee shop and substitute a response that is incompatible with eating behavior.

You can also discourage eating by lengthening the chain of behaviors that preceded it. Buy foods that require lengthy preparation. Even in preparing a hot dog, you should boil one hot dog instead of a pot of them. To eat a second hot dog, you must go through the entire chain a second time.

Altering Response Consequences

Keep stimuli that inhibit eating in full view while eating. You might eat before a mirror. This increases awareness of the amount of food being consumed. You might wish to keep a behavioral chart near the eating table. If you are making progress, the reduction in calories and pounds indicated by the charts will be immediately reinforc-

231

ing. When this occurs, you are now reinforced immediately for eating less rather than eating more. If you are too embarrassed to gorge yourself with food when other people are around, force yourself to eat in their presence. Hang on walls or in some conspicuous place photographs taken or garments worn before the weight-reduction program was undertaken. These stimuli should produce unpleasant associations with eating and thereby reduce the eating behavior.

Reward yourself when a subgoal is achieved. This can be accomplished by permitting yourself to engage in some desirable activity only when a goal has been reached. For example, if during the week you attained your goal of 2 pounds weight reduction, go to a movie, to a ball game, or bowling. Perhaps you can buy a new article of clothing; this is an excellent reinforcement for weight loss. *Do not go to a restaurant for a feast!* You should never reward success in weight reduction with food. Enlist members of the family or friends to provide social reinforcement in the form of praise or compliments for goal attainment. Social approval is a powerful reinforcer.

Activities formerly associated with eating can be made contingent on the formation and practice of good eating habits. Instead of eating while watching TV, reading, or being with friends, you can permit yourself to engage in these activities only when no more than a reasonable amount of the proper foods has been consumed.

You might want to establish an additional self-control contingency by *depositing some money or other valued possession with a friend or family member with an understanding that each time a weight-reduction goal is reached, a certain portion of the money or*

BOX 9-3. ACCELERATING DISSERTATION WRITING THROUGH PRODUCTIVE AVOIDANCE

Zimmerman (n.d.) proposed a technique of "productive avoidance" that involves having a person increase some desirable behavior in order to postpone some aversive outcome. A person deposits with someone else a sum of money or goods that will be forfeited if the person fails to achieve some self-control goal. Harris and Bruner (1971) have shown that such a productive-avoidance technique can be used in a weight-control situation. If a person fails to meet and sustain certain weight-reduction goals, he or she will eventually forfeit the entire sum of money.

Harris (1974) also reports another novel way the productive-avoidance technique can be used. She worked with a doctoral student who had postponed writing her dissertation for 2 years. This student was requested to deposit $50 with the investigator. Five dollars was returned each week to the student if five pages of writing were submitted. If no manuscript pages were submitted, the money was donated to a church organization that the student disliked. After 8 weeks, this student submitted a complete draft of her dissertation that was returned with only minor revisions.

232

merchandise can be redeemed. In other words, the other person becomes a caretaker and refunds the money according to your progress in reaching a self-control goal. If no progress is achieved within a certain period, the money is forfeited. Another possibility is to establish a contingency whereby you have to give up something of value each time you do not reach a goal. For instance, you might decide to donate a certain amount of money to some organization for which you have contempt each time you fail to reach a goal.

Increasing Motivation to Lose Weight

For many people the desire to lose weight is outweighed by the reinforcing effects of the taste of food, the actual act of eating, or the appearance of the food. Hence, a major step in any weight-reduction program is to increase motivation not to eat and decrease the motivation to eat. The following are some suggestions for increasing motivation not to eat excessively.

For many, the desire to lose weight is outweighed by the reinforcing effect of seeing, smelling, and tasting food. (Photo © Emilio Mercado/Jeroboam.)

Use mental imagery and picture yourself as a slender person. Picture yourself in several situations as this "new" person—for example, walking into a party and catching the eyes of other attractive persons. Think about the new you and all the new opportunities you could have as a slender person. Put up magazine photographs of attractive slender persons on the refrigerator and in other parts of the kitchen as rewarding cues for being slender. You may become immune to these cues, so periodically change these pictures.

Buy one piece of special clothing that will fit only after you have reached your weight goal. For women especially: Go to various department stores and look at all the new clothes. Try on a bikini or some other article of clothing that all your slender friends are wearing now but that you cannot because of your weight. (It appears that new clothes play a major part in a woman's opinion of herself. More times than not, when obese women lose weight, they begin to buy stylish clothing; therefore, it is assumed that clothing would play a major part in motivating women, and perhaps also men, to lose weight.)

Final Guidelines for Self-Modification of Eating Behavior

Set a realistic goal for weight loss. A realistic goal would be between 1 and 2 pounds per week. You can reach such a goal without upsetting your entire life-style or routine, and you also feel a sense of accomplishment when the goal is reached. These conditions increase the probability that you will continue the intervention program.

Be sure to establish accurate baselines for eating behavior and weight before the intervention program is initiated. Baselines provide a reliable standard of comparison for changes in eating behavior and weight.

Consult a physician to determine an appropriate diet and to help you set reasonable goals for weight loss.

Initiate the program step by step. You may try only one or two of the aforementioned suggestions in the initial stages of the self-control program and incorporate others as practical and appropriate. The point is that you not try too great an undertaking too soon. Start in modest degrees and progress from there.

Keep accurate and regular data as you proceed with the program. If progress is being made in decreasing food intake and weight, the recording and graphing of these results can be a most gratifying experience and ensures continued participation.

Be willing to modify your program. If, after a reasonable time, you are not getting the desired results, try to identify problem areas and make adjustments accordingly. For example, if you find that your program works at home but not at a restaurant or at a neighbor's house, develop programs for those situations. If you are still unsuccessful, it may be necessary to avoid eating in those places. Or you may find yourself becoming negligent about recording the necessary data. If this happens, you must develop a program to correct it. You might, for example, permit yourself to eat appropriate foods only after you have all charts up to date.

234

Inevitably some problems such as those described above will be encountered. The key to success is not to scrap the programs but to identify problem areas and develop appropriate reinforcement contingencies. When this process is continued, progress toward achievement of the goal is very likely.

SMOKING

We will conclude this chapter by applying the three self-control strategies to problem smoking behavior. As with eating, one must gather baseline data and determine the extent of one's smoking problem and the conditions in which it occurs. Then a self-control strategy can be used. Remember that any self-control program, to be effective, must be adaptable to one's own particular situation and personality.

Controlling Behavioral Antecedents

You might begin a self-control program in which you gradually reduce the areas and situations in which you normally smoke. You might permit yourself to smoke anywhere you desire but never in the presence of other persons. Learn to smoke alone, and refuse invitations from others to smoke in their presence. Better yet, choose a particular place in the house to smoke, and restrict all smoking to that location. You might have a "smoking chair," as Nolan (1968) has suggested. Do not allow yourself to watch TV, talk with family members, read the newspaper, or engage in any rewarding activities while smoking. Remove your smoking chair to some out-of-the-way place, such as the cellar or garage.

You should also try to restrict smoking to certain times as well as locations. You will probably find that smoking is almost irresistible at certain times but more or less a reflex action at other times. Examine your behavioral chart and determine when you smoke out of "need" and when out of "habit." Effort toward reducing smoking should be directed first toward "habit" cigarettes. Do not permit yourself to smoke while watching TV, driving your car, or on a work break. You can control the circumstances that lead to "habit" smoking. When you have learned to control your smoking in one situation, begin working on the next situation on your list, and so on until you have eliminated the "habit" cigarettes. You are now ready to work on the "need" cigarettes. To control "need" smoking, you may have to use control procedures directed toward altered thinking and feeling (that is, coverant procedures).

Whenever and wherever you smoke, monitor the frequency of smoking behavior. Only through step-by-step analysis can you learn to lower daily cigarette consumption. You may eventually restrict smoking to such a degree that you will be highly motivated to quit smoking completely.

235

Acquiring Incompatible Responses

Your analysis of baseline data should help you identify the time of day and situation in which you are most likely to smoke. It may also help you identify some of the various kinds of satisfaction derived from smoking. In developing incompatible, or competing, responses you are really trying to substitute another habit (helpful, you hope, rather than harmful) that becomes associated with either the cues or the consequences previously attached to smoking behavior. Here are some examples of things you might want to try.

The ritualistic act of reaching for a cigarette, taking it out of the pack, and lighting and puffing it may be reinforcing. If so, you might substitute something in place of the cigarette, such as a "dummy" cigarette, a piece of gum, or a toothpick. This permits you to go through virtually the same response chain without experiencing the final response of smoking.

Each time you get the urge to smoke while studying, working at your desk, or reading the newspaper, you might try walking five times around the room, doing ten pushups, jogging in place for 5 minutes, or anything that seems most reasonable in your particular case. The idea is that you engage in some behavior other than smoking in those situations that once elicited smoking behaviors. It is helpful to take up some relatively simple activity, game, or skill at which you really want to become adept and practice it instead of smoking. If you are tempted to smoke after a meal, simply excuse yourself and go for a walk or engage in some hobby you have or take a shower or wash the dishes.

When you experience the urge to smoke and seem obsessed with the thought of doing so, you might simply say to yourself (or aloud, if you prefer) "To hell with this! I am not a slave to anybody or anything, including a cigarette. I am a free person. *I do not smoke."* Then shift your thoughts and your actions to something else. This should give you a feeling of strength and self-confidence. You need to see yourself as having the strength and power to control your behavior in order to achieve self-control.

Altering Response Consequences

Some form of coverant control can be used in conjunction with the control of antecedent cues and acquisition of incompatible responses. You might imagine a scene in which you become extremely nauseated when you light a cigarette. Or you may prefer to repeat some simple statement such as "Cigarettes cause cancer," "Smoking will kill me," or "I'll have a heart attack if I don't stop." Keep searching until you find some aversive thought. It will be helpful to create an incongruence between your overt behavior and your inner thoughts. Such "cognitive dissonance"—that is, inconsistency between your behavior and your private thoughts—may bring about behavior change. It just does not make sense to smoke if smoking is harmful to your health.

236

Assuming that you desire to continue to live and have good health, you cannot enjoy that which is a threat to life and health. Such mental dissonance produces tension and discomfort, which can be relieved by either discrediting the thought (rationalization) or changing the behavior.

The logical and most beneficial way to reduce this dissonance is to stop smoking. Any dissonance you create may help motivate you to stop smoking. If you pick up a cigarette, always make yourself think of some aversive consequence; when you put a cigarette away without lighting it or have the urge but do not reach for a cigarette, reward yourself with such thoughts as "I feel so much better now," "Refusing that cigarette will add several minutes to my life," or "I feel healthier and stronger already." Think of some pleasant consequence of not smoking that is especially meaningful to you. For best results, associate pleasant thoughts with no smoking and unpleasant thoughts with smoking for a number of days. Be sure to check your behavioral chart daily for evidence of progress.

Another tactic is to start a physical-fitness program in which you set some definite goals. You may wish to run 2 miles a day without stopping. Smoking then produces a consequence that blocks you from achieving this worthy objective. You can also now think "If I smoke, I'll never be able to run 2 miles."

Some people get support from friends or acquaintances who are also trying to quit smoking. Others can lend support to you when the going is difficult and share the enjoyment of success when you are making progress.

Do not forget the Zimmerman productive-avoidance procedure, discussed in Box 9-3. Enter into a contract with someone whereby you deposit money or other valuables with the person, which you earn back by reducing your smoking behavior. Another kind of agreement is one in which each time you do not make sufficient progress in your smoking behavior, the money must be donated to some cause or organization that you intensely dislike. Or you might prefer that each time you do not smoke, you deposit some money into a "shopping fund," which you can spend on yourself once you reach a particular goal. When you do not make progress, do not permit yourself to engage in the desired activity. In other words, "pay the price" for smoking and "reap the reward" when you do not smoke.

In any contract of this sort you must make the consequences significant enough to have an effect on your behavior. For example, if you are Black and have agreed to donate $10 to the Ku Klux Klan for each cigarette you smoke, you will have second thoughts about smoking. Do not enter into a contract that is not binding, even if it is with yourself. You must follow through on every stipulation of the agreement if it is to be effective.

The techniques we have labeled as "Acquiring Incompatible Responses" and "Altering Response Consequences" are not completely independent. The acquisition of a competing response may also alter the consequences of both the original and the new response. The person who, when desiring a cigarette, tells himself or herself "I am a free person. I do not smoke" and really means it is less likely to smoke and more likely to engage in a more constructive activity. The change in self-concept (increase in self-confidence) that accompanies this "self-talk" is likely to change smoking from an enjoyable to a more aversive experience. Hence, not only has a different response been acquired, but the consequences of the old response and the new one have been altered.

It should be emphasized that you are not expected to use all the suggestions presented in this chapter. An attempt to incorporate them all would be overwhelming and self-defeating. Remember that the purpose of this chapter is to help you develop greater self-control, and that includes making your own decisions. When you decide to stop smoking, you should find some of these procedures and techniques helpful to you. Feel free to combine and/or modify them so that they are tailored to your particular situation. You should be able to use simultaneously some of the "behavioral antecedent," "response consequence," and "incompatible response" techniques.

SUMMARY

Most people would like to gain greater control over their behavior, but many do not understand the nature of behavior and how to bring it under greater self-control. Systematic plans should be developed for behavioral self-regulation. The model presented in this chapter consists of four steps: defining the problem, collecting baseline data, developing a program, and evaluating the program.

It is imperative that the behavior to be modified be clearly defined so that an adequate baseline can be established and the effectiveness of a self-control program determined. The frequency of the specific behavior should be carefully recorded, along with some description of the situation in which the behavior occurred.

Several strategies may be used in a self-control program. Three such strategies are controlling behavioral antecedents, acquiring incompatible responses, and altering response consequences. Controlling behavioral antecedents requires identifying and bringing under self-control the environmental cues that elicit some problem behavior. Altering response consequences requires us to recognize and bring under self-control the reinforcing consequences of our problem behavior.

Our thoughts and mental images exert a significant amount of control over our behaviors. This mental activity can be controlled to some extent through covariant-control procedures. Smokers should find it easier to quit if they think "Smoking causes lung cancer" every time they feel the urge for a cigarette. Coverants are particularly useful in self-control because they can be produced on demand and can serve as an immediate behavioral consequence.

In this chapter we presented suggestions for bringing smoking and eating behavior under greater self-control. These same principles and strategies can be applied to a wide variety of problem behaviors.

238

KEY CONCEPTS

Baseline phase the period in a self-control program when the frequency of the problem behavior is recorded before any attempt to modify it. The purpose of the baseline is to provide a standard of comparison for the frequency of the behavior after the treatment has been initiated.

Behavioral antecedents stimulus events that precede and serve to maintain behavior.

Coverant control a method of controlling behavior by regulating thoughts and mental images.

Incompatible responses new responses that compete with and come to replace problem behavior.

Problem behavior the specific behavior that a person desires to change.

Reinforcer a stimulus event that serves to increase the strength of some behavior.

Response consequences stimulus events that follow behavior.

Stimulus control the regulation of behavior through the control or manipulation of behavioral antecedents.

Treatment phase the period in a self-control program when the self-control strategies are in effect.

10

CHAPTER OBJECTIVES

1. To understand the nature of anxiety and anger.
2. To distinguish between two components of anxiety—emotional arousal and worry.
3. To distinguish between reality-based stress and threat-produced anxiety.
4. To become familiar with some theoretical approaches to emotional control.
5. To become familiar with some research on the control of anxiety and anger.
6. To assess the degree of one's anger problem.
7. To develop strategies for managing test anxiety, dating anxiety, and anger.
8. To formulate self-verbalizations that can be used in a cognitive/behavioral strategy for managing emotions.

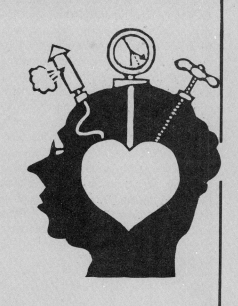

MANAGING
OUR
EMOTIONS

There seem to be an ever-increasing number of factors in our modern social environment that evoke anxiety and trigger the response of anger. People get upset over high taxes, unemployment, crowded living conditions, interpersonal relations, political issues, uncertainty about the future, perceived inequity in work assignments, and many other things. Since, obviously, not all sources of stress can be eliminated from our lives, it behooves us to learn to cope with these emotion-arousing situations. Failure to do so can result in physiological problems, such as indigestion, headaches, and cardiovascular disorders, and can have disruptive social and economic consequences, including alienation of loved ones and reduction in work performance. The purpose of this chapter is to suggest ways a person can learn to cope with stressful emotional situations that may interfere with daily living. We will particularly concern ourselves with suggestions for anxiety and anger control.

We will begin our discussion with a review of a cognitive/behavioral approach to anxiety reduction and anger management. Next we will show how a cognitive/behavioral approach might be used to reduce two important types of anxiety: test-taking anxiety and dating anxiety. We will close this chapter with some suggestions for modifying another significant emotion, anger.

ANXIETY REDUCTION THROUGH COGNITIVE CONTROL

In Chapter 5 we indicated that **anxiety** is the reaction to any circumstance that threatens one's sense of well-being. We further pointed out that threats to one's sense of well-being can originate in environmental threats, superego threats, or various unconscious influences. Whatever the origin of anxiety, it is a conscious feeling that must eventually be dealt with at a conscious level. Here we shall look at some ways that psychologists have tried to reduce anxiety.

Meichenbaum's Cognitive/Behavioral Approach

Meichenbaum and Turk (1975) have conducted research on how thinking influences the experience of anxiety. Using both a cognitive analysis of behavior and the technology of behavior modification, they suggest a three-step process for achieving greater emotional control. First is the self-observation step. In this phase the person becomes a more skilled observer of his or her own behavior. Through a heightened awareness, one learns to monitor one's thoughts, feelings, and interpersonal behaviors. This step is similar to the baseline phase of self-control programs, described in the preceding chapter.

Once the person has accurately identified the thoughts and feelings accompanying an emotion, the second step is to introduce incompatible thoughts and behavior. The person must generate thoughts that will weaken the old maladaptive behaviors. What one now thinks must serve as a trigger for a new series of more adaptive

"I've studied hard, and I know I can do well on this exam." (Photo © Cornell Capa/Magnum.)

behaviors. Since the assumption is made that thoughts in the form of mental images or silent verbalizations to oneself generally precede and/or accompany overt behaviors, the key to the success of this self-instructional approach is learning appropriate and inappropriate "self-talk." By learning a new kind of self-talk, one comes to perceive and behave in a manner consistent with such inner talk; that is, one acquires **cognitive control** over one's behavior. When taking an examination, a college student who engages in negative self-talk, such as "I'll never be able to pass this test," is likely to do poorly. However, positive self-talk, such as "I know I can do it," can have a positive effect. Positive self-talk, of course, must be combined with adequate preparation.

These are a few examples of negative self-talk statements related to test anxiety:

> I can feel my anxiety level rising.
> My stomach is beginning to get tight.
> I'll never pass this test.
> One more F and I'm out.
> I guess I'm just stupid.
> My parents will be so disappointed in me.
> I feel like everything is out of control.

And these are some positive self-talk statements:

> I have skills to deal with my anxiety.
> No negative statements; just think rationally.
> I've studied and I can meet this challenge.
> Steady, now. One step at a time.
> I'm in control. I can handle it.
> Keep focused on the present; what is it I have to do?
> I'll just stay task-relevant and not worry.
> Worry won't help anything.
> Breathe slowly; there, that's better.
> I feel better now. It's not as bad as I expected.

The third step of this process involves learning to use positive self-talk as the trigger for implementing the new coping strategy. Exercises designed to help the person acquire skills in using positive self-talk include observation and imitation of models using a cognitive/behavioral approach in problem situations, individual tutoring, and role playing. People are also encouraged to use self-talk in coping with their own problems.

Spielberger's Approach to Emotional Control

Spielberger's work on emotional control has been directed mainly toward the concept of anxiety. Spielberger recognizes a difference between **trait anxiety**, which is

244

a relatively stable personality characteristic, and **state anxiety**, which is a transitory emotional state resulting from situational factors. Much of his work has focused on state anxiety, especially in situations in which a person's performance is being evaluated. Spielberger (1972) conceptualizes test anxiety as a situation-specific anxiety trait, with the amount of anxiety experienced on a given occasion depending on how personally threatening the student perceives the test to be. Persons with a high anxiety trait are prone to perceive examinations as more threatening and hence become more anxious in test situations than low-anxious persons.

Spielberger uses the term **stress** to refer to the stimulus properties of situations that are characterized by some degree of objective physical or psychological danger and **threat** to refer to one's perception of a given situation as more or less dangerous. A person's anxiety state may vary in intensity and duration depending on the amount of stress that impinges on him or her and the persistence of his or her perception of that stressful situation as threatening.

The amount of examination stress is a function of test difficulty and the importance of the consequences of successful performance. The more difficult and important a particular test is, the more likely is that test situation to be perceived as threatening by most students. Some students, however, would be inclined to perceive an easy test of little consequence (nonstressful) as threatening and continue to experience high anxiety in this situation.

Spielberger, Anton, and Bedell (1976) concluded from an extensive review of research literature that high levels of test anxiety lower test performance both by causing a state of emotional arousal in which people are more likely to make mistakes (signs of this arousal include sweating and rapid heart rate) and by producing negative self-centered, cognitive reactions (worry)—for example, saying to oneself while taking a test "I am stupid" or "I'll probably fail."

Spielberger's review of the literature also showed that behavioral approaches, including **relaxation training** and **systematic densensitization**, were effective methods of reducing the emotional aspects of test anxiety whereas cognitive/behavioral approaches, such as those used by Meichenbaum (1972) and Wine (1971) were more effective in reducing the negative, cognitive reactions labeled "worry."

Since test anxiety seems to comprise two kinds of reactions, emotional/autonomic and cognitive, Spielberger et al. have developed the Test Anxiety Inventory (TAI), a 20-item questionnaire that includes subscales for measuring worry and emotionality. This instrument should be helpful in determining whether a person's high test anxiety results mainly from emotional or cognitive factors or both. This information would help the psychologist or counselor, and perhaps the student also, in determining what method to use in the treatment of test anxiety. As just mentioned, relaxation training and systematic desensitization have proved to be more effective with the emotional component, while cognitive approaches appear to be more effective in reducing worry. Techniques for achieving self-relaxation and self-desensitization are described in detail by Hankins (1979).

245

Novaco's Approach to Anger Management

Novaco (1975) has concentrated his efforts on the analysis and management of anger. He has developed a self-instruction strategy for anger management which is an extension of Meichenbaum's cognitive/behavioral approach. Novaco's strategy is based on a set of nine propositions for anger management, from which a package of self-statements was generated to enable people to deal more effectively with anger-arousing situations. Although not all these statements have been empirically validated, the statements do provide some intuitive and practical suggestions on anger control. In simplified form, Novaco's propositions state the following: *

1. People who can maintain a task orientation rather than an ego orientation and stay focused on what they must do to effect desired change will be more able to manage anger than those who perceive a provocation as a personal affront or challenge.

2. People with high self-esteem, when confronted with personal provocations (threats to self-worth), are less inclined toward anger arousal than people with low self-esteem. High-self-esteem persons are more apt to engage in positive self-statements and should be less susceptible to ego threats.

3. People who have learned to cope with provocations in nonantagonistic ways are less likely to become angry when provoked. Those who are able to handle provocations with nonantagonistic behaviors develop a sense of competence and learn to take charge without becoming angry. Some people become angry in provoking

*This and all other material from this source are reprinted by permission of the publisher from *Anger Control: The Development and Evaluation of an Experimental Treatment*, by Raymond W. Novaco. (Lexington, Mass.: Lexington Books, D. C. Heath and Company, Copyright 1975, D. C. Heath and Company.)

246

encounters simply because they have not acquired effective coping skills and are unaware of alternative responses to anger.

4. An awareness of one's own anger arousal increases the likelihood that one can regulate one's anger. The earlier in the course of a provocation one learns to tune in on one's arousal, the greater the improvement in ability to regulate anger.

5. Anger awareness can serve as a cue, or signal, for nonantagonistic coping strategies. We can learn to interpret the onset of anger as a signal to act in ways that are more likely to reduce tension and resolve conflicts.

6. People who perceive themselves as being in control of situations in which provocations are encountered are less likely to become angry and more likely to use alternative coping strategies than people who see themselves as helpless or powerless in these situations.

7. People who learn to dissect provocation situations into stages and to use appropriate self-instructions for each of those stages are more likely to manage their anger. Like most difficult tasks, anger control is more easily accomplished when broken down into manageable chunks.

8. As people experience success for having effectively regulated anger arousal, their ability to use nonantagonistic coping behaviors is enhanced. Self-congratulatory self-statements not only serve as reinforcers for positive coping strategies but also raise one's self-esteem.

9. People who acquire tension-reducing and relaxation skills can more effectively regulate their anger.

Much of Novaco's research has been done with police officers (Novaco, 1976). As he points out, law-enforcement officers have a uniquely difficult status with regard to anger control. They find themselves in a double bind by not only being thrust into situations having a high potential for antagonism but also being expected to behave in an objective and professional manner in these situations. Consequently, they are not afforded avenues of emotional release that are granted to other persons.

The procedure Novaco has developed for training law-enforcement personnel has three steps: (1) cognitive preparation regarding the functions of anger (some functions of anger will be discussed later in the chapter), (2) skill acquisition and rehearsal whereby participants discover and review coping processes through small-group exercises, and (3) application and practice of coping techniques during a graduated series of role-played provocations.

Cognitive Preparation. According to Novaco, the anger-management strategy is based on the conviction that anger arousal is to a significant extent determined by cognitive factors (namely, one's interpretation of a situation, attributions of intent, justifications, and self-statements), and the strategy is directed toward achieving competence in cognitive self-control skills. The first step—helping participants develop an understanding of the functions of anger as a response to provocation—is accomplished by introducing participants to a model of the functions of anger as they

247

relate to police experience. This model specifies five basic types of provocation: annoyances (for example, "spilling coffee on your uniform"), frustrations ("a citizen refuses to give you assistance"), ego threats ("you walk into a bar and someone says 'Here comes super pig!'"), assaults ("a suspect you are transporting spits on you through the screen"), and inequity ("getting a day's suspension for damage to a unit that was unavoidable").

During the second phase participants learn to view anger-arousal incidents as sequences of interrelated events, which include (1) setting events, (2) cognitive mediators, (3) situational cues, (4) the mode of response, and (5) consequences of the encounter. The provocation experience is seen as a cluster of events that triggers anger, with each succeeding event escalating the episode until "one party resigns his needs or copes constructively, or . . . sufficient coercive power is brought to bear on the antagonist resulting in his capitulation" (Novaco, 1976, pp. 9–10).

Setting events include those circumstances that affect one's mood and prime one's reactions; for example, a patrolman reports for work and finds his cruiser out of gas or in a state of disrepair. *Cognitive mediators* are memories, expectations, and self-dialogues that precede and/or accompany the response to provocation. For example, while on patrol an officer may fret about complaints that he has not written enough tickets or about his failure to get vacation time when he wanted it. This kind of frustration and resulting self-statements can play a major role in shaping emotional reactions and overt responses. *Situational cues* are those stimuli that act as elicitors of the anger response. Profanity, insults, long hair, and other stimuli can elicit and intensify anger reactions of police officers. The *mode of response* to a provocation is the way a person reacts to that situation. Overzealous interrogation and unnecessary roughness by police in response to a personal affront can result in broken bodies, including those of the police. The *consequences of the encounter* are whatever outcome results from the episode—that is, whether it is closed or whether there is further agitation and disruption of performance.

Skill Acquisition and Rehearsal. The next step in training is to acquire a set of skills or methods for self-regulation of anger. Participants describe on index cards some provocation experiences in vivid detail. In small groups each participant presents his chosen scenario for discussion, and the group examines such factors as the situational determinants, the variables that might exacerbate or ameliorate the antagonism, and potential situational hazards. The purpose is to generate some potentially useful ways of handling the situations.

Effective Control through Role Playing. After this experience and additional rehearsal of coping strategies comes a period of regulated exposure to provocative situations in which these skills can be practiced. This is accomplished through role playing. An example of a provocation incident used in role playing is presented below:

248

Role-playing situations can be used to help individuals cope with real-life provocations. (Photo ©
Hiroji Kubota/Magnum.)

> While on patrol you notice that a car ahead of you is carrying expired plates.
> You turn on your lights to pull the car over, but the driver turns at the next intersec-
> tion and continues on as if he didn't see you. Pursuing the vehicle you hit the siren,
> and he finally pulls over.
> You approach the vehicle and ask for license and registration. The driver
> states that he has misplaced the registration, so you return to your unit to radio for a
> records check and while waiting you notice that his left front tire is very worn. When
> you call his attention to this, he becomes hostile and sarcastic. At that point you
> request that he get out of the car and open the trunk to show you his spare. With a
> smirk on his face, he gets out of the car, fumbles through his pockets and claims that
> he has lost the trunk key and cannot open the trunk [Novaco, 1976, p. 16].

According to Novaco, the provocative impact of these role-playing situations
can be increased in intensity and complexity as the scenarios incorporate more ego-
threat dimensions, such as items of verbal abuse likely to be encountered in barrooms
which "challenge the officer's manhood, question his maternal ancestry, or remark on
his wife's occupation." In these role-playing episodes other group members can act as

249

observers and help provide support and corrective feedback, which facilitates the learning process. Novaco reports that these stress-inoculation workshops have been well received; both his procedure and the results are most impressive. Although his techniques have been developed specifically for police officers, these principles and procedures could be profitable to anyone with anger problems.

RESEARCH ON COGNITIVE/BEHAVIORAL PROCEDURES

Test Anxiety

Meichenbaum (1972) was successful in helping college students reduce test anxiety. In accordance with his three-step process, students were made aware of their thoughts and self-talk before and during test situations. Group discussions were used to increase their awareness of cues that produce anxiety and arousal of task-irrelevant behaviors. This "insight procedure," derived mainly from Ellis' (1963) rational-emotive therapy, helped students conceptualize the worry component inherent in test-taking situations. During the first phase of this treatment program, discussions centered on the kinds of negative self-talk experienced by group members in test situations and the consequences that such statements seemed to have.

In the second phase students tried to increase positive self-talk statements and learn how to relax in test-taking situations. Each student was asked to visualize imaginary scenes in which he or she was becoming anxious and tense and then to visualize himself or herself successfully coping with these anxiety-evoking situations. Students visualized themselves performing specified exam-related behaviors (studying at night before an exam; taking an exam), and if they became anxious, they were to begin slow deep breathing and self-instructions to relax. They were also encouraged to

---

BOX 10-2. REDUCING PHOBIC BEHAVIOR

Meichenbaum and his associates have repeatedly shown that self-talk and self-instructional training produce behavior change. He has shown that such techniques can be used not only with test-taking anxiety but even with more ingrained phobic behavior. Meichenbaum and Cameron (1973), for instance, showed that such techniques can be used in phobic-behavior modification. They studied subjects who avoided situations like camping and picnicking because of their fear of snakes or rats. When subjects had mastered the self-instructional and relaxation exercises, they were gradually presented with increasingly threatening exposures to a 5-foot corn snake and a white rat. Eventually, these phobic patients were able to move from a 15-foot distance from these animals to holding them barehanded for 1 minute.

250

use any self-talk that would facilitate their attending to the task and inhibit task-irrelevant thoughts.

Students were tested before and after the cognitive-modification treatment, and there was a control group. In comparison with the control students, those receiving the treatment showed significant improvement on several measures, including grade-point average and self-report measures of anxiety. Furthermore, the high-test-anxious students in the cognitive-modification group performed as well after the treatment as a comparable group of low-test-anxious students. Meichenbaum suggests that this finding provides further evidence of the effectiveness of cognitive-modification procedures in removing test anxiety. The superiority in performance of the treatment group over the control group was maintained at a follow-up comparison 1 month later. What we learn to say to ourselves does make a difference.

Anger Management

Participants in another study by Novaco (1975) comprised some students and staff members at Indiana University and some members of the surrounding community who had problems with anger control. The degree and extent of their anger reactions were first assessed by means of an anger inventory, personal interview, and pretreatment laboratory provocations.

After the pretreatment assessment, the participants were randomly assigned to four groups, only one of which will be discussed here—the cognitive-coping group. This group engaged in discussions on topics such as the duration and extent of their anger problems and a situational analysis to try to identify particular aspects of provocations that trigger anger. An attempt was made to help participants develop an awareness of self-talk emitted in provocation encounters by having them close their eyes, recall recent anger experiences, and report thoughts and feelings they had experienced.

These reported feelings, thoughts, and statements were used in presenting a rationale for the coping strategies used in this study. Clients were made aware of the correspondence between anger and the kinds of thoughts they had and the things they said to themselves. In other words, anger can be aroused, maintained, and inflamed by the kind of self-talk that occurs in provocation situations.

Novaco's propositions for anger management were discussed with the participants. They were encouraged to develop an awareness of their self-statements during periods of anger, to record these self-statements, and to do a situational analysis of what triggered the anger response. It was assumed that this experience would increase the clients' positive self-talk and sharpen their assessments of their own feelings and behavior.

In later sessions clients were instructed in how to view a provocation experience as a sequence of stages, including (1) preparation for the provocation, when possible, (2) the confrontation, (3) coping with anger arousal, and (4) a reflective period in which the client can reward himself or herself for coping successfully.

251

Group discussion of anger problems can provide individuals with insights into more effective anger management. (Photo © Ken Heyman.)

A sheet of self-statements serving as examples of ways to regulate anger through cognitive control was also offered to each client. These statements are presented below:

1. *Preparing for a Provocation*
   What is it that I have to do?
   I can work out a plan to handle this.

I can manage this situation. I know how to regulate my anger.

If I find myself getting upset, I'll know what to do.

There won't be any need for an argument.

Time for a few deep breaths of relaxation. Feel comfortable, relaxed and at ease.

This could be a testy situation, but I believe in myself.

2. *Confronting the Provocation*

Stay calm. Just continue to relax.

As long as I keep my cool, I'm in control here.

Don't take it personally.

Don't get all bent out of shape; just think of what to do here.

You don't need to prove yourself.

There is no point in getting mad.

I'm not going to let him get to me.

Don't assume the worst or jump to conclusions. Look for the positives.

It's really a shame that this person is acting the way he is.

For a person to be that irritable, he must be awfully unhappy.

If I start to get mad, I'll just be banging my head against the wall. So I might as well just relax.

There's no need to doubt myself. What he says doesn't matter.

3. *Coping with Arousal and Agitation*

My muscles are starting to feel tight. Time to relax and slow things down.

Getting upset won't help.

It's just not worth it to get so angry.

I'll let him make a fool of himself.

It's reasonable to get annoyed, but let's keep the lid on.

Time to take a deep breath.

My anger is a signal of what I need to do. Time to talk to myself.

I'm not going to get pushed around, but I'm not going haywire either.

Let's try a cooperative approach. Maybe we are both right.

He'd probably like me to get really angry. Well, I'm going to disappoint him.

I can't expect people to act the way I want them to.

4. *Self-Reward*

It worked!

That wasn't as hard as I thought.

I could have gotten more upset than it was worth.

My ego can sure get me in trouble, but when I watch that ego stuff I'm better off.

I'm doing better at this all the time.

I actually got through that without getting angry.

I guess I've been getting upset for too long when it wasn't even necessary [Novaco, 1975, pp. 95–96].

Clients were encouraged to generate some self-statements of their own and also to analyze their previous dialogues in provocation situations, looking in particular for self-defeating and anger-eliciting self-talk. During these sessions each client was given instructions in techniques for achieving deep-muscle relaxation.

The treatment given to the cognitive-coping group was most effective in reducing anger and increasing anger management, compared with the control group.

This procedure was effective in reducing anger not only in the laboratory but also in real-life situations.

In discussing the implications of these findings for the treatment of anger, Novaco puts it this way:

> The results of the project demonstrate that cognitive control procedures can be effectively used to regulate anger arousal. The cognitive control skills that were taught to persons having chronic anger problems involved their becoming educated about their anger patterns, learning to monitor and assess their anger, learning how to alternatively construe provocations to mitigate the sense of personal threat, and instructing themselves to attend to the task dimensions of a provocative situation. Through the making of self-statements, clients were able to influence their perception of provocations ("Maybe he's having a rough day" or "There's no need to take it personally") and to guide their response to the problem situation ("Don't act like a jerk just because he is" or "What do I want to accomplish here"). The use of such covert procedures imparts to the person an explicit sense of personal control which has the effect of diminishing the threat value of the provocation as well as increasing one's response options. Discovering that there are alternative ways of perceiving and responding to provocations plays a major role in the development of competence for anger management. Anger, or even rage reactions, follows from a person (or animal) being "cornered" or "boxed in." We frequently characterize the circumstances of anger arousal as "having reached the end of the rope." As a person acquires coping skills that enable him to resolve provocation situations to his satisfaction, he is less prone to resort to anger as the sole means of influencing the behavior of others [1975, pp. 47–48].

DEVELOPING COGNITIVE STRATEGIES FOR SPECIFIC PROBLEM AREAS

Controlling Test-Specific Anxiety

Test-taking anxiety is so widespread that all of us could use some practical self-control suggestions at one time or another. Although mild anxiety can often facilitate examination performance, for many students anxiety levels are so high as to interfere with retention and disrupt performance. One may find oneself sitting in a college classroom perspiring heavily and breathing rapidly, with a steady stream of task-irrelevant thoughts passing through one's mind. How can one get such anxiety under control?

Spielberger (1972) points out that test taking may be *stressful* and/or *threatening*. Stressful situations are characterized by some degree of objective physical or psychological danger. Threatening situations are simply situations that one perceives as dangerous.

254

Most people find stressful situations threatening, but whether a situation is interpreted as threatening by a particular person will depend on that person's perception of the situation. An objectively stressful situation may not be perceived as threatening by the person who is unaware of the danger or who has the skills to cope with it. Conversely, situations lacking in objective danger or stress may be appraised as threatening and result in increased anxiety. Nevertheless, as the difficulty of an examination and the importance of its consequences increase, it becomes more likely that most students will perceive the test situation as threatening.

Reality-Based Stress. The student who thinks he or she is experiencing an undue amount of anxiety should observe other students for signs of anxiety. When many students perceive a test situation as threatening, the test may be too hard, too much emphasis may be placed on its outcome, or both. In such cases students may need to discuss the problem with their instructor. If anxiety is not widespread, the student may need to search for individual causes that are reality-based. One may need to spend more time in study or to develop more efficient study habits, for example.

Threat-Produced Anxiety. Students whose perception of potential danger and negative consequences is incongruous with objective reality (who feel threatened when the situation does not justify it) need to develop a coping strategy to deal with their high levels of anxiety. One might begin by taking Spielberger's Test Anxiety Inventory to determine whether the high anxiety results mainly from emotional or cognitive factors or both. For anxiety caused by emotional factors, research has demonstrated the effectiveness of relaxation training and systematic desensitization. If the difficulty is a result of cognitive factors (worry), the student could begin by identifying negative thoughts that occur in test situations and substituting positive self-talk, which should serve as a cue for more adaptive behaviors. A plan based on Meichenbaum's cognitive/behavioral model should be helpful in alleviating the worry component of anxiety.

Controlling Dating Anxiety

Many young people experience anxiety in the presence of members of the opposite sex, especially in dating situations. Since our society provides little preparation for appropriate dating behavior, anxiety experienced by people in dating situations is understandable. Most people learn dating skills in a haphazard, unsystematic way, with the result that they have little knowledge and are confused about what to do. It is customary for the male to initiate contact with the female in our society. For that reason, we will examine some of the problems experienced by the male trying to initiate conversation with a female.

Shmurak has developed a program for helping males overcome dating anxiety using Meichenbaum's "self-talk" procedure. Shmurak thought that most males, particularly at the college level, have adequate dating skills but that anxiety interferes

255

Improving conversation skills can sometimes help individuals overcome dating anxiety. (Peter Vandermark/Stock, Boston.)

with effective dating behavior and enjoyment. He assumed that dating anxiety can be reduced by learning to generate positive rather than negative thoughts.

In one study, Shmurak (1974) presented male subjects with taped scenarios in which a male model verbalized what he would be saying to himself in a dating situation. This self-talk began negatively and then switched to positive self-talk, which was positively reinforced. Below are two situations in which positive self-talk was encouraged.

Situation A. Let's suppose you've been fixed up on a blind date. You've taken her to a movie and then for some coffee afterwards. Now she begins to talk about a political candidate, some man you've never heard of; she says "What do you think of him?" You say to yourself "She's got me now. I'd better impress her or she'll put me down. I hate politics anyway, so this girl is obviously not my type" (*Negative self talk*). "Boy, that's really jumping to conclusions. This is only one area, and it really doesn't show what type of person she is. Anyway, what's the point of making up stuff about somebody I never heard of? She'll see right through me if I lie. It's not such a big deal to admit I don't know something. There are probably lots of things I know that she doesn't" (*Positive self-talk*). (*Self-talk reinforcement*): "Yeah, that's a better way to think about it. She's just human, trying to discuss something intelligently. I don't have to get scared or put off by her. I'll admit I don't know anything about this candidate, and we'll talk about something I'm more comfortable talking about."

Situation B. You have enjoyed your date with this girl and would like to ask her out for the next weekend. Now you are walking her home, there is a silence, and you decide this is the perfect time to ask her. Your self-talk might be "These silences really get to me. I really want to ask her out, but what if she says no? Boy, that would really be unbearable" (*Negative self-talk*). "Yeah, but it's better than missing my chance. I wonder what she's thinking. Maybe she *wants* to see me again and is just *waiting* for me to ask her out. I *did* have a great time tonight, so maybe she did too. I'll just have to plunge ahead" (*Positive self-talk*). (*Self-talk reinforcement*): "That's it. It's so much better to take the bull by the horns than to do nothing and worry about what will happen."

These examples should help you develop greater awareness of your negative thoughts in social situations and to substitute positive thoughts, which should result in improved conversation skills.

EXERCISE 10-1. ANXIETY AND THE DATING SITUATION

Here are some hypothetical situations similar to those frequently encountered on a date. Please select the response that you would consider the best one after reading our discussion on positive self-talk.

1. This is your first date with Margaret, and the two of you are just leaving a movie. Because it is still quite early in the evening, you ask her what she would like to do next. She answers "I don't know. It's up to you." You say:
   a. We'll get a pizza.
   b. No, it's up to you.
   c. How about a pizza?
   d. It doesn't matter to me.
2. You're having lunch with Jane, a girl you don't know very well. Over lunch you've been talking politics. But every time you express an opinion, she contradicts you. Now you tell her you'd like to see Smith win the election, and she says "You're crazy." You say:
   a. I'm not half as crazy as you.
   b. You really feel strongly about it, don't you?
   c. I believe that I know more about politics than you do.
   d. I see we can't agree on politics. Let's talk about something else.
3. You've been fixed up on a blind date. You've taken the girl to a movie and then for some coffee afterward. Now she begins to talk about a political candidate, some man you've never heard of; she asks "What do you think of him?" You say:

257

a. Gee, I don't know; I'm not familiar with him. Can you tell me more about him?

b. Well, he's OK. But I really prefer Joe Johnson.

c. I never heard of the man. He must not be a very popular candidate.

d. I am not very interested in politics—or politicians, for that matter. You can't believe any of them.

4. You ask a girl to dance and she accepts. You've just succeeded in getting a good conversation going with this girl, when the music stops. You want to continue talking with her. Now, as she begins to walk away, she says "Thank you very much for the dance." You say:

a. You're welcome.

b. We're just getting to know each other. You can't leave now.

c. What are you doing after the dance?

d. Sure, I enjoyed it too. How about the next dance?

5. You're out for a big night with a person you've been dating for some time. Your date seems bored and won't tell you what's the matter when you ask. The situation gets more and more unpleasant, and you decide you must do something. You say:

a. If you don't tell me what's wrong, I'll take you home.

b. You're no fun when you get moody.

c. You seem kind of down tonight. Would you like me to take you home, and we'll talk tomorrow?

d. You are spoiling what should have been a very special evening for me.

The best responses are: 1, c; 2, b; 3, a; 4, d; 5, c. If you chose a less desirable alternative than the one indicated as "best," please review that item and see whether you can determine why your choice is less desirable. It will be helpful if you seek to determine what is implied by each response.

EXERCISE 10-2. IDENTIFYING SELF-TALK OUTCOMES

A. Try to remember some of your thinking on a first date. Do you find evidence of negative self-talk? Did you try to follow negative self-talk with positive self-talk? Did you find that such positive self-talk was reinforced?

B. Think of other real-life situations in which you might have used more positive self-talk and self-talk reinforcement. Would such thinking have led to different and possibly better consequences?

Dating enjoyment can be increased and anxiety reduced by learning to converse with one's date in a manner that is not defensive, arrogant, or domineering. Dialogue should be designed to make your partner feel at ease and show that you are concerned about her feelings and interests.

Managing Anger More Effectively

In certain provoking situations many people are rendered virtually helpless by their inability to express anger appropriately. Violence, vandalism, destruction, and homicides are most often the result of unsuccessful management of anger. Excessive inhibition of anger can also have very undesirable results. In this section we will discuss the nature and functions of anger and provide some suggestions for managing it more effectively.

EXERCISE 10-3. HOW ANGER-PRONE ARE YOU?

At this point, you might assess your need for anger management. Read the two situations described below. Read each very carefully and try to imagine yourself actually in that situation. After each scenario are four alternative courses of action that could be taken. Decide which one you would most like to take.

Situation A. In a grocery store, the checkout lines are long and the cashiers are slow in getting the customers through. Finally, you get through the line and pick up your groceries, and as you are carrying them to the door, someone comes rushing past you, knocking a bag of groceries from your arm. You turn to look at him, but he keeps right on going without stopping to apologize. Which of the following courses of action would you consider?
a. I would like to run after the person, grab him, and possibly hit or kick him.
b. I would like to shout at and possibly curse him.
c. I would stay composed, keep cool, and pick up the bag of groceries.
d. I would pick up the groceries but feel angry with myself because I did not say or do something to him.

Situation B. You have bought a pair of slacks that were on sale at a newly opened clothing store, and you discover that they have a hole in them that you didn't notice when you bought them. The next day you take the slacks back to the store, hoping to exchange them for a pair that isn't defective. You enter the store holding the pants along with your receipt, but it takes a while before someone comes to wait on you. Finally a salesperson comes along, and you explain that the slacks have a hole in them and you would like to exchange them for another pair. The following dialogue then occurs:

Salesperson: That's ridiculous! We don't sell defective merchandise.
You: Well, they were like that when I got them.
Salesperson: Then what did you buy them for?
You: Because I didn't know they had a hole in them.
Salesperson: Don't you look at what you're buying. For all we know, you could have put that hole in them yourself. You know, some people try this sort of thing all the time. It's very difficult for me to believe they were like this when you got them,

259

and besides, it's the company's policy not to take back any merchandise that was purchased on sale. Now, I'm just doing what I'm told to do.

You: May I speak to the manager?

Salesperson: The manager is out of town. This is *my* department, so I'm the one you'll have to talk to.

Which of the following courses of action would you consider?

a. I would like to throw the slacks at the salesperson and either hit or kick him.

b. I would want to tell the person off, start an argument, and demand my money back.

c. I would keep my composure, be constructive, and try to understand and analyze the situation.

d. I would withdraw and get angry with myself for not having been more assertive.

Now that you have decided what you would most like to do in these situations, compare your choices with those of a sample of 90 college students. Their choices are presented below.

Course of Action

	a	b	c	d
Situation A	6%	39%	13%	42%
Situation B	3%	48%	29%	20%

As you can see, about half these students in each case said they would most like to engage in some aggressive behavior—*a* or *b*. This finding suggests that a significant portion of this sample does have a potential problem of anger management. It is also worthy of note that a considerable percentage of these students chose *d* in each case, suggesting that they would internalize rather than externalize their anger. Since internalized anger may result in displaced aggression or self-destructive behavior, this course of action is also indicative of a need for anger management.

EXERCISE 10-4. DETERMINING THE DEGREE OF YOUR ANGER PROBLEM

Novaco (1975) has developed an anger inventory, which he has used in assessing anger-proneness. A truncated version of that inventory is presented for helping you determine the degree of your potential problem of anger control. Listed are situations that can cause some people to become provoked. Try to imagine each incident actually happening to you, and then indicate on a sheet of paper the extent to which it would make you angry, using a number from 1 through 5; a 1 indicates that the incident described would produce little or no anger, and a 5 indicates an extreme amount of anger. Numbers 2, 3, and 4 indicate degrees of anger between the two extremes.

1. On your way to go somewhere, you discover that you have lost the keys to your car.
2. Being overcharged by a repairman who has you over a barrel.
3. Being called a liar.
4. Someone borrows your car, consumes one third of a tank of gas, and doesn't replace it or compensate you for it.
5. You are waiting to be served at a restaurant. Fifteen minutes have gone by, and you still haven't even received a glass of water.
6. Watching someone bully a person who is physically smaller than he is.
7. Professors who refuse to listen to your point of view.
8. Being stood up for a date.
9. You are driving along at 45 mph, and the guy behind you is right on your bumper.
10. People asking personal questions of you just for their own curiosity.
11. Working hard on a project and getting a poor grade.
12. You accidentally make the wrong kind of turn in a parking lot. As you get out of your car, someone yells at you "Where did you learn to drive?"
13. You are trying to concentrate, and a person near you is tapping his foot.
14. Someone else's dog routinely defecating in your yard.
15. Banging your shins against a piece of furniture.
16. Being forced to do something you don't want to do.
17. Hearing that a very wealthy man has paid zero income tax.
18. You are involved in watching a TV program, and someone comes along and switches the channel.
19. Stepping on a gob of chewing gum.
20. Someone making fun of the clothes you are wearing.
21. You are in a theater ticket line, and someone cuts in front of you.
22. You use your last coin to make a phone call, and you are disconnected before you finish dialing.
23. You are at a shopping center, and two evangelistic persons stop you and want to convert you to their religious ideas.
24. Discovering that you were deliberately sold defective merchandise.
25. Being talked about behind your back.

By adding the numbers you have written down, you obtain a measure of anger-proneness. Scores may range from a low of 25 to a high of 125. A higher score indicates more anger-proneness.

We administered this inventory to a group of college students. Males averaged 79, females 83. The situations that made males feel most angry were those described in items 2, 6, 22, and 24. Those that made females feel most angry were items 2, 3, 6, 7, 11, 16, 18, 24, and 25.

Adaptive and Maladaptive Behavior. Anger arousal, though often resulting in destructive acts of aggression, has adaptive as well as maladaptive functions. In challenging and competitive situations anger allows us to act with increased vigor; it

Learning to manage those everyday irritating situations should be an important objective of anger management. (Photo © Richard Kalvar/Magnum.)

energizes behavior. When the level of anger arousal goes beyond a certain point, however, the attentional processes are distracted, and impulsive reactions interfere with task performance. In the sport of boxing, for example, anger arousal may enable a combatant to respond with increased vigor and strength, but it may also cause him to disregard his fight strategy, throw caution to the winds, and either become overly exhausted or get knocked out by his opponent. When this happens, anger *disrupts* effective behavior. People who learn to cope with anger are able to reduce its disruptive and disorganizing effects, thereby improving their personal effectiveness by remaining composed in irritating situations.

Anger is a way of communicating our feelings to others; in this sense it plays a positive role by enabling us to give others feedback about how their behavior is affecting us. It serves an *expressive* function. Problems may arise, however, depending on the mode of anger expression, or what is done when anger is experienced. People often need help in learning to express negative feelings in constructive and socially acceptable ways so that their behavior does not merely escalate a sequence of antagonism. As Novaco (1975) reminds us, the aim of anger-management strategies is not to eliminate anger but to develop competence in regulating it.

262

Anger can also serve a *defensive* function as an antidote to anxiety. Many people prefer to be perceived as angry rather than as anxious and apprehensive. If one labels one's state of arousal as "anger" rather than "anxiety," one is more likely to experience a sense of control or mastery of the situation. "If we think of hitting someone, or even killing someone, we feel far more powerful and in control of a situation than if we think of fleeing or doing nothing" (Rothenberg, 1971, p. 459). This reaction enables one to focus on something external to oneself. When anger is used to preempt anxiety in the face of an ego threat, coping strategies that enable one to interpret provocations in ways that are not ego-threatening should reduce anger arousal.

People can be trained to use anger for an additional function as a *discriminative cue*. When one develops an awareness of anger arousal, the experience of anger can be the cue to initiate one's coping strategy.

Some Principles for Managing Anger.
One objective of anger management is to learn to cope with anger-producing provocations. To accomplish this, one must learn to interpret a provocation in ways that are not ego-threatening and to become more aware of one's arousal state so that this cue can become the signal for one's coping strategy. Following are some principles derived from Novaco's (1975) propositions for anger management and from his research.

Becoming angry often has something to do with self-doubt, being unsure, or feeling threatened by someone else. It is always important to remember that you have many good qualities and that you are a worthy person. Sometimes we get angry because we take things too personally when there is no need to. Even when someone is being personally offensive and insulting, we can control and contain our anger by remaining task-oriented rather than letting that person cause us to lose our composure. Always remember that the most important thing to do in such situations is to stay focused on the issue and stick to what must be done to get the outcome you want. When you begin taking insults personally, you get distracted from your task and get caught up in unnecessary combat. Don't let yourself get sidetracked and get baited into a quarrel. Although you are aware of what the other person is doing as a provocation, stay task-oriented and issue-focused.

We sometimes get angry simply because it is the one thing we have always done in a certain kind of situation. Learning to react to provocations in alternative ways not involving anger will decrease the probability of anger.

One of the most important things we can do to control our anger is to recognize the signs of arousal as soon as they occur. As we become more and more sharply tuned to the signs of tension and emotional arousal, we will achieve greater ability to short-circuit the anger process. Heightened anger makes us agitated and impulsive. When we learn to relax, our ability to regulate anger improves.

Our anger can serve a useful function of alerting us that we are becoming upset and that effective action is called for if a positive outcome is to result. Use anger to work to your advantage. Remember, getting angry makes you agitated and

263

impulsive—and impulsive, antagonistic acts get you into trouble. Stay task-oriented and instruct yourself.

Sometimes we get angry because things look as if they are getting out of hand and we want to take charge. We may be afraid that things will not go the way we want them, and so we get angry to try to control them. When we instruct ourselves and manage our anger, we are likely to deal with the situation more effectively. The best way to take charge of a situation can be not to get angry when most people would expect or even want you to be upset.

As we learn to break down provocation experiences into chunks, or stages, we will have a better handle on things, which is another way of putting ourselves on top of the situation. We can also learn how to instruct ourselves in ways that correspond to these stages.

Learning Activities for Anger Management. On the basis of research presented in this chapter, we have developed some activities that a person with anger problems should find helpful. We recommend that you get an index card and describe in detail some of the situations in which you have trouble with temper control. As accurately as you can, recall the dialogue that occurred between you and the other person or persons involved. Either by yourself or with the help of another person or persons, examine what happened in these situations. What kind of mood were you in when the trouble started? What cue, such as profanity, yelling insults, or threats, seemed to elicit anger within you? What factors seemed to increase the antagonism and hostility? What could have been done to reduce tension and ameliorate the antagonism?

Analyze your responses in these situations to see how they could be improved. In addition to overt responses, try to identify your thoughts, or self-verbalizations, that were also occurring. Analyze these self-statements: what effect did they have on your perception of the situation, the other person, and your verbal responses? Make a list of self-statements that are less defensive and hostile and can be substituted for your previous self-statements.

From your list of situations that make you angry, have someone role-play the provocation scenes with you. First reconstruct some scene as carefully as you can, with you playing yourself and your friend playing the parts of others involved. If possible, record these role-played situations and listen to yourself as you interact with others. By now you should be able to identify several factors that caused you to become angry.

Role-play the same situation again, but this time keep in mind everything you have learned about anger control. Practice your new list of self-statements instead of those you previously experienced. Tell yourself to stay task-relevant, remember that you are a worthy person, do not take insults personally, and so on. See if you are feeling less angry now than before. Listen to the recording of the revised role-played interaction and concentrate on differences between the ways you responded to the situation in the two role-playing sessions. Congratulate yourself when you have achieved a greater degree of anger control.

264

In additional role-played scenes you may want to get involved in more intense situations and increase your competence in coping with them. Be sure to practice what you have learned in the next situation in which you are inclined to experience anger. Your feelings of success that result from your newly acquired coping skills should be sufficient reinforcement to help you maintain greater control of your anger problem.

SUMMARY

Many factors in our daily experience tend to make us feel anxious and sometimes angry. Since we cannot eliminate all of life's stresses, we need to learn how to cope more effectively with these emotion-arousing situations. Cognitive control procedures for emotional control are currently being developed and refined. Meichenbaum, one of the forerunners in development of cognitive/behavioral control techniques, operates on the assumption that thoughts precede overt behaviors and that by changing our thoughts we produce behavioral changes.

Spielberger's research on emotional control has been directed mainly toward the concept of anxiety. Spielberger distinguishes between trait anxiety (a personality characteristic) and state anxiety (a transitory emotional state). He has identified two components of anxiety, cognitive and emotional. Cognitive strategies, such as those of Meichenbaum, seem to be more effective in reducing the cognitive component; behavioristic techniques, such as systematic desensitization, are more effective with the emotional component. Spielberger is particularly interested in finding ways to reduce test anxiety.

Novaco has developed a cognitive strategy for anger management. This strategy is based on the assumption that people are less likely to become provoked and lose emotional control if they remain task-oriented, have high self-esteem, have developed coping skills, and perceive themselves to be in control of the situation. He is concerned mainly with helping people learn to cognitively restructure a potentially anger-arousing situation so that it is perceived as less threatening. Cognitive restructuring is accomplished by teaching people to emit positive rather than negative self-statements. Shmurak uses a similar strategy for dating anxiety.

The strategies of Meichenbaum, Spielberger, and Novaco yield some suggestions for managing anxiety and anger. For example, positive self-talk is recommended for both problems.

KEY CONCEPTS

Anxiety the reaction to any circumstance that threatens one's sense of well-being.

Cognitive control modifying behavior by learning to change our thoughts (self-talk).

Relaxation training instruction and practice in systematically tensing and relaxing the various muscle groups of the body.

State anxiety a transitory state of anxiety resulting from situational factors.

Stress a property of situations that are characterized by objective physical or psychological danger.

Systematic desensitization a process using classical-conditioning techniques to eliminate or reduce fear and anxiety.

Threat one's perception of a situation as dangerous.

Trait anxiety chronic anxiety as a relatively stable personality characteristic.

11

CHAPTER OBJECTIVES

1. To understand the three basic processes involved in memory.
2. To identify and describe some mnemonic devices.
3. To use mnemonic devices for memory improvement.
4. To become familiar with some research on the use of mnemonic devices.
5. To know how to reduce interference between learning tasks.
6. To understand insight learning.
7. To use a master planning schedule for better time management.
8. To learn to set priorities for tasks to be accomplished.
9. To list the six steps in the time-management program described in this chapter.

USING
MEMORY AND
TIME MORE
EFFICIENTLY

Our behavior is the vehicle through which we express our feelings and thoughts and ultimately achieve our life goals. To the extent that we can learn effective management of our behavior, we can realize our goals more readily and achieve greater self-satisfaction. This chapter will look at how goals and personal satisfaction can be attained through more efficient use of memory and time.

IMPROVING OUR USE OF MEMORY

Effectiveness in everyday living, whether it be in work or play, depends to some extent on our ability to remember instructions, directions, schedules, appointments, names, special events, and so on. Forgetting can result in lowered efficiency, embarrassment, and even occasional danger to ourselves and others. The ability to remember information is not fixed. As a matter of fact, people never achieve their full

Efficient living depends on efficient memory. (Photo © Ken Heyman.)

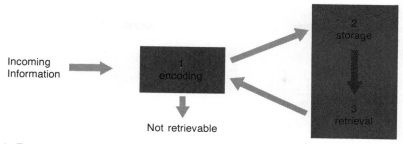

Figure 11-1. *Three processes in memory.*

memory potential. Therefore, we all can benefit from a more complete understanding of the memory process. The purpose of this section of the chapter will be to provide you with some principles and suggestions for understanding and improving memory. It will include a discussion of how memory works. The techniques discussed in this chapter apply only to words and numbers or other material that can be reduced to words or numbers. Cermak's book (1976) *Improving Your Memory* contains a more complete discussion of this topic.

In the simplest of terms, memory may be viewed as consisting of three processes. These processes are encoding, storage, and retrieval (see Figure 11-1).

Encoding

Encoding refers to what we attend to in a given situation and how it is organized in preparation for memory storage. Many problems of retention can be traced to a faulty encoding process. One of the prerequisites for efficient memory is that the individual must focus attention on the information. Since people cannot respond appropriately to large amounts of incoming information at one time, they must be able to screen out the relevant from the less relevant information.

Have you ever been introduced to a stranger at a party but found that the loud music or other distractions prevented you from adequately processing his or her name? A cardinal rule during an introduction to another person is that we must explicitly attend to and register the name clearly as it is presented. Too often we fail to attend to someone's name because we are distracted with the related tasks of smiling, shaking hands, initiating a conversation, or anticipating the next person to be met. Any stimulus not noticed or not isolated from competing stimuli will not be easily recalled. To prevent this, one must make a conscious effort to screen out other information and briefly rehearse the information one has attended to. This should serve as a beginning.

We might use the analogy of a filing system to understand how the memory process works. A file clerk may have filed information in several cabinets. Each cabinet may have several drawers containing many separately labeled folders. When new material must be filed, the clerk must put it in the appropriate slot in the

271

Remembering a stranger's name is often difficult to do because we are attending to other distracting stimuli. (Photo © Ellis Herwig/Stock, Boston.)

appropriate drawer. Customer complaints may be put in one file, personnel records in another, and unpaid bills in yet another. The file label indicates the storage category and serves as a cue for retrieval. The encoding process operates in much the same way. Incoming information must be encoded (labeled) in such a way that it is filed appropriately in memory storage and can be quickly located and retrieved from storage.

Suppose, for example, that you are given two lists of words to memorize.

List A: skyscraper, cathedral, gymnasium
List B: priest, cathedral, sermon

The common word in Lists A and B is *cathedral.* In List A, *cathedral* is likely to be labeled and categorized as a type of building. The classification concept of "building" would help you remember *cathedral* in the future. The words in List B could be associated with "worship" or "religion," and either of those labels would help you remember not only *cathedral* but the other words in the list. This process, in which an abstract category label helps one recall items within that category, is called *mediation.* The point is that the way in which material is organized, or encoded, affects the kinds of associations that will help us remember it.

Chunking and *clustering* are terms psychologists use to describe how information may be organized and placed into memory storage. These processes occur when several items are grouped together and then rehearsed as a single unit of material. It was once thought that our memory could store only a given amount of information; the more information one already had, the harder it was to pack in any more. It seems more likely, however, that the more information there is in memory storage, the easier it is to add new information.

Now look at the serial list of words in Table 11-1. After reading through this list once, check how many words you can remember. Now read the list again and see if you can place the words into categories. You will note that each item refers to an animal, a vegetable, or a profession. If these are placed into three separate categories, they should be more easily remembered. When you think of "profession," the words *teacher, doctor, lawyer,* and *minister* should come to mind. The mediational category "profession" helps you recall these items.

Table 11-1. Serial Word List

cow
pea
corn
teacher
horse
doctor
lawyer
lettuce
celery
minister
dog
cat

Sometimes information easily lends itself to internal mediational organization, as in the previous example. With some information, however, such as lists of unrelated words, mediational organization may be more difficult. Some form of external organization of the list is required. In such cases **mnemonic devices** can be helpful. Mnemonic memory is based on having an organizational plan even before seeing the material to be learned. The rule "*i* before *e* except after *c*" is a simple mnemonic device that we have learned to help us remember when to use *ie* and *ei* in spelling. Another mnemonic device is the way many of us have learned the number of days in any month. We simply recite "Thirty days hath September, April, June, and November."

Pegword Method. A simple mnemonic plan for organizing unrelated items is called the **pegword method.** It is a form of mediational learning composed of two separate steps. The first step is to associate certain words, which serve as "pegs" for further associations, with numbers. The poem below gives examples of pegwords associated with the numbers 1 through 10.

One is a bun,
Two is a shoe,
Three is a tree,
Four is a door,
Five is a hive,
Six is sticks,
Seven is heaven,
Eight is a gate,
Nine is a lion,
Ten is a hen.

The associations made in this step form the framework of this mnemonic device. The number/pegword associations should be highly overlearned until they come to your mind automatically. Practice the poem until you can recite it without error. You should be able to after a few trials. It is important that you form a clear mental image of each pegword, because the image will serve as a cue for other associations. Now see whether you can associate each pegword with its number. We will take them out of order. What is associated with the number 3? What is 8? 5?

The second step is to attach the items to be recalled to number/pegword associations. Suppose that you wish to remember the following list of unrelated words: *marble, chewing gum, radio, briefcase, wallet, dish, bouquet, paint, salt, overcoat.* The use of rote memory in the recall of these ten words would require several trials, and the list would probably be quickly forgotten. With the pegword method you should remember the list after one or two trials and for a considerable period of time. From the list of number/pegword associations contained in the poem above, you will recall that 1 is a bun. You might imagine a bun baked so hard that a marble bounces off it. Since 2 is a shoe, you could imagine yourself walking into the classroom and stepping on a large wad of gum. Three could be an image of a radio hanging from a tree, spreading music about a neighborhood. Four could be an image of a briefcase hanging on an office door. *Wallet,* the fifth word, should be easily remembered if you imagine trying to retrieve a wallet from a hive of bees without getting stung.

Now make mental images of each of the remaining words in the list interacting with the corresponding pegword in some way. Any image can be used, but try to make it as clear and detailed as possible. The more unusual or idiosyncratic the image, the easier it usually is to recall.

The number/pegword associations are used as cues for recall of the word list. Recall each association in order, along with the mental image of the interaction between it and the item to be recalled. Figure 11-2 contains pictorial illustrations of associations used in our examples.

In recalling the list of words, begin with 1, think of bun, then of a marble bouncing off a hard bun. Then think 2, shoe, chewing gum on shoe. You can now probably recall all ten words in the list. Try it.

This method facilitates memory for lists of up to ten unrelated items because it is easier to make up a mental image of an item interacting with the pegword, which

1	is a bun		marble	
2	is a shoe		chewing gum	
3	is a tree		radio	
4	is a door		briefcase	
5	is a hive		wallet	
6	is sticks		dish	
7	is heaven		bouquet	
8	is a gate		paint	
9	is a lion		salt	
10	is a hen		overcoat	

Figure 11-2. *Images of items to be recalled interacting with pegwords.*

is the name of a concrete object, than it is to imagine some item interacting with only the number, which is harder to incorporate into a mental image. A particular advantage of this method is that it makes it easier to recall the list in reverse as well as forward order and to maintain the exact position in the list of each item to be recalled. Try it. You should be able to go backward as well as forward. You should also be able to associate any word with the corresponding number, and vice versa. If asked to recall the sixth word, you should immediately remember *dish,* and when given the word *radio,* you should recall that it is item number 3. When you want to recall a different list of words, use the same number/pegword associations but form new mental images of the new list interacting in some way with your prior set of pegwords. The number/pegword associations remain constant for all lists.

Method of Loci. A similar mnemonic device is the **method of loci,** commonly called the "house method." In the method of loci you relate information to be learned to familiar locations throughout your house that have been attached to numbers in the same way as were the pegwords in the prior example. This method is preferable when lists contain more than ten items. With the pegword method it becomes harder to make the pegword rhyme with numbers greater than 10. With the house method this poses no problem, since numbers are associated with locations in the house rather than with rhyming words. With that exception the principles and steps involved in the house method are identical to those of the pegword method.

According to Bower (1973), Cicero referred to such a method as he related a story about a man named Simonicles. While attending a large banquet, Simonicles was called outside. During his absence the building collapsed, killing all inside and mangling their bodies beyond recognition. Simonicles, however, was able to identify each corpse by recalling where each person had been sitting at the banquet table before the tragedy. He was able to do this by mentally associating each victim's name with his location at the banquet table. Hence the name *method of loci; loci* means "locations."

To use the method of loci, walk through your house or some other familiar place and assign numbers to particular locations. For example, the front door to your house might be Location 1. Location 2 might be the table in the hallway, 3 the couch, 4 the TV, 5 the coffee table, 6 the mirror. As perhaps you enter the kitchen, the stove would become 7, the refrigerator 8, and so on. The number of stations you generate is limited only by the length of your mental path and the number of items identified along the way. If you exhaust all household objects, simply leave the house and visualize objects and locations in your yard or neighborhood. Initially, you should begin with not more than 20 or 25 locations. When you are more proficient in using the method of loci, you can gradually increase the number of locations. Within just a week a student of one of the authors was able to recall 100 words without error using this method. It is of critical importance that the ordering of locations be highly overlearned. Once this mental path of locations can be readily reconstructed, surprisingly large amounts of information can be stored in memory. Table 11-2 presents an example for you to consider.

Table 11-2. Using the House Method (Method of Loci) of Recall

Position	Location	Item to be recalled
1	front door	key
2	hallway table	orange
3	couch	letter
4	TV	package
5	coffee table	syrup
6	mirror	snow
7	stove	hair
8	refrigerator	football
9	sink	shirt
10	oven	pencil
11	dining table	spinach
12	cabinet	teddy bear
13	clock	wreath
14	bathtub	mud
15	commode	cat
16	bed	lion
17	dresser	smoke
18	nightstand	perfume
19	rug	bread
20	closet	water

As in the pegword method, the number/location associations serve as cues for word lists to be recalled. It may be helpful if you picture the object in some unusual or exaggerated position or "doing something interesting" at the location where it is placed. You might visualize a large key in the front door, an orange tree growing out of the hallway table, a letter from a loved one on the couch, a giant crate serving as a package enclosing the TV, syrup spilled on the coffee table, and so on. With practice you will find that you can recall your word list forward or backward. You will also be able to match any number picked at random with the corresponding item, and vice versa.

Bower (1973) cites evidence that subjects using the method of loci are able to recall two to four times as much material as subjects using traditional rote-memory techniques. In one of Bower's investigations he and a colleague had college students study five successive "shopping lists" of 20 items each. They were allowed 5 seconds to study each word. (For best results you should allow yourself considerably more time.) They tried to recall each list individually, and at the end of the session they tried to recall all five lists, a total of 100 words. Students using the method of loci recalled an average of 72 items; those using rote memory recalled only 28 items. Those using the mnemonic system were also much better at keeping the items in the correct position and the correct list.

Remembering Numbers. Pegword systems are of little value in learning such numbers as license plates, Social Security numbers, and telephone numbers. A system that is particularly helpful with numbers is a *number-to-sound* coding system. You assign a consonant of the alphabet to each number 0 through 9 and then form

277

number/consonant associations in the same manner as number/pegword and number/ location associations. For example, you can use the following code:

0—b	5—h
1—c	6—s
2—n	7—k
3—v	8—l
4—r	9—t

Next, you insert vowels between the consonants to make a word. To recall a series of numbers, you think of the word, pick out the consonants in order, and substitute the corresponding numbers. If you want to remember that an important meeting is being held in Room 234, for example, you would substitute the letters *nvr*. By adding the vowel *e* between the consonants, you have the word *never*. You are "never" to forget that the meeting is in Room 234. The telephone number 929-4986 would become *tntrtls*. By adding appropriate vowels, we have TEN TURTLES. When deciphered according to our code, the consonants become 929-4986. TEN TURTLES is much easier to recall than the phone number itself. For some phone numbers, it may be easier to make something memorable using the letters on the dial. A nearsighted woman had the number 526-5393. A friend noticed that the number became LANK EYE. Nearsighted people have long eyeballs, so this person never had to look up her nearsighted friend's number again.

Very long numbers can be broken up into a series of words to make a phrase. As with any other skill, the code needs to be rehearsed if it is to be effective. Once the code has been learned, it takes little time and effort, less than we ordinarily spend in trying to remember, copying, or looking up important numbers.

Storage

The **storage** phase of memory is "the phase between acquisition and retrieval" (Wickelgren, 1977, p. 363). Storage processes are of two kinds: constructive processes and destructive processes. Constructive storage processes include conscious rehearsal and other, largely unconscious processes that facilitate memory; destructive processes include interference that leads to memory decay. In the following pages, we will suggest some ways that interference and decay can be reduced and memory retention facilitated.

Interference in Learning. In our discussion of the pegword system you learned ten number/pegword associations and used them to memorize ten words, which you may still recall. Suppose you are now given a second list of words, shown in Table 11-3. You will probably find this list somewhat harder to remember because the items in the previous list keep getting in the way. For example, when you think of bun, you remember *marble* instead of *clock*. This kind of interference, in which prior learning hinders later learning, is called **proactive inhibition** and can occur with manual skills as well as cognitive material. Figure 11-3 shows the research design for studying proactive inhibition. Laboratory experiments to determine how prior learning interferes with new learning necessitate two groups: an experimental group and a control group. The experimental group, having learned the first list of words (Task A), would probably find it harder to learn the second list (Task B) than the control group.

Table 11-3. An Example of Interference in Learning when Two Lists Are Attached to the Same Pegwords

Number	Pegword	List I	List II
1	bun	marble	clock
2	shoe	chewing gum	leaf
3	tree	radio	automobile
4	door	briefcase	smoke detector
5	hive	wallet	gasoline
6	sticks	dish	potato
7	heaven	bouquet	butterfly
8	gate	paint	shirt
9	lion	salt	hospital
10	hen	overcoat	garbage can

Figure 11-3. Research Design for Studying Proactive Inhibition

Experimental group	Learn Task A	Learn Task B
Control group	Rest	Learn Task B

Real life provides many examples of proactive inhibition. The United States is replacing our traditional system of measurement with the metric system. People who have grown up with the present system will have more difficulty making the transition to the metric system than those who are trained early in the metric system. A lifetime of experience with the familiar system will be hard to overcome. Americans, who drive on the right side of the road, face a formidable task when driving in England. They must adjust to driving on the left side of the road and using a steering wheel on the right side of the car. If the gearshift is in the floorboard of the car, it must be operated with the left hand. The driver must be extremely cautious when making a right turn lest he or she cut across into incoming traffic. Even pedestrians, when crossing the street, must look to the right instead of the left to avoid blindly stepping into the path of an unnoticed vehicle. People who learn new languages or try to count money in a foreign currency must also confront the problem of proactive inhibition.

When two lists of words—or two related tasks of any kind, for that matter—are learned, both may be harder to recall. In verbal-learning tasks, the first

279

Americans, who drive on the right side of the road, find that such learning interferes with driving on the left side of the road in England. (Photo © Erich Hartmann/Magnum.)

list can be harder to recall than the second list. When new learning interferes with the retention of old learning, we say that **retroactive inhibition** has occurred. Figure 11-4 presents the experimental design for testing retroactive inhibition.

Figure 11-4. Research Design for Studying Retroactive Inhibition

Experimental group	Learn Task A	Learn Task B	Recall Task A
Control group	Learn Task A	Rest	Recall Task A

As you recall the ten pegwords presented above, along with the two lists of items to be associated with them, you should begin to understand some of the difficulty in remembering List I. When you think of the pegword *bun*, you may wonder whether the item in the first list was *marble* or *clock*. For *shoe* you may not recall whether your association was *leaf* or *chewing gum*. At this point you may want to see how many of the items in List I you can recall. If some of the words in that list are hard to recall, you have probably experienced retroactive inhibition.

280

Reducing Interference in Learning and Retention. It is frequently advantageous to retain several lists of words simultaneously, including grocery lists, schedules, appointments, important events, and lists of daily activities. What can be done to prevent proactive or retroactive inhibition among the various lists of items? If you need to recall several lists, the method of loci is preferable to the pegword method because it more easily lends itself to very long lists or multiple lists of words. The first step is to assign numbers to at least 50 locations in your house and form number/location associations for each of the 50 places. Then divide the 50 locations into five categories each containing ten locations. The first ten locations, represented by numbers 1–10, can be reserved for grocery lists, the second set of ten, represented by numbers 11–20, can be reserved for appointments, the third set (numbers 21–30) for daily activities, and so on. This procedure creates separate categories of number/location associations to be used with different kinds of lists and decreases the interference from one list to another.

Another way to reduce interference is to use the method of loci and have several sets of number/location associations. One set could be developed for your house, as we have suggested. Another set of number/location associations can apply to locations at school or work, and yet another to locations on the block where you live. Associations connected with your house can be used for grocery lists, those connected with the place of work can be used for activities or appointments, and those connected with the block where you live can be reserved for important events.

A final suggestion helps when the pegword method is being used to facilitate recall of more than one list of items. To illustrate how interference between lists can be reduced, let us return to Table 11-3, where two lists of items were associated with the same set of pegwords and might interfere with each other. We will now show how inhibition can be reduced or possibly eliminated by an extension of the mediation techniques we have discussed.

Examine the words in Table 11-3. To recall both Lists I and II you might imagine two items interacting in some way with a pegword. For example, you could visualize a marble clock being dropped on a bun, a wad of chewing gum and a leaf stuck to a shoe, a radio from an automobile dangling from a tree, and a briefcase containing information about smoke detectors hanging on the door. Try your own associations for the remaining items in the lists.

Bugelski, Kidd, and Segman (1968) suggest that it is helpful to give yourself enough time to generate a clear mental image of both items interacting with the pegword before proceeding to the items connected with the next pegword. When you have formulated mental images of interactions between each pegword and both items connected to it, you should be able to recall correctly the items in both lists without experiencing the usual interference that occurs when each list is learned independently. In fact, you will probably discover that retention of one list makes it easier to remember the other. From your mental image of the marble clock falling on the *bun*, it is easy to recall that *marble* is the first word in List I and *clock* is first in List II. The image of chewing gum and a leaf stuck to a *shoe* provides sufficient stimulation for you to recall *chewing gum* and *leaf* as the second words in the respective lists. The third

281

word in each list is suggested by the association of the *radio* from an *automobile* dangling from a *tree*. These mental images involving two items interacting with each pegword should improve recall of both lists and increase ability to recall each list in the exact order that it was presented.

When the second list is made easier to recall by having learned the first list, the effect is called **proactive facilitation**; when the second list aids in the recall of items contained in the first list, the effect is called **retroactive facilitation**. In the preceding discussion we have shown how mediation techniques can reduce interference in recall and help the items in one list facilitate recall of the other.

BOX 11-1. LEARNING A FOREIGN LANGUAGE

Laboratory demonstrations of the effectiveness of mnemonics and mental imagery in verbal learning have led to methods of teaching foreign-language vocabulary. Atkinson (1975) has shown how mnemonics can facilitate the learning of both Russian and Spanish. He describes a *keyword method* in which you first pronounce the foreign word and then think of an English keyword that has phonetic similarity. For example, the Spanish word *caballo,* meaning "horse" and pronounced "cob-eye-yo," might be associated with the English keyword *eye.* Then you think of a visual image that relates the keyword *eye* and the English translation "horse" in some way. Atkinson suggests that you might produce a mental image of a horse with one huge eye protruding from the middle of its forehead or a horse kicking someone in the eye. You first think of the English word *horse,* then the keyword *eye,* and then the Spanish word *caballo* ("cob-eye-yo"). Or take the Spanish word for duck, *pato* ("pot-o"). With *pot* as the keyword, one could imagine a duck hiding under a pot with its feet and tail sticking out.

Students using the keyword method for studying Russian-English pairs were able to recall 72% of the foreign words correctly, whereas a control group using rote memory recalled only 46% of the words. Differences between the experimental and control groups were even more striking in the study of Spanish-English word pairs: the keyword method resulted in 88% retention and the rote-memorization method only 28%—an improvement of over 200% for the experimental group. This is a good illustration of how learning principles identified in the laboratory can be applied to a practical learning situation.

Retrieval

In the phase of memory called **retrieval**, the memory trace is brought from storage into awareness. Quite frequently most of us meet someone we know rather well only to find ourselves in the embarrassing situation of not being able to recall the person's name. When we forget something, it does not necessarily mean that the

282

memory is lost. It may well be that situational or mediational cues fail to retrieve the appropriate file in memory storage. Tulving and Thomson (1973, p. 353) put it this way: "What is stored is determined by what is perceived and how it is encoded, and what is stored determines what retrieval cues are effective in providing access to what is stored." As mentioned earlier in this chapter, a former student of one of the authors used the method of loci to recall without error a list of 100 words. The author came to know this student well and invited him on several occasions to demonstrate the use of mnemonic procedures in the classroom. However, when they recently met in a shopping mall and the student tried to introduce the author to his wife, he could not recall the author's name. This was a terribly embarrassing situation for him because he had become widely known in the department as a memory expert. The student's memory problem was mainly one of retrieval. He "knew" the author's name, but he was unable to retrieve it at that instant and in that unfamiliar setting.

The fact that the student saw the author in a very different context (both geographic location and manner of dress) than the one in which they had interacted on previous occasions disrupted his recall. This shows just how important the situational cues can be in memory retrieval. Had this student had more time to scan his memory, he would have been able to recall the name correctly. He could have asked himself "What is unusual or conspicuous about his appearance?" "Where have I seen him before?" Eventually he would have identified the appropriate file cabinet: "He is a teacher at East Tennessee State University." From the correct file cabinet he would have been able to retrieve the appropriate folder, such as the department of psychology and a particular course. At that point there is a good probability that the author's name would have emerged into awareness. A task that would have required only a split second in one setting produces that embarrassing delay in another.

We have literally thousands of memory traces that are activated and retrieved when appropriate cues are present. Old friends who have not seen each other in years tend to reminisce about "old times" when they get together. The sight of the other person, the sound of his or her voice, and mannerisms are sufficient cues for rapid retrieval of dust-covered memories. One of the authors recently returned to his grade school after more than 20 years. As he walked from room to room, he could clearly recall the faces and many names of former students and teachers. He became keenly aware of how efficient one's memory can be when information is well encoded.

Generally, the greater the similarity between cues present at the time of recall and the original learning (that is, the encoding), the easier to retrieve the memory. Students might find, for example, that it is beneficial to study in the classroom where they are to take an examination. The greater the correspondence between the learning and recall situations, the easier the recall.

Cues can also serve to associate memories with past feelings. Merchants and chambers of commerce seem to recognize this. They put up Christmas decorations weeks before Christmas to create an atmosphere that helps us remember to do our Christmas shopping. Such cues serve to remind us that we have only so many shopping days before Christmas. In our minds these same cues elicit feelings of good cheer and a need to spend money.

Photographs serve as reminders of good times experienced in days gone by. Many people regard cameras as necessities at such events as proms, weddings, homecomings, and family reunions. These events are associated with happiness, good health, and pleasant times; photographs help us preserve those memories. Souvenirs gathered from faraway places or famous people serve the same purpose.

Sometimes memories are associated with negative feelings. One who has lost a loved one through death, divorce, or simply a lovers' quarrel may encounter environmental cues that remind one of the person. A widow or widower may find articles of clothing and other reminders that continually elicit memories of the recently deceased spouse. By moving to another residence, he or she may find it easier to begin storing new memories rather than dwelling on past memories.

In summary, we must accept the fact that life requires that we remember many things. It is in our own best interest to acquire learning and retention skills that make this human capability less painful and more efficient. By applying the principles and techniques described above, you may be able to spend less time with the mundane chores of memory and free yourself for more creative thought. Bower (1973) concludes an article with this sobering advice: "We ought to take advantage of what we know about memory, forgetting, and mnemonics, and we ought to do it soon. You are already beginning to forget the material you just read" (p. 70).

BOX 11-2. MASSED PRACTICE VERSUS DISTRIBUTED PRACTICE

When learning is scheduled on a continuous and sustained basis, with a single period of practice extending to complete acquisition of the material, the practice is "massed." When learning takes place over a number of learning periods interspersed with periods of rest or other activity, the practice is "distributed," or "spaced." The father of modern learning psychology, Hermann Ebbinghaus (1885), concluded that distributed practice is more effective for most tasks than massed practice. This conclusion has since been substantiated many times. The advantage of distributed practice is most likely due to the dissipation of fatigue during the rest periods. A schedule of massed practice, having no rest intervals, produces fatigue, which interferes with learning and retention.

Remembering More Complex Material

Psychologists have also been concerned with understanding the principles that make for more efficient learning and memory of complex material. One form of cognitive structuring is that which may lead to creative, or "insightful," thought, in

284

which a person tries to organize thinking in such a way that novel ideas emerge. Let us look at one example of how cognitive restructuring may lead to creative ideas.

A number of years ago, Wolfgang Köhler performed a series of learning experiments with chimpanzees. These learning experiments, unlike the previous ones mentioned, concerned trying to solve a particular problem. Köhler presented chimpanzees with a variety of problems that they could not solve through simple trial-and-error efforts. In one such problem, Köhler presented his most intelligent chimpanzee, Sultan, with a problem involving three sticks of varying lengths. In order to reach a piece of fruit placed outside his cage beyond arm's reach, Sultan had to "perceive" that the shortest stick, which was inside the cage but was too short to reach the fruit, could be used to get the middle-sized stick lying outside the cage. In turn, the middle-sized stick could be used to retrieve the longest stick, also lying outside the cage but further away. Finally, the longest stick could be used to retrieve the fruit. For us this would be a most simple task. And even a 3-year-old child could solve this problem with some effort. However, this turned out to be a very complex task for chimpanzees, even the chimpanzee prodigy Sultan. He, like the other chimpanzees, initially tried to reach the fruit through trial and error. His efforts gave rise to frustration and a series of temper tantrums and self-punitive behavior.

After a number of unsuccessful attempts at reaching the fruit, Sultan's behavior became less aggressive and he assumed a "meditative" posture. It was almost as if one could hear him saying to himself "How in the world am I going to get that fruit?" Then suddenly, after a long pause, Sultan jumped up, grabbed the short stick, and used it to pull in the next stick. He then used the middle-sized stick to get the longest stick, with which he managed to retrieve the long-awaited fruit. Unlike the spastic and impulsive behavior during the trial-and-error efforts, this behavior was characterized by a smooth and coordinated sequence. It looked as though Sultan had been retrieving fruit this way for years. Köhler called this type of learning "insight learning." Insight learning involves perceiving the solution to a problem mentally. Suddenly, one has that "aha" experience in which, as though a light bulb had come on, one has complete understanding of the solution to the problem.

There are some general features of this type of learning. First, insight usually follows from one's actively seeking out relations that might lead to the solution. Learning to solve a problem by insight is generally hard work. However, a second feature of insight learning is that once one solves a problem by way of insight, that learning is hard to forget. Unlike much of our learning, which becomes hard to remember almost immediately after we acquire it, insight learning stays with us. Another feature of insight is that one learns not only the solution to a particular problem but also a principle that can be applied to similar situations in the future. This is often true in learning logical chemistry and algebra problems. Although understanding these problems is a difficult chore, once they are solved the person finds that he or she has also learned a principle that can be applied to similar problems.

Insight learning is also the basis of much creative thought. We often think of creativity as involving the "discovery" of new things. However, many creative contributions have come from individuals who merely perceived existing knowledge in a new way. It may have been that traditionally facts were viewed in one particular sequence, such as A-B-C-D. Then some creative thinker broke away from the traditional thinking and viewed these same facts in a new sequence—say, A-C-B-D. The result may be a whole new way of viewing the world—just as happened with Albert Einstein. He may not have had any more knowledge and facts than other physicists, but he did choose to view what he had within different categories of thought. His result was a new law of relativity, which changed our whole way of thinking about the nature of the physical universe.

Every college professor has given identical grades to essays written by two different students because they both have the necessary information. However, while one is able to present the factual information, another student exhibits evidence of greater understanding of the material. Such a student has made an effort to perceive the relations that make the concrete material meaningful. For the student of history, memorizing names, dates, and events is a tedious and laborious task. Only when the student comes to see meaningful relations among such data can the study of history become enjoyable.

EXERCISE 11-1. SOLVING PROBLEMS THROUGH INSIGHT

Humans by nature do not like to be confronted with problems they cannot solve. Problems create stress that pushes us to find a solution. That is why we will energetically work toward the solution of a puzzle or a riddle even if we are not given an external reward for solving the problem.

Below is a problem that must be solved by mentally perceiving the relations essential to the solution. See whether you can solve this problem. As you work at the problem and eventually solve it, check on the following:

1. Do you find such problems stressful while working on them?
2. Do you feel a sense of great relief once you perceive the solution?
3. Once you have solved a problem, do you think you might be able to solve it 6 months later even if you have no further practice?
4. If you see a similar type of problem later in, say, a magazine, will you have benefited from solving this earlier problem?

Problem

Below are five boxes that have been constructed from toothpicks. Your task is to rearrange these toothpicks so that you finish with only four boxes that are the same size as the five below. However, in solving this problem you must:

1. not move more than three toothpicks,
2. not lay one toothpick on top of another, and
3. finish the problem with the same number of toothpicks you started with (that is, 16). Each toothpick must form a side of one or more boxes.

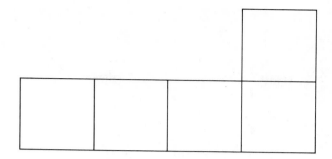

The solution to the problem is given at the end of the chapter.

Note: You should not arrive at a solution in which there are four boxes but also some extra toothpicks left over, such as

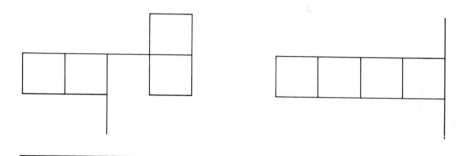

MANAGING TIME MORE EFFICIENTLY

How often we hear ourselves and others remark "I'd love to, if I only had the time!" The fact is that each of us, regardless of age, status, or wealth, has exactly the same amount of time in a given period to do the things we want and need to do. For each of us there are 24 hours in a day, no more and no less. There are exactly 168 hours in any week, and once gone, this time can never be regained.

Time is one of our most valuable possessions. A person who lives to age 70 will have lived 25,550 days (plus a few more for leap years), or 613,200 hours. If we subtract the amount of time we spend growing to adulthood, sleeping, or incapacitated owing to declining health, opportunity to achieve what we want out of life is much more limited. The more we procrastinate, goof off, and follow a generally undisciplined life-style, the more we shorten our productive lives. In the final analysis, what you accomplish in life is a function of how you manage your time. Since

287

What you accomplish in life is a function of how you manage your time. (Photo © Elizabeth Crews/ Icon.)

time is such a precious commodity, it is in our best interest to use it as wisely and effectively as we can.

Establishing Life Goals

In order to manage our time effectively, we must decide what is of real importance in life. Clearly stated goals are a prerequisite to effective time management. Without definite goals to be accomplished, a problem of time management does not exist. The person who is drifting through life aimlessly and without purpose has no problem with time. For most of us, a time problem exists only when there are more things to be done in a given time period than can be done in that period. However, to make maximum use of our time, we must learn to establish priorities and set definite short-range and long-range goals.

288

All of us have goals, but they may not be very specific or clearly defined. Lakein (1973) recommends that one might begin to use time effectively by listing lifetime goals on a piece of paper. Writing goals down helps you clarify them and decide what you really want to accomplish in life. A written list of goals should increase your commitment to them and make you determined to achieve them.

Lakein suggests that one ask the following questions: "What do I really want to accomplish in life?" "How would I like to spend the next 3 years?" "If I had only 6 months to live, how would I spend that time?" These questions can help you articulate both short-range and long-range goals. Then identify the three most important goals under each of the three categories above. This will result in a total of nine goals. Next select the *three most important goals* from this list of nine. This constitutes what Lakein calls one's "Life Goals Statement." The Life Goals Statement is not carved in marble, but is merely one's present perception. As a matter of fact, the LGS should be reviewed periodically, perhaps at the beginning of the calendar year or on your birthday. Take these times to reassess the value of these goals in your life. The changes in your statement of goals over the years can reflect the degree to which you are growing and maturing. Table 11-4 shows LGSs for a hypothetical person at age 19 and at age 21. The goals, both long- and short-range, at age 21 are much more specific and realistic than those at age 19. They reflect greater self-understanding and maturity than the earlier list.

Table 11-4. Life Goals Statements

	Age 19
Long-range goals:	1. To become successful and rich
	2. To be popular and well-liked
	3. To be important and powerful
Short-range goals:	1. To find something more interesting
	2. To get out of school
	3. To be happy
	Age 21
Long-range goals:	1. To become an airplane pilot
	2. To feel competent as an aviator and have the respect of colleagues
	3. To develop satisfying leisure activities
Short-range goals:	1. To complete my college program
	2. To complete flight-training school
	3. To secure employment with an airline

Setting Priorities for Activities

Once top-priority goals have been identified, you need to make a list of activities that will help you achieve these goals. Goals are more likely to be achieved if you clearly identify what you must do to reach them. Next you should set activity priorities and start immediately on the most important activity. This means that in addition to listing life goals, you must proceed with specific plans of action to reach these goals. Lakein offers a simple suggestion for listing the priority of activities. He uses what he calls the "ABC Priority System," whereby an A is assigned to those activities having highest value, a B for medium value, and a C for little value. A-priority activities should always have precedence over those of lower value and importance. The values of activities may change; what is today a high-priority activity may on a later occasion be relegated to the B or C list. Keep in mind that the assigned values depend on the immediacy of the goal and its priority relative to other goals.

Let us suppose that a high-priority goal in your LGS is to become a success in your chosen profession. Further, you want to have completed the requirement for a college degree in the next 3 years. A compatible short-term goal would be doing your best in the courses you are taking during the present quarter or semester. You know that to reach these goals, you probably will have to engage in such activities as writing term papers or making class presentations in addition to passing the tests in each course. Once you have identified the activities that must be completed in order to maximize your performance, you will find it helpful to arrange daily schedules into a system of ABC priorities. Evening is a good time to plan the schedule for the following day. Lakein believes it is a good idea to list more activities than you may get completed; the important thing is that you complete all the A-priority activities on your daily schedule. Completing the list is less important than making the best use of your time. A schedule can help you achieve the latter. Figure 11-5 shows a daily schedule of activities for a student, with priorities indicated for that day. Remember that a low-priority activity today may become a high-priority activity at a later time.

Figure 11-5. Daily Activity List

Priority	
B	Do some background reading in history
C	Wash the car
A	Study for tomorrow's biology exam
A	Make an outline for a term paper in psychology
C	Read some graduate school catalogues
C	Answer the letter from a friend
A	Get a bulb for the lamp in the study room
B	Make an appointment with the math teacher to discuss a grade

---

For those who feel frustrated by their failure to complete all their low-priority tasks, regardless of the amount of work accomplished, Lakein suggests the 80/20 rule, which states: "If all items are arranged in order of value, 80 percent of the value would come from only 20 percent of the items" (p. 84). According to this rule, one who has a daily "to do" list of ten items should find the completion of the two most important ones yielding about 80% of the value of having completed them all. The amount of value realized from the scheduled tasks that one does complete is more important than the number of tasks completed. You may spend a whole day on low-priority activities and yet realize very little value from your day's efforts.

A Master Planning Schedule

In planning a daily schedule, a master planning schedule (Hankins, 1979) should be helpful. Figure 11-6 shows a master planning schedule for one week's activities. This planning schedule breaks the normal working day into 1-hour units. One may, however, block time according to one's own particular schedule or routine. The schedules of homemakers, for example, may be quite different from those of salespersons or business executives. Homemakers probably have set times for doing laundry, cooking, shopping, and housecleaning. Many are also active in organizations and activities outside the home. Figure 11-7 shows hypothetical schedules for a student and a homemaker on a particular day.

	Day of Week						
	Sun.	Mon.	Tue.	Wed.	Thur.	Fri.	Sat.
7:00 A.M.							
8:00							
9:00							
10:00							
11:00							
12:00							
1:00 P.M.							
2:00							
3:00							
4:00							
5:00							
6:00							
7:00							
8:00							
9:00							
10:00							
11:00							

Figure 11-6. Master planning schedule for a 1-week period.

Daily Schedule
Monday

7:00 A.M.	Get up, dress, eat, prepare for class	Get up, dress, prepare breakfast, get children off to school
8:00	History class	Clear table, wash dishes, clean up kitchen
9:00	Physical education	Make beds, general cleaning of house
10:00		Laundry
11:00		Laundry
12:00	Lunch	Prepare lunch, eat, clean up dishes
1:00 P.M.	Psychology	
2:00		
3:00		Fix snack for children, spend time with them listening to their activities of the day
4:00		
5:00		Prepare dinner
6:00	Dinner	Eat, general cleanup of kitchen
7:00	Fraternity meeting	Spend time talking with spouse
8:00		Prepare children for bed, read nighttime story, and so on
9:00		
10:00		
11:00		

Figure 11-7. *Daily schedules for a hypothetical student and a hypothetical homemaker.*

292

Using our time efficiently requires setting goals and establishing their priorities. (Photo © Robert Eckert.)

You will note that the student has unscheduled time blocks between 10:00 A.M. and noon, between 2:00 and 6:00 P.M., and after 8:00 P.M. During these 9 hours, assuming that the person goes to bed at 11:00 P.M. the student could plan additional activities. The high-priority activities indicated in Figure 11-5 (study for biology exam, make outline for term paper in psychology, get bulb for lamp) could be scheduled in these time blocks. The homemaker has no unscheduled time in the morning but has some free time between lunch and the preparation of the evening meal. He or she also has additional unscheduled time between 9:00 P.M., the children's bedtime, and his or her own bedtime.

It is probably not a good idea to block out all your waking hours with obligations. People need leisure time. We will present in a later chapter some suggestions on how to use leisure time for personal enrichment and satisfaction. A full and inflexible schedule will give rise to a feeling that you are a slave to the clock. Remember that the purpose of the schedule is to help you gain greater control of your time, not to create a feeling of helplessness or being out of control. Lakein suggests that one reserve at least 1 hour of uncommitted time a day. This allows some time for unexpected events, which can never be scheduled in advance. Tasks of highest prior-

CHAPTER 11   USING MEMORY AND TIME MORE EFFICIENTLY

ity should be completed early in the day so that you will be less annoyed by interruptions, which inevitably occur.

The priority system should help you to clarify your thinking with respect to both long-term and short-term goals and to identify and organize specific tasks that are necessary for achieving the goals you have set. It is important that you use this method as a tool that serves you rather than becoming a slave to it. Once you get accustomed to setting goals and establishing priorities, you may find that you do not have to spend a lot of time writing them down; a mental listing may be all that is necessary to help you make more efficient use of your time. Setting goals and establishing priorities will certainly make you more time-conscious. Time awareness is a prerequisite to efficient time management. The steps we have recommended can be summarized as follows:

1. Set goals; establish priorities.
2. Make a daily "to do" list.
3. Make a master planning schedule and daily schedules.
4. Look at daily schedule to see what time is already allocated.
5. Insert daily "to do" list in unscheduled time periods.
6. Always perform A activities before doing Bs and Cs.

BOX 11-3. HOW TO MAKE A LIST

Lists are in nowadays. But of course there always have been lists. A favorite list of one of the authors was Satchel Paige's six rules to follow in order to live to be 100. Everyone is familiar with his "Don't look back; something may be gaining on you." But equally endearing are his "Avoid fried meats, which angry up the blood" and Satch's advice "Keep your juices flowing by jangling around gently as you move."

More recently, a book by John Gall called *Systemantics: How Systems Work and Especially How They Fail* offers a list of 32 axioms to carry us through the contrariness of complex systems. Among these are "If it isn't official, it hasn't happened" and "If a system is working, leave it alone."

There is even a *Book of Lists,* compiled by Irving Wallace, Amy Wallace, and David Wallechinsky. If you want to contemplate a list of the ten greatest political films ever or ten famous people whose parents were ministers, this is the book for you. The spinoffs of such a book are endless; one of them might even provide a list of ten psychologists who changed their last names during adulthood otherwise than by marriage (for example, Krech, Appley, the Hartleys) or ten major cities in the United States that will never be the site of the American Psychological Association convention (Houston? Newark?).

But such dilettantish perversions are not the purpose of this essay. Rather, the authors wish to convince you of the joys and benefits of organizing your own life through making lists of your forthcoming tasks. Now, we realize that the world can be divided into two groups of people: the few who organize their lives in such a way and the many who do not. And we well remember the reactions when they suggested elsewhere that people keep simplified records of how much time they spend on different tasks ("too compulsive"; "too hard to do"; "too depressing").

But many people probably avoid making lists of their anticipated tasks because they do not fully understand the secrets of successful list making. With the help of Patti Keith-Spiegel, another committed list maker, the authors offer now a list of ten secrets of successful list making:

1. The "completion ratio" is perhaps the most important quality of a list of tasks. Many people avoid making daily or weekly lists of tasks because they assume that within that time interval they have to complete every one on the list. This is looking at the list in the wrong way. Rather, putting the task on a written list means that it will be done sooner or later. It reflects an existential promise to oneself to do the task, but not a rigidly time-bound promise.

2. Point #1 implies that list making is not primarily an organizational activity but rather a commitment mechanism, a way of distinguishing for oneself those activities that must eventually be accomplished from those that are better forgotten.

3. Within the designated time interval, a completion percentage of around 80% is probably most desirable. If you complete 100% of your listed tasks, either you do not have enough to do, or you are leaving no room for unexpected interruptions or unplanned time, or you have not mastered the art of what kinds of tasks to list. (See #4.)

4. When considering which tasks to list, we know that some novice list makers have been encouraged to begin with routine or essential activities ("get up in the morning," "go to the bathroom at least once today"). Such advice is well-meaning and is offered with the expectation that the completion of such mundane chores will give the novice list maker the confidence to take on the listing of more challenging tasks. However, we believe it is better not to coddle incipient list makers; rather, they should plunge, "cold turkey," into the listing of *meaningful* tasks.

5. When considering which tasks to list, it is mandatory to include only those tasks whose completion can be clearly identified. Once a daily or weekly list is memorialized on paper, there are strong pressures to complete each item. If tasks are not operationally defined, there is a self-deceptive tendency in which one compromises what is defined as "completion." For example, we have known of other people—never ourselves—who have on weekly lists such items as "write chapter for Fenwick's book" and have drawn a line through the item upon completion of *only the outline for their chapter.* We have heard such people muttering to themselves that "after

295

all, organizing the work was the hard part; writing the chapter will only be a straightforward fleshing out of the skeleton." Now, friends, such statements are tacky subterfuges that do a discredit to mature list making. If your real intention this week is only to do the outline for the chapter, then say so on your written list.

6. In planning a daily, weekly, or monthly list, a proper "mix" of tasks differing in subjective probability of accomplishment is important. Balance each task that is unpleasant or time-consuming with one that is quickly done or un-challenging. In such a way, the achievement of the 80% "hit rate" can be maintained.

7. In deciding the order in which tasks are to be done, the mix of subjective probabilities is again important. It is good to begin the list with a difficult task. There is a sad but human tendency among list makers to do the easy thing first. Such actions give a false sense of accomplishment when, half-way through the time period, the list maker discovers that he or she has "already" completed 50% of the items on the list. A frequent topic of conversation among dedicated list makers is how to avoid this response of "premature effectualization," or shooting all one's energy on the completion of the few trivial items on one's list. One solution is to make two lists, varying in difficulty level, and choose items alternately from the easy list and the hard list.

8. Some tasks lack a definable difficulty level because they will be "accomplished" whether one lifts a finger or not. For example, the list item "get ready for 2:00 class" may be accomplished by walking to the classroom and refreshing oneself on the topic during the walk. The inclusion of too many such unspecified "accomplishments" means that one has not really created a list but rather an appointment schedule. As we said before, tasks must be operationally defined. Sometimes the use of subjective criteria is unsatisfactory. Consider the task "get adequately prepared for class today." If the topic of the 2:00 lecture is Jung's theory of personality, one could read for days and still not feel adequately prepared. Therefore, in such cases, a time criterion probably is wisest; the task should state: "spend X number of hours preparing for Jung lecture."

9. Another way to mix the order is to use certain tasks as reinforcers. It is important to riddle the list with potential reinforcers so you can say to yourself "If I do three uninteresting tasks first, then I can do this interesting one." Some of us, however, use cookies or candy rather than interesting tasks as reinforcers. As you become an inveterate list maker, you will find that the act of crossing off a list item can have tremendous reinforcing value all by itself. You might give some thought to how this is done; one of us prefers to use a bright felt-tip pen that makes a broad swipe through the

item. (By using this rather than cookies or M&Ms as the reinforcement, one does not risk tooth decay or weight gain.)

10. Always remember that list making and list monitoring (pulling out your list to see how you are doing so far) are private matters. Most people are not sympathetic to public displays of one's private lists. They avoid lists because they are basically disorganized, and this disorganization is some kind of ingrained personality characteristic that serves some odd need. (We figure that at this point we can be that blunt; if you have read this far, you are not one of "those people.") Such people cannot face up to the fact that list making makes one's responsibilities very salient. So flash your lists only in the privacy of your car or the restroom; otherwise people will misunderstand.

From the *Society for the Advancement of Social Psychology Newsletter*, November 1977, 4(1), 9. Reprinted by permission.

SUMMARY

Increased efficiency in memory and time management enables us to accomplish more with less effort. Specific techniques exist that can help us improve in each of these areas. Some knowledge of how memory works makes it easier to use memory-improvement techniques, such as mnemonic devices. Memory may be viewed as consisting of three processes: encoding, storage, and retrieval. Interference, the primary cause of forgetting, can be reduced by following certain guidelines. The pegword method and the method of loci are examples of mnemonic devices that can greatly reduce interference between lists of words.

Stating specific long-range and short-range goals helps us establish priorities for the completion of daily tasks and activities. A master planning schedule is useful in helping us budget our time and schedule activities of high priority. When we are overwhelmed with what we feel we need to accomplish in a given time period, a priority system forces us to decide what is really important. Having priorities enables us to direct maximum effort to tasks of greatest concern. The six steps for time management listed in the chapter are so essential for anyone with time-management problems that they are repeated here. (1) Set goals; establish priorities. (2) Make a daily "to do" list. (3) Make a master planning schedule and daily schedules. (4) Look at the daily schedule to see what time is already allocated. (5) Jot daily "to do" list in unscheduled time periods. (6) Always perform high-priority activities first.

297

Solution to "insight" problem in Exercise 11-1

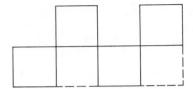

KEY CONCEPTS

Encoding the mental organizing of material in preparation for memory storage.

Method of loci a popular mnemonic device based on the principle of making mental associations between objects to be recalled and locations, usually in one's house.

Mnemonic device a system or plan for helping a person organize and remember unrelated material.

Pegword method a mnemonic device in which material to be recalled is associated with "pegwords" listed in a fixed numerical order.

Proactive facilitation the process in which prior learning makes later learning or recall easier.

Proactive inhibition the process in which prior learning makes later learning or recall harder.

Retrieval the memory phase in which the memory trace is brought from storage to the level of awareness.

Retroactive facilitation the enhancement of a prior memory or skill by subsequent experience.

Retroactive inhibition the deterioration of a prior memory or skill as a result of subsequent experience.

Storage the memory phase between acquisition and retrieval when the memory trace is largely below the level of awareness.

CHAPTER OBJECTIVES

1. To identify some long-range goals.
2. To understand some of the relatively complex and changing motives for work.
3. To identify some of the widely used instruments for measuring interests.
4. To distinguish between aptitude and achievement tests.
5. To become familiar with various sources of occupational information.
6. To develop some skills in applying for and getting a job.
7. To identify some traits and abilities that are necessary for holding and advancing in a job.

CHOOSING
A VOCATION

The choice of a vocation is one of the most important decisions that anyone ever makes. It is far more important than many people seem to realize. Many young people take the first entry-level job they can with the idea that they can change later should they so desire. One buys a home and a car, usually with the aid of a finance company, and suddenly one is overly dependent on a job to meet financial obligations. Add possible marital and family responsibilities, and one finds it difficult to change jobs or seek more education. The result of these circumstances is a trapped feeling and boredom at the job. Our assumption is that careful vocational planning can help you avoid this kind of dilemma.

MAKING A CAREER DECISION

A successful vocational choice is important for numerous reasons. Most of us spend 30 to 40 years at work. Vocational activities can provide opportunities for us to develop meaning and satisfaction in life—or they can become a source of dissatisfaction. Imagine spending 30 years, one day at a time, doing something you do not enjoy! Not only can a satisfying job serve as a basis of self-identity, but it can form the basis of our life-style, our relationships with people, and our perception of how others view us. One's vocation can be an important means of self-expression and a source of fulfillment.

Choosing a career should be viewed as a process rather than an event. Many factors must be carefully considered, including long-range and short-range goals, one's philosophy of life in general, and such personality factors as interests, motivation, and abilities. One might begin by asking the following questions:

What are my basic lifetime goals?
What must I do to realize these goals?
What values and principles do I stand for?
What are my particular interests and abilities?
What kind of life-style do I want?
How important are money, prestige, recognition, and power to me?
Do I prefer working with people, data, or things?

These are not questions that can be quickly or easily answered. Later in the chapter we will present information and provide some exercises that should be helpful in this regard. To the extent that you can find some answers, you have a clearer conception of who you are, where you are going, and what you are trying to do.

Vocational decisions no longer are of interest and concern to just the young who are entering the labor market for the first time. Vocational choice eventually becomes a concern of nearly every adult. More and more it may become a concern at different stages of one's life. Middle-aged persons who may have reared their children or have retired from some career are returning to school in increasing numbers to

An interview with a personnel officer is often the most important phase of getting a job. (Photo © Ellis Herwig/Stock, Boston.)

acquire new marketable skills. Others who are employed full-time but in an unfulfilling job are also reevaluating their career alternatives.

BOX 12-1. INTERNAL/EXTERNAL CONTROL AND CAREER DECISIONS

Farmer (1978) has been engaged in research examining the role of personality variables in making career decisions. She investigated the relation between internal or external locus of control and career goals. Internally oriented persons with high self-esteem were found to choose more career goals that promise intrinsic satisfaction, whereas externally oriented persons tended to ignore this aspect of career choice. Internally oriented, high-self-esteem persons were also found to (1) assess themselves more accurately, (2) develop more feasible plans for obtaining needed resources and overcoming obstacles to their career goals, and (3) be more likely to try out new behaviors and to persist in new behaviors even when faced with initial failure. This characteristic suggests that internally oriented persons with high self-esteem are more adequate decision makers. They acquire more information, make more attempts at acquiring it, retain information better, and are better at utilizing information and devising rules to process it. They are more likely to show greater school and career achievement and to attribute success to effort and work rather than to luck. They are more interested in finding a job to fit their interests and abilities and are more realistic in their plans, knowing where they have a greater probability of success or failure in academic and career pursuits.

In contrast, externally oriented persons with low self-esteem tend to view the world as determined by chance, outside their personal control, or otherwise unpredictable. Consequently, they avoid seeking new information and trying out new behaviors related to their career goals. They perceive little or no connection between their individual effort and educational and career success. These perceptions seem to be particularly pronounced in persons of lower socioeconomic status.

Farmer believes that such legislation as Equal Pay for Equal Work, Equal Employment Opportunity, and Equal Access to Education can provide avenues for changing individuals' belief that their life is under the control of fate or chance. Through such legal and environmental changes, lower-class children, adolescents, and adults would change their perceptions of who is in charge of their destiny.

SURVEY OF OCCUPATIONAL CONTENTMENT

Renwick and Lawler (1978) conducted a survey of readers of the magazine *Psychology Today* and found that a majority of those readers appeared to be having

304

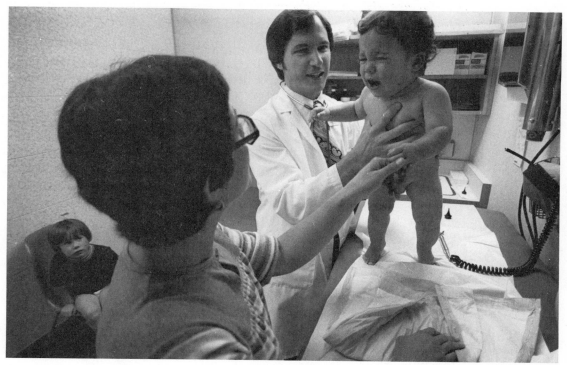

Occupational contentment is more likely if the job responsibilities fulfill one's psychological needs. (Photo © Robert Eckert.)

second thoughts about their occupations. These readers expressed several reasons for their occupational discontent. Many people experienced a midcareer crisis in which they felt a need to reexamine their values and life goals. Others felt that technological advances had rendered their skills obsolete and that they were therefore less useful. Forty percent of the participants in this survey indicated that they had entered an occupation without much deliberation; another 16% indicated that they had settled in their occupation because opportunities in another occupation, which they would have preferred, were limited. Forty-four percent felt "locked into" their jobs because of seniority and fringe benefits.

Other important findings in this survey were that (1) many young people devote insufficient time and effort to vocational choice and (2) a majority of people consider changing careers and many of these do so. To the extent that *Psychology Today* readers are representative of the work force, it appears that modern workers feel less committed to their employers and their occupations. Today's workers seem ready to change jobs if they think they can improve their circumstances. Many appear to be constantly in search of job situations that will fulfill a broad spectrum of needs.

305

CHANGING JOBS

Yet a person should not take changing jobs too lightly. It should be done only after careful consideration. Janis and Wheeler (1978) suggest an exercise that a person might use in evaluating potential risks or benefits in a job change. They suggest using a balance sheet that identifies various courses of action along with expected consequences of each course of action. They point out that one should consider how a course of action will influence (1) utilitarian gains or losses for self, (2) utilitarian gains or losses for significant others, (3) self-approval or disapproval, and (4) approval or disapproval from significant others. For each course of action the decision maker fills out a balance sheet that explicitly identifies both the positive and negative potential outcomes in each of these four categories.

Assume that a middle-aged man has worked as an architect for a large, successful architectural firm for a number of years. He is considered by superiors to be a competent employee, and he is making a good salary; however, he feels that he has reached his performance peak, and he is considering going into business for himself. This man might develop two balance sheets, one for his current job and another for his anticipated job. (Table 12-1 is the balance sheet for his present job.) By comparing the two balance sheets, he can determine the feasibility of changing jobs. The balance sheets help the decision maker develop an awareness of his or her alternatives and their advantages and disadvantages. They also help him or her to make a more comprehensive appraisal of possible trade-offs, to concentrate on the major differences among alternatives, and to assess the importance of crucial pros and cons.

PREDICTING OCCUPATIONAL SUCCESS

Psychologists have identified three influences on occupational performance: interests, abilities, and motivation.

Measuring Interests

For a person to be satisfied with a job and perform optimally at that job, he or she should have interests that are congruent with the job. For instance, a person who has a high need for social interaction and conversation would probably not enjoy being a house painter. Or a person who enjoys privacy and a secluded life would not enjoy politics. This is a facet of occupational success that is too often ignored. Psychologists have, however, developed a number of **interest inventories** that identify one's interests and may also determine what occupations might be consistent with those interests. Interest inventories can help people learn about themselves and enable them to make better occupational decisions.

306

Table 12-1. A Hypothetical Example of an Architect's Balance Sheet for Present Job

	Positive expectations	Negative expectations
Tangible gains and losses for self	1. Satisfactory pay	1. Poor prospects for advancement
	2. Opportunity to use my skills and training	2. Undesirable relations with superiors
		3. Constant pressure— deadlines too short
		4. Lack of opportunity to make decisions
Tangible gains and losses for others	1. Adequate income for family	1. Too little time with family
	2. Wife and children have security because of my position with the firm	2. Wife must tolerate my irritability after disagreement with boss
Self-approval or self-disapproval	1. Pride in my achievement	1. Cannot make full use of my potentialities
	2. Sense of accomplishment when I see what our firm has done	2. Feel like a fool putting up with these deadlines and demands
		3. Feel hypocritical working for people I can't respect
Social approval or disapproval	1. Approval of my colleagues and one superior who wants me to stay	1. Possible skeptical reaction of my wife, who wonders whether I would be happier working for myself
	2. Approval of my secretary and assistant, who with myself have formed an effective work team	2. A friend in another firm has been wanting me to consider a job with his firm. He may be disappointed

In our discussion of some of the more widely used interest inventories, it is important not to confuse interest with ability. If a person expresses high interest in a given vocation, this does not guarantee that he or she has the necessary ability for that vocation. Interest and ability are two distinct aspects of fitness for a field of study or work. There is some relation between measured interest and ability, but this relation is much too slight for one measure to serve as a substitute for the other. Both kinds of information are needed for any meaningful assessment of a person's suitability for a particular vocation.

307

We will discuss three of the leading measures of interest patterns: the Strong-Campbell Interest Inventory, the Kuder Preference Records, and the Ohio Vocational Interest Survey.

Strong-Campbell Interest Inventory. One of the most widely used interest inventories is the Strong Vocational Interest Blank (SVIB), first published in 1927. The latest edition of this test is the Strong-Campbell Interest Inventory (SCII Form T 325). The major change in the newer edition is the merger of the forms for men and women into a single inventory. Previously there was a completely separate form for each sex. Because a substantial difference exists between the sexes in some areas, the separate norms for each sex are still maintained.

The SCII is a questionnaire with items about types of occupations, occupational activities, school subjects, relationships with people, and preference for various activities. It is based on the fact that people in a particular profession or vocation tend to have common interest patterns. For example, a high score on the Psychologist scale indicates that the respondent has interest patterns similar to those of successful psychologists. A low score on this scale indicates interest patterns that are dissimilar to psychologists'. It should be emphasized that a high score for a particular profession does not indicate interest in that area specifically; it does, however, indicate interest patterns similar to those of people working in that profession.

According to the SCII test manual, interests for most people begin to solidify at age 17 or 18, so that test results can be used as reliable predictors for career-planning purposes. By age 25 interest patterns have become well established for almost everyone.

BOX 12-2. OCCUPATIONAL INTERESTS AS PREDICTORS OF OCCUPATIONAL CHOICE

There is some evidence that interests can be used as predictors of vocational choice. Campbell (1966) selected from a pool of 2500 high school seniors a group of students who had high ratings on the Life Insurance Salesman scale of the Strong Vocational Interest Blank. Ten years later a survey of their current occupations was made. Of this group, 10% were in the life-insurance business, 32% were in other sales jobs, 12% were in business-contact jobs, such as public relations, 22% were in social-service persuasive jobs, such as lawyer or minister, and 24% were in essentially unrelated jobs. These results show that about three fourths of these people were working in an area related to their high-interest area 10 years earlier. Although only 10% of this sample were working in the specific area measured by the inventory, about 65% were working in a related area.

Adapted from "Occupation Ten Years Later of High School Seniors with High Scores on the SVIB Life Insurance Salesman Scale," by D. T. Campbell, *Journal of Applied Psychology*, 1966, *50*, 369–372. Copyright 1966 by the American Psychological Association.

308

Kuder Preference Records. Another widely used set of interest inventories is the Kuder Preference Records, which classify interests in the following categories: Vocational, Personal, and Occupational. The Vocational form measures ten broad areas of interest: outdoor, mechanical, computational, scientific, persuasive, artistic, literary, musical, social service, and clerical. The Personal form measures five kinds of preferences, called sociable, practical, theoretical, agreeable, and dominant. The Occupational Interest Survey (OIS), the newest form, is designed for use in grades 11 and 12 and by adults. It permits a person to compare his or her interest preferences with those of people in various occupational groups and people pursuing various college majors. The Kuder General Interest Survey (GIS) is an updated version of the original Vocational form and gives a picture of the person's interests in the ten general interest areas listed above.

Ohio Vocational Interest Survey. The OVIS is an interest inventory designed to assist students in grades 8–12 with educational and vocational plans. It is probably more appropriate for younger adolescents (ages 12–17) than the SCII. It encourages a broad exploration of vocational opportunities. This inventory, consisting of 280 items, is based on the assumption that most jobs involve an interest in data, people, things, or some combination of these. Areas of high interest are analyzed according to the degree to which they require working with data, people, or things. The results are used largely for counseling purposes as an aid to vocational exploration and self-understanding.

Measuring Abilities

There are two types of ability tests: those designed to measure some present level of knowledge or skill (called **achievement tests**) and those designed to measure the potential for some future level of performance (called **aptitude tests**). The college or university course examinations that are so familiar to you are types of achievement tests. You read certain designated chapters in your textbook and study your notebook, and then an instructor gives you an examination to test your knowledge of this material. Your instructor uses such tests to examine your present level of knowledge about the assigned subject matter.

Some types of ability tests, however, are used to predict how well one might perform in the future if given training. These tests, called "aptitude tests," require measuring something other than what is being predicted. For example, most college students have taken college entrance tests, such as the American College Test (ACT) or the Scholastic Aptitude Test (SAT). The purpose of these tests is to predict how well students might perform in college if given the opportunity to go to college. Since the students are not in a position to take college achievement tests (that is, college examinations), another test must be given in hopes of predicting how they might do on such college examinations.

Many kinds of decisions require prediction of future performance. Psychologists have developed aptitude tests for a wide variety of abilities. Tests have been developed for determining mechanical aptitude, clerical aptitude, musical aptitude, and even what individuals might make successful pilots. Perhaps the most widely used aptitude tests, however, are general intelligence tests.

Successful intelligence testing began with the construction of a scale by a French psychologist, Alfred Binet, in 1905. This scale eventually immigrated to the United States, where Lewis Terman at Stanford University constructed a revision of the Binet test, called the Stanford-Binet. The concept of an intelligence quotient (IQ) was incorporated into a revision of the Stanford-Binet test. Today the Stanford-Binet test is one of our best measures of general intelligence. Two other widely used tests of general mental ability were developed by David Wechsler. These tests consist of a general intelligence scale for children (the Wechsler Intelligence Scale for Children) and one for adults (the Wechsler Adult Intelligence Scale). The two Wechsler scales and the Stanford-Binet are administered by psychologists to single individuals, and they have been found to have high reliability and validity.

Since most occupations appear to require certain minimal levels of general intellectual ability, these tests can be useful in helping one identify occupations that are appropriate for one's ability level. Sometimes a person needs more-specific information on his or her capacity for occupational performance. Many aptitude tests are available that might be suited to one's needs. A student might determine whether such ability testing is available at his or her institution or at local state employment agencies. Moreover, there are very high correlations between some standardized achievement tests, such as the ACT, and standard intelligence tests. One may wish to find qualified counselors who can interpret one's standardized-test scores in terms of vocational concerns.

Measuring Motivation

Motivation is a particularly difficult dimension of personality to measure because it can vary considerably over time. A person may be highly motivated and study hard for an examination today, and tomorrow that same person just cannot seem to make even a minimal effort at study. In some courses we work hard and in others we do not. Although motivation can vary over time, it does seem that the more explicit one's goals and the stronger one's desire to reach them, the more persistent one's motivation.

As suggested earlier in this chapter, individuals should clearly establish what their short-range and long-range goals are. And they should arrange appropriate priorities in attaining goals. Many freshmen, for instance, want to become teachers, engineers, or physicians, but the thought of having to work 4 or possibly 8 or more years to reach such goals may have a discouraging effect on the student's study. Obviously, one must also work toward short-range goals that can provide more-immediate rewards. For many, working for good grades on examinations serves this

310

purpose. Others may have to generate additional sources of support. One might find it helpful just to be able to talk with a person in the profession to which one aspires. Sometimes faculty members at colleges and universities fail to realize how important occasional faculty/student conferences can be in sustaining a student's interest in a discipline. You should use your own creative capacity to think of various short-range goals that can keep you striving week to week toward your long-range goals.

EXERCISE 12-1. INCREASING OCCUPATIONAL INTEREST BY ESTABLISHING SHORT-RANGE GOALS

Identify your occupational goal.

Now list at least three things you can accomplish over the next week that might help you reach your occupational goal. In addition to your required course work, you may wish to talk with some person in your anticipated occupation. You may wish to read a magazine or view a TV program that relates to your anticipated occupation. What agencies or organizations might you write to for information on this occupation? Whatever you do, actively seek out situations that might sustain your interest in long-range occupational goals. You will also be surprised to find that much learning can take place outside the classroom.

Psychologists have found that even though motivation is somewhat variable over time, some people are characterized by more persistent motivation than others. McClelland (1961), for instance, has identified a relatively stable dimension of a person called **achievement motivation**. Achievement motivation is the general tendency for a person to approach those goals which culture recognizes as evidence of success. High achievement motivation seems to be established by aspects of the socialization process. For example, studies have shown that firstborn children have higher achievement motivation than later-borns (Schachter, 1963), that males generally have higher achievement motivation than females (Chance, 1965), and that people from upper socioeconomic classes have higher achievement motivation than people from lower socioeconomic classes (Rosen, 1956).

EXERCISE 12-2. PREDICTING OCCUPATIONAL SUCCESS

The previous discussion has indicated that three factors (interest, ability, and motivation) combine to produce occupational success. Certainly, the more objective information one can obtain about these areas (as through interest, ability, or motivation tests), the more knowledgeable one can be in setting realistic occupational goals.

Although an individual's self-perceptions cannot completely substitute for objective measurement of interest, ability, and motivation, you might wish to try this exercise. On the following scales, estimate the extent of your interest, ability, and

311

motivation relative to your occupational goal. On the first scale, entitled "Interest," indicate the extent to which you feel your interest patterns are similar to those of successful people in your anticipated occupation. On the second scale, "Ability," indicate your level of ability compared with successful people in your anticipated occupation. On the third scale, "Motivation," indicate the level of your motivation to succeed compared with successful people in your anticipated occupation. These three scales range from 0 to 10, 0 being the absence of interest, ability, or motivation and 10 being the highest value. Now rate yourself on these three dimensions.

Interest   *High*
0   1   2   3   4   5   6   7   8   9   10
Ability
0   1   2   3   4   5   6   7   8   9   10
Motivation
0   1   2   3   4   5   6   7   8   9   10

Now take the three values that you assigned to these three factors and multiply them. For example, your values might have been $4 \times 6 \times 10$, which would equal 240. What was your total score? Scores can range from 0 ($0 \times 0 \times 0 = 0$) to 1000 ($10 \times 10 \times 10$). The higher the score, the greater your perception of your chances of success in your anticipated occupation.

You will note that these three factors are in a multiplicative relationship. Therefore, if the value on any one factor is 0, the total score for occupational success will be 0. For instance, one may have high interest (10) and high ability (10) but no motivation (0), and the result is no occupational success.

WHERE TO GET OCCUPATIONAL INFORMATION

The Occupational Outlook Handbook is a very valuable source of occupational information providing descriptions of more than 850 occupations. This biannual publication of the U.S. Department of Labor describes jobs in the sales, professional, managerial, craft, service, and clerical areas, among others. The handbook contains occupational briefs written by experts in various fields arranged in 13 clusters of related jobs. Examples of clusters are office, service, education, sales, and construction. An occupational brief in a cluster contains information on (1) the nature of the work, (2) places of employment, (3) training, other qualifications, and advancement, (4) the employment outlook, (5) earnings, and (6) working conditions. Most of the occupational briefs suggest organizations you can write to for additional career information. The *Occupational Outlook Handbook* provides clear instructions on how it can be used. It is available at the reference desk of most libraries and can be bought from the Superintendent of Documents, U.S. Government Printing Office, Washington, D.C. 20402.

312

Other sources of career information can usually be found in public school or college libraries and vocational-guidance offices. Ask the personnel there for books, pamphlets, and magazine articles with occupational information. Many business and industrial establishments are willing to supply information about job descriptions and qualifications and the kinds of jobs they have available. Professional organizations and trade unions have publications that may carry announcements of job vacancies and job qualifications. Many such organizations have full-time staff members who supply career information on occupations or industries with which they are associated. Private employment agencies can provide helpful information and assistance for their clients. (They generally charge a fee for their services.) Most colleges and universities have placement offices, which can provide information about careers appropriate for college graduates and help in setting up interviews with prospective employers. Most colleges also provide students with career counseling. State employment-service agencies can help job seekers find employment and help employers find qualified workers. They can also provide information about hiring standards and local wage scales. State employment services also provide employment-counseling opportunities, referrals to training programs (such as apprenticeship programs or vocational and technical schools), and placement services. The employment service also has special programs and opportunities for veterans, disadvantaged youths, graduating seniors, the handicapped, and other groups.

GETTING A JOB

When you learn of an appropriate job vacancy, your primary goal is to obtain that job. In this section we will offer some suggestions on how to get a job. Each employment situation is different, but there are some general features of virtually every job-getting situation: (1) writing a letter of application, (2) completing an application form, (3) preparing a résumé, and (4) often participating in a job interview.

The Letter of Application

A letter of application is often the initial communication with a prospective employer and should show that you can communicate well in writing. The letter should also communicate your vocational goal as well as some knowledge of the company and its operations.

You may also wish to summarize your credentials in a brief paragraph, but do not try to present all supporting information; leave that to your résumé. Your letter might include such information as your training and education, prior work experience, and work-related interests. A final paragraph of your letter might try to elicit a response from the employer. However, you should not appear too demanding or desperate in the letter. Too many letters of application are written around the theme "I need a job; please do me a favor and hire me." Prospective employers are interested in what you can do for *them*, and they are on the lookout for good employees. The letter should state what services you can offer the employer.

Write clearly and to the point. Remember that the quality of this first communication may determine whether the employer wishes to know more about you. You hope that it will result in an application blank and an interview with someone in the company. Books with sample letters of application can be found at the reference desk of most school libraries.

The Application Blank

What we have to suggest in completing the application blank may seem self-evident and even trite, but failure to give sufficient attention to such matters may determine whether you get a job. Application blanks should be typed if possible, otherwise done in ink. You should make some response to all items on the form. Failure to answer relevant items might be viewed as revealing a blasé attitude on your part or a desire to withhold information. When the form contains a question that does not pertain to your particular situation, you should draw a neat horizontal line or write "N/A" (for "not applicable") in that space. If asked about salary and you are not sure about the appropriate salary range, you should probably respond with "open" or "negotiable." Otherwise you may either price yourself out of the position or commit yourself to a lower figure than might have been negotiated. If you have some way of determining the salary range for a position, you should indicate that range or an amount within that range.

The Résumé

The résumé is probably the most important source of information the employer has about you in the early stages of job seeking. Serious consideration and effort should be given to developing a résumé. Moreover, if one is seeking employment at more than one place, the résumé should be tailored to each employment situation. Figure 12-1 gives an example of the types of information that would be appropriate in a résumé. Résumés should never be "padded." Most employers can see right through one's attempts to oversell oneself. Yet when you are preparing a résumé, it is not the time to be overly modest about one's accomplishments or competencies. Be terse, objective, and clear about your credentials.

Every résumé should be accompanied by a cover letter designed to introduce the employer to the résumé. The same considerations used in writing a letter of application may be applied here. In fact, in many situations these two letters are one and the same. In any case, the following guidelines might be helpful:

314

```
                              James A. Bowlen
                              223 Sequoyah Drive
                              Salem, Virginia  36213
                              Telephone:  (703)  929-1642

OBJECTIVE          (Name and describe the position you are seeking)

AREAS OF           (List the kinds of experience that would qualify you for
EXPERIENCE           this position)

PERSONAL           (Birthdate and state of health)

EDUCATION          (Include all vocational or professional training, including
                     the name of each school, location, the degree received,
                     and the date the degree was received)

EDUCATIONAL        (List particular courses you have had that relate to your
HIGHLIGHTS           vocational objective)

STUDENT            (List any organizations to which you belonged and offices
ACTIVITIES           held, honors received, and so on)

WORK               (Start with the most recent job and continue through your
EXPERIENCE           first job.  Include part-time experience and any hobbies
                     that may be relevant)

SALARY             (Open to discussion within a stated range)
TRAVEL             (State whether you are willing to travel)
LOCATE             (State whether you are willing to relocate for right offer)
AVAILABILITY       (State when you will be available)
REFERENCES         (References on request)
```

Figure 12-1. *Sample résumé.*

1. Address the letter to a particular person by name when possible.
2. Use the first paragraph to attract the reader's interest.
3. Emphasize the contribution you feel you can make to the employer.

315

4. Be sure to call attention to the résumé.
5. Keep the cover letter short.
6. Let your letter reflect your individuality, but remember that this is your first contact with a stranger about a subject that is very important to both of you.

Figure 12-2 is a sample letter from a hypothetical person with limited work experience. How would you react to such a letter if you were an employer? Try preparing a cover letter that would be submitted to a prospective employer in your anticipated occupation. Rewrite it several times. You will probably find that each rewrite brings some degree of improvement in your communication.

The Initial Interview

If an employer invites you for a personal interview, he or she is probably interested in hiring you. Yet it is quite common for more than one person to be interviewed for a position. Therefore you need to maximize this opportunity. Before going into an interview, you should—

Do some research about the company and become as knowledgeable as you can about its operations.

Anticipate possible questions in the interview and formulate your responses to these questions ahead of time.

Clearly identify your vocational goals and be able to verbalize them succinctly.

Make a list of questions you would like answered in the interview.

Role-play an interview with a friend or relative so that you have some experience being interviewed.

Never underestimate the importance of your physical appearance. Use good judgment in deciding what to wear. Be on time for the interview. Make direct eye contact with the employer and give a firm handshake. It is probably a good idea not to smoke during the interview. The interviewer will take the initiative in the beginning, but you should be alert to cues that you should take up the ball. Poise and the ability to express oneself verbally are assets to any job seeker, and these traits can be enhanced by careful preparation for the interview. Avoid lengthy answers. The nature of the work and your qualifications for the job should be discussed before you raise questions about salary or fringe benefits. At the close of the interview, express your appreciation for the opportunity to be interviewed, and later write a short letter of appreciation even before you learn of the employer's decision.

Below are some areas you should be prepared to comment on in an interview:

1. Work experience
   A. duties and responsibilities in prior jobs
   B. work demands—closeness of supervision, accuracy, quantity, working with people, and so on

```
                                        223 Sequoyah Drive
                                        Salem, Virginia 36213
                                        October 18, 1979




Slonaker Studios
Commercial Photographers
154 W. Main Street
Johnson City, Tennessee  37601

Attention: Director of Personnel

Dear Sir or Madam:

     I know I am short on experience, but please read on.  I am long on
potential and enthusiasm.

     As shown in the attached résumé, I do have some experience in the
field of photography, even though it is limited.  In addition to the
part-time job I have listed, please note the courses I have taken in
preparation for a career in this most exciting profession.

     I am eagerly anticipating working for a highly respected company
such as yours and will do my utmost to make a competent, productive,
and trustworthy employee.  I would very much appreciate an opportunity
to be interviewed for the position.


                                        Sincerely,



                                        James Bowlen
```

Figure 12-2. *Sample cover letter.*

C. demands of jobs that are liked and disliked
D. reasons for changing jobs
E. evaluations by prior employers
F. reasons for choosing your vocation

317

2. Educational training
   A. schools attended
   B. extracurricular activities and experiences
   C. reasons for choice of school, subject, and so on
3. Other activities
   A. hobbies
   B. membership in organizations
   C. leadership positions held
   D. military record
4. Health
   A. extent of sick leave
   B. past and present need for medical care
   C. health of family

HOLDING A JOB

Once a person has obtained a job, he or she must demonstrate some necessary traits and skills in order to hold it. Although the specific demands of jobs vary widely, a few identifiable qualities are necessary for success in any vocation. They include dependability, interpersonal skills, willingness to accept legitimate authority, and emotional stability.

Dependability

To be an asset to an employer, an employee must be dependable. He or she should be able to conform to schedules—for example, in reporting to work on time and having a good work attendance record. Good employees must accept responsibility for their conduct in the workplace and be honest in discharging their responsibilities. Inattention, lack of concentration, and other forms of carelessness can lead to increased costs as well as personal injury.

Interpersonal Skills

Ability to get along with people is a requirement of practically all jobs. Employees must be able to communicate effectively with supervisors, coworkers, subordinates, and, in many cases, the general public. Many jobs require ability to communicate both in writing and orally. The employee who cannot get along with coworkers is less likely to be productive and to hold a job.

Acceptance of Legitimate Authority

Employers have definite goals that they seek to achieve. This does not mean that the goals of the organization and those of the employee are incompatible. More often than not, group goals and individual goals are very congruent. Nevertheless, any organized effort must have some form of authority. For effective functioning, organization members must respect that authority. A good employee, for example, must be able to take instructions from supervisors and to function within the framework established by the governing body of any institution or enterprise.

Emotional Stability

To hold most jobs, an employee must be reasonably stable emotionally. The person who cannot tolerate ordinary work pressures, experiences frequent crying spells, becomes severely depressed, or experiences rage and throws temper tantrums is not likely to be productive. Readers who have problems with control of emotions, particularly anxiety and anger, are encouraged to apply some of the techniques described in Chapter 10.

GETTING AHEAD ON THE JOB

Education and relevant experience are prerequisites to advancement in many jobs. In addition to these requirements, there are certain indications of "maturity" that should enhance job advancement. A mature person, as the term is used here, is an individual who has formulated specific life goals, is willing to assume responsibility, and is sensitive to the needs and desires of other people. The mature person has some understanding of his or her strengths and weaknesses and is able to make a rational evaluation of capabilities and set goals accordingly.

The person who works efficiently and uses time wisely is more likely to get ahead. One must know how to establish priorities for activities that need to be completed within a designated time period. Some of the ideas presented in Chapter 11 should be helpful in this area.

The person desiring to move ahead should study carefully the organizational structure and the "psychological climate" of the organization. Psychological climate includes the personalities and attitudes of important officials in the organization. Some administrators and supervisors, for example, respect innovation by subordinates, whereas others prefer those who follow established practices or customs. It is also helpful to know whether companies promote mainly on the basis of merit or seniority. If a merit system is used, one should understand clearly the criteria by which merit is determined, since these criteria differ from place to place.

319

REACHING THE OCCUPATIONAL PLATEAU

Whether one works for promotion is an individual matter. Among those who do seek promotion, not everyone can get to the top. It is important to know when to stop trying to move higher in the organizational hierarchy. Peter and Hull (1970), in a book titled *The Peter Principle*, humorously make the point that some employees who have achieved competence at a given level are promoted to levels at which they become incompetent. Although competence at a lower level might be one of the best predictors of higher-level competence, it is not a guarantee of increased performance or satisfaction. Many people find a level at which they feel comfortable and probably should not attempt further advancement. How does one know when one has reached this level? The following questions should be helpful in making this determination: "Is my present job producing a genuine sense of accomplishment? Do I have an opportunity to use my abilities in this job? Am I currently functioning at my optimal level? Do I want increased responsibility? Am I comfortable in my present position?"

One who seeks advancement should also analyze one's motives for doing so. If one feels that one's ability or expertise is not presently being used to the maximum, a promotion might be beneficial to everyone. If the motive is simply a need for greater power or prestige, which one feels can be satisfied by the status of the position, the decision to push for advancement should be reexamined.

SUMMARY

The choice of a career is a most important decision because (1) we devote so much of our lives to a career, (2) it is a basis for self-identity and life-style, and (3) our relationships with others are influenced by the work we do. Surveys show that many people are not satisfied with their career choices and they are changing careers, even during middle age, in increasing numbers.

To some extent occupational success can be predicted from a person's interests, abilities, and motivation. Interest inventories can help people learn about themselves and make better occupational choices. Three of the leading measures of interest patterns are the Strong-Campbell Interest Inventory, the Kuder Preference Records, and the Ohio Vocational Interest Inventory. Abilities are generally measured by achievement and aptitude tests. Motivation is generally inferred from one's long- and short-term goals and from one's behavior in various settings. The person who is not interested in a particular field, has little ability in it, or is lacking in motivation is not likely to be successful in that area. The person who has each of these characteristics is much more likely to succeed.

Adequate information makes possible better decisions regarding vocational choice. Some of the best sources of career information are the *Occupational Outlook*

Fortunately, some individuals may find satisfaction doing work that others find dissatisfying. (Photo © Donald C. Dietz/Stock, Boston.)

Handbook, state employment services, college and university placement offices, career-counseling centers, and private employment agencies.

Those who can write a good letter of application, prepare an attractive and complete résumé, and show composure and skill during an employment interview are more likely to obtain the job of their choice. After one obtains a job, one must demonstrate some desirable characteristics in order to hold a job and to progress in it. These characteristics include dependability, interpersonal skills, willingness to accept legitimate authority, emotional stability, willingness to assume responsibility, and sensitivity to the needs and desires of other people.

KEY CONCEPTS

Achievement motivation the general tendency for a person to approach goals that culture recognizes as evidence of success.

Achievement test a test designed to measure some present level of knowledge or skill.

Aptitude test a test designed to measure potential for some future level of performance.

Interest inventories instruments designed to identify interest patterns and in many cases to determine what occupations might be consistent with a person's interests.

13

CHAPTER OBJECTIVES

1. To better understand the changing nature of motivation for work.
2. To become familiar with several theories of intrinsic motivation.
3. To identify some needs that may be satisfied through one's job.
4. To demonstrate knowledge of several theories of work motivation.
5. To define and give examples of job enrichment.
6. To become familiar with some research exploring the relation between job satisfaction and performance.

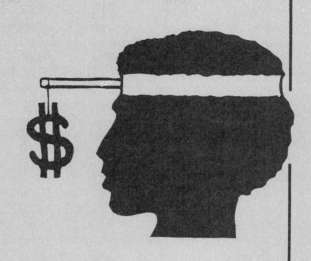

MOTIVATION
AND WORK
BEHAVIOR

Work is important in people's lives for several reasons. One function of work is to provide some form of reward in exchange for services rendered. Whether these rewards are mainly extrinsic, in the form of money, or intrinsic, in the form of personal satisfaction, one has certain expectations about the type and amount of reward one should receive for one's services.

Work may serve several social functions. The workplace provides opportunities for meeting people and developing friendships. A person's job can also be a source of status both within the organization and in society at large. For example, a bank president may have high status in the community because of his or her position within the organization.

Work can be an important source of identity, self-esteem, and self-fulfillment by giving an employee a sense of purpose and demonstrating his or her value to society. Many people tend to evaluate themselves according to what they have been able to accomplish at work. If they see their job as impeding progress toward the realization of their full potential, it is hard for them to maintain a sense of purpose at work. The result can be less job involvement, decreased job satisfaction, and a lowered desire to perform. The nature of the job and the meaning it has for an employee can have a profound effect on one's self-concept and feelings of personal worth as well as on work performance.

Because of the many kinds of needs that can be met or fail to be met on the job, worker motivation is recognized as one of the most complex problems confronting business and industry today. In the past, industry has relied mainly on monetary incentives to induce workers to increase their productivity. Recently researchers have questioned the effectiveness of monetary incentives alone in motivating people to work. According to Herzberg (1968), the promise of money can *move* a person to work, but it cannot *motivate* that person to work. Herzberg believes that money is the primary motivator to work only when workers are below a subsistence living level. The motivation to perform well comes from an inner desire. Such a desire is rooted in an innate need for self-fulfillment and a need for accomplishment. Whether such needs are innate is a moot question. However, there is no doubt that modern workers expect a job to fulfill their human needs.

Yankelovich (1978) describes a new breed of worker born out of the youth social movements of the 1960s. Such workers find the present work-incentive system so unappealing and dissatisfying that although they want to hold a job, they are not motivated to work hard. Consequently, they withdraw emotionally from work and try to substitute pay increases and fringe benefits for the fulfillment of intrinsic needs. The less they give to the job, the more they seem to demand from the employer. Yankelovich attributes this state of affairs to the failure of the old money incentive system to keep pace with new worker needs.

Below are some of the assumptions of the old money incentive system:

1. Workers will tolerate many drawbacks of a job so long as the job provides them with a decent living and some degree of economic security.
2. Money and status are the main reasons people work.

For some people, work may serve as the basis for self-identity. (Photo © Will McIntyre/Photo Researchers, Inc.)

3. Loyalty to the organization is at least as important to job commitment as providing security for one's family.
4. One's work role is the basis for defining one's self-identity.
5. Women who can afford to stay home do not work at a paid job.

The "new breed" of workers do not readily accept these assumptions. For them work has grown less important while family and leisure activities have become more important. In addition, many women are no longer satisfied with being "just a housewife" but may seek work as a means of achieving autonomy and independence and a new sense of self-worth. Workers of this new breed are less likely to subordinate and submerge their personalities in a work role. They are more likely to demand that their individuality be recognized. From his survey Yankelovich found that the need to be recognized as an individual and the opportunity to be with pleasant people were more important than the features of the work itself.

It seems that among newer members of the work force a closer correspondence is needed between incentives and motivation. A job must meet not only one's need for income but also one's needs for self-respect, independence, and belonging to society. Otherwise people will work without taking their working seriously. Yankelovich suggests that the main lesson to be learned from changes shaped by these new, emerging values is that we need to pay greater attention to the human side of the work situation.

INTRINSICALLY MOTIVATED BEHAVIOR

Psychologists describe two reasons that a behavior may occur. The behavior may be carried out because it is enjoyable to do (**intrinsic motivation**) or because the behavior leads to some externally rewarding outcome (**extrinsic motivation**). That is, behavior may be performed because it is either intrinsically rewarding or extrinsically rewarding. For example, many behaviors of children are performed for no other reason than that they are enjoyable. A child may climb the steps of a playground slide and slide down one, two, perhaps 20 times. No one is standing at the end of the slide giving the child an M & M candy after each response. Rather, the child derives satisfaction from the activity itself, not what the activity results in.

Many of the activities children enjoy doing (such as play, exploration, or doing math), however, can be brought under the control of external rewards. For instance, a child may enjoy finger-painting and find this activity intrinsically satisfying. But once the child learns that he or she can receive some reward for this activity (for example, a smile or a pat on the head), the child may lose interest in the activity except when a reward is expected. If the teacher does not come around and reward the child's effort, he or she may feel the work was not worth the effort.

Educators like to believe that students are intrinsically motivated to learn. They read books, write papers, and take tests because they enjoy these activities. However, we must admit that in actuality students would not generally do these things if it were not for the expectation of some future external reward (a high grade on a test; a well-paying job). It is perhaps unfortunate that our education system has created the attitude that learning is something that must pay off in external rewards. Many find that once they find a suitable paying job, the incentive to work cannot be sustained day after day solely by such rewards. In the final analysis, people must enjoy their work to be completely satisfied with the job.

Theories of Intrinsic Motivation

Several approaches have been used in the study of intrinsic motivation. De Charms (1968) defines *intrinsic motivation* and *extrinsic motivation* not by the presence or absence of external reinforcement but by the locus of perceived causality. De

Charms suggests that a behavior is extrinsically motivated when the individual perceives himself or herself as a puppet, with the controlling influence located in the environment. As indicated in Chapter 1, a person with these perceptions is called a "pawn." Intrinsically motivated behavior occurs when the person perceives himself or herself as the originator of the behavior—that is, the behavior is under internal control. Such a person is called an "origin." De Charms postulates an interaction effect between the locus of causality and internal and external motivation. Receiving an external reward for an intrinsically motivated behavior would shift one's perception of the controlling influence to the external environment and decrease intrinsic motivation. He believes that humans are motivated to control their environments and to exercise personal causation—that is, to become origins rather than pawns.

Deci (1975) has proposed a cognitive-evaluation theory to account for changes in intrinsic motivation following exposure to external rewards. This theory focuses on one's cognitive evaluation of the reasons for engaging in an activity. It suggests that when a person performs an intrinsically motivated task for money, his or her perception of the reason for performing the task shifts from "intrinsically motivated" to "extrinsically motivated." Since the person is then performing for money, an external reward, intrinsic motivation decreases.

According to Deci's theory, monetary rewards and social rewards, such as verbal praise, have different effects on intrinsic motivation. Verbal praise, for example, should strengthen a person's sense of competence and increase intrinsic motivation. These predictions have been supported by Deci's (1971), research. The general findings of these studies suggest that one who seeks to develop and enhance intrinsic motivation in other people (children, students, employees, or whomever), rather than concentrating on external rewards like money, should focus on creating situations that are intrinsically interesting and then be interpersonally supportive of persons in those situations. Deci suggests that people who experience social approval will continue to be intrinsically motivated because their feelings of competence are enhanced and because they are less likely to think of affection or verbal approval as a control mechanism.

BOX 13-1. DESTROYING INTRINSIC MOTIVATION WITH MONEY

An old man lived on a street where boys played noisily each afternoon. On one especially noisy day, he called the boys into his house and told them that he liked to listen to them play, but his hearing was failing and he could no longer hear their games. He offered them a quarter each if they would come around each day to the front of his house and engage in their noisy games. The youngsters raced back the following day and made a tremendous racket in front of the house. The old man paid them and requested that they return the next day, which they did. But this time he gave each boy only 20 cents, explaining that he was running out of money. After the noisy

329

games on the third day, each boy received only 15 cents. Furthermore, the old man told them he would have to reduce the fee to five cents on the fourth day. The boys became angry and told the old man they would not be back. It was not worth their effort, they said, to make noise for only five cents a day (Casady, 1974).

Important Job-Related Needs

In this section of the chapter we will look at some of the important human needs that must be considered in a total view of work motivation. We will discuss three important work-related needs: the need for satisfying work, the need for competence, and the need for a sense of control over one's life.

Need for Satisfying Work. When the University of Michigan's Research Center for Group Dynamics interviewed 2000 workers, it was found that jobs requiring long hours, heavy workloads, and pressing responsibilities produce less mental and physical illness than jobs with easier work conditions (Horn, 1975). For instance, family doctors, despite working 55 hours a week, expressed the most satisfaction with their work. They also ranked low in depression, anxiety, and irritation. At the other end of work satisfaction were assembly-line workers. Most worked normal hours at a regular pace and had very little responsibility. Yet they were found to be least satisfied with their workload and complained most about depression, poor appetite, insomnia, and physical problems.

Need for Competence. Some psychologists view motivation as arising from a search for competence and mastery over some element of the environment (White, 1959) or from a need to become self-actualized (Maslow, 1954); that is, people have an inherent need to reach their potential or to become that which they are capable of becoming. Some people look on life as a process of developing and bringing to fruition those talents and potential abilities with which they were born. Such potentiality, however, cannot be achieved without the person's being intrinsically motivated.

The difference in work satisfaction among physicians and assembly-line workers may be a result of the difference in feelings of mastery and competence between these two groups. Physicians may be able to endure long hours and heavy workloads with less stress because they feel that their efforts are contributing to the welfare of others. They perceive themselves as needed, responsible, and valued members of society.

Need for a Sense of Control over One's Life. Many years ago, Richter (1957), a psychologist at Johns Hopkins University, observed that a wild rat, when dropped into a tank of warm water, managed to stay afloat for about 60 hours before finally becoming exhausted and drowning. With a second rat he tried something

330

different. Before dropping it into the tank of water, he held it firmly in his grasp until it ceased to struggle. In this situation the rat learned that it was helpless. When placed in the water, this rat swam around excitedly for a few minutes before passively sinking to the bottom, never to resurface.

Ferrari (1962), in a study of perceived freedom of choice in old age, interviewed 55 women over 65 who had applied for admission to a home for the elderly. Each lady, upon admission, was asked how much freedom of choice she had in the decision to move to the home, whether she had been given other alternatives, and how much pressure had been applied by relatives to get her to enter the home. Thirty-eight women reported that they had other alternatives and sought admission on their own volition; 17 indicated they had no other choice. At the end of the first 10 weeks in the home, only one resident who had had a choice had died; 16 of the 17 with no choice were deceased. Although it is possible that these data are contaminated by different levels of health between the groups (the sicker you are, the more your relatives may seek to put you out of sight), Seligman (1975) attributes the results of Ferrari's study to a feeling of helplessness by those without perceived freedom of choice.

The desire to exert some control over one's environment or at least to have some perceived freedom of choice seems to be a very powerful motive for most people. There is also some evidence of a relation between perceived control and the state of one's health, mental and physical (Seligman, 1975).

On the basis of the research presented here, it seems reasonable to conclude that positive relations exist among intrinsic motivation, the need for competence or control over aspects of the environment, job satisfaction and productivity, and physical and mental health. In the remainder of this chapter, we will show how the development of intrinsic motivation and perceived internal control can facilitate job satisfaction and productivity.

THEORIES OF WORK MOTIVATION

The attempt by researchers to understand more fully the nature of motivation and particularly the relation between motivational factors and job performance has produced several theories of work motivation. Before discussing some of the current methods being used to increase the degree to which human needs can be met on the job, let us review three of those theories: equity theory, expectancy-valence theory, and motivation-hygiene theory.

Adams' Theory of Inequity

Adams (1965) has developed an **equity theory** of work motivation on the basis of individuals' perceptions of input/outcome ratios for themselves and others. *Input* refers to any contribution, skill, or knowledge that one brings to the work

331

situation. Inputs may include one's age, previous work experience, education, or desire to do well at the job. Equity theory assumes that workers feel that job-related outcomes, such as payment or promotion, should be roughly parallel to their inputs. Therefore, worker satisfaction and worker productivity are directly tied to the worker's perceptions of the equitable input-outcome ratios for self and others.

One interesting aspect of Adams' theory is that one's perception of fair payment is determined by the input/outcome ratios of fellow workers. For instance, Adams (1965, p. 280) says that inequity is experienced when a person perceives that his or her own input/outcome ratio is unequal to another's input/outcome ratio. Such inequity may be in the direction of the person's being overrewarded or underrewarded. Consequently, inequity exists whenever a person feels he or she is receiving too much or too little for his or her level of inputs. If such inequity is perceived, one is then motivated to alleviate this tension state by means of adjustments in one's own input/outcome ratio or in one's perception of the ratios of others. The theory does state, however, that one has a lower reactive threshold for adjusting to underpayment than to overpayment.

Several hypotheses deduced from Adams' inequity theory have been tested experimentally. Goodman and Friedman (1969) have reviewed the empirical studies on equity theory and found adequate support for the following:

1. Inequity does produce a tension state, and the greater the perceived inequity, the greater the motivation to resolve it.
2. The threshold for underpayment is lower than the threshold for overpayment.
3. Individuals will resist changing input/outcome cognitions that are central to their own self-concepts.
4. Overpaid hourly workers will produce more than equitably paid workers.
5. Overpaid piece-rate workers produce less quantity but higher quality than equitably paid workers.
6. Underpaid hourly workers will invest lower inputs than equitably paid workers.

Adams' theory of inequity is conceptually simple in defining both the conditions that lead to perceived inequity and the conditions that may lead to the resolution of perceived inequity. Researchers have found this model to be of particular value in investigating the cognitive influences on workers' performance. Such research suggests that a reasonable effort by management to understand workers' perceptions of inequity can often lead to minor organizational changes that result in greater worker satisfaction and productivity.

Expectancy-Valence Theory

Expectancy-valence theory is a cognitive theory of motivation that views people as thinking, reasoning beings who have beliefs and expectations about future events in their lives. This theory assumes that human behavior results mainly from

332

the interactive processes between characteristics of the person and his or her perceived environment.

From this theoretical perspective, Steers and Porter (1975) see performance in organizational settings as a function of at least three variables: motivational levels, abilities and traits, and role perceptions. First, a person must want to perform, to direct his or her behavior toward particular tasks or outcomes. A basic prerequisite for task performance on most jobs is a desire of an employee to do assigned tasks.

Desire alone, however, is insufficient to ensure task performance; one must also have the necessary abilities and skills. The purpose of much testing, education, and training is to ensure that employees have the skills and abilities to perform the tasks required of them. Personality traits should also be compatible with the demands of the job. Very introverted persons may make poor salespersons, for example.

The third factor in this analysis of the concept of motivation is role clarity. In order for an employee to devote full and efficient energy to a job, he or she must have an accurate understanding of the job requirements. Without a clear understanding of the occupational role, the person who is highly motivated and has the necessary skills and abilities is likely to perform poorly. Thus, there appear to be at least three factors that significantly influence performance: one must be motivated, one must have the necessary abilities and traits, and one must have fairly clear role prescriptions.

Most of the theoretical and empirical work by expectancy-valence theorists has focused on the "motivation" variable of the above equation. In essence, the expectancy-valence theory predicts that the motivational force to perform (effort) is a multiplicative function of the expectancies that people have concerning future outcomes times the value they place on those outcomes. An expectancy is the extent to which one believes that a certain action will result in a particular outcome. Valence is the value one places on a particular outcome. For example, if a person has a high expectancy that increased performance will lead to a pay increase and if that person places great value on that monetary reward, work motivation should be high. If this person with higher motivation also has the necessary abilities and skills and a clear understanding of job requirements, an increase in job performance should occur.

This analysis of work motivation suggests that job performance is a function of at least three factors: motivation, ability, and role clarity. To maximize job performance, employers should find persons who want to work, fully understand the requirements of their job, have the abilities and skills required by the job, and believe that increased performance on the job will produce desirable outcomes.

This approach should be helpful in diagnosing the motivational aspects of a performance situation and in modifying appropriate aspects of that situation so as to obtain higher levels of performance from employees. Once a diagnosis has been made, Mitchell and Biglan (1971) suggest, changes in the job situation can involve (1) instituting new outcomes which employees will value and which will be perceived as resulting from hard work, (2) changing the expectancies of existing outcomes so that the link between hard work and positively valued outcomes is strengthened and the link between hard work and negatively valued outcomes is weakened, or (3) changing the valences of existing outcomes. The third alternative would be most difficult to

333

accomplish; the first two would be more practical, because it should be much easier to change aspects of the situation so that the employee will perceive it differently than it would be to change the evaluations that an employee makes of various outcomes.

Herzberg's Motivation-Hygiene Theory

Herzberg has developed such an approach within the framework of his **motivation-hygiene theory**. He begins with the assumption that the factors that produce job satisfaction (and motivation) are distinct from the factors that produce job dissatisfaction. Feelings of job satisfaction and dissatisfaction are not opposites, but

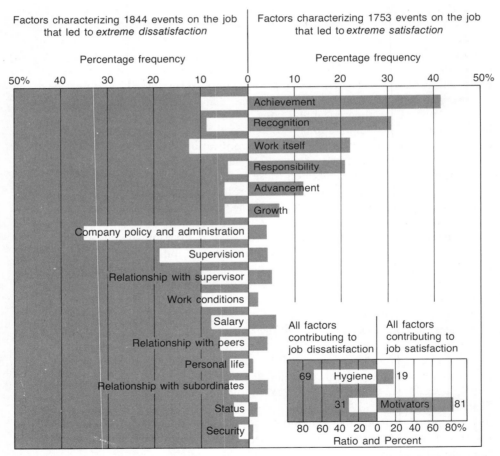

Figure 13-1. *Factors related to job dissatisfaction and satisfaction.* (From "One More Time: How Do You Motivate Employees?" by Frederick Herzberg, *Harvard Business Review,* January–February 1968, p. 57. Copyright © 1967 by the President and Fellows of Harvard College; all rights reserved.)

Why is this boxer enduring such physical punishment? The answer may lie in intrinsic motives (such as enjoyment of boxing) or in extrinsic rewards (such as a million-dollar paycheck). (Photo © Bob Henriques/Magnum.)

are independent of each other. He insists that one who experiences job satisfaction may also experience some job dissatisfaction. Either, both, or neither of these feelings may be experienced by any employee at any given time. This is true because two different sets of human needs are involved. One set (associated with job dissatisfaction) can be thought of as stemming from man's animal nature—hunger, pain avoidance, and so on. Since hunger, a biological drive, makes it necessary to earn money, the need for money also becomes a specific drive. The other set of needs (associated with job satisfaction) relates to a uniquely human characteristic—the need to achieve and experience psychological growth. The potential for satisfaction of animal-based needs in the work setting is to be found in the *job environment,* while the potential for meeting psychological-growth needs originates in the *job content.*

The growth factors (job satisfiers) that are intrinsic to the job are achievement, recognition for achievement, the work itself, responsibility, and growth or advancement. The hygiene factors (job dissatisfiers) related to the job environment include company policy and administration, supervision, interpersonal relationships, working conditions, salary, status, and security. (See Figure 13-1.) Growth factors are

335

more directly related to the nature of the work, while hygiene factors are tied to the environment in which the work is performed.

JOB ENRICHMENT

Job dissatisfiers, according to Herzberg, are not an intrinsic part of the task but rather are related to the conditions under which a task is to be performed. A good hygienic environment can prevent job dissatisfaction, but it cannot create true job satisfaction or happiness. Like physiological needs, hygiene needs are cyclical: when relieved, they immediately begin to develop again. If a worker wants a pay increase, for example, she is unhappy until she gets it. However, once she gets it, she will soon feel the need for another raise, just as she did before. A lack of money can cause unhappiness, and a raise can temporarily make one feel better. But such happiness is of short duration compared with the satisfaction obtained from actual work achievement or recognition. In other words, Herzberg points out that the relief of hygienic needs merely creates a temporary absence of dissatisfaction, but this cannot provide an enduring basis of work satisfaction, which is essential to psychological growth.

Herzberg credits psychology with identifying important work-related psychological needs, such as the need to learn, the need to discover new things, and the need to develop one's potentialities. He found that many people, however, attempt to receive job satisfaction solely from hygiene factors. In addition, industry contributes to the lack of personal growth in employees by ignoring people's psychological needs for growth and creativity. Herzberg suggests that industry might give greater attention to the conditions that would generate more job satisfiers, rather than devoting attention to conditions that reduce job dissatisfiers. The result could be a happier and more productive worker.

Herzberg calls attention to the fact that some college graduates go into business careers that offer high salaries but little job satisfaction. The doctor-in-training, in contrast, may start his or her career with relatively poor working conditions—low pay, long working hours, no pension plan or fringe benefits—but be highly satisfied with the work. In other words, the intern's morale and job satisfaction may be high even though the working conditions are thoroughly dissatisfying. The reason is that interns are given real responsibility with live patients and the kind of supervision that enables them to learn and develop professionally and psychologically. Of course, the expectation of large monetary rewards in a year or two also makes less-than-satisfactory working conditions more tolerable.

DEVELOPING JOB-ENRICHMENT PROGRAMS

Job enrichment is an attempt to increase job satisfaction by increasing responsibility, diversifying activities, providing variable work schedules, and so on. As an example of what can be done to make industrial jobs more satisfying, Herzberg describes how one large company assigned employees to new and important work responsibilities. They were assigned to answer technical questions submitted by shareholders. Each employee was trained to be an expert in a particular area of inquiry and was given full responsibility for handling inquiries and complaints in such areas as transfer taxes and dividend income. Each employee set his or her individual work pace and composed and signed the letters in his or her area of expertise. The result was that morale rose, productivity improved, and employee turnover and absenteeism decreased. It is interesting that this was accomplished not by increasing salary but by giving employees more responsibility and opportunity for personal growth.

The Volvo company, a Swedish automobile manufacturer, was one of the first companies to use job enrichment on a wide scale. In designing the Kalmar plant, Volvo decided to create a work situation in which assembly lines were removed and employees worked in teams while assembling autos (Gyllenhammar, 1977). This plan was based on the assumption that work should be made congruent with individuals' social needs.

Each team worked in quiet surroundings and was responsible for constructing a particular portion of the car—for example, electrical systems, interiors, or doors. Each team established its own work pace, and team workers determined when the work required individual or group effort. Responsibility for the work was enhanced by permitting each team to perform its own quality inspection. After a car passed three group stations, specially trained inspectors examined the work. Later a computer provided feedback to particular groups about recurring problems or the absence of problems. Union surveys showed that employees favor these new working patterns. Volvo now has five plants constructed on this plan, and productivity has been high.

The US Eaton Corporation has attempted another approach to job enrichment by trying to establish a climate of responsible industrial freedom among plant workers. According to Scobel (1975), it began when the manager of Eaton's Battle Creek, Michigan, engine-valve plant decided to build a new facility at Kearney, Nebraska. He asked his managerial staff how he might avoid the problems in employee/management relations in Nebraska that had occurred in a Michigan plant.

In their response members of his managerial staff discussed and evaluated traditional policies and practices that affected employee relations. Their composite critique was summarized in the form of a letter written as if by a factory employee who is explaining why he brings so little of himself to his workplace. The letter read as follows (Scobel, 1975, pp. 133–135):*

> Dear Sir:
> What you are asking me, as I see it, is why was I not giving you my best in exchange for the reasonable wages and benefits you provide me and my family.

337

First, I'm not trying to blame anybody for why you don't see the "whole" me. Some of the problem is company policy, some is union thinking, some is just me. Let me tell you why, and I'll leave it to bigger minds than mine to figure out blames and remedies.

I'll begin with my first day on the job eleven years ago—my first factory job, by the way. I was just 19 then. Incidentally, my cousin started work in your office on the same day. We used to drive to work together. She still works for you, too.

The first thing I was told that day by the personnel manager and my foreman was that I was on 90 days' probation. They were going to measure my ability and attendance and attitude and then make up their minds about me. Gee, that surprised me. I thought I'd been hired already—but I really wasn't. Although the foreman tried to make me feel at home, it was still sort of a shock to realize I was starting out kind of on the sidelines until I proved my worth. In fact, the only person who told me I "belonged," without any strings attached, was my union steward.

You know, that first day my foreman told me all about the shop rules of discipline as if I were going to start out stealing or coming to work drunk or getting into fights or horseplay. What made it even worse was when I later found out that no one told my cousin she was on probation. I asked her if she had seen the rules, and here it is eleven years later and she still doesn't know there are about 35 rules for those of us working in the factory.

What it boils down to is that your policies—yes, and the provisions of our union contract—simply presume the factoryman untrustworthy, while my cousin in the office is held in much higher regard. It's almost like we work for different companies.

After I had been here about eight months, a car hit my car broadside on the way to work. My cousin and I were both taken to the hospital right away and released several hours later. As soon as I was released by the hospital, I called the plant to tell them what happened. I couldn't get through to my foreman, so I told my tale to a recording machine. When my cousin didn't show up by nine o'clock, her boss got worried and called the house and then the hospital. When he found out my cousin had a broken arm and some cuts, but was basically okay, he sent for a taxi to take her home.

Both my cousin and I ended up missing four days' work. On each of the next three days, I called and told the tape recorder I would not be in. I never heard from anybody in the company and when I got back to work later that week, my supervisor said, "Sure glad to see you're okay . . . it's a shame you spoiled your perfect attendance record. . . ."

Sir, I don't come to work to be worried about by someone. But I have some difficulty understanding why, when I'm absent, nobody really cares. It seems as if the company's just waiting for me to do something wrong. When I got back to work from that car accident, you started getting another little chunk less from me. Does that sound crazy? Or does it seem selfish?

Sir, why must I punch a time clock? Do you think I'd lie about my starting and quitting times? Why must I have buzzers to tell me when I take a break, relieve myself, eat lunch, start working, go home? Do you really think I can't tell time or would otherwise rob you of valuable minutes? Why doesn't the restroom I must use provide any privacy? Why do I have to drive my car over chuckholes while you enjoy reserved, paved parking? Why must I work the day before and after a holiday to get holiday pay? Are you convinced I will extend the holiday into the weekend—while, by the way, my cousin is thought to have more sense than that?

I guess I'm saying that when you design your policies for the very few who need them, how do you think the rest of us feel?

Sir, do you really think I don't care or don't know what you think of me? If you are convinced of that, then you will never understand why I bring less than all of myself to my workbench.

You know, sir, in my eleven years, I've run all kinds of machinery for you, but your company has never even let me look at what the maintenance man does when he has to repair one of my machines. No one has ever really asked me how quality might be better or how my equipment or methods might be improved. In fact, your policies drum it into me good and proper that you really want me to stay in my place. And now, you want to know why I don't pour it on? Wow! Don't you realize that I may want to contribute more than you let me? I know the union may be responsible for some of this—but again, I'm trying to explain why, not whose fault it is.

You know, sir, I would like a more challenging job, but that isn't the heart of the matter, not for me at least. If there were a sense of dignity around here, I could not hold back the effort and ideas within me, even if my particular job was less than thrilling. Many of my buddies do not want their modest contributions respected.

You know, my neighbor is a real quiet, sweet old man who just retired from here last month. When I ask him how he sums up his life's work, he says—and I can almost quote him exactly—"A pretty good place to work—only thing that really bothered me was that warning I got 26 years ago for lining up at the clock two and one-half minutes early."

Well, sir, I suspect that 26 years ago, you may have corrected this quiet, nice guy for lining up early at your clock. But the price you paid was making him a "clock watcher" for 26 years. I wonder—was that warning all that necessary? Why couldn't you have just told him why lining up early isn't a good idea and then relied on him to discipline himself? I wonder.

It has been said, sir, that factory people look upon profit as a dirty word. I don't feel that way, but you know, it's almost as if love is the dirty word here.

Why don't I give my best? Well, I guess I have a kind of thermostat inside me that responds to your warmth. Do you have a thermostat inside you?
Very truly yours,

As a result of this letter, which all but spells out its own solutions, management at the new Eaton plant puts out a written handbook that commits the company to a counseling rather than rules-and-penalties process, to weekly departmental meetings that encourage employee input, to a uniform benefit system for office and factory workers, and to a managerial policy that emphasizes trust and employee participation. These are some of the policy changes instituted:

1. A new hiring process in which applicants and their families were invited to the plant for plant tours and encouraged to speak openly and frankly about their

impressions and concerns. Newcomers could also express special job preferences within their ability and experience.

2. No probationary period. New employees were evaluated individually. The company policy assumes that people are eager to work and be dependable employees.
3. No time clocks. Employees were responsible for recording their own work time.
4. A standard sanction system for plant employees, the same as for office and supervisory employees.
5. An "open floor" concept that made the factory worker's workplace as important as the supervisor's office. Territorial and status barriers were eliminated, so that managerial people often conducted business at the employee's workplace as well as their own office.
6. Involvement of factory, supervisory, and lower-level office personnel in managerial meetings, functions, and planning sessions. Many important issues, such as whether to shorten the work week or lay off some employees, were decided by unanimous decision.

As a result of these policy changes, it was found that many employees wanted to learn new ways to improve their work performance as well as learn more about the entire company production process. Moreover, many wanted to take on new responsibilities. One custodian persuaded his boss that he, rather than the purchasing department, should order local cleaning supplies, since he was more directly aware of the needs.

About 7 years after this approach was implemented, absenteeism was about 1–3%, compared with 6–12% at other company locations. Employee turnover was similarly reduced. The major problem with this new approach was getting supervisory personnel in some plants to accept this new managerial philosophy, and of course a few employees exploited this new freedom. This approach required a lot of close cooperation of management, employees, and the union. Advantages of this plan are that it is simple and cheap. Certainly the improvement in employee attitudes and productivity makes the Eaton plan an attractive form of job enrichment.

Job Enrichment through Flextime

Flextime is any system that provides employees some measure of control over their working hours. Flextime permits the worker to adjust the work schedule to accommodate individual preferences and personal needs. Fixed times of arrival and departure are replaced by a workday composed of *core time* and *flexible time*. Core time consists of the hours within the workday during which all employees must be on the job. Flexible time is that portion of the workday, before and after the core hours, within which the employee may choose his or her time of arrival and departure. Flextime allows employees to vary their starting and quitting times, but they continue to be required to work a specified number of hours per day or week and must be on the job during the core hours.

The concept of flexible working hours is simple and easily applied. For instance, working hours may be scheduled from 7:00 A.M. to 6:00 P.M. The core time

340

is usually about four or five hours—say, from 10:00 A.M. to 3:00 P.M. In this example the flexible time would therefore be 7:00–10:00 A.M. and 3:00–6:00 P.M.

Flextime is intended to increase the worker's job satisfaction, motivation, and attendance, with the goal of increasing productivity. Being able to adjust one's work schedule to personal needs and desires not only should decrease the dissatisfaction that can result from the routine repetition experienced in many jobs but also allows the worker to perform personal business, such as meeting banking or medical appointments, without using vacation or sick leave. About 1000 American companies and government agencies, having more than 300,000 workers, have adopted some form of flextime.

In the United States, the Social Security Administration (part of the Department of Health, Education and Welfare) has been among the pioneers in initiating flextime schedules. Since the experiment began in April 1974 with the Data Processing Bureau, Baltimore, Maryland, about 12 more components of the Social Security Administration have changed to flextime programs. The program was expanded because of positive results of the experimental group in four evaluation categories: effectiveness; job satisfaction and morale; leave use and tardiness; and energy use. Today between 4000 and 5000 Social Security Administration employees work under flextime.

The most commonly anticipated organizational advantages of flextime are minimizing of tardiness in reporting for work, reduction in overtime and sick leave, increase in productivity, improved morale, more concentrated work and thought, and reduction in rush-hour traffic. Since flexible work hours allow time adjustments for personal business, employees should use less work time for personal purposes. It may also be that a worker is more likely to continue a task to completion, thus reducing downtime and start-up time. It is also possible that the worker will choose work hours that coincide with his or her period of peak efficiency.

Experiences with Flextime

Harriet Weinstein (1975) relates the experiences of three firms using some variation of flexible work hours. Two of the organizations are insurance companies, and the third is the corporate headquarters of a Fortune 500 company. The implementation of flexible work hours had an obvious impact on all three companies. Tardiness and 1-day absences declined. One company, which had experienced a turnover problem in personnel, noted greater stability in their labor force.

One of these companies adopted flexible working hours after successful experimentation with flextime at its worldwide headquarters in Switzerland. Employees were allowed to choose their arrival and departure times on a daily basis, arrival time being between 8:00 and 9:30 A.M. and departure time being between 4:00 and 6:00 P.M. The Nestlé Company's program was reported to be well received by management and employees. The system is credited with increasing both morale and productivity.

341

Two firms found no change in the level of efficiency or productivity, but one of the insurance companies found that productivity, measured by the number of applications processed per day of work, increased.

A recent survey of over 23,000 readers of the magazine *Psychology Today* indicated that over 78% would like to be able to set the hours that they start and leave work (Renwick & Lawler, 1978). This finding suggests strong support for flextime plans.

CORRELATES OF JOB SATISFACTION

Job Satisfaction and Performance

As Ben walked by smiling on his way to his office, Ben's boss remarked to a friend: "Ben really enjoys his job, and that's why he's the best damn worker I ever had. And that's reason enough for me to keep Ben happy." The friend replied: "No, you're wrong! Ben likes his job because he does it so well. If you want to make Ben happy, you ought to do whatever you can to help him further improve his performance."

This story typifies the controversy over the cause-and-effect relations between job satisfaction and job performance. Some people might argue that job satisfaction causes increased productivity, but Porter and Lawler (1968) remind us that it is possible for a worker to be simultaneously satisfied and nonproductive. They suggest that it is wiser to think of job satisfaction as something that results from job performance than as the cause of good or bad performance. Job satisfaction is a function of the degree to which the employee receives rewards, both intrinsic and extrinsic, from his or her job situation. The problem is that in many organizations the rewards received are not tied to job performance.

Porter and Lawler's research in five companies showed that managers who were ranked high by their superiors reported significantly greater satisfaction than low-ranked managers. The relation between high performance and high satisfaction, however, was not very great. The best-performing managers did not report receiving much greater rewards in pay or security, but they did report more rewards in areas concerned with opportunities to express autonomy and to obtain self-realization in the job. The implication of this finding was that the companies seemed to be allowing their best management performers to gain more self-fulfillment and self-realization from their work than low performers, but in giving monetary rewards they were not making significant discriminations between high and low performers.

Porter and Lawler imply that organizations should actively and visibly give rewards in direct proportion to the quality of job performance for employees at all levels. When this is done, high satisfaction should be more closely associated with

Hard work that leads to positive outcomes is likely to be sustained. (Photo © Janet Fries/Icon.)

superior performance, and, in turn, the best performers will be the employees who believe they are receiving the most rewards.

A company's failure to find a positive relation between job satisfaction and performance for its employees could mean that it is not differentially rewarding its best performers. The aim of the employer would not necessarily be to increase everyone's satisfaction; it would be to make sure that the best performers were the most satisfied employees—that is, to maximize the relation between satisfaction and performance. To accomplish this, Porter and Lawler suggest, management should make sure that (1) rewards given are those highly desired by those who perform well, (2) superior performers are given more extrinsic rewards (salary, bonuses, and so on) and more opportunities to gain intrinsic rewards (challenging work, autonomy, and so on) than inferior performers, and (3) employees see and believe that good performance leads to greater rewards, both extrinsic and intrinsic.

Companies must make sure that the rewards they provide are ones widely desired by the persons receiving them. They also need to find more objective methods of discriminating between good and poor performance and of providing commensurate rewards for high performance. A boss may be reluctant to discriminate among employees by giving rewards for good performance because those who fail to get what they wanted may complain. In such cases it is the function of higher management to provide concrete rewards to superiors who do not shrink from evaluating and reward-

343

ing outstanding performance. The right types of reward policies at the top can have positive impacts on those practiced throughout the organization.

Greene (1972) agrees that the use of differential rewards may require courage on the part of the manager but that failure to give differential rewards can have worse consequences. An employee is likely to repeat that behavior which was rewarded, regardless of whether it resulted in high or low performance. Not only will the rewarded low performer continue to perform poorly, but the high performer, with knowledge of this inequity, will eventually reduce his or her level of performance or seek a new employer. To be most effective, a reward system must also have credibility. This means that the basis on which evaluations are made is made known to all employees and that there is no secrecy about the rewards received. Secrecy about who gets what in salary and bonuses tends to reduce confidence in the objectivity and fairness of the system and thereby undermines the motivational possibilities of linking higher pay to better performance.

Job Satisfaction and the Need for Achievement

An employee's need for achievement is related to job satisfaction. McClelland (1961) has found that people with a high need for achievement (1) like situations that allow personal responsibility for finding solutions to problems, (2) tend to set moderate achievement goals and take calculated risks, and (3) want frequent and concrete performance feedback. Adams and Stone (1977) hypothesized that people whose need for achievement is not satisfied on the job would be more likely to engage in highly achievement-oriented leisure-time activities than those whose need for achievement was satisfied on the job. Their data supported this hypothesis. They suggest that organizations might reduce employee turnover either by increasing achievement characteristics of various jobs or by encouraging and/or providing achievement-oriented leisure-time activities for those whose need for achievement is not satisfied on the job. Organizations might also consider the degree of achievement opportunity afforded by various positions and seek better matches between jobs and employees' levels of need for achievement.

IMPLICATIONS FOR MANAGEMENT

The data presented in this chapter have implications for managers who want to improve performance and work attitudes. They could begin by increasing their sensitivity to individual differences in motivation. They should recognize that different employees have different preferences for the rewards available for good performance. For example, money as a reward is much more important to some than to others. A greater awareness of these differences would encourage managers, within

344

policy limitations, to reward good performance with those things more desirable to employees.

Employees should see a clear relation between successful performance on their part and the receipt of desired rewards. Managers should identify superior performers and reward them. When rewards are not tied to performance, motivational levels would be expected to decrease markedly.

So far as possible, employees should be provided with jobs that offer greater challenge, diversity, and opportunities for personal satisfaction. They should also clearly understand the demands of the job, since role clarity generally facilitates job performance.

Efforts should be made to involve employees in cooperative ventures aimed at improving production. Data presented in this chapter indicate that a very important factor in motivating employees is fuller participation in the decision-making processes aimed at improving organizational effectiveness.

In this chapter we have emphasized some of the techniques and procedures that have resulted in increased satisfaction that can be derived from one's work. We do not intend to imply that all work can become completely satisfying or pleasurable or even that all workers should be satisfied with their work. It may be that many jobs, by their nature, will always remain routine, repetitive, and monotonous. Practically all kinds of work, for that matter, have a great deal of routine and require some "hard" work—physically, mentally, or both. The term *work*, by definition, implies that we must exert sustained effort and be performing our duties and assignments when we would rather be doing something else. Work means that we are not completely free to choose how we will spend our time. An effective and productive worker must be capable of following instructions, accepting responsibility, completing assignments, and meeting deadlines. This requires self-discipline and an ability to put business before pleasure in situations in which the task is not intrinsically satisfying. Since almost no one finds his or her work completely satisfying, the next chapter will deal with the use of leisure time. We will present concepts and ideas which we hope will enable you to more adequately meet those needs not met in a work situation and which will help you reach a higher state of personal and social development.

SUMMARY

Work continues to be an important source of identity, self-esteem, and self-fulfillment for most people. Some of the incentives for work, however, are changing. People are demanding more from their jobs than a means of survival. One of the problems for managers is to increase the intrinsic motivation of workers and the extent to which some of their needs can be met on the job. This requires some understanding of intrinsic motivation and how it can be facilitated. A manager needs to be aware of some basic human needs that can be satisfied through work and how various incentives and motivational devices are perceived by employees. An understanding of the relations between job satisfaction and job performance is also needed by managers.

In this chapter we have presented three theories of work motivation which have contributed to our understanding motivation on the job. They are the inequity theory, the expectancy-valence theory, and the motivation-hygiene theory. We have also discussed some of the needs that can be satisfied through work including the need for satisfying work, the need for competence, and the need for a sense of control over one's life. Although the relationship between job satisfaction and job performance is complex and not completely understood, we have presented some ideas and research on this relationship.

KEY CONCEPTS

Equity theory a theory of work motivation that says workers feel that job-related outcomes, such as payment or promotion, should correspond to what the worker contributes.

Expectancy-valence theory a theory based on the assumption that behavior is a function of the interactive processes between personal characteristics and the person's perceived environment. This theory predicts that effort expended is a function of expected outcomes times the value placed on those outcomes.

Extrinsic motivation motivation originating in one's external environment. Extrinsically motivated behavior occurs in order to produce some desirable consequence or to prevent some aversive consequence. Such behavior is a means to an end.

Flextime a system that provides employees some measure of control over their working hours.

Intrinsic motivation motivation originating within the individual. Intrinsically motivated behavior is engaged in for its own sake, not for the result it may have. The behavior is an end in itself.

Job enrichment an attempt to increase job satisfaction by increasing responsibilities, diversifying activities, providing variable work schedules, and so on.

Motivation-hygiene theory a theory of motivation based on the assumption that causes of job satisfaction (motivation factors) and causes of job dissatisfaction (hygiene factors) are distinct from each other.

346

CHAPTER OBJECTIVES

1. To understand the problems of leisure-time use at various stages of life.
2. To examine various theories of why people need leisure time.
3. To understand the distinction between leisure time and nonleisure (or work) time.
4. To understand the interaction between leisure-related needs and leisure activities.
5. To learn how to plan one's leisure-time use.

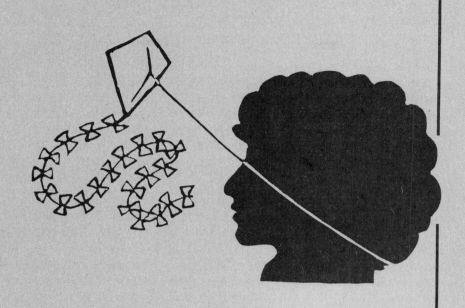

LIVING
WITH
LEISURE
TIME

Leisure-time activities have become big business. In 1977 leisure was the number-one industry in the United States, with Americans spending over $160 billion on leisure and recreational activities that year. *U.S. News & World Report* ("How Americans Pursue Happiness," 1977) describes how the American people are bombarded with promises of pleasure once they purchase a Hula Hoop, a minibike, a CB radio, a South Seas vacation, or any of a thousand other attractions. Disneyland-type entertainment parks have sprung up across the country. The interstate highways overflow with vacationers. Major sporting events draw capacity crowds. Millions of dollars are spent on equipment and opportunities to participate in weekend sporting activities like tennis or golf. Colleges and universities are offering courses in leisure-time use, and many courses in higher education have solely a recreational objective. People are more involved in nonwork-related activities than ever before, and one expert predicts that the desire for summertime recreational facilities will be four times as great in the year 2000 as it was in 1960.

Most people today consider that modern living entitles them, as a right, to more leisure time and less work time. In fact, the World Leisure and Recreation Association, in conjunction with other international recreational agencies, has developed a charter for leisure (see Box 14-1). Generally researchers have found that automation, more "flextime" work schedules, better pension plans for the retired, better health of the elderly, and a general increase in the affluence of the average American have created more nonwork time. However, as Box 14-2 indicates, there is some evidence that the freeing of the average worker for more nonwork time is not as great as supposed.

BOX 14-1. CHARTER FOR LEISURE

Preface

Leisure time is that period of time at the complete disposal of an individual, after work and other routine obligations are completed. Leisure hours are periods of freedom, when an individual can enhance life as a human being and as a productive member of society. Moreover, the World Leisure and Recreation Association believes that recreation and leisure activities can play an important part in establishing good relations among the nations of the world. Below is this organization's charter for leisure.

Article 1

Every man has a right to leisure time. This right comprises reasonable working hours, regular paid holidays, favorable traveling conditions and suitable social planning, including reasonable access to leisure facilities, areas and equipment in order to enhance the advantages of leisure time.

Article 2

The right to enjoy leisure time with complete freedom is absolute. The prerequisites for undertaking individual leisure pursuits should be safeguarded to the same extent as those for collective enjoyment of leisure time.

Article 3

Every man has a right to easy access to recreational facilities open to the public, and to nature reserves by lakes, seas, wooded areas, in the mountains and to open spaces in general. These areas, their fauna and flora, must be protected and conserved.

Article 4

Every man has a right to participate in and be introduced to all types of recreation during leisure time, such as sports and games, open-air living, travel, theatre, dancing, pictorial art, music, science and handicrafts, irrespective of age, sex, or level of education.

Article 5

Leisure time should be unorganized in the sense that official authorities, urban planners, architects and private groups of individuals do not decide how others are to use their leisure time. The above-mentioned should create or assist in the planning of the leisure opportunities, aesthetic environments and recreation facilities required to enable man to exercise individual choice in the use of his leisure, according to his personal tastes and under his own responsibility.

Article 6

Every man has a right to the opportunity for learning how to enjoy his leisure time. Family, school, and community should instruct him in the art of exploiting his leisure time in the most sensible fashion. In schools, classes, and courses of instruction, children, adolescents, and adults must be given the opportunity to develop the skills, attitudes and understandings essential for leisure literacy.

Article 7

The responsibility for education for leisure is still divided among a large number of disciplines and institutions. In the interests of everyone and in order to utilize purposefully all the funds and assistance available in the various administrative levels, this responsibility should be fully coordinated among all public and private bodies concerned with leisure. The goal should be for a community of leisure. . . . Where feasible, special schools would train leaders to help promote recreational programs and assist individuals and groups during their leisure hours, in so far as they can without restricting freedom of choice. Such service is worthy of the finest creative efforts of man.

Jogging is a favorite leisure-time activity for many people. (Photo © Cary Wolinsky/Stock, Boston.)

BOX 14-2. IS LEISURE TIME INCREASING?

Although most assume that the answer to this question is yes, the truth is that it is very hard to know whether leisure time has increased significantly in our society over the past couple of decades. Godbey and Parker (1976) point out that it is difficult to compare amounts of leisure time in society over the years because researchers use different definitions of *leisure*.

Investigators who believe that workers have more free time today than yesteryear point to the short work week, earlier retirements, more efficient technology, and a decline in the Puritan ethic, which holds that what is pleasurable is sinful. But other investigators think there are good reasons to suspect that leisure time has not dramatically increased in our society. Both De Grazia (1962) and Linder (1970) suggest that even though work hours have apparently dropped over the last half century, these figures do not take into consideration the part-time and overtime work of many American workers. Some spend less time at a particular job, but many have found it necessary to moonlight to maintain their middle-class status. Moreover, these figures would change if work around the home or travel time were included as work time. In addition, another study (Walker, 1969) has shown that even with more efficient technology in the home, time spent in household duties has not substantially decreased in the last 40 years.

Whether nonwork time is increasing or not, the belief that one is living in a society with more leisure time can have a profound influence on one's behavior. Linder (1970), for instance, believes that most of us have been caught up in the myth that the American society is a society of leisure. The result is that people have become virtually obsessed with finding new ways to fill in periods of free time. Moreover, many have come to feel that work can never bring complete fulfillment and personal happiness, which therefore must be accomplished by way of leisure and recreational activities.

Unfortunately, many of us do not know how to use leisure time effectively or meaningfully. Moreover, the concept "leisure" has different meanings to different people. For some, leisure time means the opportunity to do absolutely nothing. It is simply a time to relax or be with one's thoughts or perhaps just read the newspaper. For others, every moment of one's life must be devoted to productive activity, whether it be work-time activities or nonwork-time activities. For still others, nonwork time is not so much devoted to productive endeavors as to activities that are intrinsically satisfying and meaningful. In other words, the most rewarding use of leisure time is when one is just having fun doing something.

Obviously, leisure time can be used in many ways—some that bring productivity, self-fulfillment, and satisfaction and some that do not. Too often in our society the leisure time is used for self-depreciating or self-defeating behavior, such as drug abuse, or even antisocial behavior. Hence, knowing more about the psychologically healthy use of leisure time can be more than just a superficial study. In this chapter we will examine some of the things we know about leisure-time use and make some suggestions on how to live more effectively with leisure time.

LEISURE AT VARIOUS STAGES OF LIFE

In this section we will examine how people tend to use leisure time at three stages of life in our society: childhood, adolescence, and adulthood.

353

Leisure in Childhood

A substantial portion of leisure-time activity for most people is likely to take place in a family setting. The home is the place where most people of all ages—except perhaps adolescents and nonmarried adults—spend most of their nonwork time.

In our society it is generally assumed that as children get older, less time should be free time and more time should be devoted to work-related activities. Therefore, the attitudes that parents hold about leisure and work will have an important influence on their own lives and the way they socialize their children. For instance, some individuals may grow up believing that leisure time is synonymous with laziness. For others, leisure time is evidence of being successful in society.

It is somewhat difficult to apply the term *leisure* to the activities of preschool children. Part of a young child's day is occupied by structured activities, such as eating, sleeping, and dressing, but the rest of the day consists of play. Most of the preschooler's day consists of energetic play with a few brief relaxation periods. Parents usually provide toys or other materials to occupy the child's time. However, whether the play is with toys, siblings, other children, or parents, the behavior is almost always of a spontaneous and free-moving character.

Each parent must decide what his or her role will be in the young child's play time. It is probably desirable for parents to strive for some balance between completely dominating the child's play time and giving the child complete freedom to use play time in his or her own way. Psychologists have found that children's play-time activities are not just ways they occupy time. A tremendous amount of learning occurs during play. The nature and quality of play activities will have an important impact on the child's emotional, social, and intellectual growth. Children develop a sense of security and enjoyment from structured play activities during the day. A child will come to anticipate a scheduled "reading time" or "puzzle time" and even a scheduled "mental time" (see Box 14-3). Children cannot express or develop their potentialities by spending endless hours watching television or being entertained with toys and mechanical gadgets. Parents should recognize that there is no better assurance of a child's effective personality development than for the parents to be an active part of the child's life—even during play time.

BOX 14-3. A NEED FOR MENTAL TIME

Activity is desirable. As pointed out in Chapter 4, we need to explore and know our world. By nature, we are stimulation-seeking organisms. Accordingly, people need to be provided with opportunities and meaningful activities that provide an outlet for this need. However, the psychiatrist William Glasser points out ("How Americans Pursue Happiness," 1977) that the human organism does not need constant environmental stimulation. Rather, he believes the human brain is set up in such a way that it requires periods of "mental time" each day. These periods of "mental time" provide the brain with temporary relief from sensory bombardment so that it may be free for thinking and fantasy. The brain needs these opportunities for internal stimulation as well as external stimulation. Glasser emphasizes that watching television or listening to the radio cannot provide the flexible and creative stimulation provided by our own thoughts and fantasies.

As a child grows older, he or she uses play to try out sex-appropriate behavior. The impact of sex-role training can easily be seen in a child as early as age 3. Around age 4 or 5, children become interested in sex-role games. Pretending to be a father, a mother, a doctor, a nurse, or a soldier may help children to explore new ways of coping with the world.

As a child enters late childhood (approximately age 6 to puberty), leisure activities change both in quantity and in quality. The child's leisure activities become more structured, more recreationally oriented, and more social. More rules and regulations come to govern the child's play activities. There is a greater acceptance of "give and take" and "leader/follower" play conditions. Moreover, the more or less impulsive play of early childhood gives way to generally more orderly and more passive recreational activities.

BOX 14-4. SEX DIFFERENCES IN LATE CHILDHOOD PLAY

Developmental psychologists have noted that boys and girls often progress somewhat differently in the development of play activities. Child and Child (1974), for instance, report that girls' play activities proceed from creative-imaginative play (that is, pretend games) to more physical and competitive play in late childhood. Boys, however, tend to devote most of their energy to physical and competitive play, and although creative-imaginative play tends to increase during childhood, the amount of time devoted to such play never exceeds time devoted to physical play.

Later childhood can be more meaningfully divided into "leisure time" and "nonleisure time." Children at this stage come to delineate time into "school time," "work or study time," and "free time." For the most part, getting home from school is the dividing point between "work time" and "nonwork time." As the child gets older and progresses through the educational system, more and more time must be given over to homework and constructive play as the child prepares for the arrival of adolescence.

355

Leisure in Adolescence

In Chapter 4 we mentioned that rather stable and consistent behavior patterns of late childhood are abruptly disrupted by the onset of puberty. For the young adolescent, free time is usually devoted to daydreaming and a general withdrawal from activity. As the adolescent becomes older, a heightened interest in people develops, particularly in regard to the opposite sex, as do concerns about an occupation.

Most adolescents live at home. However, their interests are not directed toward family activities, although the parents still have an important influence on the adolescent's leisure behavior. Parental values are experienced in regard to part-time work, selection of dates and friends, and the acceptability of certain recreational activities. The major parent/adolescent conflict may be in regard to how the adolescent should use his or her free time. Many adolescents feel a need to pay their way or at least provide some spending money, which will give them some freedom in controlling leisure time.

Most schools recognize students' need for recreation and make recreational opportunities available. There are usually readily available recreational activities at school at little or no cost to the student. Some students cannot afford frequent non-school-related recreational activities—movies, sporting events, and the like.

Although there may be an emphasis on "having fun" in adolescence, it is also a time when the individual must establish some order in life and set some life goals. For the most part, modern adolescents have more free time than in the past. They have fewer home responsibilities and chores, and some adolescents have difficulty determining what to do with their free time. The "youth culture" may emphasize group activities, and withdrawal from home involvement is common. Free time may be used just to congregate, listen to music, or sometimes use drugs. A striving for freedom and independence may be expressed through a protest against the broader culture.

As adolescents approach young adulthood, they tend to be more selective in their social relationships and their leisure activities. Usually in adolescence work and family obligations have not greatly curtailed leisure time. However, adulthood brings more obligations and responsibilities and less and less leisure time.

Leisure in Adulthood

The socialization process does not end when a person reaches adulthood. Learning in childhood and adolescence establishes a foundation for adult functioning, but such learning cannot prepare one for all adult roles or provide strategies for meeting all adult life demands. As we pointed out, in sheer number and variety of adjustments, early adult years are often the most demanding years of one's life. Early adulthood is the age of decision. Decisions about continuing one's education, what career to pursue, whether to marry, whether to have children, whether to buy a home

356

As an individual grows older, his or her leisure-time activities become more orderly and more social. (Photo © Cary Wolinsky/Stock, Boston.)

or rent, and so on are constant concerns in one's thoughts. Moreover, one must be a doer as well as a thinker.

Perhaps the most important influences on the quality and quantity of the young adult's leisure time are (1) one's marital status, (2) whether one has children, and (3) one's economic status. The young unmarried adult will generally have both more money and more time to spend on leisure activities. For the young married couple without children, simply enjoying the companionship of each other is a form of leisure. As one couple said, "For us a big time is watching *Hawaii Five-O* and eating a bowl of popcorn." Most recreational activities may simply be carryovers from the dating relationship. Once the young married couple has a child, however, free time will be greatly curtailed, and most recreational activities will be directed toward the child's interests. Havighurst and Feigenbaum (1959) have identified two patterns of adult use of leisure. Adults' leisure activities are either **home-centered** or **community-centered**. Home-centered recreational activities are pursued mainly with family members and include things like going on picnics, playing games, or simply watching TV together. Community-centered recreational activities are related to interests outside the home and include things like going to concerts or theaters or participating in social clubs.

A number of studies have shown that adult leisure-time use is related to socioeconomic status. In lower-class families, recreational activities are more outside the home environment and are less home-centered. Middle-class families' recreation is more prone to be home-centered, although such families can better afford commercial entertainment financially. Moreover, fathers from lower-class homes are less likely to be involved in the family's leisure-time and recreational activities. Members of the upper-middle class often devote more time to work activities.

In middle age (approximately ages 40 to 60), most people are at their peak earning capacity and have fewer family and financial obligations. They usually have more free time to enjoy. For many people this is the first time in their lives that leisure-time use is important. Education is out of the way, children are grown and probably have interests outside the home or are married, and work activities are probably stable. Even the housewife may find for the first time in her married life that domestic demands do not require all her time. Consequently, many middle-aged adults find themselves with more time and more money available for leisure activities.

For many, such leisure time is a problem. Most people at this age prefer more sedentary recreational activities. Many activities used to fill up free time in early adulthood, such as tennis, golf, and dancing, may be less desirable. Moreover, many people were involved as young parents in home-centered leisure activities and find that without children free time is not fulfilling. Some couples continue to seek out activities together, while others become more involved in social or community or civic groups. For many, church activities become especially important at this time. However, as Hurlock (1968) reported, the forms of recreation that are most popular among middle-aged American men and women are reading, movies, radio, television, visiting, trips, sports, and hobbies. Hobbies are a particularly popular way of using leisure time in middle age, as well as in later years.

BOX 14-5. HOBBIES

Hobbies have always been a means by which one could find self-expression and self-satisfaction. Most people select a hobby that requires a modest amount of time and energy and can be engaged in at one's convenience. Some care for old cars. Others find pleasure in a genealogical study to trace their "roots." Many are finding self-expression and self-satisfaction in college courses. Today most colleges and universities provide both credit and noncredit courses in recreational and hobby-development areas. Some people are even making a hobby of creative writing. More

Games are satisfying leisure-time activities at all ages. (Photo © Andrée Abecassis.)

and more people over 40 are finding that college and university environments have much to offer the student who wishes to grow in self-development areas.

Hobbies may become an outlet for leisure needs at virtually any age, but they are particularly popular in middle and old age. Research shows that the earlier one has developed a meaningful hobby, the more satisfying the hobby tends to be in later years. Hobbies may be purely intrinsically motivated activities, or they can compensate for an unfulfilling life. Generally, women have more hobbies and a greater variety of hobbies than men.

For those interested in developing a hobby, a number of books describe types of hobbies as well as how to begin a hobby. One excellent "how to" book is Alvin Schwartz's *Hobbies* (1972). Schwartz presents a survey of some popular and some not so well-known hobbies that one might take up. Below are some hobbies you might wish to explore:

1. *Crafts:* ceramics, making prints, developing a printing press, photography, puppetry, woodcarving, and woodworking.

2. *Collections:* autographs, coins, postage stamps, bottles, and over 20 other lesser-known types of collections.
3. *Nature studies:* birds, fishes, fossils, insects, plants, rocks, and seashells.
4. *Science and communication:* archeology, astronomy, "ham" radio, weather forecasting, and others.

In Chapter 4 we mentioned that there are two prevailing attitudes about the elderly in our society. One attitude is that the elderly are just as young as they feel. The other attitude is that the elderly should "act their age" and resign themselves to a sedentary life-style. The point here is that how an elderly person uses leisure time may very well be influenced by the attitude he or she adopts about what he or she should do.

Surprisingly, the leisure-time behavior patterns of the elderly are not significantly different from those of the middle aged. Most elderly persons are generally capable of carrying out the same types of recreational activities as the middle aged. Of course, some factors can curtail certain activities. Such influences as physical health, whether one still lives in one's home, and one's financial situation may require some adjustments in leisure-time use. In general, however, it seems that if a person has made wise and meaningful use of his or her leisure time in prior stages of life, adjustments to leisure time are less pronounced in old age. Most older people appear capable of meeting the demands of this stage of life, including how to use free time, if they have successfully coped with the demands of preceding stages of development.

EXERCISE 14-1. PLANNING LEISURE-TIME USE

On the basis of the information presented in this chapter so far, how might you identify and develop appropriate leisure-time activities for the following individuals:

1. Imagine that some friends of yours will be leaving their 5-year-old daughter with you for the day. What activities would you plan for this child? What if this child were a 5-year-old boy?
2. Imagine that you have volunteered for some community service work and you have been asked to entertain a 70-year-old man for the day. What activities would you plan for this gentleman? What if this were an elderly woman?

Try to imagine other situations in which you would be called on to develop use of leisure and recreational time for another person. What kinds of information about that person would help you in planning and scheduling daily activities?

Once you have completed reading Chapter 14, see whether you can improve on your suggestions for planning leisure-time use in the above situations.

360

THE CONCEPT OF LEISURE

Like the layperson, researchers have thought of the concept of leisure in a number of ways. Godbey and Parker (1976) have identified two main ways of defining *leisure*. The **residual method** is to subtract from the 24 hours in a day all required activities, such as working, sleeping, eating, and attending to physiological needs. What time is left over is leisure time. This approach can lead to some ambiguity, since some people perceive some required activities, such as gardening, as leisure activities. The second way of defining *leisure*, called the **activity method**, assumes that leisure is not a period of time but depends on one's perception of the desirability of the activity engaged in. In other words, pleasurable activities are a form of leisure, and less pleasurable activities are a form of work. Godbey and Parker point out that combining these two approaches—time plus perception of the activity—may be the best approach to defining the concept of leisure. Gist and Fava (1964) express a similar view by defining *leisure* as "the time which an individual has free from work or other duties and which may be utilized for purposes of relaxation, diversion, social achievement, or personal development" (p. 411).

Kaplan (1960) has suggested additional guidelines for whether to consider an activity a form of leisure. To him, leisure may range from relatively insignificant activities to activities of personal and social significance. However, such activities must not serve an economic function, and the person must carry out the activity freely and feel under no social obligation.

Why Do People Need Leisure Time?

Suits (1967) has described some of the major theories about why people need leisure time. Although most of these theories have been generated for understanding children's play, they are applicable to adult nonwork-time activities as well.

Surplus Energy. One theory assumes that people have a particular amount of energy that must be expended in behavior, and although for most people work and daily routine activities use up most of one's energy, some residual energy may exist. This theory assumes that play and various leisure-time activities serve as good avenues for this surplus energy.

Preparation for Adulthood. Another theoretical notion assumes that childhood play serves to prepare the individual for adult living. The child learns how to give and take in social situations and learns to adopt and abide by rules and expectations. Childhood play is not just an outlet for excessive energy but is also a necessary learning experience for preparing individuals for the adult world of give and take. One weakness of this notion is that little attention is given to adult play or

361

leisure-time activities. Such activities are thought to have fulfilled their usefulness by adulthood.

Need for Relaxation. Another view is that people need a change in daily routines in order to relax. Here it is felt that work-time activities may increase tension and therefore increase the need for energy release. Implicit in this theory is the view that people often need a change of pace in order to relax. The relaxing activity may even be more vigorous than one's work-time activities, as long as it is different from them (playing golf, working in the yard or garden, running).

Need for Catharsis. A theoretical notion somewhat related to the need for relaxation is the need for **catharsis**. The concept, which originated in the psychoanalytic view of human personality, assumes that people need an outlet for their emotional tensions. Such emotional tensions may be precipitated or aggravated by situational influences like stress in one's work or home environment, but such tensions are mainly the result of unconscious (repressed) memories associated with childhood fantasies and traumas. Many of these repressed fantasies and traumas have a sexual or aggressive character. The catharsis notion assumes that such energy may be worked off in small amounts and in socially acceptable ways (for example, in sexual activity in marriage or exercise) or through socially unacceptable activity (abnormal sexual activity, such as rape or voyeurism, or excessive and violent physical action).

Need for Self-Expression. Another view about play or leisure-time activity is that it provides an opportunity to fulfill one's inner potentials and achieve self-actualization. Here leisure-time activities serve to increase self-understanding, self-awareness, and self-expression. This theory assumes that both work and nonwork activities can be used to fulfill one's need for self-expression. Both breadth and depth of interests at work and play are assumed to be important in achieving the goal of self-fulfillment.

Leisure Time versus Work Time

Although researchers have tended to break one's life into "work time" and "leisure time," it is probably best not to think of these as independent categories. Many people's work activities and leisure activities are distinctively different, but for many work and leisure fulfill the same needs. In Chapter 4 we identified some important human needs, such as the need for a favorable self-concept, the need for sensory stimulation, and the need to know and understand the world. The truth is that people may find fulfillment of these needs in both the work situation and the nonwork situation. Probably the most effective person is the one who derives satisfaction from, and has a sense of accomplishment in, both his or her leisure-time activities and work-time activities.

It is certainly possible, however, that one may overidentify with the work situation or the leisure situation. We would expect that if one is not deriving pleasure and a sense of accomplishment from one area, one might try to compensate in the other area for the lack of fulfillment. Yet, on the other hand, it may be that satisfaction with one's work role is a prerequisite for complete self-fulfillment. From this viewpoint, leisure-time activities can probably further enrich the productive worker's life, but an unhappy worker probably cannot achieve complete personal fulfillment through compensatory leisure-time activities.

There is some evidence that a balance between leisure-time activities and work activities is more typical of individuals in higher-status jobs than lower-status jobs. Reissman (1954), for example, found that people in high-status professions were more active and diverse in their social and leisure participation than people in low-status jobs. Further, Graham (1959) noted that nearly twice the number of professional workers engaged in strenuous exercise programs as unskilled workers. These studies perhaps suggest that people in more self-fulfilling occupations tend to engage in more and a wider variety of leisure activities than those in less fulfilling occupations.

Yet people who are not in self-fulfilling work situations may try to compensate through nonwork activities. Adams and Stone (1977) report that people with a high need for achievement that was not satisfied on the job did seek out achievement-oriented leisure-time activities. And there is evidence in one study (see Box 14-6) that the less rewarding a job, the more workers engaged in recreational activities if made available.

BOX 14-6. RELATION OF JOB BOREDOM TO LEISURE-TIME ACTIVITY

Grubb (1975) examined the relation between job boredom and recreation participation in auto assembly-line workers. His study included three groups whose work ranged from repetitive tasks (installing a single vehicle part) to tasks that involved assembling the entire vehicle. This study did find relations among task repetitiveness, job boredom, and frequency of participation in recreational activities. Grubb found that the less demanding the task, the higher was a worker's job boredom. Moreover, the workers who were bored with their jobs appeared to want to engage more frequently in recreational activities.

LEISURE ACTIVITIES AND LEISURE-RELATED NEEDS

In an attempt to identify and classify the variety of leisure activities, researchers have used a statistical procedure called "factor analysis." Factor analysis provides the smallest number of dimensions that will account for similarities among subjects' responses to attitudinal questionnaires about their leisure activities. Bishop (1970), using the factor-analysis technique, identified three general categories of leisure activities. The first was Active-Diversionary activities, which were a variety of activities that were simple to do and were readily accessible to a person. Dancing, listening to the radio, and playing baseball in one's backyard are examples of Active-Diversionary activities. They serve to provide a person with relatively brief distractions. A second factor, called the Potency factor, included more energetic activities, such as golf, tennis, and swimming. These activities require more time and preparation as well as energy. A Status factor included such activities as reading a book, attending a concert or play, or attending a public lecture. These activities all serve a self-edification function.

Using different attitudinal questionnaires, other investigators have identified other leisure-activity categories. For instance, McKechnie (1974) identified seven leisure activities, which he labeled Mechanics, Crafts, Intellectual, Slow Living, Fast Living, Neighborhood Sports, and Glamour Sports. And again, Ritchie (1975) identified categories he called Active Sports, Relaxing Entertainment, Social Interaction, Achievement-Oriented Hobbies, and Shopping.

Other investigators have been more interested in identifying leisure-related personality needs than in identifying leisure activities. London, Crandall, and Fitzgibbons (1977) have argued that the search for leisure-related personality needs will probably be a more profitable line of research than identifying categories of leisure activities. They reason that people may be attracted to a variety of leisure activities that satisfy the same basic need. Their research has led to the identification of three important personality needs that can be satisfied by leisure activity:

Feedback—an activity gives a person information about his or her efforts, thereby, perhaps, serving as an opportunity for increasing one's self-esteem.
Liking—an activity provides a person with intrinsic enjoyment.
Positive interpersonal involvement—an activity provides an opportunity for social interaction.

From the personality-needs perspective, people may participate in the same leisure-time activity—say, playing tennis—for different reasons. One person may either enjoy the game or enjoy the fellowship with others. For another, success or failure at the contest may be the most important concern. Knowing one's needs, according to London, Crandall, and Fitzgibbons (1977), can be used to guide and implement leisure activities for individuals and groups. Perhaps persons who are low in feedback needs but high in interpersonal-involvement needs could be paired in sporting activity. Similarly, it might be undesirable to pair a person high in the need for feedback with a person high in the need for interpersonal involvement. The person high in feedback need may constantly be concerned with task activities, while the person high in interpersonal-involvement need may be less patient with the continual push toward goals and more concerned with the satisfaction being derived from the interaction.

A LEISURE ACTIVITIES × LEISURE NEEDS MODEL

From the previous discussion, we can see that some investigators have tried to understand leisure behavior from the perspective of *leisure activities* and others from the perspective of *personality needs*. It might be helpful to the reader to examine his or her own leisure behavior using both conceptions. Figure 14-1 presents an activities × needs model for understanding leisure behavior.

Figure 14-1. Activities × Needs Model of Leisure Behavior

		Types of leisure activities			
Activity dimension		Passive		Active	
Interpersonal dimension		Solitary	Group	Solitary	Group
Type of satisfaction	Intrinsic need	Type 1	Type 2	Type 3	Type 4
	Extrinsic reward	Type 5	Type 6	Type 7	Type 8

The activities × needs model of leisure behavior shown in Figure 14-1 identifies two dimensions of leisure activities (an *Activity* dimension and an *Interpersonal* dimension) and one dimension of personality needs (*Type of Satisfaction*). Each of these three dimensions contains two categories. On the Activity dimension, leisure activities are classified as either *passive* or *active*, and on the Interpersonal dimension they are classified as either *solitary* or *group*. The type of satisfaction derived from the leisure activities is classified as due to either **intrinsic need** or **extrinsic reward**. A leisure activity performed simply for the enjoyment of engaging in that activity would be a form of intrinsic-need satisfaction, whereas a leisure activity performed in order to receive some external reward (such as winning a bet or receiving public accolade) would be a form of extrinsic-reward satisfaction.

The model in Figure 14-1 yields eight general types of leisure behavior. For example, Type 1 behavior would be a passive leisure activity performed alone for intrinsic-need satisfaction. Type 5 leisure behavior would be a passive leisure activity performed alone for some external reward. You can similarly list the characteristics of the remaining types of leisure behavior. You will be using this model as you respond to Exercise 14-2.

EXERCISE 14-2. IDENTIFYING YOUR TYPES OF LEISURE BEHAVIOR

Using the activities × needs model of leisure behavior given in Figure 14-1, try to identify your own types of leisure behavior. Using the time balance sheet in Figure 14-2, identify the leisure activities you have engaged in over the past week or more.

365

Now try to classify each leisure activity in accordance with the model in Figure 14-1.

Let us say that this statement describes a leisure activity that you have engaged in recently: "Played tennis with a friend and the loser had to buy the winner a drink." Using the activities × needs model of leisure behavior, you should be able to identify this as an *active* and *group* leisure activity. And since you were playing for an external reward, this activity might be viewed as a source of extrinsic reward. Therefore, this would be a Type 8 leisure behavior. Of course, it is hard to judge another's motive for doing something, because motivation is not directly observable—but you should be able to determine your own reason for doing something. It may be, for instance, that the main reason for playing tennis with your friend was not to win the bet but just to enjoy the fellowship and interpersonal reaction. Then this would be a Type 4 leisure behavior—that is, *active, group, intrinsic need*.

Try to classify each of your leisure activities into one of the eight types given in Figure 14-1. Moreover, you may wish to count the leisure activities you engaged in within each type. This may give you some information on the "type" of leisure person you are. No research is available on the trustworthiness of this activities × needs model of leisure behavior, but future investigations may determine whether there are "types" of leisure people and whether certain types of leisure behavior are related to more or less effective personality functioning.

Time is an abstract. Iron does not rust simply because of the passage of time; rather, it is what happens during time that determines this consequence. Within two identical periods of time, various influences may speed up or slow down this oxidation process, so that one piece of iron has little rust while another is highly rusted. Therefore, although we find it useful to delineate time into measurable units, it is really what goes on *within* time that makes measurement meaningful. Similarly, to understand leisure behavior, one needs to know not only *how much* leisure time one has but also *how* such leisure time is used.

In studying your leisure time, it might be helpful to use the balance sheet used for identifying your daily routine in Chapter 11 (Figure 11-7). This balance sheet can then be used to understand how you use time during the course of a day. Figure 14-2 is a version of a balance sheet that may be used to record your daily activities. This balance sheet provides categories for listing "leisure" activities and "nonleisure" activities. As we have seen, researchers disagree on the definitions of leisure and nonleisure activities. Perhaps the best approach would be to rely on your own definition. However, it is probably advisable to treat necessary and routine daily activities, such as personal care, housework, shopping, and traveling from place to place, as nonleisure activities.

SUMMARY

This chapter was concerned with defining and understanding leisure time. Most Americans assume that leisure time is increasing, but research indicates that it

	Leisure activities	Nonleisure activities
6:00–7:00 A.M.		
7:00–8:00		
8:00–9:00		
9:00–10:00		
10:00–11:00		
11:00–12:00		
12:00–1:00 P.M.		
1:00–2:00		
2:00–3:00		
3:00–4:00		
4:00–5:00		
5:00–6:00		
6:00–7:00		
7:00–8:00		
8:00–9:00		
9:00–10:00		
10:00–11:00		
11:00–12:00		
12:00–1:00 A.M.		
1:00–2:00		
2:00–3:00		
3:00–4:00		
4:00–5:00		
5:00–6:00		

Figure 14-2. Balance sheet for recording leisure and nonleisure activities.

may not be. Still, people are spending a sizable portion of their incomes on leisure activities.

This chapter examined how people at stages of life from childhood to old age use their leisure time. A young child's use of leisure time (play time) is important in personality development. As children get older, their play becomes more structured and less active. Increased interest in the opposite sex and increased pressures toward more responsible adult behavior generally result in a more selective use of leisure time by the adolescent. How young adults use their leisure time is influenced by marital status, economic status, and whether they have children. The middle aged, freed from the pressing financial and family demands of young adulthood, may find themselves with more leisure than they are comfortable with. Leisure-time use is quite similar from middle age to old age, and leisure is more satisfying for the elderly who have developed leisure interests earlier in life. For many, leisure time appears to be a mixed blessing, and what is "leisure" is a matter of personal definition.

Psychologists have speculated on why people need leisure time and have offered five theories: surplus energy, preparation for adulthood, need for relaxation, need for catharsis, and need for self-expression. People may seek in leisure activities what their work fails to provide, such as achievement or sensory stimulation. In addition, leisure activity fulfills three important personality needs: feedback, liking, and positive interpersonal involvement.

This chapter presented a leisure activities × leisure needs model to help readers identify their own types of leisure behavior.

KEY CONCEPTS

Activity definition of leisure a definition of *leisure* in terms of an individual's perception of the desirability of the activity.

Catharsis the release of pent-up emotional tension; in one view, this is the purpose of leisure activities.

Community-centered leisure activities recreational activities that are related to social interests outside the home.

Extrinsic-reward leisure activity an activity that is engaged in in order to receive some external reward, such as money or fame.

Home-centered leisure activities recreational activities that are related to social interests within the family.

Intrinsic-need leisure activity an activity that is engaged in merely for the enjoyment of the activity.

Residual definition of leisure a definition of *leisure* as time remaining after subtracting all required activities in a 24-hour period.

368

CHAPTER OBJECTIVES

1. To understand the role of advertising in a complex economy.
2. To distinguish between implications and assertions contained in advertising claims.
3. To identify advertising claims that are misleading.
4. To develop greater awareness of the use of euphemism and hyperbole in advertising.
5. To more fully understand how emotional appeals are used to create psychological needs for products and services.
6. To recognize flimflam techniques and other methods used by bargain hucksters and con artists.
7. To identify the main characteristics of quacks.
8. To develop skills for coping with impulsive buying behavior.

BECOMING
A MORE
KNOWLEDGEABLE
CONSUMER

Tens of billions of dollars are being spent each year in the United States on advertising. The spending of such immense sums of money on advertising has one main object: to influence human behavior. Dr. Samuel Johnson, the celebrated man of letters, made the following statement in a 1759 essay: "Advertisements are now so numerous that they are negligently perused, and it is therefore become necessary to gain attention by magnificence of promises, and by eloquence, sometimes sublime and sometimes pathetic. Promise, large promise, is the soul of advertising."

Today people tend to be suspicious of advertising. The general negative view of American advertising is understandable. However, advertising is of indispensable value to the modern consumer. In our complex economy, advertising serves to introduce new products and helps the consumer meet daily needs of modern living. Advertising should benefit both the buyer and the seller. Reasons that producers and consumers make use of advertising can be complementary. By advertising the seller can increase the market for a product, and the consumer is given information on which to make a purchase judgment.

However, not all advertising is designed to help the consumer make the wisest and most economical judgment. This is particularly true when many manufacturers are producing virtually the same product. When this happens, each producer must attract the buyer through various advertising techniques. Since no one clearly superior product exists, advertising must create an illusion of superiority and establish a "need" in the consumer for just that product. Some of the largest advertising budgets are devoted to parity products, such as gasoline, beer, pain relievers, and soaps; these are called "parity products" because virtually no difference exists among them.

The purpose of this chapter is to help you differentiate between misleading advertising claims and those providing useful consumer information. In the discussion that follows, it is not our intention to imply that all or even most advertising is deceptive or misleading. There are a number of fine products and services around that are represented by truthful and straightforward advertising. But, as Wrighter (1972) reminds us, a sincere and honest sales attempt, when put up against a "rock 'em, sock 'em" commercial that tries to gloss over the real truths, generally gets less attention. As Box 15-1 shows, we do not always find that claims in TV commercials are correct.

BOX 15-1. THE FANTASTIC WORLD OF TV COMMERCIALS

Boy, television commercials are really something.

The other night I watched a car tear across a rock-studded field, forge a river, scale a mountain, speed through a desert, and pass five stranded autos in a snowstorm to prove how put-together it was.

I have the same make and model in my driveway.

Creating a desirable product image is a goal of many advertising campaigns. (Photo © Jan Lukas/Photoresearchers, Inc.)

That car has a battery in it that, according to television, can light up an entire airstrip at 50 degrees below zero.

It has four tires on it that have been tested on four-inch spikes.

It's so airtight you could ride through a war and not hear a sound.

The suspension is so smooth you could cut a diamond in the back seat.

There's enough trunk room to carry a five-tiered wedding cake.

The brake system is so terrific, anyone would be a fool not to stand in front of it.

There's only one problem. The car doesn't start.

A lot of things are like that. I've seen commercials where they glue two pieces of wood together and make a diving board out of them and this guy springs from them into a pool. I've used the same glue and can't get a picture to stick in a photo album.

Bought a sweeper once that when demonstrated sucked up pennies, pins, metal, nails, garbage, and a small dog that wasn't paying attention. It won't pick up dust.

373

And a watch that I saw rescued from a sandy beach after three years, stopped running for me one night when I spilled a drink on it.

Maybe it's me. I want to believe that a kid can take a hammer to my kitchen floor and the shine won't crack. Or that my perfume will drive men within a radius of three miles up the wall.

I wanted to believe there was such a thing as a childproof toy, so when I saw an elephant stand on a truck one day, I went right out and bought it. (The truck, not the elephant.)

Two hours later the truck was in a heap on the floor. Two kids were crying, and once again my faith had been shattered.

When they show me a truck that can come in contact with a brother's head and still remain intact, I'll go back to believing.

From *At Wit's End,* by Erma Bombeck. Copyright 1978 Field Enterprises, Inc. Courtesy of Field Newspaper Syndicate.

THE LANGUAGE OF ADVERTISING

At some point in our lives, all of us are probably influenced by the excessive and misleading claims of advertising. Consequently, we all can benefit from becoming more knowledgeable consumers. One fundamental rule in analyzing an advertising claim is that if any product is truly superior, the ad will contain a forthright statement to that effect. Such superiority can be documented by convincing evidence. When an ad hedges in the least about a product's advantage over the competition, you can almost certainly assume that the product is not superior—possibly equal to the competition, but not superior. When a product or service is superior, you may rest assured that the ad will say so in no uncertain terms.

When a forthright claim cannot be made, an advertiser may try to persuade by keeping us from thinking rather than encouraging us to use our intellects. A typical example of an advertisement that tries to persuade without providing any useful information or making any forthright claim and consequently falls into the category of "say-nothing" advertising is the commercial that begins in the midst of a discussion between two persons. One asks: "What does *your* broker say?" The other responds: "*My* broker is E. F. Hutton, and E. F. Hutton says . . ." There is then complete silence and absence of movement as many other people stop to listen. The commercial ends with the announcer telling us that "when E. F. Hutton talks, people listen." What useful information does this commercial contain? What advantage, if any, does E. F. Hutton offer over other brokers? What do we really learn about E. F. Hutton? Although this is undoubtedly an effective advertisement for the company, its effectiveness is achieved without making any claim or giving us any information. It is effective because we, as consumers, respond to the message's implications without making a critical analysis of the message.

374

Robert Blake, the star of the TV series *Baretta,* comes sliding and skidding into your TV screen in an old car, reminding young viewers not to drive like that. He tells us that he uses STP in all his vehicles. He then asks: "Why do I use STP?" and provides us with the answer: "On account of it works. And that's the name of that tune." This is another example of "say-nothing" advertising. What is not said but clearly implied, however, is that such old cars can withstand the rough treatment because of STP.

In our analysis of the language used in advertising, it is very important that we distinguish between **assertions** and **implications**. An assertion is a direct and forthright statement that can clearly be determined to be true or false. False assertions in advertising are illegal. It is not illegal, however, to imply false or misleading information in advertising. There are no specific laws dealing with implications in ads. Consequently, each case is individually reviewed and judged, making it possible for advertisers to introduce subtle implications into ads. The knowledgeable consumer should therefore be discerning of differences in advertising messages.

Some courts, however, are beginning to hold that implications contained in commercials are, in effect, a part of the warranty of the product. For example, in 1978 the Ford Motor Company was sued after a driver put a dent in his four-wheel-drive truck during a rough trip through mud and sand. He contended that Ford should be required to pay $500 in repairs. The driver, who had bought the truck for hunting trips, contended that his driving was mild compared with the workouts he had seen on television. "In no way did I ever jump it through the air or race it over sand or across rocky terrain like they do in those television ads," he said.

A Ford staff lawyer argued that the only warranty on vehicles is the "express warranty" given in writing to buyers at the time of purchase. This argument failed to convince a jury in Minnesota, which insisted that "a television commercial showing pick-up trucks dashing over rough terrain and sailing through the air is as much a warranty as the paper an owner gets when he puts down his money ("Ford Commercial Implies Warranty," 1978, p. 7).

Different Kinds of Implications

There are many ways in which an advertisement can imply a false claim. One way is the use of hedges, or **weasel words**—words designed to weaken or nullify an assertion while leaving a strong implication. They are used as qualifiers in order to avoid direct assertions that can be proved or disproved. Commonly used weasel words include *helps, fights, works, virtually,* and *may be.* These are examples of weasel claims:

> Listerine *fights* bad breath.
> Allerest *may help* you live as if you *barely* had hay fever.
> For *virtually* spotless dishes nothing can beat Cascade.
> Aim *fights* tooth decay. Take Aim instead of cavities.
> Black and Decker *just might* be the finest saw *for the money* in America.

Comparative adjectives may be used without ever specifying the subject of the deleted clause in the underlying syntactic structure. These implied claims fall into the category of **unfinished claims**. These are statements that claim a product is better or has more of something but do not finish the comparison. When you are confronted with such claims, your first question should be "Better or more than what?" Examples:

> Chore gives you a whiter wash.
> Magnavox gives you more.
> BC is stronger and faster-dissolving. It has 30% more pain reliever.

An ad for Colgate fluoride toothpaste claimed that "most Colgate kids get fewer cavities" without stating fewer than what, hoping that readers would infer that kids using Colgate would get fewer cavities than those using other fluoride toothpastes and others, perhaps, who did not brush their teeth at all.

Imperatives may be carefully juxtaposed in such a way as to imply a causal connection between two activities without making an assertion to that effect. Harris (1977) lists hypothetical examples of **juxtaposition of imperatives**:

> Moo Moo milk tastes great. Keep your family healthy. Buy Moo Moo milk.
> Get through a whole winter without colds; take Eradicold.

A negative question can be a useful device for implying an answer that may not be true. The question is usually stated in such a way that an affirmative answer that implies something good about a product is elicited. The correct answer may be no, but the assumption is yes. Examples:

> Isn't quality the most important thing to consider in buying aspirin?
> Plymouth, isn't that the car America wants?
> If you can't trust Prestone, who can you trust?
> Haven't you done without a Toro [lawn mower] long enough?

Some advertisements stress the uniqueness (We're different) of a product, implying that uniqueness means superiority:

> Colt 45: A completely unique experience.
> Allstate's different. When it takes being different to be better, Allstate will do it.
> Nobody makes telephones like Western Electric.
> There are lots of investment firms; there is only one Merrill Lynch.
> Today's Monte Carlo is an original. There's no other car quite like it.

Consumers can also be misled through *incomplete, inadequate, or inappropriate reporting of survey or test results.* Such practices as reporting only the number of respondents indicating a certain preference without the percentage or sample size, or vice

376

WHY YES, AS A MATTER OF FACT — I WAS IN THE TV COMMERCIAL FOR THIS CAR ... WHY?

versa, can be very misleading. Biased sampling techniques, reporting only the number responding to a survey when the number questioned was much larger, and failure to specify the competition in comparative tests are similar deficiencies. Reporting of piecemeal results to imply an unwarranted conclusion is also a misuse of test results—for example, stating "A Cramp Leprechaun has more front headroom than a Datsun B-210, more rear-seat hiproom than a Chevette, and a larger trunk than a Ford Pinto" (Harris, 1977, p. 604) to imply that the car has more interior room by all measures than the three competitors. In an actual commercial the Plymouth Duster was compared to a Datsun 610 with this claim: "Our small car is $754.50 less than their small car." In addition, the claim was made that the Duster was larger inside and had a longer wheel base than the Datsun 610. What was so misleading was that the 610 was the top of the Datsun line and the Duster was the bottom of the Plymouth line. A more realistic comparison would have been between the Duster, the cheapest Plymouth, and the Datsun B-210, the cheapest Datsun. Incidentally, the Datsun 210 was priced slightly lower than the Duster.

In television commercials the Ford Motor Company advertised its LTD as "quieter than even the most expensive imports," implying a comparison with the famed quiet of Rolls-Royce. When the Federal Trade Commission ordered an independent substantiation of this and other claims made in auto advertisements, it was disclosed that comparison tests showed that the new Ford LTD was quieter than a 1963 model Daimler with 37,225 miles clocked on it and also quieter than a 1964 Jaguar with over 20,000 miles.

Some ads claim a difference between parity products when the difference is negligible. A cigarette ad that claims that Brand A is lower in tar and nicotine than other brands implies that this difference is a significant one. Bayer aspirin made the claim that government tests had proved that no nonprescription pain reliever was stronger or more effective than Bayer aspirin. That much was true. This claim could be interpreted to imply—although it did not assert—that Bayer was superior to the others. What this commercial failed to mention was that the gov-

377

ernment tests, sponsored by the Federal Trade Commission, had actually found no difference at all among the five headache preparations tested, either in speed or in effectiveness of pain relief. Although it was true that no pain reliever was any more effective than Bayer aspirin, it was equally true that none was any less effective than Bayer. Adding that second comparison puts the conclusion in a quite different light.

An advertisement showing the faces of Harry Reasoner and Barbara Walters, who were at that time the coanchors of the ABC Evening News, said "On the network more people are watching." Although the reader could easily be led to conclude that more people were watching Harry Reasoner and Barbara Walters than the CBS Evening News or the NBC Nightly News, they were not. The Nielsen ratings did indicate that more people were watching some programs on ABC than on the competing networks, but the Reasoner/Walters show consistently received the lowest ratings of the three evening news programs. This ad was misleading because it implied that the Reasoner/Walters show was the most popular evening news program of the three major networks when, in fact, it was the least popular.

Many claims do not fit into any of the preceding categories but nevertheless make implications of superiority without making a direct assertion. The claims are usually very vague and, like those we have previously discussed, cannot withstand the scrutiny of logical analysis. Examples:

> Don't compromise—Midasize.
> Coke adds life to just about everything you do.
> Stokely's—so fresh that when you open our green beans you taste the sunshine.
> If you can find a better-built small car than Toyota, buy it.
> A steak without A-1 is a mistake.
> Seven out of eight Volvo drivers purchase Volvo after a test drive. Maybe you should test-drive a Volvo.
> Pearl Beer, made from the water from the land of 1100 springs.

The first claim implies that if you use Midas mufflers, you are not compromising with an inferior product. The claims for Coca-Cola and Stokely's contain the phrases "adds life" and "taste the sunshine," which are so vague as to render those claims completely meaningless. The implication of the Toyota claim is that you cannot find a better-built car than Toyota, so why search? Go ahead and buy a Toyota without bothering to make comparisons. The next claim implies that, if you do not use A-1 steak sauce, you are settling for less than the best.

The Volvo claim begins with what is probably a factual statement. It is quite probable that seven out of eight people who buy a Volvo have test-driven one first. But is it logical for the listener to conclude that he or she should test-drive a Volvo? Although this claim implies that you are likely to buy a Volvo after a test drive, it provides no information on how many people test-drive a Volvo and then do not buy one. Without thinking, you might conclude that only one out of eight test-drivers does not buy a Volvo, but the claim does not say that.

378

Without a very careful reading, one might interpret the Pearl Beer claim to be that this beer is made from water from 1100 different springs. Instead it says that the beer is made from water from the *land* of 1100 springs. Even if it were made from water from 1100 different springs, so what? Would it be any better than if all the water came from one spring? Although the answer is probably no, this claim clearly implies otherwise.

Sylvania uses this argument to persuade listeners to buy its products: "Sylvania was willing to bet $100,000 that no other television was superior to theirs. Now this doesn't prove that Sylvania is superior, but don't you owe it to yourself to find out why they were willing to bet $100,000 on their product?" This claim does not say that Sylvania made a bet but only that it was willing to. With whom? We do not know. The Sylvania people go on to say that this willingness does not prove the superiority of their product. That certainly is a true statement! But they do suggest that since they were willing to bet on their product (with whom we don't know), we are obligated to find out why by purchasing their product. This kind of argument could appear logical only to those who are either intellectually inadequate or too lazy to think.

Recalling Implications versus Assertions: What Does Research Say?

Harris (1977) examined the comprehension and memory of asserted and implied claims in commercial advertising to determine whether people can discriminate between asserted and implied claims. Subjects in his study heard tape-recorded mock commercials that either directly asserted or implied claims about some fictitious products. After listening to the commercials, the subjects (college students) were given test sentences derived from the advertising claims and asked to indicate whether they were true or false. Examples of such commercials are given in Table 15-1.

Students who heard the implication commercials were almost as likely to agree with the test statements as those who heard the assertion commercials. This finding indicates that people process and remember implications very much like direct assertions. Specific instructions about implications did produce some improved discriminations between assertions and implications.

Preston (1967) found that subjects who were asked to judge a statement as accurate or inaccurate, based on an ad they had read, erroneously judged implied claims as accurate more than 75% of the time. Harris (1977) discovered that subjects tended to remember implications as though they were asserted facts. For example, subjects hearing the claim "Crust toothpaste fights cavities" generally remember it as "Crust toothpaste prevents cavities." These findings stress the importance of educating consumers about implications so they can guard against accepting an implied claim as asserted fact.

Bruno (1977) has shown that people can be taught to discriminate between implications and assertions. The advertisements in Box 15-2 are adapted from Bruno's test materials. Please note the difference between the "Implication" version and "As-

379

Item 1   *Assertion Commercial:* Aren't you tired of the sniffles and runny noses all winter? Tired of always feeling less than your best? Taking Eradicold Pills as directed will get you through a whole winter without colds.

         Implication Commercial: Aren't you tired of the sniffles and runny noses all winter? Tired of always feeling less than your best? Get through a whole winter without colds. Take Eradicold Pills as directed.

         Test Sentence: If you take Eradicold Pills as directed, you will not have any colds this winter.

Item 2   *Assertion Commercial:* Ladies, don't you really want to look your very best? Women who use Roy G. Biv Hair Color really care about looking their very best. Think of yourself in any one of Roy G. Biv's seven beautiful and natural shades of hair color. Don't you deserve such rich and vibrant color?

         Implication Commercial: Ladies, don't you really want to look your very best? Women who really care about looking their very best use Roy G. Biv Hair Color. Think of yourself in any one of Roy G. Biv's seven beautiful and natural shades of hair color. Don't you deserve such rich and vibrant color?

         Test Sentence: If a woman uses Roy G. Biv Hair Color, she must really want to look her very best.

Item 3   *Assertion Commercial:* In a survey of 500 doctors, over half reported that they recommended Knockout Capsules.

         Implication Commercial: In a survey of 500 doctors, over half reported that they recommended the ingredients in Knockout Capsules.

         Test Sentence: A majority of doctors in a survey recommended Knockout Capsules.

Item 4   *Assertion Commercial:* Crust prevents cavities.

         Implication Commercial: Crust fights cavities.

         Test Sentence: If you brush regularly and properly with Crust Fluoride, you will have few, if any, cavities.

Item 5   *Assertion Commercial:* Gargoil can't promise to keep him coldfree, but it will help him prevent colds.

         Implication Commercial: Gargoil can't promise to keep him coldfree, but it may help him fight off colds.

         Test Sentence: Gargling with Gargoil Antiseptic helps prevent colds.

sertion" version of each ad. Implications and assertions are enclosed in parentheses, the implication appearing first.

BOX 15-2. CHEAPMARKET SPECIALS

Cheapmarket asks this question: Where can you go to get high quality and low prices these days? The answer? (Come down to see us and find out/Cheapmarket). Here are only a few great buys at Cheapmarket:

Dippy chips, the great new corn chips (were made to go with/taste great with) dip. Dippy chips were made strong so they won't break when you dip into your favorite dip! So try Dippy chips, the delicious new corn chips. Are you tired of staring at the same boring white paper when you're doing your schoolwork? Rainbow, the brightly colored notebook paper, is designed to (make your schoolwork more exciting/improve your schoolwork). So try the peppy paper—Rainbow!

If you're the star on the basketball court until the fourth quarter gets you down, you need Instant Energy. Instant Energy is a delicious snack that will give you the energy to (keep you on that court/be the fourth-quarter star, too)! So stay in the game with Instant Energy. Do you love chocolate, but it doesn't love you? I'm talking about the way your face breaks out every time you eat your favorite chocolate snack. Here's good news from the makers of Sweetenall, the sugar substitute: Introducing new Fake-olate, the delicious new snack that tastes like chocolate without pimple-causing fat. Try Fake-olate. Not only will your mouth love it, but (your face will love it, too/your face won't break out, either).

It's annoying to have to worry about getting stains on your clothes when you're sliding into home plate. That's why we've invented Alloff. Alloff puts a protective coating on your clothes. If you want your uniform to always be stainfree, use Alloff. (It'll help prevent/It'll prevent) your clothes from becoming stained. . . .

Tipsi-Cola is the refreshingly different soft drink. (People of the Now Generation drink Tipsi-Cola/People who drink Tipsi-Cola are of the Now Generation). Oh, I see you drink Tipsi-Cola. . . .

When anyone in my family is sick, I want the very best care possible for him or her. That's why I buy St. Abraham's, the coconut-flavored aspirin. After all, (isn't quality the most important thing to consider in buying aspirin?/quality is the most important thing to consider in buying aspirin). If quality care is important to your family like it is to mine, buy St. Abraham's aspirin. . . .

Has your love life been "on the rocks" recently? Do you need some "magnetism" to pull those beautiful blondes and brunettes back to you? What you need is Tarzan After Shave. Make all those Janes go wild over that fresh, manly scent. They will love the attractive effect it has on you. Get your love life back on course where it belongs. (Have the girls come flocking to you like birds around the jungle water hole. Slap yourself with Tarzan After Shave/Tarzan After Shave will bring the girls flocking to you like birds around the jungle water hole). In a survey conducted by a leading university, doctors were asked what they used to relieve pain from aching muscles. (The majority of those reporting said/75% of those questioned reported) that they themselves used Biceptennial Cream Rub. So buy what the doctors use themselves—Biceptennial Cream Rub for those tired, aching muscles.

These are only a few of the bargains you'll find this week at Cheapmarket. (People who shop at Cheapmarket really care about their families/People who really care about their families shop at Cheapmarket). So hurry down to Cheapmarket today!

From "Training the Distinction of Pragmatic Implications from Direct Assertions in Adolescents and Adults," by K. J. Bruno. Unpublished master's thesis, Kansas State University, 1977. Reprinted by permission of the author.

Some prospective customers are attracted by words like "special" and "bargain." (Photo © Ellis Herwig/Stock, Boston.)

Euphemism and Hyperbole in Advertising

Communication in advertising may also be distorted or exaggerated through the use of euphemism and hyperbole. **Euphemism** is the substitution of a word with pleasant connotations for a word that is more blunt and possibly closer to the truth. Euphemism can be a handy tool to avoid offending or shocking others. For most of us it is perfectly acceptable for a young woman at a party to ask for directions to "the powder room" when she actually is in search of the toilet. Some euphemisms can be used to produce psychological benefits. The self-concept of an awkward teenager may be less distorted if he thinks of himself as having some "facial blemishes" rather than being afflicted by "pimples." The label "For motion discomfort" that airplanes place on paper containers helps passengers keep better control of their squeamish stomachs on a bumpy flight than if the containers were called "vomit bags."

The use of euphemism, however, can lead to forms of deception. If deteriorating slum areas are made to appear more livable or inevitable when called "substandard housing," then our perceptions of large cities have been distorted and our ability to evaluate the effects of poverty has been diminished. The young person who gains increased self-acceptance by thinking of himself or herself as a "swinger" rather than as promiscuous is engaging in a form of self-deception.

The language of advertising often employs euphemism and **hyperbole** (exaggeration for effect). Car dealers may refer to their autos as "preowned" rather than "secondhand." A "large half-quart" bottle of Coca-Cola sounds like a lot more than a pint bottle. A foreign observer was said to have remarked that in America there are no "small eggs; only 'medium,' 'large,' 'extra large,' and 'jumbo.'" The story is told that a Russian athletic organization once placed an order with an American shoe manufacturer for some size 18 shoes for its Olympic athletes. After learning of this request, one of our athletic associations immediately sent a requisition to Russia for some T-shirts, size 82 "medium." "Dentures" sounds preferable to "false teeth." Women may use "rinses" or "tints" on their hair when the thought of "dyeing" their hair would be very unsettling. By enlisting in the Navy, you get not just a job but an "adventure."

Advertisements are loaded with such words as *amazing, whopping, first, new, improved, better than ever, big, mild, expensive, exclusive,* and *fashionable.* Below are some additional examples of euphemistic double talk used in commercials.

problem skin	eczema *or* psoriasis
bathroom tissue	toilet paper
consumer	buyer
thrift shop	day-old bakery store
night soil	human excrement
planned community	real-estate development
mobile estate	trailer park
mobile home	house trailer
ladies' lounge	women's toilet
senior citizen	old person
waste water	sewage

Over time the euphemism may replace the original word and the user may fail to appreciate it as a euphemism.

EMOTIONAL APPEALS IN ADVERTISING

Advertising may try to bring about behavior change by influencing our emotions. **Emotional appeals,** as we shall see, easily lend themselves to some subtle—and

383

sometimes not so subtle—implications about products or services. Here we will examine several commonly used emotional appeals in advertising.

Fear and Threat

Some advertisements are designed to motivate us to buy by eliciting fear. Life-insurance commercials, for example, may show wives and children trying to get along without their deceased husbands and fathers. Fear arousal is used in selling merchandise ranging from smoke detectors and fire alarms to mouthwashes and deodorants. Commercials for Scope mouthwash play upon the threat of being rejected by others if you do not use Scope. Manufacturers of denture grips play upon denture wearers' fear of losing their upper plates in delicate social and romantic situations. A television ad for a punctureproof automobile tire shows a beautiful woman driving alone late at night through a remote wooded area when her tire runs over a large nail lying in the road. A close-up photograph shows the nail entering the tire while someone asks: "What if the person you saw driving the automobile were you or your wife?" The next scene shows this woman driving safely into her driveway at home and entering the house. Fortunately for her, she had a set of the punctureproof tires. The implication is that these tires served to avert a major disaster.

Fram oil-filter commercials use a similar tactic by having a mechanic show us a Fram oil filter and the low cost for which it can be installed. He then shows us a ring-and-valve job and the resulting costs. As he pulls the chain hoisting out the burnt-out motor so that a new one can be installed, he says something like "You can get a new oil filter for four dollars or a new engine for four hundred dollars. The choice is yours. You can pay me now—or pay me later." Such a thought of potential trauma arouses many car owners to immediate action.

Scare tactics should be recognized for what they are: attempts to frighten you into buying something to prevent a catastrophe. This approach is appropriate when a product or service is designed to prevent disaster. Fear arousal may be appropriate in encouraging people to purchase fire alarms and smoke detectors and to stop smoking.

Nostalgia

A desire for some products can be created through emphasis on pleasant memories of days gone by. Such appeals are based on nostalgia. Bakery products are frequently advertised as "the kind Grandma used to make." Manufacturers of cameras make frequent use of this emotional appeal. Typical commercials show children in family settings, usually on special occasions, interacting with their parents or grand-parents. With pleasant music in the background, the announcer reminds us that children grow into adults so fast and that we all grow old too soon. We are reminded that we cannot capture these precious moments. If we buy a camera, we can reexperience these pleasant moments again and again.

384

Sexual Appeals

One of the most frequent types of emotional appeals is sexual appeals. No product seems to have been immune from this approach. The use of sexual appeals is often subtle. A facial expression can provide subtle sexually arousing cues. Faces of men on billboards advertising cigarettes are good examples. These male models are chosen not because of their love of cigarettes but rather because they are attractive and exhibit masculine traits. Many viewers may identify with such persons and feel that by smoking a particular brand of cigarettes they will also have these desired traits.

Many advertisements may make absolutely no reference to sex, but if you did not know what the announcer was referring to, a sexual meaning could easily be inferred. For instance, a recent two-page magazine advertisement for Beautyrest mattresses showed four beautiful women, each lying on a mattress. The ad was captioned with "Beautyrest support now comes in four different firmnesses. So you can go from mattress to mattress, until you find the one you want." An English Leather men's toiletry ad paired the product with the face of a pretty woman. This woman states: "My men wear English Leather or they wear nothing at all." Many advertisements contain slogans or statements that intentionally have double meanings. A camera ad, for example, showed a photograph of a woman in a seductive pose and a picture of a camera below the photograph. Directly above the photograph were the words "One guy got her on the first try." In smaller print we are told that the photograph "caught this doll—in just one exposure. Without a flash!"

Probably the most extensive use of sexual appeals has been in automobile advertisements. The male owner of a new car is shown either driving away with the girl of his dreams or driving off leaving an admiring woman wishing she were in the seat beside him. Glamorous women are often used to point out positive features of a particular car, usually the interior. Cameras are placed at just the right angle to show their legs as they slide under the steering wheel into the driver's seat. Their soft hands sliding over the seat, fondling the gadgets on the instrument panel, and caressing the

385

gearshift knob can be quite enticing. When we repeatedly are exposed to a shiny new car and a sexy woman, we associate the two. We may then purchase an automobile with the expectation of satisfying sexual needs. Although the use of erotic or sexual appeals in advertisements is hardly new, what is new is the intensity and number of such appeals used to sell a variety of products.

BOX 15-3. THE EFFECT OF EROTIC STIMULATION ON ATTITUDES TOWARD A PRODUCT

Peterson and Kerin (1977) experimentally examined the influence of three levels of erotic stimulation on attitudes toward a personal feminine product (bath oil) and an impersonal masculine product (a ratchet-wrench set). Advertisements were prepared that presented each product alone or paired with one of three female models. A demure model was dressed in a long-sleeved, completely buttoned, dark blouse and a pair of tan slacks. A seductive model was dressed in similar attire, but the blouse was knotted at the waist, exposing some midriff and some "cleavage." A third model was completely undressed.

Male and female subjects viewed the advertisements; each subject saw one of the ads for each product. Subjects were then asked to express their attitudes toward the quality of the advertisement and product as well as the respectability of the company offering the product. Males' attitudes were generally more favorable than females' attitudes when a nude model was used. The most favorable attitudes toward advertisement, product, and company resulted when the feminine product (bath oil) was paired with the seductive female model. Least favorable attitudes were expressed when the bath oil was advertised by a nude female model.

Peterson and Kerin feel that advertisements should be characterized by product/model congruency. The model selling the product should "fit" with the product being sold. Moreover, although seductive models may have a positive influence on some products, nude models appear to harm attitudes toward both the product and the company offering the product. In fact, some products might best be advertised without any model, let alone a sexually arousing one. For example, the most favorable evaluations of the ratchet-wrench set occurred when no model was used in the advertisement.

Testimonials

Another form of emotional appeal frequent in advertising is the **testimonial**. In a testimonial, someone unknown to the public, speaking as a typical consumer, attests to the quality and/or superiority of a particular product. Testimonials are often

386

used by smaller companies whose markets are limited to a particular region of the country. But they have become more widely used for selling products nationwide. Testimonials, which use ordinary people posing as consumers, are usually less expensive to produce than endorsements.

Endorsements

An **endorsement** uses a famous person to sell a product. Endorsements are particularly popular when advertising parity items—that is, products or services for which there is virtually no difference among competitors. Do you want a Hamilton Beach popcorn popper, for example, because it is the best popcorn popper on the market or because Joe Namath uses one? Farrah Fawcett-Majors tells us that we get "great balls of comfort" from a can of Noxzema shaving cream.

O. J. Simpson attempts to get us to use Hertz rent-a-cars. The effectiveness of this commercial is enhanced because of the similarity between the image Hertz is trying to project and the speed of a famous halfback. Karl Malden, with his "tough cop" image, is also effective in commercials for American Express Travelers Cheques; Joe Dimaggio and Sophia Loren for Mr. Coffee; Pelé, the former great soccer player, for American Express cards; Bruce Jenner for Wheaties; and the list goes on and on.

Sometimes, however, famous people do not have the desired impact on the sales of a product. One reason may be lack of the *product/model congruency* that Peterson and Kerin (1977) discussed. Mark Spitz, the winner of seven Olympic gold medals in swimming, was less successful as an endorser. To push its Flexamatic razor in competition with Remington's Mark III, Schick signed Spitz to a lifetime contract of $100,000 a year for the first 5 years and $50,000 a year for the remainder of his life. However, Spitz's only successful promotion came with his life-size poster showing him in a form-fitting bathing suit, wearing his seven gold medals. Schick overexpanded its marketing efforts, lost $6 million, and wound up with Mark Spitz for life, but not for long in commercials.

Evel Knievel, the motorcycle daredevil, has so much power to excite the imagination of the public that many companies have tried to cash in on the Knievel craze. No fewer than nine companies have acquired rights to manufacture Knievel toys and accessories ranging from watches, radios, and hobby kits to motor-bike accessories for bicycles, tank tops and other boys' clothing, and even drinking straws. The Ideal Toy Company began having second thoughts about its investment, however, after making a large stockpile of Knievel toys, only to learn that Evel Knievel was in jail for hitting a former associate across the wrists. Although the effects of this incident on his appeal as an endorser have not been determined at this time, Ideal has ceased production of these toys.

Endorsements are effective because we, as consumers, allow them to be. Our desire to identify with famous persons makes the products they endorse more appealing. In evaluating the claims of these commercials, we should ask ourselves whether the endorsement is in any way related to the quality or performance of the product.

387

Slogans and Melodies

Slogans are communication devices used to present an idea rapidly and concisely. One important feature of the slogan is that it is designed to be easily remembered. A slogan or melody needs to have a "catchiness" that will encourage readers or listeners to repeat it to themselves. These techniques are particularly effective with children, who, in turn, can often influence parents to buy a particular product. They tend to be more widely used on television and radio than in printed advertisements. On radio, where no visual impression is possible, the value of a good slogan increases. The best slogans emphasize some important aspect of a product or service. Some examples of well-known slogans are these:

Ford has a better idea.
Things go better with Coke.
When you're out of Schlitz, you're out of beer.
When you say Budweiser, you've said it all.
Bayer works wonders.
You asked for it, you got it, Toyota.
At Texaco, we're working to keep your trust.
You're in good hands with Allstate.

Note how frequently the word *you* occurs in these slogans. Most of us respond favorably when the message appears to be directed to us in a personal way.

Competitor Putdown

When a company has an existing effective image or campaign, a competitor may attempt to diminish its competition's claims. Hertz used to claim proudly: "We're number one!" Avis countered with the slogan "When you're number two, you try harder." More recently, Hertz commercials show O. J. Simpson running through airports, demonstrating how quickly one can get out of the airport into a waiting car. Advertisements by Avis show a middle-aged, bald-headed man rushing through an airport, wiping the perspiration from his forehead, as someone taps him on the shoulder, takes his luggage, and reminds him that "at Avis you don't have to run through airports."

The Chrysler Corporation manufactured a small car called the "Roadrunner," a name that symbolizes speed and agility. Ford Motor Company came out with a similar small car called the "Cobra" and used the slogan "Eats birds for breakfast."

For years the blimp has been recognized as a symbol of the Goodyear Tire and Rubber Company. When we think of the blimp, we think of Goodyear. Recent commercials by the B. F. Goodrich Company show people in various situations discussing Goodrich. Invariably, one of them will blunder and ask about the blimp only to be reminded that Goodrich does not have a blimp, because "we're the other guys."

388

The intent is to capitalize on a symbol made famous by Goodyear. At the sight or mention of the blimp, the Goodrich people want us to think "Not Goodyear. Goodrich. We're the other guys." They are, in effect, trying to capitalize on the competitor's trademark.

We previously referred to the claim that "when E. F. Hutton talks, people listen." Another broker now makes this claim: "When people talk, we listen." The implication is that E. F. Hutton tells people what is best for them, whereas the other company learns what is best for the people by listening to them. The Budweiser people refer to Budweiser as the "king of beers." A competitor makes this claim: "For about what you would pay for the king of beers, you could have Tuborg Gold, the golden beer of Danish kings."

Symbolism

Have you ever wondered why so many automobiles have been named after animals? The Mercury Cougar, Audi Fox, Mustang, Pinto, Maverick, Bronco, Colt, and others are very familiar names to most of us. Why are names like Pinto, Mustang, Bronco, and Colt preferable to Mule or Donkey? The answer is obvious. Probably no car will ever be called the Mule or Donkey because these names suggest slowness, stupidity, and stubbornness. Names like Pinto and Mustang are used because they suggest something small yet fast, wild, free, undomesticated. This more clearly reflects the image small-car makers want their products to have.

The Exxon Company has had great success with its picture of a tiger and the slogan "Put a tiger in your tank." The makers of men's toiletries selling under the trade name of English Leather have recently marketed a cologne called Musk. Their radio commercials for this product begin with a sound like the roar of a lion at mating time. We are then reminded that Musk by English Leather is a "civilized way to *roar!*" Many perfumes and aftershave lotions are given names with sexual overtones, such as Brut, Temptation, and My Sin.

DECEPTION IN ADVERTISING[1]

The standard used by the Federal Trade Commission for **deception** in advertising has been whether an advertising claim is false or could mislead the "average" or "ordinary" person in the audience addressed by the advertisement, taking into account that many who may be misled are unsophisticated and unwary. It is possible for an advertisement to be regarded as nondeceptive to an adult audience and deceptive to an audience of children. In deciding whether an ad is deceptive, the total impression it

[1] The material in this section is summarized from "Developments in the Law—Deceptive Advertising," *Harvard Law Review*, 1967, *80*, 1005–1159.

389

generates is considered more important than its literal truth. Vague claims and even silence can be legally considered deceptive when reasonably likely to be understood in a way that is false by a substantial portion of the audience. If an ad can be interpreted in more than one way, and one of those interpretations is false and likely to mislead a substantial portion of the audience, the ad is unlawful.

Some advertising claims are so vague that they cannot be measured and are not considered deceptive. Claims like "Bayer works wonders," "Coca-Cola is the real thing," "Exxon puts a tiger in your tank," and "When you're out of Schlitz, you're out of beer" are not intended by the advertisers to be taken seriously, and it is hard to imagine a significant number of sensible consumers being deceived by such claims.

Deceptive advertising may take various forms, one of which is an inappropriate use of *mock-up* advertising. In mock-up advertising, the product actually has the qualities perceived by the TV viewer, though the means used in the studio to create the image are different from what is perceived on the home screen; for example, mashed potatoes may be used in place of ice cream because ice cream would quickly melt under the heat from TV lights. This kind of advertising has not been found by the FTC to be deceptive. Mock-up advertising is deceptive when an advertiser distorts characteristics of its own or competitive products in order to create in the mind of the consumer a perception of product qualities that the product does not have—for instance, by using lens angles that distort the size or speed of a toy racing car.

The FTC was successful in prosecuting a case against Colgate, which sought to demonstrate that Rapid Shave had moisturizing properties that permitted the shaving of sandpaper, implying that it would be effective in shaving the toughest beards. Since sandpaper appears in television transmission as plain colored paper, the shaving cream was applied instead to Plexiglas covered with sand, which was then swept clean by a razor. What the Supreme Court found deceptive about this commercial was not only that it was a mock-up but that the sandpaper could not be shaved unless it had been soaked by the cream for some 80 minutes. The court went on to find that even if sandpaper could be shaved as shown in the commercial, the commercial was still deceptive, since the advertiser was found to have represented to the public that it was presenting an actual demonstration of its product's qualities.

Not all mock-up advertisements are clearly deceptive. A classic example is the automobile-windshield commercial that demonstrated the distortion free properties of the glass by filming passing scenery with the auto windows rolled down. The advertiser justified this practice on the ground that technical difficulties in filming necessitated the practice to make the advertiser's point. Simulated demonstrations made necessary by technical aspects of television broadcasting are permissible as long as the simulation is disclosed.

The Federal Trade Commission has taken the position that it may be unlawful to make a statement in advertising that, though true, does not support the claim it purports to prove. This stand occurred as a result of a demonstration designed to show the heat- and cold-resistant qualities of a finish given by an auto wax. Gasoline was poured on a waxed auto hood, lighted, and then doused with cold water. Since the fire did not last long enough to heat the surface significantly, the fact that the car suffered no damage from the dramatic fire actually showed nothing about the protective properties of the wax.

BOX 15-4. THE GREAT PAPER-TOWEL DECEPTION

Several years ago an advertisement for paper towels showed Rosie the waitress demonstrating that a soaking-wet Bounty—a two-ply paper towel made by Procter & Gamble—can hold not just one but *two* coffee cups piled one atop the other. This feat clearly impresses the customers in Rosie's diner, and the intent is that the viewer will also be sufficiently impressed to use Bounty rather than some cheaper paper towel. According to Field (1975), this commercial reminded one viewer by the name of Ray Howard, a columnist for a Chicago newspaper, of a demonstration used against him some 20 years earlier, when he was a Kleenex salesman. A competitor from Scott Paper would tour grocery stores and show their managers how soaking-wet Scotties would hold an apple while Kleenex would not. Mr. Howard, conducting an experiment of his own, discovered that the secret to the success of this demonstration is in the way the paper is held. The fibers in paper tend to line up in the direction the papermaking machine is running, forming a "grain." Paper tears more easily along the grain than across the grain.

Recalling this experience, Mr. Howard promptly fetched a roll of Bounty and tried Rosie's coffee-cup test. As he suspected, when held by its perforated edges, the wet Bounty held two cups, just as it had for Rosie; but held by its nonperforated side edges, it could not hold even a single cup. Mr. Howard's experiment not only failed to impress Procter & Gamble but also resulted in the loss of two Wedgwood cups and saucers.

BOX 15-5. EDICT OF LOUIS XI, KING OF FRANCE, A.D. 1481

Anyone who sells butter containing stones or other things (to add to the weight) will be put into our pillory, then said butter will be placed on his head until entirely melted by the sun. Dogs may lick him and people offend him with whatever defamatory epithets they please without offense to God or King. If the sun is not warm enough, the accused will be exposed in the Great Hall in front of a roaring fire, where everyone will see him.

Recent developments in federal regulation of advertising involve efforts to devise a set of effective sanctions for deceptive or unfair claims. Previously, the standard prescription for deceptive advertising was a "cease-and-desist order," defining those categories of claims that were illegal and threatening fines for subsequent violations. One of the more recent remedies is to impose **corrective advertising** on the

391

offender—that is, to require the offender to correct in future advertisements any misleading claims or implications made in previous ones. For example, the Warner-Lambert Company had for many years proclaimed that Listerine mouthwash was effective in ameliorating, preventing, and curing colds and sore throats. When it was demonstrated that Listerine did not cure colds and sore throats, Warner-Lambert was ordered to explain in subsequent commercials that Listerine did not have these properties. Corrective advertising is currently the standard remedy for deceptive advertising.

TECHNIQUES OF BARGAIN HUCKSTERS AND CON ARTISTS

If you believe the bargain huckster, the ways to "get rich quick" are practically limitless. It seems that the supply of people who can be baited with that promise is also practically inexhaustible. Thousands of persons, particularly the elderly, are swindled each day by various schemes, including home repair, door-to-door sales techniques, charity abuse, mail-order schemes, auto repair, burial insurance, and real-estate development, to name only a few. Since it is impossible to give adequate coverage to this topic in a portion of one chapter, our discussion will be limited to chain referral schemes, flimflam techniques, appeals to vanity, quackery, and techniques of land developers. The principles and caution emphasized here, however, are applicable to other unethical or questionable practices.

Chain Referral Schemes

A **chain referral scheme** entices one to purchase some product or service by promising the purchaser commissions on similar sales to friends, relatives, and neighbors. Victims are led to believe that by selling a product to their friends, they can receive commissions not only on the sales they make but also on the sales made by their customers, their customers' customers, and so on. According to a publication of the U.S. Government, thousands of families annually end up paying exorbitant prices for such popular appliances as central vacuum-cleaning systems, color TVs, intercom systems, and burglar-alarm units because they were lulled into believing that there is an unlimited market for this "wonderful new product" and that "with all our friends we won't have any trouble getting enough $50 commissions to reimburse us for our purchase."

Some schemes suggest much more than reimbursement for purchases. One such scheme was called "Multiprogression." Participants were encouraged to fill out an order form and enclose a check for $15, for which they would receive by mail seven pairs of men's socks. Along with the socks were ten brochures explaining "Multiprogression," ten computer cards that served as order forms for customers of the recipient, and a letter. The brochures explained that the usual marketing plan employs a retail salesman who does not share his earnings, which, in this instance, would be $5, or one third of the total purchase price. With this "addition" method he is limited to earning only from those sales he personally completes. With "Multiprogression" a participant shares his earnings, receiving only $1 on each sale personally sponsored but "multiplying" his earning potential with the "continually expanding and unlimited number of sponsors whose earnings he will share." The process progresses as follows: One participant sponsors ten sales and receives $10. Then his ten customers sponsor ten sales each (100 sales), and he receives $100. These 100 customers sponsor ten sales each, and he receives $1000. These 1000 customers sponsor ten sales each, and he receives $10,000. These 10,000 customers sponsor ten sales each and he receives $100,000. With $1 commission on each of the above sales, the original participant's total earnings are $111,110.

A typical letter soliciting participation might read as follows:

Thank you for your order; and welcome to the excitement of MULTI-PROGRESSION! This could be the beginning of a "dream come true" for you. We know you will enjoy your purchase and eagerly share the good news with friends. Your total benefits are not dependent entirely upon your actions; however, they are dependent upon you alone for a beginning. If you do not tell your friends about the GOLD-N-SOX opportunity, they will have no way of knowing (until someone else passes on the information and adds your friend to *their* MULTIPROGRESSION!). Would you believe the greatest handicap you will encounter is an unbelieving "It's too good to be true!"??! Most of us have become so saturated with "FREE if" or "FREE with" etc., that we automatically look for "the catch" when it appears something might be too easily obtained.

Happily, there are no strings attached with MULTIPROGRESSION. MULTIPROGRESSION was introduced by selling to my own friends; and after five days, with hardly any effort, I had completed 28 sales! If these 28 friends shared my enthusiasm, with each of them sponsoring 28 sales in five days and this rhythm continuing throughout the five progressions, in only five weeks my $1.00 commissions would total $17,847,788.00! This kind of success could start a "run" on the sock market!

Being realists, certainly we don't anticipate a monopoly on socks! MUL-TIPROGRESSION is entirely dependent upon the human variable. There are "winners" who will immediately understand their potential and jump at the GOLD-N-SOX opportunity. At the same time there are "born losers," determined to fail, who will find an excuse not to get involved with winning. In between are those who may have hesitation for one of the following reasons; and with your clarification of any doubt, this group will readily move to the "winners' circle."

Because of some similarity to a "chain letter," some may wonder "Is it legal?" IT HAS TO BE! Subject as it is to public scrutiny, this business could not otherwise exist. Apart from satisfying the demands of our own ethics, had our lawyer vetoed the legality of the presentation it would not be offered by us. There is far too much available in legitimate opportunity in our country for anyone to resort to illegal methods. Each individual remains free to check with his own legal counsel, of course.

Often opportunity comes along only to be overlooked or, worse, discarded. You came into the MULTIPROGRESSION program because one of your friends told

393

you it was a fun way to make a lot of money. Regardless of how good something is, however, there is always someone to "knock" it. The first friend you approach might be such a person. For instance, when I explained MULTIPROGRESSION to one of my friends, his first words were "It won't work"! Even though this was a blow to my efforts I did not quit. Instead, that afternoon I talked to seven more friends; and six of them eagerly wrote a check for the SOXcess package. Should you run into one of these "born losers," don't let *him* make *your* decision. Don't lay your cards on the shelf, saying "Well, I got some good socks anyway." Just tell another friend about the GOLD-N-SOX opportunity. When he thanks you and writes a check for his order your enthusiasm will be renewed.

Should you fail to continue this progression, of course, you limit your own Sponsor as well as three Sponsors before him—And though we can't say you will lose a fortune, you certainly may fail to gain one!

It's easy! It's fun! And it *DOES* work! Let's SOCKITO'EM!!

Although it is theoretically possible to make $111,110 from an initial investment of $15, one's chances of doing so are practically zero. Yet many find even the slight possibility of reaping large monetary rewards so enticing they cannot resist the urge to take a chance. A government publication (*Mail Fraud Laws,* 1970) reminds consumers that those with a couple of thousand dollars, no selling experience, and a yen to get rich are prime targets for such "fabulous," "new" marketing plans. Such plans frequently include buying a distributorship for selling a consumer product. In one case, in which the promoter received a 10-year sentence, victims paid as much as $7500 for the right to distribute a household cleaning solution in a Southwestern city. The big profits were to come from recruiting agents and dealers to sell the solution to retail outlets and from house to house. As a distributor, one was promised a percentage of the money one's dealers put into the scheme plus commissions on their sales.

Not all multilevel distributorships are fraudulent, but the pyramid type resembles the illegal chain-letter scheme. The profits come not from selling the product but from inducing others to put their life savings into a distributorship. When a scheme flourishes, the supply of fresh victims is soon exhausted, and the new investors are left with a faded dream and a garage full of merchandise.

Postal inspectors recommend the following:

1. Be wary if the promoters are more interested in selling distributorships than they are in selling a product or service that consumers need.
2. Ask those selling vending-machine routes or franchises for the names and addresses of those making the "fabulous profits." Ask to see their business records, and interview those actually operating a franchise.
3. Check the company with your Better Business Bureau.

Flimflam Techniques

Flimflam techniques involve outright deception and are designed to appeal to our desire to "get something for nothing" or to "get rich quick." The less educated

394

and the elderly seem especially vulnerable to these schemes. Following are some typical examples summarized from various newspaper reports.

1. An elderly man was approached by three men in a supermarket parking lot. They told the old man that he would "get rich quick" by participating in an insurance deal in which he would put up $4000 and they would ante $22,000. The swindlers took his money, apparently wrapped it with theirs in a bandana, and gave it back to him for safekeeping. When they left to check on some "details" of the insurance deal, he decided to examine the money, only to discover that he was holding a handkerchief full of tissue paper.

2. Three men came to the home of an elderly couple and said they were painters who had finished a large painting contract, had some paint left over, and would give them a good price if allowed to paint their house. The couple agreed, and the painters went to work with a spray gun, partially painting three sides of the house, along with the glass in the windows and the shrubbery, with a substance similar to whitewash.

Meanwhile, one of the men went inside the house and demanded payment. When the wife opened her pocketbook, the man reached in and took the couple's Social Security checks and all their cash, an amount estimated to total $335. The men left, saying they would check back the next morning to make sure their customers were satisfied. They never returned.

3. City merchants were approached by advertisers saying they planned to sponsor, in conjunction with the local VFW post, a book of coupons for giveaway items. Some merchants were told part of the money would go to disabled veterans. Others heard no mention of such use of the money but were told the number of coupons printed would be limited in both number and duration of usability. Some merchants signed "contracts" (often only blank pieces of paper), and most were told they would be given final approval of the coupon advertising.

Suddenly the merchants faced a deluge of coupons and were forced to begin giving out the promised items or services. They banded together in search of a way out, only to discover that the "company" that had sold them on the plan had skipped town. Meanwhile, customers are still presenting coupons, and merchants are still gritting their teeth and handing out free goods and services. The end is not in sight.

Appeals to Vanity

Many people are flattered by seeing their names in print. Some publishers capitalize on this desire by obtaining lists of names from legislators and other public officials, businesses, colleges and universities, and professional, business, and civic organizations. A package of materials including a flattering letter, a brief biographical questionnaire, a brochure describing a book that contains the names of outstanding people, including the recipient of the letter, and a reply envelope is sent to the persons whose names appear on these lists. The recipient is encouraged to complete the questionnaire, giving name, address, occupation, and so on and to place an order for a

395

book containing thousands of people's names, addresses, and occupations and little else. These books usually sell for at least $25.

Following is a sample letter of this type.

> Dear Distinguished Citizen:
>
> In 1776 Mr. William Coleman was a merchant in Philadelphia. He held the position of provincial judge and was a member of a debating club called "The Junto" whose members had formerly included a printer named Benjamin Franklin.
>
> How do we know about Mr. Coleman? His name and his contribution to his community appear in one of the reference books of his day. His name does not appear in history books . . . his portrait is not preserved in a museum . . . yet we know something of his life and time because he *shared* it with others.
>
> In commemoration of the 200th anniversary of our nation's founding, we are continuing this tradition by publishing a comprehensive directory of *Distinguished Citizens of Bicentennial America.* We congratulate you on your role, your activities, and outstanding achievements in this 200th year of our nation's history. To recognize and permanently preserve your important part in America's heritage, you have been selected by our Bicentennial Committee to appear in *Distinguished Citizens of Bicentennial America.*
>
> Outstanding personalities from each of the fifty states—including senators, representatives, mayors, judges, homemakers, educators, civic leaders, creative and professional people—have been selected for this honor.
>
> To receive your official Bicentennial Plaque and the directory of *Distinguished Citizens of Bicentennial America,* simply indicate the number of each you desire on your order form. While ordering, remember parents, children, and other relatives and friends to whom you may wish to present gift copies of the Bicentennial Plaque and the commemorative directory.
>
> Congratulations to you and your family for the high level of achievement you have attained, and we extend to you our best wishes for all your future endeavors.

Perhaps the best way to avoid being unduly influenced by this sales technique is to ask the question "Is this a personal letter sent directly to me genuinely recognizing some unique feat I have accomplished or contribution I have made, or is this a form letter designed to sell me a book through flattery?"

Quackery

Some people claim to have competence in fields in which they have little or no training. The fields of medicine and psychology, in particular, seem to attract these self-styled experts, or **quacks**. A large share of sales by the medical quack are through the mail. Without having to face his or her victims, a promoter can peddle nostrums to those with incurable diseases. He or she can also use mailing lists to prey upon families not receiving modern medical care and faddists seeking unusual cures for real or fancied afflictions. *Mail Fraud Laws* (1970) describes some of the schemes that affect the health of thousands of persons. For example, the operator of a mail-order testing laboratory in Texas falsely claimed he had perfected an effective urine test for cancer. More than 15,000 tests were made at $10 each before investigations disclosed that the tests were fake and this scheme was stopped.

One of the greediest schemes directed against the elderly was one of selling hearing aids at prices from $2000 to $7000 to persons confined to wheelchairs and those so disabled by strokes they could hardly speak.

The poor, often not knowing how to get proper medical care, were the target of mail-order ads and other promotions of a New York chiropractor's free "medical" clinic. Frightened by false medical diagnoses, thousands of poorly educated persons signed long-term contracts for unneeded and worthless medical products and treatments. When victims fell behind in their payments, debt collectors—claiming to be health officials—told them they would lose their welfare or other public assistance if they did not pay up.

In this and in most other medical frauds that bring heavy physical and financial losses, postal inspectors seek criminal indictments, which can result in prison sentences of up to 5 years.

There are many other illegal medical schemes in which the individual's financial losses are not too great but the product is of little or no value. In these instances, the Postal Service can call upon the false-representation statute to deny the promoter the right to receive money or orders through the mail.

An Oregon company preying upon persons crippled by arthritis was selling a supply of worthless pills for $31. Because there is no medical evidence that these pills could reduce the pain of arthritis, the Postal Service was able to stop this scheme promptly and protect thousands of sick persons.

Another target of the swindler is men worried over the loss of their hair. A typical promotion was for a $10 "miracle formula" consisting of instructions for massaging the scalp and a high-mineral-and-vitamin diet. The company falsely claimed this would produce a thick, luxuriant head of hair.

This problem is sufficiently pervasive that the Food and Drug Administration has prepared for consumers an *FDA Fact Sheet* (1971) on quackery. The following information is taken from that publication.

What Is Quackery? The term *quackery* encompasses both people and products. The "health practitioner" who has a "miracle cure" but no medical training is a quack; the drug or food supplement promoted with false health claims is a quack product; the machine that has impressive knobs and dials but does nothing except take money out of the pockets of the unsuspecting is a quack device. Broadly speaking, quackery is misinformation about health.

What Kinds of Quackery Are There? Three types of quackery are common: false claims for drugs and cosmetics; silly food fads and unnecessary food

supplements; and fake medical devices. Their promoters' interest is not to protect or restore your health—but to separate you from your money.

Quackery in drugs includes cures for baldness among men, which is incurable; chemical "face peels" that promise new youth but may bring permanent disfigurement; "prompt relief" from colitis through laxatives, which can seriously worsen this condition; drugs that "melt away" fat without dieting. Most cruel and dangerous of all are unproved treatments for cancer, which rob the patient of the one element that can save his or her life—valuable time during which really effective treatment could still be administered.

Food fads are the second common type of quackery. Contrary to what self-appointed "nutrition experts" say, American farm land is not "depleted"; chemical fertilizers and modern food processing have not deprived our food supply of its high nutritive quality. Americans are the best-fed people in the world; diseases caused by dietary deficiencies, which once killed thousands, are no longer encountered.

Device quackery is the third type. The electrocardiograph records the action of the heart; a special gauge shows the blood pressure; X rays record abnormalities within the body. But there is no machine that can diagnose or treat different diseases by simply turning a knob or flashing lights; no apparatus can reduce excess weight by vibration; no glove or bracelet can cure arthritis by radiation. Sometimes quackery even involves legitimate devices. It is practically impossible to get properly fitted eyeglasses or dentures by mail order, for example.

How Can Quackery Be Recognized? Quackery has some well-defined characteristics. If your answer to any of the following questions is yes, it is very likely that you are one of the thousands of people who are being victimized by quackery.

Is the product or service being offered a "secret remedy"?

Does the sponsor claim that he is battling the medical profession, which is trying to suppress his wonderful discovery?

Is the remedy being sold from door to door by a self-styled "health adviser" or promoted in lectures to the public, from town to town?

398

Is this "miracle" drug, device, or diet being promoted in a sensational magazine, by a faith healer's group, or by a crusade organization of laypersons?

Does the promoter show you "testimonials" on the wonderful miracles his product or service has performed for others?

Is the product or service good for a vast variety of illnesses, real or fancied?

What Can You Do? If you suspect that you are the victim of quackery, there are a number of things you can do:

See your physician or inform your county medical society.

Get in touch with the Food and Drug Administration either at its district office in your area or at headquarters, 5600 Fishers Lane, Rockville, Maryland 20852.

Ask the Better Business Bureau about the reputation of the promoter.

If the drug or device was promoted through the mail, inform your local post office.

Techniques of Land Developers

Have you ever received a letter with a fancy color brochure inviting you to come visit some exotic-sounding place and promising free prizes and possibly cash bonuses just for showing up, or have you been notified that you are the winner of a free vacation to some resort area? Perhaps you have also received a phone call from an inviting female whose mellifluous voice invites you and your spouse to free drinks, a gala dinner, and "a chance to show you our wonderful new way of life at our mountaintop retreat and reasonably priced homesites and condominiums, a place to get away from it all in the recreation community of tomorrow."

The chances are that you have been approached in some such manner, and the chances are also that if you accepted these invitations, you were exposed to some high-pressure land-sales pitches. Some land-development operations are legitimate, and others thrive on outright fraud. In an effort to control the growing number of land developers, Congress in 1968 established the Office of Interstate Land Sales Registration (OILSR) in Washington, D.C. Testimony by victims of land swindlers before this agency has often been appalling. A couple vacationing in New Orleans, for example, were approached by a salesman who offered them a free lunch and a tour of the city if they would listen to his land-sales presentation. Several months before their visit to New Orleans, a perfectly legitimate company had bought England's famed London Bridge, transported it to Arizona, and resurrected it amidst great publicity at Lake Havasu City. Almost simultaneously, on a large section of remote, barren desert some 40 miles away, another development sprang up with the name Lake Havasu Estates. This development consisted of a few dirt "streets" through a cactus-covered area remote from utilities and adequate water and sewage systems. The promoters began selling lots sight unseen all over the United States.

Only after the vacationing couple in New Orleans had bought a lot in Lake Havasu Estates, made a down payment, committed themselves to a sizable monthly payment for 7 years (after which they would acquire a deed), and returned home did they realize their mistake. By that time it was too late. They were stuck with one and one-fourth acres of Arizona desert far removed from their dream, Lake Havasu City, which was located in a beautiful area overlooking the Colorado River.

This case is by no means an anomaly. Others report similar experiences daily. The OILSR suggests that you take three steps before buying real estate.

1. Ask to see a federal property report, which by law is required of all developers. Take it home and study it carefully. It should contain such things as title, nature of the land and surroundings, description of facilities to be provided, liens, and water and sewer restrictions. Under federal law, if purchasers are not given the property report, they may void their purchase and get their money back. You also have the right to cancel your agreement of purchase within the 48-hour period following that agreement.
2. Show a lawyer your contract before signing anything. If you are still not satisfied, OILSR will provide a free bulletin defining your legal rights.
3. Never buy land without first seeing it! It is better to pay travel expenses and personally visit the real-estate location than to lose your life savings or get yourself committed to a long-term financial commitment.

BUYING ON IMPULSE

A significant percentage of sales, especially of clothing and food products, is a result of impulse buying. Many stores are laid out to encourage this behavior. There are several methods of reducing the amount of impulse buying that we do. A very simple but effective method is making a shopping list before entering a store and buying only items on the list. This technique is especially helpful when grocery shopping. Those who wish to avoid impulsive purchases in the grocery store should enter only when armed with a shopping list and after eating a full meal.

A second technique is to avoid credit cards and pay cash for each purchase. It is extremely tempting to buy impulsively when we have only to toss out a credit card, sign our name, and walk away with the merchandise. Paying cash increases our awareness of how much money we are spending.

Many clothes are bought on momentary impulse and may only occasionally, if ever, be worn. It is probably not a good idea to buy an expensive article of clothing at first sight unless you have known exactly what you were looking for for a long time. A good rule to follow when tempted to make an impulsive purchase of clothes is to walk out of the store and consider the potential purchase for at least several hours, if not a day or so. It may be that when you are no longer around the garment or at a later time

400

you will find that it is not nearly so appealing. You should also ask such questions as "What do I have that will match this garment?" and "Will I have to buy other clothes that will blend with it?" People have been known to purchase a multicolored shirt or pair of trousers, only to discover that they now need a jacket and tie to make the outfit complete. If you find that a day or so later you still have a strong desire for the garment and if you feel that you can justify the purchase, go ahead.

Candy, gum, and other small items are placed near the checkout counters in many stores so that customers—and especially the children of customers—find something that appeals to their impulses as they pass through the cashier's aisle. Automobile dealers place their bright-colored and expensive sports cars in the most conspicuous positions on the car lot. These cars attract attention and help create a desire for a different auto. It may well be that when customers make their purchase, it is a more conservative car than the one that "caught their eye." The sporty car, nevertheless, has served its purpose, since it attracted a customer who otherwise would have waited much longer to buy a car. Cars are frequently redistributed on the lot to give the impression that they are moving fast.

Another technique to create a desire for a product is through planned obsolescence—that is, implying that a product is out of date or no longer fashionable when it is still serviceable. Clothing styles, for example, change on an annual and sometimes even seasonal basis. Few people actually wear out their clothes; most are discarded because they are perceived to be out of style. The styles of most automobiles are changed with each new model. Many people like to feel that they have the latest in both fashion and technology, to the extent that they are willing to trade in a serviceable vehicle for the later model.

Many merchants use such techniques as free gifts, prizes, and contests to get people into their place of business. They realize that if they can attract people to the store, those people will see something they want, and many will make a purchase before they leave.

SUMMARY

Although many advertisements contain some useful information, not all advertising is designed to help the consumer make the wisest and most economical choice. We become more knowledgeable consumers when we learn to distinguish between useful information in advertising and claims that are deceptive or misleading. The knowledgeable consumer is able to distinguish between assertions and implications. Research has shown that even college students remember claims only implied in advertising as if they had been asserted. Implied claims may contain weasel words, juxtaposition of imperatives, unfinished claims, or incomplete reporting of test results. Communication may be distorted through euphemism and hyperbole. Some advertising seeks to produce conviction through emotional appeals, including fear and threat, nostalgia, sex, testimonials, endorsements, slogans and melodies, competitor putdown, and symbolism.

Bargain hucksters frequently resort to unscrupulous methods designed to appeal to the greedy. Some of the more common methods are chain referral schemes, flimflam techniques, appeals to vanity, quackery, and fraudulent land-development schemes.

An awareness of the kinds of persuasive methods described in this chapter can help us become more knowledgeable and discriminating consumers. Armed with this information, we should be inoculated against some of the gimmickry, subtle manipulation devices, and even outright deception to which naive and less informed persons are more susceptible.

KEY CONCEPTS

Assertion a direct statement that can clearly be determined to be true or false.

Chain referral scheme a sales technique that entices one to purchase some product or service by promising the purchaser commissions on similar sales to friends, relatives, and neighbors.

Corrective advertising the practice of requiring offenders to correct in future advertisements any misleading claims or implications made in previous commercials.

Deception the use of advertising claims that are not true or are reasonably likely to be misunderstood by a substantial portion of the audience.

Emotional appeal an attempt to influence behavior through emotional arousal.

Endorsement the use of a famous person to extol the virtues of a product or service.

Euphemism the substitution of a word with pleasant connotations for a word that is more blunt and possibly closer to the truth.

Flimflam techniques sales methods which involve outright deception and which are designed to appeal to our desire for something for nothing.

Hyperbole using words that exaggerate the truth for the purpose of producing greater effect or impact.

Implication the use of language or pictures to suggest a claim without making a direct statement.

Juxtaposition of imperatives arranging imperative statements in such a way as to imply a causal connection between using a product or service and receiving some benefit without making an assertion to that effect.

Quacks persons claiming to have competence in a field in which they have little or no training.

Testimonial an advertising technique in which some ordinary person, speaking as a consumer, attests to the quality of a product or service.

Unfinished claim an advertising claim of product superiority that does not indicate what the product is superior to.

Weasel word a qualifying word inserted to avoid a direct assertion that can be proved or disproved.

REFERENCES

Adams, A. J., & Stone, T. H. Satisfaction of need for achievement in work and leisure time activities. *Journal of Vocational Behavior,* 1977, *11,* 174–181.

Adams, J. S. Inequity in social exchange. In L. Berkowitz (Ed.), *Advances in experimental social psychology* (Vol. 2). New York: Academic Press, 1965.

Adorno, T. W., Frenkel-Brunswik, E., Levinson, D., & Sanford, N. *The authoritarian personality.* New York: Harper & Row, 1950.

Alexander, F., & French, T. M. *Studies in psychosomatic medicine.* New York: Ronald Press, 1948.

Allen, B. P. Social distance and admiration reactions of "unprejudiced" whites. *Journal of Personality,* 1975, *43,* 709–726.

Altman, I., & Haythorne, W. W. Interpersonal exchange in isolation. *Sociometry,* 1965, *28,* 411–426.

Altman, D., Levine, M., Nadien, M., & Villena, J. Trust of the stranger in the city and the small town. Unpublished research, Graduate Center, City University of New York, 1969. Cited in S. Milgram, The experience of living in cities. *Science,* 1970, *167,* 1461–1468.

American Psychiatric Association. *The diagnostic and statistical manual of mental disorders* (2nd ed.). Washington, D.C.: Author, 1968.

Anderson, L. R., Karuza, J., Jr., & Blanchard, P. N. Enhancement of leader power after election or appointment to undesirable leader roles. *Journal of Psychology,* 1977, *97,* 59–70.

Asch, S. E. Studies of independence and conformity: A minority of one against a unanimous majority. *Psychological Monographs,* 1956, *70*(9, Whole No. 416).

Aslin, A. L. Counseling "single-again" (divorced and widowed) women. *The Counseling Psychologist,* 1976, *6*(2), 37–41.

Atkinson, R. C. Mnemotechnics in second-language learning. *American Psychologist,* 1975, *30,* 821–828.

Bahr, H. M., & Chadwick, B. A. Conservatism, racial intolerance, and attitudes toward racial assimilation among whites and American Indians. *Journal of Social Psychology,* 1974, *94,* 45–56.

Bailey, R. C., & Bartchy, D. *Ninth-grade male and female attitudes toward the acceptability of a male or female candidate for the presidency of a company.* Unpublished manuscript, East Tennessee State University, 1976.

Bailey, R. C., DiGiacomo, R. J., & Zinser, O. Length of male and female friendship and perceived intelligence in self and friend. *Journal of Personality Assessment,* 1976, *40,* 635–640.

Bailey, R. C., Finney, P., & Bailey, K. G. Level of self-acceptance and perceived intelligence in self and friend. *Journal of Genetic Psychology,* 1974, *124,* 61–67.

Bailey, R. C., & Mettetal, G. W. Perceived intelligence in married partners. *Social Behavior and Personality*, 1977, *5*(1), 137–141.

Bailey, R. C., & Price, J. P. Perceived physical attractiveness in married partners of long and short duration. *Journal of Psychology*, 1978, *99*, 155–161.

Bales, R. F. *Interaction process analysis: A method for the study of small groups*. Reading, Mass.: Addison-Wesley, 1950.

Bales, R. F. Task roles and social roles in problem solving groups. In E. E. Maccoby, T. M. Newcomb, & E. L. Hartley (Eds.), *Readings in social psychology* (3rd ed.). New York: Holt, Rinehart & Winston, 1958.

Bandura, A. *Aggression: A social learning analysis*. Englewood Cliffs, N.J.: Prentice-Hall, 1973.

Bandura, A., Ross, D., & Ross, S. A. Transmission of aggression through imitation of aggressive models. *Journal of Abnormal and Social Psychology*, 1961, *63*, 575–582.

Bardwick, J. M. *Psychology of woman: A study of biocultural conflicts*. New York: Harper & Row, 1971.

Barker, R. C., & Wright, H. F. *The Midwest and its children: The psychological ecology of an American town*. New York: Harper & Row, 1954.

Barocas, R., & Vance, F. L. Physical appearance on social responsiveness. *Psychological Reports*, 1974, *31*, 495–500.

Bath, J. A., & Lewis, E. C. Attitudes of young female adults toward some areas of parent-adolescent conflict. *Journal of Genetic Psychology*, 1962, *100*, 241–253.

Berkowitz, L., & Macaulay, J. R. Some effects of differences in status level and status stability. *Human Relations*, 1961, *14*, 135–148.

Berman, E. M., Miller, W. R., Vines, N., & Lief, H. I. The age-30 crisis and the 7-year itch. *Journal of Sex and Marital Therapy*, 1977, *3*, 197–204.

Berscheid, E., & Walster, E. Physical attractiveness. *Advances in Experimental Social Psychology*, 1974, *7*, 157–215.

Bickman, L., & Henchy, T. *Beyond the laboratory: Field research in social psychology*. New York: McGraw-Hill, 1972.

Birchler, G. R., Weiss, R. L., & Wampler, L. D. *Differential patterns of social reinforcement as a function of degree of marital distress and level of intimacy*. Paper presented at the meeting of the Western Psychological Association, Portland, Oregon, April 1972.

Bishop, D. W. Stability of the factor structure of leisure behavior: Analyses of four communities. *Journal of Leisure Research*, 1970, *2*(3), 160–170.

Bohannan, P. (Ed.). *Divorce and after*. New York: Doubleday, 1970.

Bohannan, P. The six stations of divorce. In J. Bardwick (Ed.), *Readings on the psychology of women*. New York: Harper & Row, 1972.

Bogardus, E. S. Social distance and its origins: Measuring social distances. *Journal of Applied Sociology*, 1924–1925, *9*, 211–308.

Bogardus, E. S. Changes in racial distances. *International Journal of Opinion and Attitude Research*, 1947, *1*(1), 55–62.

Bower, G. How to . . . uh . . . remember! *Psychology Today*, October 1973, pp. 62–70.

Bronfenbrenner, U. The changing American child: A speculative analysis. *Journal of Social Issues*, 1961, *17*, 6–18.

Bruno, K. J. *Training the distinction of pragmatic implications from direct assertions in adolescents and adults*. Unpublished master's thesis, Kansas State University, 1977.

Bryan, J. H., & Test, M. A. Models and helping: Naturalistic studies in aiding behavior. *Journal of Personality and Social Psychology*, 1967, *6*, 400–407.

Bugelski, B., Kidd, E., & Segman, J. Image as a mediator in one-trial paired associate learning.

Journal of Experimental Psychology, 1968, *76,* 69–73.

Buys, C. J. Humans would do better without groups. *Personality and Social Psychology Bulletin,* 1978, *4,* 123–125.

Byrne, D. The influence of propinquity and opportunities for interaction on classroom relationships. *Human Relations,* 1961, *14,* 63–69.

Byrne, D., London, O., & Reeves, K. The effects of physical attractiveness, sex, and attitude similarity on interpersonal attraction. *Journal of Personality,* 1968, *36*(2), 259–271.

Campbell, D. T. Occupation ten years later of high school seniors with high scores on the SVIB Life Insurance Salesman scale. *Journal of Applied Psychology,* 1966, *50,* 369–372.

Campbell, D. T., & Stanley, J. C. *Experimental designs for research.* Chicago: Rand McNally, 1966.

Caplow, T., & Forman, R. Neighborhood interaction in a homogeneous community. *American Sociological Review,* 1950, *15,* 357–366.

Carlson, R. Stability and change in the adolescent's self-image. *Child Development,* 1965, *36,* 659–666.

Casady, M. The tricky business of giving rewards. *Psychology Today,* September 1974, p. 52.

Cash, T. F., Begley, P. J., McCown, D. A., & Weise, B. C. When counselors are heard but not seen: Initial impact of physical attractiveness. *Journal of Counseling Psychology,* 1975, *22,* 273–279.

Cash, T. F., Gillen, B., & Burns, D. S. Sexism and "beautyism" in personnel consultant decision making. *Journal of Applied Psychology,* 1977, *62,* 301–310.

Cash, T. F., Kehr, J. A., Polyson, J., & Freeman, V. Role of physical attractiveness in peer attribution of psychological disturbance. *Journal of Consulting and Clinical Psychology,* 1977, *45*(6), 987–993.

Cates, J. Psychology's manpower: Report on the National Register of Scientific and Technical Personnel. *American Psychologist,* 1970, *25,* 254–263.

Chance, J. *Independence training and children's achievement.* Paper presented at the meeting of the Society for Research in Child Development, Minneapolis, March 1965.

Chapple, E. D. Measuring human relations: An introduction to the study of the interaction of individuals. *Genetic Psychology Monographs,* 1940, *22,* 1–47.

Child, E., & Child, J. Children and leisure. In M. A. Smith et al. (Eds.), *Leisure and society in Britain.* London: Allen Lane, 1974.

Chodoff, P., & Lyons, H. Hysteria, the hysterical personality, and hysterical conversion. *American Journal of Psychiatry,* 1958, *114,* 734–740.

Cimbalo, R. S., Anzelone, P. A., & Younkers, M. P. Attitude, cognitive structures, and emotional reactivity to sex and security: Sex differences. *Psychological Reports,* 1974, *34,* 715–725.

Cimbalo, R. S., Faling, V., & Mousaw, P. The course of love: A cross-sectional design. *Psychological Reports,* 1976, *38,* 1292–1294.

Clark, H. The crowd. *Psychological Monographs,* 1916, *49,* 311–313.

Clark, K. B., & Clark, M. P. Racial identification and preference in Negro children. In T. M. Newcomb & E. L. Hartley (Eds.), *Readings in social psychology.* New York: Holt, Rinehart & Winston, 1947.

Clarke, A. C. An examination of the operation of residential propinquity as a factor in mate selection. *American Sociological Review,* 1952, *17,* 17–22.

Clarke, J. H. Race: An evolving issue in Western social thought. *Journal of Human Relations,* 1970, *18,* 1040–1054.

Coates, B., & Pusser, H. E. Positive reinforcement and punishment in "Sesame Street" and

"Mister Rogers." *Journal of Broadcasting,* 1975, *19,* 143–151.

Coates, B., Pusser, H. E., & Goodman, I. The influence of "Sesame Street" and "Mister Rogers' Neighborhood" on children's social behavior in the preschool. *Child Development,* 1976, *47,* 138–144.

Coleman, J. C., & Hammen, C. L. *Contemporary psychology and effective behavior.* Glenview, Ill.: Scott, Foresman, 1974.

Cook, S. W. A preliminary study on attitude change. In M. Werheimer (Ed.), *Confrontation psychology and the problems of today.* Glenview, Ill.: Scott, Foresman, 1969.

Courtney, A., & Shipple, W. Women in TV commercials. *Journal of Communication,* 1974, *24*(2), 110–118.

Crowley, J. E., Levitin, T. E., & Quinn, R. P. Seven deadly half truths about women. *Psychology Today,* March 1973, pp. 94–96.

Darley, J., & Berscheid, E. Increased liking as a result of the anticipation of personal contact. *Human Relations,* 1967, *20,* 29–40.

Darley, J., & Latané, B. Bystander intervention in emergencies: Diffusion of responsibility. *Journal of Personality and Social Psychology,* 1968, *8,* 377–383.

Darley, S. A. Big-time careers for the little woman: A dual-role dilemma. *Journal of Social Issues,* 1976, *32*(3), 85–98.

De Charms, R. *Personal causation: The internal affective determinant of behavior.* New York: Academic Press, 1968.

De Charms, R. Personal causation training in the schools. *Journal of Applied Social Psychology,* 1972, *2,* 95–113.

Deci, E. L. Effects of externally mediated rewards on intrinsic motivation. *Journal of Personality and Social Psychology,* 1971, *18,* 105–115.

Deci, E. L. *Intrinsic motivation.* New York: Plenum, 1975.

DeFleur, M. L., & Westie, F. R. Verbal attitudes and overt acts: An experiment on the salience of attitudes. *American Sociological Review,* 1958, *23,* 667–673.

De Grazia, S. *Of time, work, and leisure.* New York: Twentieth Century Fund, 1962.

Dermer, M., & Thiel, D. L. When beauty may fail. *Journal of Personality and Social Psychology,* 1974, *31,* 1168–1176.

Dion, K. K. Physical attractiveness and evaluation of children's transgressions. *Journal of Personality and Social Psychology,* 1972, *24,* 207–213.

Dion, K. K., Berscheid, D., & Walster, E. What is beautiful is good. *Journal of Personality and Social Psychology,* 1972, *24,* 285–290.

Dion, K. K., & Dion, K. L. Self-esteem and romantic love. *Journal of Personality,* 1975, *43*(1), 39–57.

Dion, K. L., & Dion, K. K. Correlates of romantic love. *Journal of Consulting and Clinical Psychology,* 1973, *41,* 51–56.

Dutton, D. G., & Lake, R. A. Threat of own prejudice and reverse discrimination in interracial situations. *Journal of Personality and Social Psychology,* 1973, *28,* 94–100.

Eagly, A. H. Sex differences in influenceability. *Psychological Bulletin,* 1978, *85,* 86–116.

Ebbinghaus, H. *Über das Gedächtnis.* Leipzig: Altenburg, 1885.

Edinger, J. D., Bailey, K. G., & Lira, F. T. Effects of team play on racial prejudice. *Psychological Reports,* 1977, *40,* 887–898.

Elbing, A. O., Gadon, H., & Gordon, J. R. M. Flexible working hours: The missing link. *California Management Review,* Spring 1975, pp. 50–57.

Ellis, A. *Humanistic psychology: The rational-emotive approach.* New York: Julian Press, 1963.

Emswiller, T., Deaux, K., & Willits, J. E. Similarity, sex, and requests for small favors.

Journal of Applied Social Psychology, 1971, *1*, 284–291.

Epstein, C. F. *Woman's place: Options and limits in professional careers*. Berkeley: University of California Press, 1970.

Erikson, E. H. *Childhood and society*. (2nd ed.). New York: Norton, 1963.

Fagot, B. I. Sex-related stereotyping of toddlers' behaviors. *Developmental Psychology*, 1973, *9*, 429.

Fagot, B. I. Sex differences in toddler's behavior and parental reaction. *Developmental Psychology*, 1974, *10*, 554–558.

Farmer, H. Career counseling implications for the lower social class and women. *Personnel and Guidance Journal*, 1978, *56*, 467–471.

FDA fact sheet no. 72-1004. Washington, D.C.: U.S. Government Printing Office, 1971.

Feather, N. T. Positive and negative reactions to male and female success and failure in relation to the perceived status and sex-typed appropriateness of occupations. *Journal of Personality and Social Psychology*, 1975, *31*(3), 536–548.

Ferrari, N. A. *Institutionalization and attitude change in an aged population: A field study on dissidence theory*. Unpublished doctoral dissertation, Case Western Reserve University, 1962.

Ferster, C. B., Nurnberger, J. J., & Levitt, E. B. The control of eating. *Journal of Mathematics*, 1962, *1*, 87–109.

Festinger, L. Informal social communication. *Psychological Review*, 1950, *57*, 271–282.

Field, R. The great paper towel deception. *Science Digest*, May 1975, pp. 86–88.

Fine, G. A., & Rosnow, R. L. Gossip, gossipers, gossiping. *Personality and Social Psychology Bulletin*, 1978, *4*, 161–168.

"Ford commercial implies warranty, county jury says." *Johnson City Press Chronicle*, February 6, 1978.

Freedman, J. L. Role playing: Psychology by consensus. *Journal of Personality and Social Psychology*, 1969, *13*, 107–114.

Freedman, M. B., Leary, T. F., Ossorio, A. G., & Coffey, H. S. The interpersonal dimension of personality. *Journal of Personality*, 1951, *20*, 143–161.

Fromm, E. Selfishness and self-love. *Psychiatry*, 1939, *2*, 507–523.

Gaertner, S. L. Helping behavior and racial discrimination among liberals and conservatives. *Journal of Personality and Social Psychology*, 1973, *25*, 335–341.

Gaertner, S. L. *Racial attitudes of liberals*. Paper presented at the convention of the American Psychological Association, New Orleans, September 1974.

Gilbert, G. M. Stereotype persistence and change among college students. *Journal of Abnormal and Social Psychology*, 1951, *46*, 245–254.

Gist, N. P., & Fava, S. F. *Urban society*. New York: Thomas Y. Crowell, 1964.

Godbey, G., & Parker, S. *Leisure studies and services: An overview*. Philadelphia: Saunders, 1976.

Goldstein, M. A., Kilroy, M. C., & Van de Voort, D. Gaze as a function of conversation and degree of love. *Journal of Psychology*, 1976, *92*, 227–234.

Golembiewski, R. T., Hilles, R., & Kango, M. S. A longitudinal study of flexi-time effects: Some consequences of an OD structural intervention. *Journal of Applied Behavioral Science*, 1974, *10*, 503–532.

Goodman, P. S., & Friedman, A. An examination of quantity and quality of performance under conditions of overpayment in piece rate. *Organizational Behavior and Human Performance*, 1969, *4*, 365–374.

Goranson, R., & Berkowitz, L. Reciprocity and responsibility reactions to prior help. *Journal of Personality and Social Psychology*, 1966, *3*, 227–232.

409

Graham, S. Social correlates of adult leisure-time behavior. In M. B. Sussman (Ed.), *Community structure and analysis*. New York: Crowell, 1959.

Gravitz, M. A., & Gerton, M. I. Public prestige and preferred gender of mental health providers. *Journal of Clinical Psychology*, 1977, *33*(3), 919–921.

Green, J. A. *Attitudinal and situational determinants of intended behavior to Negros*. Paper presented at the meeting of the Western Psychological Association, Vancouver, June 1969.

Greenberg, B. S., & Parker, E. G. (Eds.). *The Kennedy assassination and the American public: Social communication in crisis*. Stanford, Calif.: Stanford University Press, 1965.

Greene, C. N. *Source and direction of causal influence in satisfaction-performance relationships*. Paper presented at the annual meeting of the Eastern Academy of Management, Boston, May 1972.

Grimes, M. D., Pinhey, T. K., & Zurcher, L. A. Note on students' reaction to "streakers" and "streaking." *Perceptual and Motor Skills*, 1977, *45*, 1226.

Grubb, E. A. Assembly line boredom and individual differences in recreation participation. *Journal of Leisure Research*, 1975, *7*(4), 256–269.

Guthrie, E. R. *The psychology of learning*. New York: Harper & Row, 1935.

Gyllenhammar, P. How Volvo adapts work to people. *Harvard Business Review*, 1977, *55*, 102–113.

Hallenstein, C. B. Ethical problems of psychological jargon. *Professional Psychology*, 1978, *9*, 111–116.

Hankins, N. E. *How to become the person you want to be*. Chicago: Nelson-Hall, 1979.

Harris, M. B. Accelerating dissertation writing: Case study. *Psychological Reports*, 1974, *34*, 984–986.

Harris, M. B., & Bruner, C. G. A comparison of a self-control and a contract system for weight control. *Behavior Research and Therapy*, 1971, *9*, 347–354.

Harris, R. J. Comprehension of pragmatic implications in advertising. *Journal of Applied Psychology*, 1977, *62*, 603–608.

Harris, R. J., Dubitsky, T., & Thompson, S. Learning to identify deceptive truth in advertising. In J. H. Leigh and C. R. Martin (Eds.), *Current issues and research in advertising*. Ann Arbor: University of Michigan, Graduate School of Business Administration, 1978.

Harvey, O. J., & Consalvi, C. Status and conformity to pressures in informal groups. *Journal of Abnormal and Social Psychology*, 1960, *60*, 182–187.

Haskell, S. D. Desired family-size correlates for single undergraduates. *Psychology of Women Quarterly*, 1977, *2*(1), 5–15.

Havighurst, R. J., & Feigenbaum, K. Characteristics of home-centered and community-centered use of leisure time. *American Journal of Sociology*, 1959, *64*, 396–404.

Heider, F. *The psychology of interpersonal relations*. New York: Wiley, 1958.

Helm, B. *Interperceptions and interpersonal behaviors*. Unpublished manuscript, Oklahoma State University, 1974.

Heron, W. Cognitive and physiological effects of perceptual isolation. In P. Soloman et al. (Eds.), *Sensory deprivation*. Cambridge, Mass.: Harvard University Press, 1961.

Heron, W., Doane, B. K., & Scott, T. H. Visual disturbances after prolonged perceptual isolation. *Canadian Journal of Psychology*, 1956, *10*, 13–18.

Herzberg, F. Motivation, morale. *Psychology Today*, March 1968, pp. 42; 45; 66–67.

Hetherington, E. M. Effects of parental absence on sex-typed behaviors in Negro and White preadolescent males. *Journal of Personality and Social Psychology*, 1966, *4*, 87–91.

Hetherington, E. M., & Deur, J. L. The effects of father absence on child development. *Young*

410

Children, 1971, *26,* 233–248.

Hilgard, E. R., Atkinson, R. C., & Atkinson, R. L. *Introduction to psychology* (6th ed.). New York: Harcourt Brace Jovanovich, 1975.

Hill, K. A., & Hill, C. I. Children's concepts of good and bad behavior. *Psychological Reports,* 1977, *41,* 955–958.

Hinkle, L. E., Jr., Redmont, R., Plummer, N., & Wolff, H. G. An examination of the relation between symptoms, disability, and serious illness, in two homogeneous groups of men and women. *American Journal of Public Health,* 1960, *50,* 1372.

Hollander, E. P. *Principles and methods of social psychology.* New York: Oxford University Press, 1967.

Holmes, T. H., & Rahe, R. H. The Social Readjustment Scale. *Journal of Psychosomatic Research,* 1967, *11,* 213–218.

Homme, L. E. Perspectives in psychology: XXIV. Control of coverants, the operants of the mind. *Psychological Record,* 1965, *15,* 501–511.

Homme, L. E., de Baca, D. C., Devine, J. V., Steinhurst, R., & Rickert, E. J. Use of the Premack principle in controlling the behavior of nursery school children. *Journal of the Experimental Analysis of Behavior,* 1963, *6,* 544.

Horn, J. Bored to sickness. *Psychology Today,* May 1975, p. 92.

Horner, M. S. *Sex differences in achievement motivation and performances in competitive and non-competitive situations.* Unpublished doctoral dissertation, University of Michigan, 1968.

Horowitz, I. A. Effect of choice and locus of dependency on helping behavior. *Journal of Personality and Social Psychology,* 1968, *8,* 373–376.

Hovland, C., Janis, I., & Kelley, H. H. *Communication and persuasion.* New Haven, Conn.: Yale University Press, 1953.

Hovland, C. I., & Weiss, W. The influence of source credibility on communication effectiveness. *Public Opinion Quarterly,* 1951, *15,* 635–650.

How Americans pursue happiness. *U.S. News & World Report,* May 23, 1977, pp. 60–76.

Hurlock, E. B. *Developmental psychology.* New York: McGraw-Hill, 1968.

Iwao, S. Internal versus external criticism of group standards. *Sociometry,* 1963, *26,* 410–421.

Janis, I. L., & Feshbach, S. Effects of fear arousing communications. *Journal of Abnormal and Social Psychology,* 1953, *48,* 78–92.

Janis, I. L., & King, B. T. The influence of role-playing on opinion change. *Journal of Abnormal and Social Psychology,* 1954, *49,* 211–218.

Janis, I. L., & Wheeler, D. Thinking clearly about career choices. *Psychology Today,* May 1978, pp. 67–68ff.

Jones, M. C. The elimination of children's fears. *Journal of Experimental Psychology,* 1924, *7,* 382–390.

Jourard, S. M. *The transparent self.* Princeton, N.J.: Van Nostrand, 1971.

Kaplan, M. *Leisure in society: A social inquiry.* New York: Wiley, 1960.

Kaplan, R. M., & Singer, R. D. Television violence and viewer aggression: A reexamination of the evidence. *Journal of Social Issues,* 1976, *32,* 35–70.

Karling, M., Coffman, T. L., & Walters, G. On the fading of social stereotypes: Studies on three generations of college students. *Journal of Personality and Social Psychology,* 1969, *13,* 1–16.

Katz, D. The functional approach to the study of attitudes. *Public Opinion Quarterly,* 1960, *24,* 163–204.

Katz, D., & Braly, K. Racial stereotypes in one hundred college students. *Journal of Abnormal*

411

and Social Psychology, 1933, *28*, 280–290.

Kelman, H. C. Human use of human subjects: The problem of deception in social psychological experiments. *Psychological Bulletin*, 1967, *67*, 1–11.

King, B. T., & Janis, I. L. Comparison of the effectiveness of improvised versus nonimprovised role-playing in producing opinion changes. *Human Relations*, 1956, *9*, 177–186.

Knoff, W. A history of the concept of neurosis, with a memory of William Cullen. *American Journal of Psychiatry*, 1970, *77*, 80–84.

Kohn, M. L., & Carroll, E. E. Social class and the allocation of parental responsibilities. *Sociometry*, 1960, *23*, 372–392.

Konecni, V. J. Some effects of guilt on compliance: A field replication. *Journal of Personality and Social Psychology*, 1972, *23*, 30–32.

Korte, C., & Kerr, N. Response to altruistic opportunities in urban and nonurban settings. *Journal of Social Psychology*, 1975, *95*, 183–184.

Kutner, B., Wilkins, C., & Yarrow, P. R. Verbal attitudes and overt behavior involving racial prejudice. *Journal of Abnormal and Social Psychology*, 1952, *47*, 649–652.

Lakein, A. *How to get control of your time and your life.* New York: Wyden Books, 1973.

Lamb, M. E. The development of parental preferences in the first two years of life. *Sex Roles*, 1977, *3*, 495–497.

Landy, D., & Sigall, H. Beauty is talent: Task evaluations as a function of the performer's physical attractiveness. *Journal of Personality and Social Psychology*, 1974, *29*, 299–304.

LaPiere, R. T. Attitudes versus action. *Social Forces*, 1934, *13*, 230–237.

Latané, B., & Darley, J. M. Group inhibition of bystander intervention in emergencies. *Journal of Personality and Social Psychology*, 1968, *10*, 215–221.

Latané, B., & Rodin, J. A lady in distress: Inhibiting effects of friends and strangers on bystander intervention. *Journal of Experimental Social Psychology*, 1969, *5*, 189–202.

Leeds, R. Altruism and the norm of giving. *Merrill-Palmer Quarterly*, 1963, *9*, 229–240.

Levine, M. E., Villena, J., Altman, D., & Nadien, M. Trust of the stranger: An urban/small town comparison. *Journal of Psychology*, 1976, *92*, 113–116.

Lewin, K. Problems of research in social psychology, 1943. In K. Lewin, *Field theory in social science: Selected theoretical papers.* New York: Harper & Row, 1951.

Lieberman, S. The effects of changes in roles on the attitudes of role occupants. *Human Relations*, 1956, *9*, 385–402.

Lilly, J. C. Mental effects of reduction of ordinary levels of physical stimuli on intact, healthy persons. *Psychiatric Research*, 1956, *5*, 1–9.

Linder, S. B. *The harried leisure class.* New York: Columbia University Press, 1970.

Lindsley, D. R. A reliable wrist counter for recording behavior rates. *Journal of Applied Behavior Analysis*, 1968, *8*, 77–78.

Locke, E. A. Toward a theory of task motivation and incentives. *Organizational Behavior and Human Performance*, 1968, *3*, 157–189.

London, M., Crandall, R., & Fitzgibbons, D. The psychological structure of leisure: Activities, needs, and people. *Journal of Leisure Research*, 1977, *9*(4), 252–263.

London, P. *The modes and morals of psychotherapy.* New York: Holt, Rinehart & Winston, 1964.

Lorenz, K. *On aggression.* New York: Harcourt Brace Jovanovich, 1966.

Lund, F. H. The psychology of belief. *Journal of Abnormal and Social Psychology*, 1925, *20*, 174–196.

Lynn, D. B., & Cross, A. R. Parent preferences in preschool children. *Journal of Marriage and the Family*, 1974, *36*, 555–559.

Maccoby, E. E., & Jacklin, N. J. *The psychology of sex differences.* Stanford, Calif.: Stanford University Press, 1974.

Mahoney, M. J. Self-reward and self-monitoring techniques for weight control. *Behavior Therapy,* 1974, *5,* 48–57.

Mahoney, M. J., & Mahoney, K. Fight fat with behavior control. *Psychology Today,* May 1976, p. 43.

Mahoney, M. J., Moura, N. G., & Wade, T. C. The relative efficacy of self-reward, self-punishment, and self-monitoring techniques for weight loss. *Journal of Consulting and Clinical Psychology,* 1973, *40,* 404–407.

Mail fraud laws. Washington, D.C.: U.S. Government Printing Office, 1970.

Marcia, J. E. Development and validation of ego identity status. *Journal of Personality and Social Psychology,* 1966, *5,* 551–558.

Marmor, J. *Psychiatrists and their patients: A national study of private office practices.* Washington, D.C.: American Psychiatric Association, National Association for Mental Health, 1975.

Martin, J. Surveying attitudes on marriage, divorce, the family, and sex. *Washington Post,* October 3, 1974, p. 131.

Maslow, A. H. *Motivation and personality.* New York: Harper & Row, 1970.

McClelland, D. C. *The achieving society.* Princeton, N.J.: Van Nostrand, 1961.

McClelland, D. C., Atkinson, J. W., Clark, R. A., & Lowell, E. L. *The achievement motive.* New York: Appleton-Century-Crofts, 1953.

McDavid, J. W., & Harari, H. *Psychology and social behavior.* New York: Harper & Row, 1974.

McKechnie, G. E. The psychological structure of leisure: Past behavior. *Journal of Leisure Research,* 1974, *6*(1), 27–45.

McKegney, F. P., Gordon, R. O., & Levine, S. M. A psychosomatic comparison of patients with ulcerative colitis and Crohn's disease. *Psychosomatic Medicine,* 1970, *32*(2), 153–166.

McKenna, W., & Morgenthau, S. Urban-rural differences in social interaction: A study of helping behavior. Unpublished research, 1969. Cited in S. Milgram, The experience of living in cities. *Science,* 1970, *167,* 1461–1468.

Meichenbaum, D. Cognitive modification of test anxious college students. *Journal of Consulting and Clinical Psychology,* 1972, *39,* 370–380.

Meichenbaum, D., & Cameron, R. *Stress inoculation: A skills training approach to anxiety management.* Unpublished manuscript, University of Waterloo, 1973.

Meichenbaum, D., & Turk, D. *The cognitive-behavioral management of anxiety, anger, and pain.* Paper presented at the Seventh Banff International Conference on Behavior Modification, 1975.

Michelini, R. L., Wilson, J. P., & Messé, L. A. The influence of psychological needs on helping behavior. *Journal of Psychology,* 1975, *91,* 253–258.

Milgram, S. The experience of living in cities. *Science,* 1970, *167,* 1461–1468.

Milgram, S. *The individual in a social world: Essays and experiments.* Reading, Mass.: Addison-Wesley, 1977.

Mitchell, T. R., & Biglan, A. Instrumentality theories: Current uses in psychology. *Psychological Bulletin,* 1971, *76,* 432–454.

Morrison, J. K., Bushell, J. D., Hanson, G. D., Fentiman, J. R., & Holdridge-Crane, S. Relationship between psychiatric patients' attitudes toward mental illness and attitudes of dependency. *Psychological Reports,* 1977, *41,* 1194.

Morrison, J. K., & Nevid, J. S. Attitudes of mental patients and mental health professionals about mental illness. *Psychological Reports*, 1976, *38*, 565–566.

Munro, G., & Adams, G. R. Ego-identity formation in college students and working youth. *Developmental Psychology*, 1977, *13*, 523–524.

Murstein, B. I. Physical attractiveness and marital choice. *Journal of Personality and Social Psychology*, 1972, *22*, 8–12.

Murstein, B. I., & Christy, P. Physical attractiveness and marriage adjustment in middle-aged couples. *Journal of Personality and Social Psychology*, 1976, *34*, 537–542.

Newman, E. *Strictly speaking*. New York: Warner Books, 1975.

Nolan, J. D. Self-control procedures in the modification of smoking behaviors. *Journal of Consulting and Clinical Psychology*, 1968, *32*, 92–93.

Novaco, R. W. *Anger control: The development and evaluation of an experimental treatment*. Lexington, Mass.: Heath, Lexington Books, 1975.

Novaco, R. W. A stress inoculation approach to anger management in the training of law enforcement officers. *American Journal of Psychiatry*, 1976, *133*(10), 1124–1128.

Nye, F. I. Emerging and declining family roles. *Journal of Marriage and the Family*. 1974, *36*, 238–245.

O'Donnell, W. J., & O'Donnell, K. J. Update: Sex role messages in TV commercials. *Journal of Communication*, 1978, *28*, 156–158.

Olson, D. H. Marriage of the future: Revolutionary or evolutionary change? *Family Coordinator*, 1972, *21*, 383–393.

Orlofsky, J. L., Marcia, J. E., & Lesser, I. M. Ego identity status and the intimacy versus isolation crisis of young adulthood. *Journal of Personality and Social Psychology*, 1973, *27*, 211–219.

Orne, M. On the social psychology of the psychological experiment: With particular reference to demand characteristics and their implications. *American Psychologist*, 1962, *17*, 776–783.

Pavlos, A. J. *Consumer ripoff: Effects of physical attractiveness and financial status on cost estimate for a service*. Paper presented at the annual meeting of the Southeastern Psychological Association, Atlanta, March 1978.

Pavlos, A. J., & Newcomb, J. D. *Effects of physical attractiveness and severity of physical illness on justification seen for attempting suicide*. Paper presented at the 82nd Annual Convention of the American Psychological Association, New Orleans, September 1974.

Pavlov, I. P. *Conditioned reflexes*. London: Oxford University Press, 1927.

Penick, S. B., Filion, R., Fox, S., & Stunkard, A. J. Behavior modification in the treatment of obesity. *Psychosomatic Medicine*, 1971, *33*, 49–55.

Peter, L. J., & Hull, R. *The Peter principle*. New York: Bantam, 1970.

Peterson, R. A., & Kerin, R. A. The female role in advertisements: Some experimental evidence. *Journal of Marketing*, 1977, *41*, 59–63.

Piaget, J. *The origins of intelligence in children*. New York: International Universities Press, 1952.

Piliavin, J., & Piliavin, I. Effects of blood on reactions to a victim. *Journal of Personality and Social Psychology*, 1972, *23*, 353–361.

Piliavin, I., Rodin, J., & Piliavin, J. Good Samaritanism: An underground phenomenon? *Journal of Personality and Social Psychology*, 1969, *13*, 289–299.

Platt, J. Social traps. *American Psychologist*, 1973, *28*, 641–651.

Pollis, N. P., & Doyle, D. C. Sex-role status and perceived competence among first graders. *Perceptual and Motor Skills*, 1972, *34*, 235–238.

Porter, L., & Lawler, E. What job attitudes tell about motivation. *Harvard Business Review*,

414

1968, *46*, 118–126.

Preston, I. L. Logic and illogic in the advertising process. *Journalism Quarterly*, 1967, *44*, 231–239.

Reissman, L. Class, leisure, and social participation. *American Sociological Review*, 1954, *19*, 76–84.

Renwick, P., & Lawler, E. What you really want from your job. *Psychology Today*, May 1978, pp. 53–65; 118.

Richter, C. P. On the phenomenon of sudden death in animal and man. *Psychosomatic Medicine*, 1957, *19*, 191–198.

Rimm, D. C., & Somervill, J. W. *Abnormal psychology*. New York: Academic Press, 1977.

Ritchie, J. R. B. On the derivation of leisure activity types—a perceptual mapping approach. *Journal of Leisure Research*, 1975, *7*(2), 128–140.

Rogers, C. R. A theory of therapy, personality, and interpersonal relationships, as developed in the client-centered framework. In S. Koch (Ed.), *Psychology: A study of a science*. New York: McGraw-Hill, 1959.

Rosen, B. The achievement syndrome. *American Sociological Review*, 1956, *21*, 203–211.

Rosenthal, R. *Experimenter effect in behavioral research*. New York: Appleton-Century-Crofts, 1966.

Rosnow, R., & Robinson, E. (Eds.). *Experiments in persuasion*. New York: Academic Press, 1967.

Rothbart, M. Perceiving social injustice: Observations on the relationship between liberal attitudes and proximity to social problems. *Journal of Applied Social Psychology*, 1973, *3*, 291–303.

Rothenberg, A. Anger, American. *Journal of Psychiatry*, 1971, *128*, 454–460.

Rotter, J. B. Generalized expectancies for internal versus external locus of control of reinforcement. *Psychological Monographs*, 1966, *80*(1, Whole No. 609).

Rubin, Z. Measurement of romantic love. *Journal of Personality and Social Psychology*, 1970, *16*(2), 265–273.

Rubin, Z. *Liking and loving*. New York: Holt, Rinehart & Winston, 1973.

Ruch, F. L., & Zimbardo, P. G. *Psychology and life* (8th ed.). Glenview, Ill.: Scott, Foresman, 1971.

Santrock, J. W. Influence of onset and type of paternal absence on the first four Eriksonian developmental crises. *Developmental Psychology*, 1974, *3*, 273–274.

Sapira, J. D., Scheib, E. T., Moriarty, R., & Shapiro, A. P. Differences in perception between hypertensive and normotensive populations. *Psychosomatic Medicine*, 1971, *33*(3), 239–250.

Schacht, T. E., & Nathan, P. E. But is it good for psychologists? Appraisal and status of DSM-III. *American Psychologist*, 1977, *32*, 1017–1025.

Schachter, S. *The psychology of affiliation*. Stanford, Calif.: Stanford University Press, 1959.

Schachter, S. Birth order, eminence, and higher education. *American Sociological Review*, 1963, *28*, 757–767.

Schneider, D. J. *Social psychology*. Reading, Mass.: Addison-Wesley, 1976.

Schultz, D. P. The human subject in psychological research. *Psychological Bulletin*, 1969, *72*, 214–228.

Schultz, D. P. *Growth psychology: Models of the healthy personality*. New York: Van Nostrand, 1977.

Schwartz, A. *Hobbies*. New York: Simon & Schuster, 1972.

Scobel, D. Doing away with the factory blues. *Harvard Business Review*, 1975, *53*, 132–142.

415

Scott, W. A. Attitude change through reward of verbal behavior. *Journal of Abnormal and Social Psychology*, 1957, *55*, 72–75.

Selby, J. W., Calhoun, L. G., & Johnson, R. E. Perceived causes of psychological problems: An exploratory study. *Journal of Community Psychology*, 1977, *5*, 290–294.

Seligman, C., Brickman, J., & Koulack, D. Rape and physical attractiveness: Assigning responsibility to victims. *Journal of Personality*, 1977, *45*, 554–563.

Seligman, M. E. P. *Helplessness: On depression, development, and death.* San Francisco: W. H. Freeman, 1975.

Severy, L. J., Brigham, J. C., & Schlenker, B. R. *A contemporary introduction to social psychology.* New York: McGraw-Hill, 1976.

Sexton, P. C. *The feminized male: Classrooms, white collars, and the decline of manliness.* New York: Random House, 1969.

Sherif, M., & Sherif, C. *Social psychology.* New York: Harper & Row, 1969.

Shmurak, S. *Design and evaluation of three dating behavior training programs.* Unpublished doctoral dissertation, University of Indiana, 1974.

Sidman, M. *Tactics of scientific research: Evaluating experimental data in psychology.* New York: Basic Books, 1960.

Sigall, H., & Ostrove, N. Beautiful but dangerous: Effects of offender attractiveness and nature of the crime on juridic judgment. *Journal of Personality and Social Psychology*, 1975, *31*(3), 410–414.

Sigall, H., & Page, R. Current stereotypes: A little fading, a little faking. *Journal of Personality and Social Psychology*, 1971, *18*, 247–255.

Simon, B., & Lawton, M. P. *Proximity and other determinants of friendship formation in the elderly.* Paper presented at the meeting of the Eastern Psychological Association, Boston, April 1967.

Skinner, B. F. *The behavior of organisms.* New York: Appleton-Century-Crofts, 1938.

Solomon, S., & Saxe, L. What is intelligent, as well as attractive, is good. *Personality and Social Psychology Bulletin*, 1977, *3*, 670–673.

Spielberger, C. P. Current trends in theory and research on anxiety. In C. P. Spielberger (Ed.), *Anxiety: Current trends in theory and research* (Vol. 1). New York: Academic Press, 1972.

Spielberger, C. P., Anton, W. D., & Bedell, J. The nature and treatment of anxiety. In M. Zuckerman and C. D. Spielberger (Eds.), *Emotions and anxiety: New concepts, methods, and applications.* New York: LEA/Wiley, 1976.

Steers, R. M., & Porter, L. W. *Motivation and work behavior.* New York: McGraw-Hill, 1975.

Suits, B. What is a game. *Philosophy of Science*, 1967, *34*, 148–156.

Sullivan, H. S. *The interpersonal theory of psychiatry.* New York: Norton, 1953.

Surgeon General's Scientific Advisory Committee on Television and Social Behavior. *Television and growing up: The impact of television violence.* Washington, D.C.: U.S. Government Printing Office, 1972.

Szasz, T. The myth of mental illness. *American Psychologist*, 1960, *15*, 113–118.

Taylor, D. A. The development of interpersonal relationships: Social penetration processes. *Journal of Social Psychology*, 1968, *75*, 79–90.

Terry, R. L., & Macklin, E. Accuracy of identifying married couples on the basis of similarity of attractiveness. *Journal of Psychology*, 1977, *97*, 15–20.

Thoresen, C. E., & Mahoney, M. J. *Behavioral self-control.* New York: Holt, Rinehart & Winston, 1974.

416

Thorndike, E. L. *Animal intelligence: Experimental studies.* New York: Macmillan, 1911.

Tulving, E., & Thompson, D. Encoding specificity and retrieval processes in episodic memory. *Psychological Review,* 1973, *80,* 352–373.

U.S. Bureau of the Census. *Number, timing, and duration of marriages and divorces in the United States: June 1975* (Current Population Reports, Series P-20, No. 297). Washington, D.C.: U.S. Government Printing Office, 1976.

Valins, S., & Nisbett, R. E. *Attribution processes in the development and treatment of emotional disorders.* New York: General Learning Press, 1971.

Walker, K. Homemaking still takes time. *Journal of Home Economics,* 1969, *51,* 621–625.

Walster, E. The effect of self-esteem on romantic liking. *Journal of Experimental Social Psychology,* 1965, *1,* 184–197.

Walster, E. *Passionate love.* Paper presented at a conference on Theories of Interpersonal Attraction in the Dyad, New London, Conn., October 1970.

Walster, E., Aronson, V., Abrahams, D., & Rottmann, L. Importance of physical attractiveness in dating behavior. *Journal of Personality and Social Psychology,* 1966, *4*(5), 508–516.

Walster, E., & Berscheid, E. Adrenaline makes the heart grow fonder. *Psychology Today,* 1971, *5*(1), 46–50.

Watson, D. L., & Tharp, R. G. Self-directed behavior: Self-modification for personal adjustment. Monterey, Calif.: Brooks/Cole, 1972.

Watson, J. B., & Rayner, R. Conditioned emotional reactions. *Journal of Experimental Psychology,* 1920, *3,* 1–14.

Weiner, B., Frieze, I., Kukla, A., Reed, L., Rest, S., & Rosenbaum, R. M. *Perceiving the causes of success and failure.* New York: General Learning Press, 1971.

Weinstein, H. G. *A comparison of three alternative work schedules: Flexible work hours, compact work week, and staggered work hours.* Philadelphia: University of Pennsylvania, 1975.

White, R. W. Motivation reconsidered: The concept of competence. *Psychological Review,* 1959, *66,* 297–333.

Wickelgren, W. *Learning and memory.* Englewood Cliffs, N.J.: Prentice-Hall, 1977.

Wiggins, J. A., Dill, F., & Schwartz, R. D. On "status-liability." *Sociometry,* 1965, *28,* 197–209.

Williams, J. E., & Edwards, C. D. An exploratory study of the modification of color and racial concept attitudes in preschool children. *Child Development,* 1969, *40,* 737–750.

Williams, R. M., Jr. *Strangers next door.* Englewood Cliffs, N.J.: Prentice-Hall, 1964.

Wilson, W., & Nakajo, H. Preference for photographs as a function of frequency of presentation. *Psychonomic Science,* 1965, *3,* 577–578.

Winch, R. F. *Mate-selection: A study of complementary needs.* New York: Harper & Row, 1958.

Wine, J. Test anxiety and direction of attention. *Psychological Bulletin,* 1971, *76,* 92–104.

Wortman, C. B., Adesman, P., Herman, E., & Greenberg, R. Self-disclosure: An attributional perspective. *Journal of Personality and Social Psychology,* 1976, *33,* 184–191.

Wrighter, C. P. *I can sell you anything.* New York: Random House, 1972.

Wrightsman, L. S. *Social psychology in the seventies.* Monterey, Calif.: Brooks/Cole, 1972.

Wunderlich, E., & Willis, F. N. The youth of victims as a factor affecting the probability of receiving aid. *Journal of Psychology,* 1977, *97,* 93–94.

Yankelovich, D. The new psychological contracts at work. *Psychology Today,* May 1978, pp. 46–50.

Zajonc, R. B. Attitudinal effects of mere exposure. *Journal of Personality and Social Psychology*

417

Monograph, 1968, *9*, 1–27.

Zimbardo, P., & Ruch, F. L. *Psychology and life* (9th ed.). Glenview, Ill.: Scott, Foresman, 1975.

Zimmerman, J. *Application of productive avoidance to the problem of accelerating "productive" behavior in humans: Rationale, some data, and some speculations.* Unpublished manuscript, Indiana University, n.d.

Zubek, J. P. *Sensory deprivation: Fifteen years of research.* New York: Appleton-Century-Crofts, 1969.

418

NAME INDEX

Coleman, J. C., 16, 155, 158
Consalvi, C., 167
Cook, S. W., 198
Courtney, A., 191
Crandall, R., 364
Cross, A. R., 73
Crowley, J. E., 192

Darley, J., 143, 206
Darley, S. A., 194
Deaux, K., 205
De Baca, D. C., 26
De Charms, R., 10, 328–329
Deci, E. L., 329
De Fleur, M. L., 201
De Grazia, S., 353
Dermer, M., 149
Deur, J. L., 73
Devine, J. W., 26
DiGiacomo, R. J., 152
Dill, F., 167
Dion, K. K., 147, 149, 154
Dion, K. L., 154
Doane, B. K., 97
Doyle, D. C., 194
Dutton, D. G., 202

Eagly, A. H., 173
Ebbinghaus, H., 284
Edinger, J. D., 198
Edwards, C. D., 196
Ellis, A., 250
Emswiller, T., 205
Epstein, C. F., 192
Erikson, E. H., 81, 85

Fagot, B. I., 192
Faling, V., 157
Farmer, H., 304
Fava, S. F., 361
Feather, N. T., 194, 195
Feigenbaum, K., 357
Fentiman, J. R., 127
Ferrari, N. A., 331
Ferster, C. B., 222
Feshbach, S., 184
Festinger, L., 166
Field, R., 391

Filion, R., 230
Fine, G. A., 145
Finney, P., 146
Fitzgibbons, D., 364
Forman, R., 143
Fox, S., 230
Freedman, J. L., 57
Freedman, M. B., 58
Freeman, V., 147
French, T. M., 117
Frenkel-Brunswik, E., 171
Freud, A., 104
Freud, S., 16, 104–106
Friedman, A., 332
Frieze, I., 139
Fromm, E., 154

Gaertner, S. L., 202
Gerton, M. I., 125
Gilbert, G. M., 198
Gillen, B., 148
Gist, N. P., 361
Glasser, W., 354–355
Godbey, G., 352, 361
Goldstein, M. A., 152
Goodman, I., 77
Goodman, P. S., 322
Goranson, R., 206
Gordon, R. O., 117
Graham, S., 363
Gravitz, M. A., 125
Green, J. A., 201
Greenberg, B. S., 49
Greenberg, R., 146
Greene, C. N., 344
Grimes, M. D., 122
Grubb, E. A., 363
Guthrie, E. R., 222
Gyllenhammer, P., 337

Hallenstein, C. B., 129
Hammen, C. L., 16, 155, 158
Hankins, N. E., 216, 245, 291
Hanson, G. D., 127
Harari, H., 54
Harris, M. B., 323
Harris, R. J., 376, 377, 379, 380
Harvey, O. J., 167

420

421

NAME INDEX

Sanford, N., 171
Santrock, J. W., 73
Sapira, J. D., 117
Saxe, L., 149, 150
Schacht, T. E., 111
Schachter, S., 141, 311
Scheib, E. T., 117
Schlenker, B. R., 207
Schneider, D. J., 145
Schultz, D. P., 50, 98, 99
Schwartz, A., 359
Schwartz, R. D., 167
Scobel, D., 337
Scott, T. H., 97
Scott, W. A., 57
Segman, J., 281
Selby, J. W., 128
Seligman, C., 149
Seligman, M. E., 331
Severy, L. J., 207
Sexton, P. C., 195
Shapiro, A. D., 117
Sherif, C., 198
Sherif, M., 198
Shipple, W., 191
Shmurak, S., 28, 255–256
Sidman, M., 52
Sigall, H., 148, 149, 198
Simon, B., 143
Singer, R. D., 77
Skinner, B. F., 224
Solomon, S., 149, 150
Somervill, J. W., 111
Spielberger, C., 244, 245, 254–255, 265
Stanley, J. C., 62
Steers, R. M., 333
Steinhurst, R., 26
Stone, T. H., 344, 363
Stunkard, A. J., 230
Suits, B., 361
Sullivan, H. S., 71
Szasz, T., 129

Taylor, D. A., 145
Terman, L., 210
Terry, R. L., 149
Test, M. A., 206
Tharp, R. G., 226

Thiel, D. L., 149
Thompson, D., 283
Thoresen, C. E., 51
Thorndike, E. L., 224
Tulving, E., 283
Turk, D., 242

Valins, S., 128
Vance, F. L., 147
Van de Voort, D., 152
Villena, J., 207
Vines, N., 88

Wade, T. C., 224
Walker, K., 353
Wampler, L. D., 155
Walster, E., 147, 148, 149, 153, 154
Walter, G., 198
Watson, D. L., 226
Watson, J. B., 22
Wechsler, D., 210
Weiner, B., 139
Weinstein, H. G., 341
Weise, B. C., 147
Weiss, R. L., 155
Weiss, W., 187
Westie, F. R., 201
Wheeler, D., 307
White, R. W., 26, 330
Wickelgren, W., 278
Wiggins, J. A., 167
Wilkins, C., 201
Williams, J. E., 196
Williams, R. M., 201
Willis, F. N., 207
Willits, J. E., 205
Wilson, J. P., 205
Wilson, W., 143
Winch, R. F., 146
Wine, J., 245, 246
Wolff, H. G., 108
Wortman, C. B., 146
Wright, H. F., 58
Wrighter, C. P., 373
Wrightsman, L. S., 203
Wunderlich, E., 207

Yankelovich, D., 9, 326

NAME INDEX

SUBJECT INDEX

Stimulus, 32
Stimulus control, 222, 239
Storage, 278–282, 298
Stress, 245, 266
Strong-Campbell Interest Inventory, 308
Success, motive to avoid, 193
Superordinate goal, 198, 211
Surgeon General's report on TV violence, 77
Survey method, 58–59, 64
Symbolism, in advertising, 389
Systematic desensitization, 245–266

Tabula rasa, 29
Task leader, 168, 178

Test anxiety, 250–251, 254-255
Testimonials, 386–387, 403
Threat, 245, 266
Time management, 287–297
Trait anxiety, 244, 266
Transient situational disorder, 123, 132

Unconditioned Response, 22
Unconditioned Stimulus, 22

Validity, 59, 64

Weasel words, 375, 403
Work motivation, theories of, 331–336

To the owner of this book:

We hope that you have enjoyed *Psychology of Effective Living* as much as we enjoyed writing it. We'd like to know as much about your experiences with the book as you care to offer. It is our hope that with your comments and the comments of others we can make *Psychology of Effective Living* a better book for future readers.

School: _____   Your Instructor's Name: _____

1. What did you like *most* about *Psychology of Effective Living?* _____

_____

_____

2. What did you like *least* about the book? _____

_____

3. Were all of the chapters of the book assigned for you to read? _____

(If not, which ones weren't?) _____

4. How interesting and informative were the Boxes, Figures, and Tables for you? _____

_____

_____

_____

5. If you used the Key Concepts, how helpful were they as an aid in understanding psychological concepts and terms? _____

_____

6. How useful were the book's graphics (figures, tables, cartoons, and photographs) in helping you learn more about psychology and its concepts? _____

_____

7. In the space below or in a separate letter, please feel free to make any further comments about the book. We'd be delighted to hear from you!

Optional:

Your Name: _____ Date: _____

May Brooks/Cole quote you, either in promotion for *Psychology of Effective Living* or in future publishing ventures?

Yes _____ No _____

Sincerely,

Norman E. Hankins

Roger C. Bailey

CUT PAGE OUT

FOLD HERE

| | | | |

BUSINESS REPLY MAIL
FIRST CLASS   PERMIT NO. 84   MONTEREY, CALIF.

NO POSTAGE
NECESSARY
IF MAILED
IN THE
UNITED STATES

POSTAGE WILL BE PAID BY ADDRESSEE

NORMAN E. HANKINS
ROGER C. BAILEY
BROOKS/COLE PUBLISHING COMPANY
MONTEREY, CA 93940